The Ceramics of Champotón, Campeche, Mexico

Frontispiece. Dr. William J. Folan, Director of the Centro de Investigaciones Históricas y Sociales of the Universidad Autónoma de Campeche since its foundation in 1981, working with Centro personnel. Dr. Folan directed the personnel of the CIHS and other scholars in the investigations at Champotón.

PAPERS
of the
NEW WORLD ARCHAEOLOGICAL FOUNDATION
NUMBER EIGHTY-FOUR

The Ceramics of Champotón, Campeche, Mexico

by

Donald W. Forsyth

Volume Editor

Mary E. Pye

New World Archaeological Foundation
nwaf.byu.edu

Brigham Young University Press
PMPC, Provo, Utah 84602

ISBN 978-0-9855198-4-1

ACKNOWLEDGMENTS

I wish to acknowledge the tremendous aid and support of Dr. William J. Folan, Lynda Florey Folan, and Dr. María del Rosario Domínguez Carrasco in carrying out this work. I also wish to thank all of the other personnel of the Centro de Investigaciones Históricas y Sociales of the Universidad Autónoma de Campeche. These colleagues include Abel Morales, Raymundo González Heredia, José Antonio Hernández Trujeque, Cosme Domínguez Aké, Leticia Caballero Mass, Rosario Cervantes Domínguez, Pascale Marie Villegas, Patricia del Carmen Estrella Magaña, Juan José Cosgaya Medina, María Isabel Rosel Hernández, Juan Carlos Díaz Angulo, Julieta Angélica Chablé Pérez, Filipencio Tuyub Huchin, and Tomás Arnábar Gunam, among others. They not only provided intellectual stimulation and support, but always went out of their way to aid me and my students in carrying out the analysis of the Champotón ceramics. Without their aid in both financial backing, and especially in the use of the Center's physical facilities, it would not have been possible to complete this study.

I also wish to thank students who worked with me in the analysis of the ceramics. These include Aaron Jordan, Scott Brian, Cady Waldrom, Emily Wise, Craig Freeman, and Trent Noble. Jerald Ek and Roberto Rosado Ramírez also aided in the analysis during the 2003 season.

I am also grateful to Sylviane Boucher and Yoly Palomo Carrillo of the Ceramoteca of the Centro INAH in Mérida, Yucatán, who kindly allowed me and my students to examine comparative collections stored in the Ceramoteca. Thanks also go to the personnel of the Centro INAH Campeche who allowed me to examine collections stored there and who facilitated my work. Likewise, the personnel of the Dirección de Difusión Cultural of the Universidad Autónoma de Campeche also aided in the production of this work.

I am also grateful to the editors at the New World Archaeological Foundation, particularly Arlene Colman and Mary Pye, for their helpful guidance, and for working with a less than ideal manuscript version that I submitted to them. Other personnel at the NWAF also greatly aided this work.

I would also like to thank the College of Family, Home, and Social Sciences and the Department of Anthropology, particularly the Rust Memorial Fund, of Brigham Young University for the financial backing and other support without which this study would not have been possible. I am also grateful to the Univerisdad Autónoma de Campeche for financial and logistic support.

CONTENTS

FIGURES

TABLES

CHAPTER 1

INTRODUCTION

Donald W. Forsyth and William J. Folan

Dr. William J. Folan provided most of the information on the excavations and their interpretation, as well as the basis for most of the figures for this Introduction. Dr. Forsyth's role was primarily to summarize it, and to describe how the ceramic analysis of the Champoton collection took place. When the text uses the first person, "I", it refers to Forsyth.

With the exception of the island of Jaina, the coastal zone of Campeche has not generally been the object of intensive archaeological investigations. To the contrary, the principal efforts have been directed toward large sites in the interior of the state, including Edzná, Calakmul, Becán, among others. One reason why coastal sites have not received much archaeological attention may be due to the fact that these sites often continued to be occupied into the colonial and modern era, and thus have suffered significant modification and destruction as a result of urban growth and transformation. This greatly exacerbates problems in the investigation of Precolumbian occupations at such sites, transforming it into a form of urban archaeology—something not commonly practiced in Maya Lowland archaeology. Nevertheless, it is clear that some of these sites played a significant role in the past.

Champotón is one of these coastal sites of particular importance in Maya civilization (Figure 1.1). According to Dr. William Folan and colleagues (2002:11):

> Even though Champotón was one of the most important cities and ports discovered by the Spanish on the Yucatan Peninsula, the site had only been investigated by means of stratigraphic test pits and surface collection...

Champotón was occupied by a substantial population at the time of Spanish contact, exploration, and conquest of the region. It continued to be occupied continuously throughout the colonial and modern periods and remains a significant settlement today. Until relatively recent times, the most important investigation along the Campeche coast was that of Alberto Ruz Lhuillier (1969), who in 1943 excavated test pits at six coastal sites—Xicalango (Aguacatal), Los Guarixés, Tixchel, Champotón, and Campeche. He also analyzed ceramics recovered by others, particularly Raúl Pavón Abreu, from Jaina (Ruz 1969:75, 77). At sites he investigated, Ruz collected surface materials and dug a number of test pits and an occasional test trench. Despite the very small-scale nature of Ruz's investigations, and the 76 years since his field work, his report still constitutes one of the best fonts of information about a number of these sites. Xicalango, or Aguacatal, was the object of investigation by Brigham Young University (BYU) in the 1950s and 1960s (Jakeman 1952; n.d.; Christensen n.d.). The only extensive report on these excavations, however, is found in Matheny (1970), who analyzed the ceramics from the site.

Unfortunately, Aguacatal is the only site in the area of the Peninsula of Xicalango and of the extreme southwest of Campeche that has provided data concerning the chronology and cultural development of the inhabitants of the region derived from extensive excavations. Nevertheless, due to the efforts of Lorenzo Ochoa, Ernesto Vargas, and many others from the Centro de Estudios Mayas (CEM) of the Universidad Nacional Autónoma de México, it is possible to affirm that the region had a long and significant occupation (Jiménez Valdez 1987; Ochoa and Terreros 1997; Vargas 1994, 2001:48–52). Still, more detailed information is not available because their investigations were limited principally to settlement pattern studies based on surface survey and mapping (Ochoa and Terreros 1997:24–27). Very limited investigations carried out at Santa Rita, which

Figure 1.1. Map of the Yucatan Peninsula showing the location of Champotón and related sites.

lies about 10 km west of Aguacatal, and which the CEM investigators supposed to be the famous site of Xicalango (Ochoa and Terreros 1997:24–27), were reported on by Jiménez (1987:118ff.), although it is not possible to specify the size or nature of the occupation at this time. However, she does report a Late Preclassic and Classic presence (Jiménez Valdez 1987:124).

Nearby a very brief investigation at Los Guarixés was subsequently published by Álvarez (1985).

Ruz (1969) excavated a couple of test pits and a test trench between the lighthouse and the market near the mouth of the Champotón River. He also dug three test pits to the west of the Pozo del Monte, as well as a couple of excavations on a small island near the mouth of the river (Figure 1.2). From these excavations he recovered approximately 13,000 sherds, all but a handful of them pertaining to the Postclassic period. Due to Contact period accounts, and to Ruz's investigations, the site of Champotón was considered by the archaeological community to be a predominately Postclassic phenomenon.

A later investigation of the Campeche coast was carried out by Jack Easton in 1967 on behalf of the Middle American Research Institute of Tulane University (Eaton 1978; Ball 1978). Eaton carried out surface collections and limited test operations at many sites along the coast of Yucatan and Campeche. Champotón was among those investigated by Eaton. According to Ball (1978:93), the ceramics recovered by Eaton belonged exclusively to the Postclassic period (but see Eaton 1978:26–27).

The only area of coastal Campeche that, until recently, has received significant archaeological investigation, other than Agaucatal, has been the site of Jaina—the object of numerous investigations undoubtedly due to the famous figurines that have been recovered. Ruz analyzed ceramics from that site excavated by Pavón Abreu, as well as other collections from the island (Ruz 1969:75–76). Subsequently, much more intensive investigations have been carried out there (Piña Chán 1968; Benavides 2002; Zaragoza and Martínez 2002; Barba 2003). Likewise, Uaymil (Inurreta 2004), and Isla Piedras (Inurreta 2006) have been investigated in more recent years. The area to

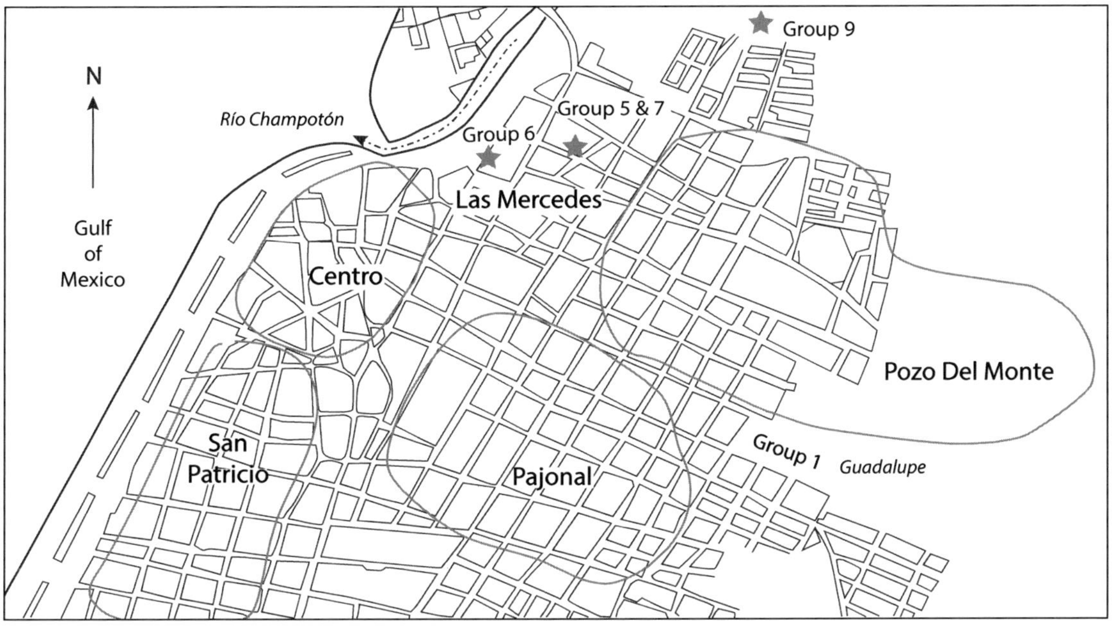

Figure 1.2. Plan of parts of the city of Champotón showing the major areas of investigations by the Universidad Autónoma de Campeche, Centro de Investigaciones Históricas y Sociales (redrawn from Folan et al. 2004).

the south of these islands has received relatively little investigation prior to the 21st century. In 1980 the Misión Arqueológica Española (Rivera et al. 1982) undertook a small investigation at Haltunchen to the north of Champotón. In 1991 and 1993 members of the Centro INAH Campeche (Zapata 1997) carried out survey and excavations in parts of the coastal zone between Campeche and Champotón as part of a road construction project. Limited excavations were carried out at the site of Villa Madero. More recently, investigations have been carried out at Villamar and Playa Esmeralda a short distance south of Champotón (Ancona et al. 2010).

In 2001, William Folan and colleagues from the Universidad Autónoma de Campeche (UAC) began intensive excavations and mapping in and around a large mound (Structure 1) situated in the current Barrio de Guadalupe in the city of Champotón (Figure 1.3), as well as in a large platform across the Champotón River in an area called Moquel (Folan et al. 2002). Late in 2001 I was invited by Dr. Folan to visit Campeche to examine the ceramic collection recovered from the first season of investigation and determine the value of undertaking a full-scale analysis of the ceramics. It was not until August of 2002, however, that Forsyth and BYU graduate student, Aaron Jordan, spent two weeks in Champotón reviewing the recovered ceramics. Based on this preliminary investigation, I decided to analyze the ceramics from Folan's investigations at Champotón. Thus, during the summer of 2003 I worked with two graduate and two undergraduate students analyzing the ceramics from the 2001 and 2002 seasons. Jerald Ek, a doctoral candidate from SUNY-Albany, also worked with us in the lab analysis that summer. In subsequent years I continued work with various BYU students, including Craig Freeman and Trenton Noble. The latter spent two summers working specifically on the large numbers of anthropomorphic censers recovered from Structure 1 of the Group 1 building.

The ceramics analyzed for this study came almost exclusively from architectural contexts, which, although excavated stratigraphically, resulted in a complicated stratigraphy, one not readily adaptable to extremely fine chronological distinctions. Nevertheless, the fact that the

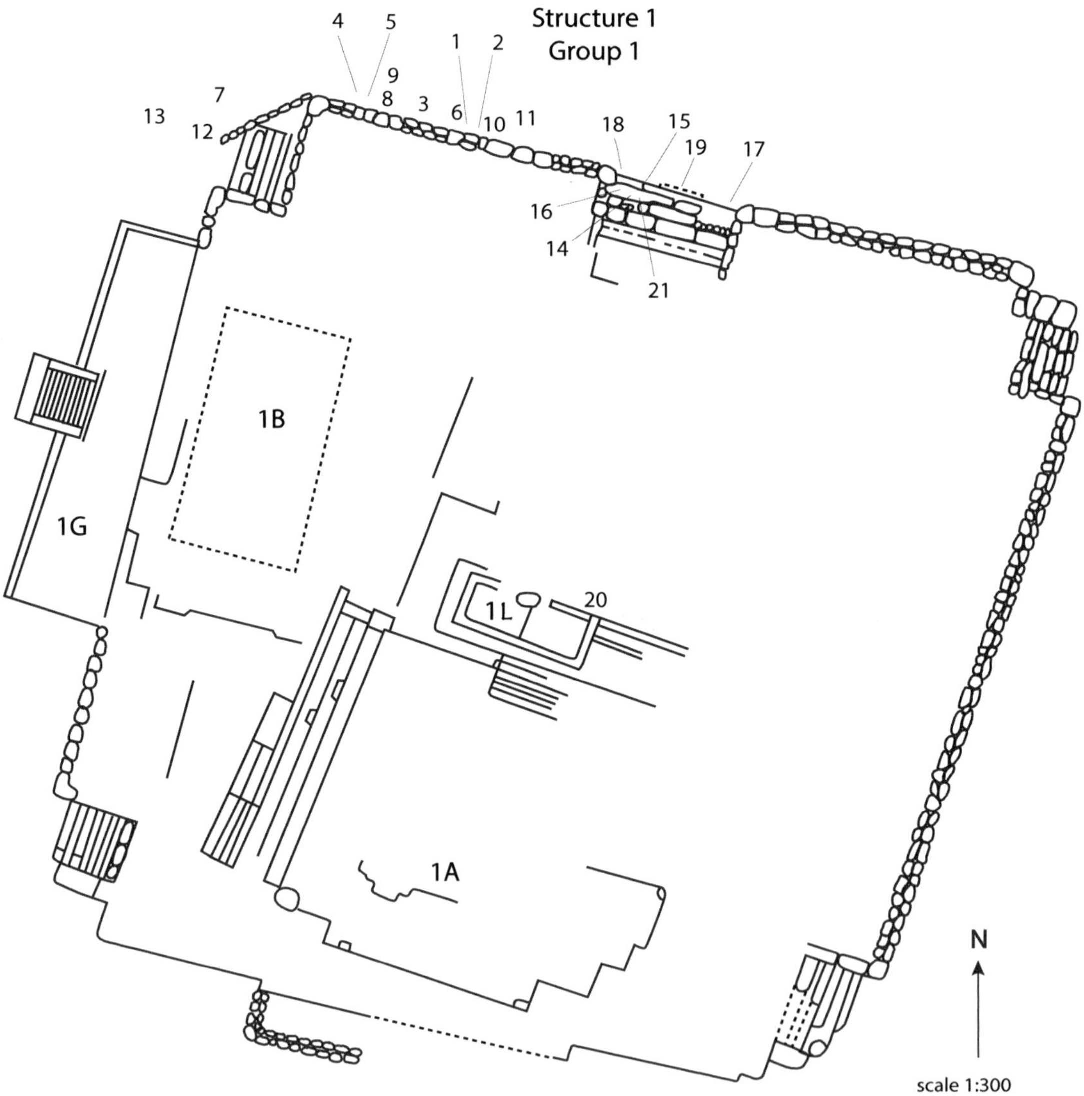

Figure 1.3. Plan of Structure 1, Group 1 in the Guadalupe Barrio of Champotón (redrawn from Folan et al. 2002).

ancient Maya shared many patterns of ceramic manufacture over wide areas and that these often changed through time in similar ways has often facilitated the dating of an unknown site by means of strong correspondences between the unknown site and others that have been relatively well investigated. Thus, it has been possible to outline a set of provisional complexes for Champotón. Because they are provisional the names that I have assigned to these complexes should not be reified, but subject to change as new data emerge.

At the present moment probably the best interpretation of the ceramic sequence in the region of Champotón has been made by Jerald Ek (2015) who carried out detailed small-scale stratigraphic excavations at numerous sites in the region around Champotón. As a result he has been able to present a ceramic sequence that is both longer than the one evidenced in the Champotón excavations and more detailed.

That is, Ek had some more detailed stratigraphic contexts. He used numbers to designate a series of seven ceramic complexes that he was able to differentiate, and this classification may end up being a better foundation for the complexes of the Champotón area. The current study, however, has a much larger sample of ceramic manufactures, which is the strength of the current study. Still, Ek (2015) has made an attempt to work out a detailed chronology, particularly for the difficult period of the Late Classic/Terminal Classsic—something that I have not been able to do on the basis of the Champotón ceramics. Another strength of the current study is that it emphasizes detailed type descriptions, something that Ek's study, provided as part of a much larger exposition of regional archaeology, does not do. Anyone interested in the archeology of the Champotón region should read Ek's work carefully, as it contributes significantly to the study of the Champotón region in general, and to the ceramics of the region specifically. It adds to the vitally important investigations carried out by Dr. Folan and the UAC investigators at Champotón. As with all early attempts in working out the archaeology of a relatively unknown region, the results reported here should be used with caution and discernment and are subject to revision in the light of new data. Hence, I expect changes, modifications, and reinterpretations as further research advances in this very interesting and key region of Campeche.

THE EXCAVATIONS

This description of the investigations at Champotón is not a comprehensive account of the excavations. Rather, it is a brief overview to provide the reader an indication of where the ceramic collections analyzed here came from. For more information on the excavations, see Folan et al. (2002, 2003, 2004, 2015).

In 2001 and 2002, Dr. William Folan and his associates from the Universidad Autónoma de Campeche (UAC) began excavations in the city of Champotón, Campeche, Mexico. Supported by the University and by the Municipio de Champotón, and under a permit from the Consejo de Arqueología of the Instituto Nacional de Antropología e Historia, Folan undertook excavations at a large mound on the edge of the modern city of Champotón. This mound, largely, but not completely intact, was designated as Structure 1 of Group 1. It should be remembered that Champotón has been occupied continuously since before European contact and is today a thriving small city. Much of the Precolumbian evidence is buried under the modern city. Structure 1, however, lay on a piece of ground adjacent to residential construction in the Barrio of Guadalupe, where it had only partially been damaged by modern activities. In addition, mounds at Moquel, to the northeast of Champotón proper, and on the other side of the Champotón River were mapped. Abel Morales López carried out a program of test pits in these platforms (Figures 1.3–1.4).

Structure 1 in Group 1 was a monumental platform (Figure 1.5) measuring 54 by 54 m and 8 m high at its highest remaining point. It was constructed of enormous cut-stone blocks weighing 250 to 500 kg each and cut so finely there was no need for wedges or mortar (Figures 1.6–1.9). According to Folan et al. (2003:67):

> The Great Platform, that represents a jewel of Maya archaeology, [was] constructed with five distinct sets of megalithic stairs, all different in their details, with the largest on the north face [of the building and] measuring seven meters wide at its base. The other four megalithic stairways [are] inset in each corner [of the structure]....

On this platform, originally constructed in the Late Preclassic, the builders erected triadic structures, the central one labeled 1-A-sub, and the western one 1-B-sub (see Figure 1.5, a reconstruction of Preclassic platform & buildings). The easternmost platform was not excavated, and, in fact, the eastern side of the platform had previously been partially damaged by a bulldozer in the past. Subsequent occupation of the platform partially destroyed and covered up these original structures. The Great Platform was occupied during the Classic and Postclassic periods, with considerable Postclassic activity on this platform. Structure 1-G, 25 by 5.50 m in size, was attached or placed against the west side of the Great Platform at

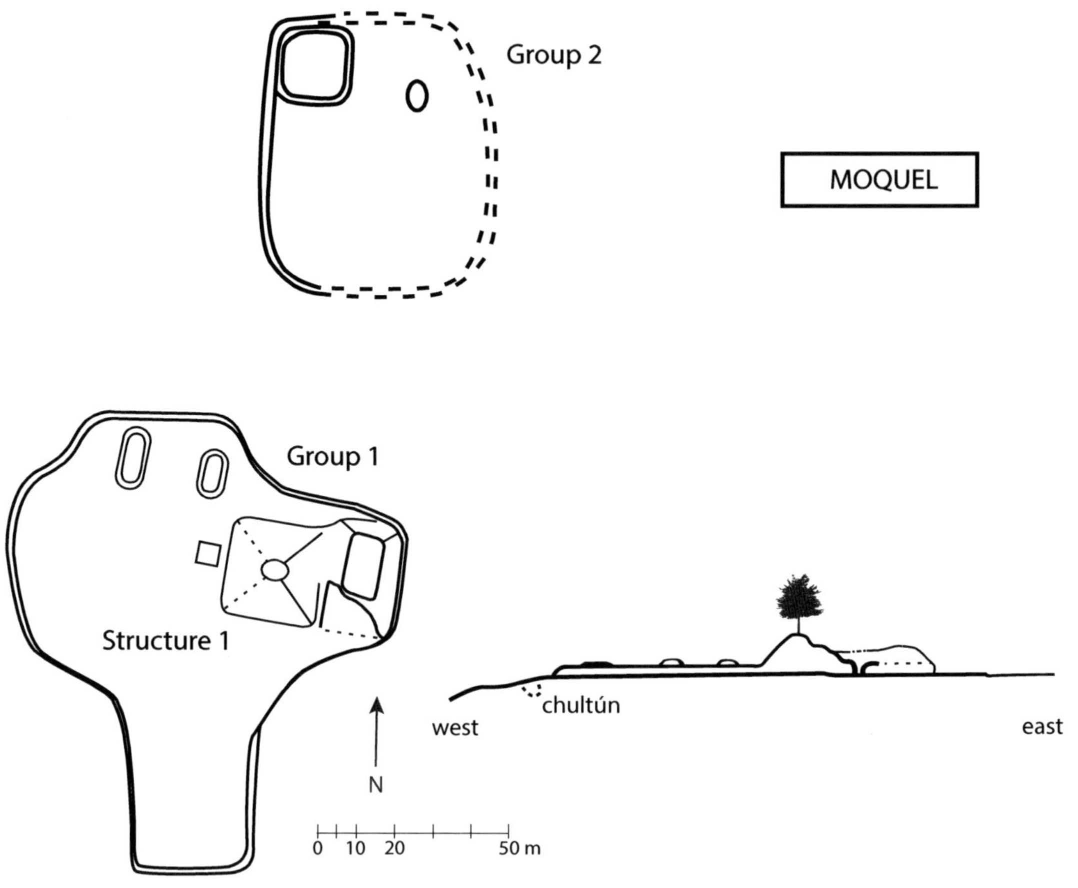

Figure 1.4. Plan of Groups 1 and 2 at Moquel and a section drawing of Group 1 (redrawn from Folan et al. 2003).

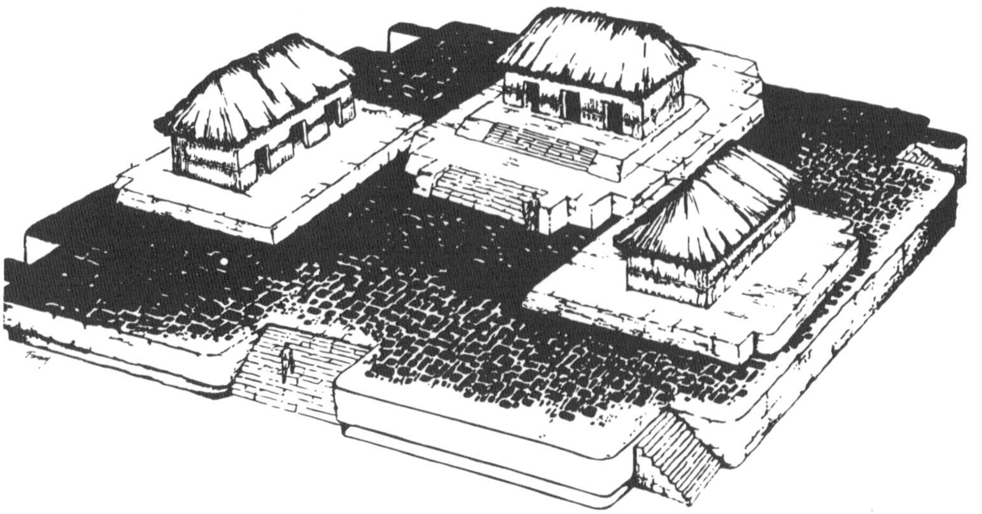

Figure 1.5. Hypothetical reconstruction of Structure 1, Group 1, during the Late Preclassic (digitally redrawn from Folan et al. 2004).

Figure 1.6. Group 1, Structure 1 platform showing the northeast stairway and east wall of the platform. Note the monumental size of the stones forming the platform (courtesy of Lynda Florey Folan).

Figure 1.7. Excavation of a section of the platform of Structure 1, Group 1 in the Guadalupe Barrio of Champotón (courtesy of Lynda Florey Folan).

Figure 1.8. Main stairway of Structure 1, Group 1 platform (courtesy of Lynda Florey Folan).

Figure 1.9. Large stone blocks forming the wall and stairways of Structure 1, Group 1 platform.

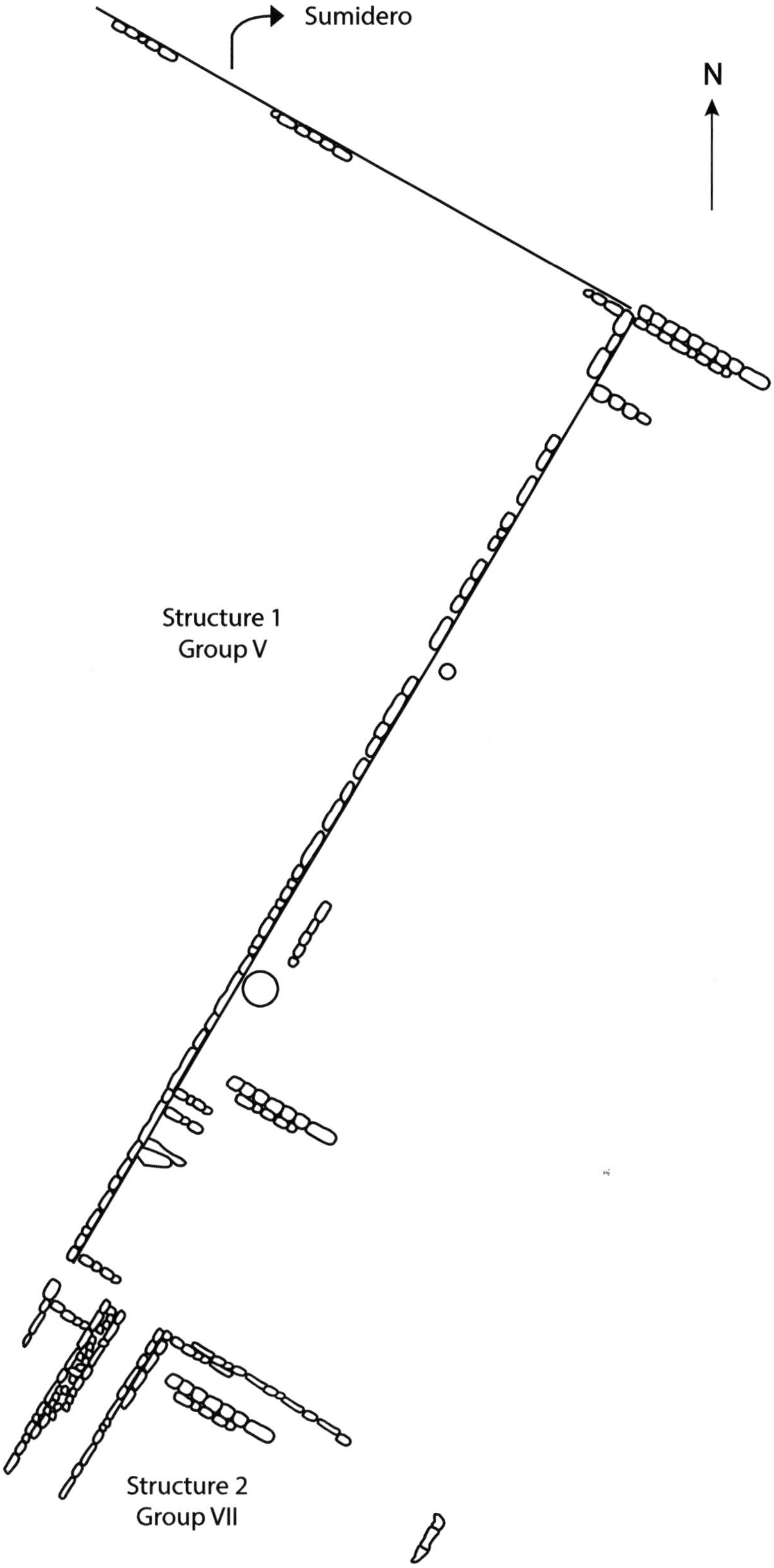

Figure 1.10. Plan of Structure 1, Group 5 and Structures 1 and 2 of Group 7 in the Mercedes Barrio of Champotón (redrawn from Folan et al. 2004).

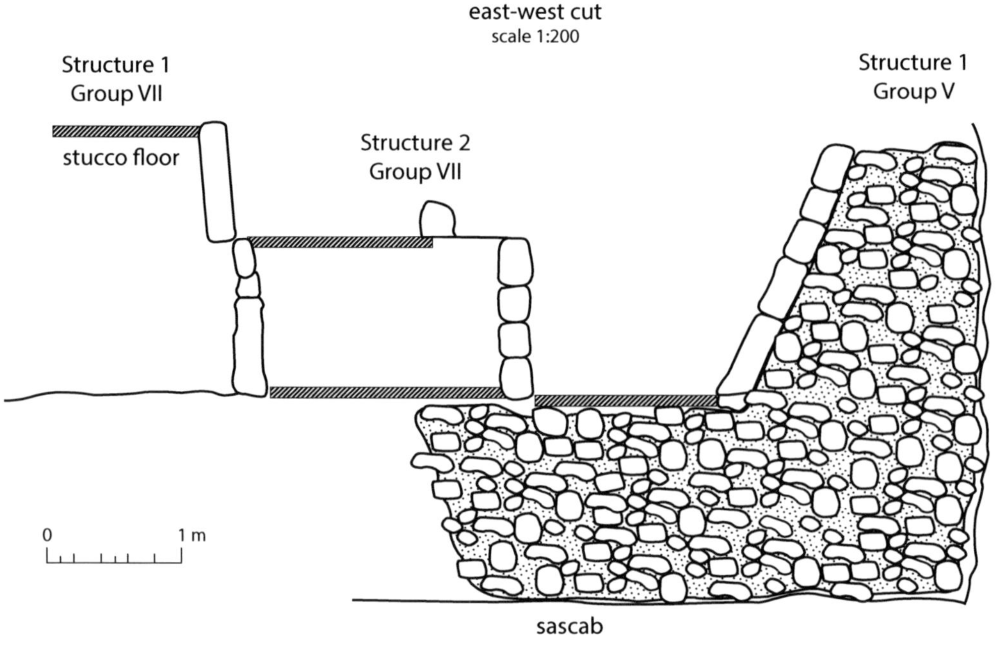

Figure 1.11. Section drawing of Structure 1, Group 5 and Structures 1 and 2 of Group 7 in the Mercedes Barrio of Champotón (redrawn from Folan et al. 2004).

this time (Figure 1.3). In addition, 21 burials from this period were uncovered near the base of the platform from the northwest corner along the northern edge to the central stairway. In addition, a very large amount of Mayapan style effigy censer fragments were deposited in two locations on Structure 1. These would seem to be special deposits in that they do not appear to have been broken in situ. Finally, a huge amount of fill material, 3 m high of earth and *sascab* were piled up on the east side of the old platform running north and south for 10 m; however, if this material was intended as fill for a structure, such structure was never constructed.

Excavations carried out at Structure 1 in Group 1 in the 2001 and 2002 seasons at Champotón completely uncovered the megalithic base of the platform and its stairways, as well as investigating the construction sequence of buildings in as much of the undamaged portion of the superstructure as possible.

In the 2003 season, the Champotón Project investigated what appear to be several ancient very large artificial levelings in the northern part of the modern city (Figure 1.2). These include levelings in the barrios of Pozo del Monte, las Mercedes, El Centro, Patricio-La Playa, and el Tajonal-El Cardenal. But the investigations were only able to demonstrate the existence of these levelings in Pozo de Monte and El Centro (Folan et al. 2004:41). In addition, Folan and associates carried out several excavations where property owners allowed them to do so. Since they were investigating in a modern built-up city, this limited the extent of such investigations. Nevertheless, they were able to partially uncover a Postclassic platform wall and three successive floors in the Barrio Las Mercedes (Figures 1.10–1.11).

Project members excavated portions of five architectural groups in this area of the city (Figure 1.2), uncovering as much as they could given the restrictions imposed by working in an urban context. Virtually all of these excavations yielded materials dating to the Postclassic (see Folan et al. 2015).

CHAPTER 2

CERAMIC TYPE DESCRIPTIONS, PRECLASSIC PERIOD

The type descriptions here follow the classification I used in the Edzná and El Mirador ceramic volumes (Forsyth 1983; 1989). Consult those works for a description of the type-variety system and for the type description format. The classification of the ceramics, particularly for the Late/Terminal Classic, should be understood as preliminary. For various reasons this period was one of the most difficult to sort, given the nature of the collections, and so modifications may be necessary as future work provides better evidence for the typology. A classification can only address the collection at hand, whatever its strengths or weaknesses may be. The strength of the Champotón collection is that it represents a large sample of ceramics from the site, but the sample is also somewhat restricted in terms of coverage. Excavating in an urban context places significant limitations on where excavations may be placed and often leads to sampling coverage problems. Fortunately, the evidence from Group 1, Structure 1 indicates that it was utilized from at least Late Preclassic times through the Postclassic period.

The ceramic collections upon which this classification is based are currently stored in the Archaeology laboratory of the Centro de Investigaciones Históricas y Sociales (CIHS) of the Universidad Autónoma de Campeche (UAC) in Campeche City, Campeche, Mexico. The work was carried out under the direction of William J. Folan, the Administrative Coordinator of the CIHS and assisted by personnel of the CIHS. The Archaeology lab is directed by Dr. María del Rosario Domínguez Carrasco. The descriptions are ordered in terms of earliest to latest.

Sherd counts are given for each ware, ceramic group, and type. For the first two, these are given in parentheses, or occasionally brackets, after the name of the ware or group. For the types, the counts are given under the *Frequency* heading. Following the number of sherds for a type are two percentage numbers in parentheses. The first one represents what percentage that type makes up of the ceramic group to which the type belongs. The second one represents the percentage that type makes up for the whole ceramic complex. For example, if a type had listed a frequency of "100 sherds (40%; 15%) it would mean that the 100 sherds made up 40 per cent of the sherds identified from that ceramic group, and 15 per cent of the sherds belonging to that ceramic complex.

THE LA MANTILLA CERAMIC COMPLEX

The earliest ceramics so far identified within our collections pertain to the Middle Preclassic Mamom horizon. It is probably somewhat inaccurate to define these materials as a complete ceramic complex as I have here, as it does not reflect what Richard E. W. Adams (1973:133–134) called "usage complementarity," by which he meant that "ceramic complexes represent the total number of functional needs for pottery in a specific time and place." The La Mantilla complex does not fit that definition. Nonetheless, given that some of the major types generally associated with the Mamom horizon in many other sites are present in small quantities at Champotón, leads me to believe that there probably was a full complex in use at the site. Unfortunately, due to the small sample size, we did not recover evidence of all of the types that would have made up that probable complex; hence, the La Mantilla complex remains tentative for the moment.

Paso Caballo Waxy Ware (see Forsyth 1989:7)

Juventud Ceramic Group

Juventud Red: Variety Unspecified
Guitarra Incised: Variety Unspecified
Desvario Chamfered: Variety Unspecified

Chunhinta Ceramic Group

Chunhinta Black: Variety Unspecified
Desprecio Incised: Variety Unspecified

Pital Ceramic Group

Pital Cream: Variety Unspecified
Paso Danto Incised: Variety Unspecified

Muxanal Ceramic Group

Muxanal Red-on-cream: Variety Unspecified

Ajal Ceramic Group

Ajal Resist: Variety Unspecified

PASO CABALLO WAXY WARE [164]

Juventud Ceramic Group (70)

Juventud Red: Variety Unspecified (Figure 2.1, a–e)

Frequency: 48 sherds (69%; 29%)

Established: Smith and Gifford (1966:170) as Joventud Red (see Forsyth 1993:34 for an explanation of the name change). This material is also similar to Chatel Orange-red at Edzná (Forsyth 1983:17–20); the latter should probably be considered as Juventud Red: Chatel Variety, rather than as a separate type. Due to the small sample size in the Champotón area, no variety designation is suggested. It is clear that the Juventud vessels at Moquel represent the tail end of the Mamom horizon, and thus are late Mamom.

Description:

Principle Identifying Attributes: (1) red to red-orange slip; (2) waxy, lustrous vessel surfaces; (3) dishes or bowls with flaring walls and wide, horizontal everted rims; (4) dishes or bowls with wide, downturned everted rims.

Paste, Firing, and Temper: The paste is generally medium-textured with crushed limestone inclusions. Paste color is usually red to reddish brown (10R 4–5/8; 10R 4/6), but an occasional example is more orangish (2.5YR 6/6). Dark cores are not common, but a few sherds have a darker core that is a strong brown color (2.5YR 3/4), and one has a brownish yellow core (10YR 6/4). Juventud Red was fired in an oxidizing atmosphere resulting in the red to brown paste color. That oxidation was normally quite complete, or nearly so, in the few recovered examples of this type. Temper appears to be white to gray calcite. Crushed sherd may also have been used as temper together with the calcite, but it is often difficult to determine this with the weak 10X magnification available. The crushed sherds shows up much more readily in the darker cores.

Surface Finish and Decoration: Slipped surfaces are generally a red to reddish orange color (10R 3–5/8; 10R 3.5/6; 2.5YR 5.5/6). The slip was applied after smoothing of the surface. Unrestricted forms are the only ones known for this type, probably due to the small sample size. Thus, the slip was generally applied to both the interior and exterior surfaces, and presumably on the interior base as well. No examples of bases were recovered, however, so it is not possible to determine if the exterior base was slipped or not. The slip was highly polished to achieve a lustrous finish. The slip color is essentially the same as that on Sierra Red vessels, so that body sherds are impossible to differentiate. Juventud sherds can be separated, therefore, primarily on the basis of diagnostic characteristics that occur only in the Middle Preclassic.

Forms:

1. Everted rim dish or bowl with wide horizontal rims and flaring walls (Figure 2.1, a–b).
2. Everted rim dish or bowl with wide downcurved rims and flaring sidewalls (Figure 2.1, c–d). No bases, supports, or appendages were noted.

Intrasite Locations and Contexts: The vast majority of Juventud Red sherds were recovered from Moquel at the base of a large platform in Group 3, Structure 1, especially Areas P2 and Qu. 3–4.

Intersite Locations and Contexts: Juventud Red occurs throughout much of the southern Maya Lowlands as the dominant slipped red

Figure 2.1. Juventud, Chunhinta, Pital, and Muxanal Ceramic Groups profile drawings—a–e. Juventud Red, f–m. Guitarra Incised, n–o. Desvario Chamfered, p–r. Chunhinta Black, s–t. Desprecio Black, u–y. Paso Danto Incised, z–bb. Muxanal Red-on-cream.

monochrome type of the Middle Preclassic horizon; however, the type can be found at many sites in the Maya Lowlands. It is the dominant Middle Preclassic slipped type in the southern Maya Lowlands and in the southern part of the northern Maya Lowlands. Sites from which it has been reported to be a major type (often listed as Joventud Red) include: Uaxactún (Smith 1955; Smith and Gifford 1966:158, 170), Altar de Sacrificios (Adams 1971:20–21), Seibal [Ceibal] (Sabloff 1975:61–62), Becán (Ball 1977:17–18), Barton Ramie (Gifford 1976:78–79), Piedras Negras (Forsyth and Hruby 1997; Muñoz 2004); northern Belize (Pring 1977; Valdez 1987:80, 82; 1988:43), Cuello (Kosakowsky 1987:42–43), Tikal (Culbert n.d.:E-18–20), Topoxté (Hermes 2000:166), Yaxhá-Sacnab (Rice 1979:22, 26–27), Tayasal (Chase and Chase n.d.:78, 121; Chase 1984:29), Flores (Forsyth 1996, 2009), Calakmul (Boucher and Dzul 2006:587, 600), Balamkú (Pierrebourg 2003), Río Azul (Adams, type list), Holmul (Kosakowsky 2001), and in the Petexbatún (Foias 1996:216–219). In the Mirador Basin, it occurs at El Mirador (Forsyth 1989:13, 15) and La Florida (Mirador Basin, 2002, personal observation), although it is known to be present at other sites as well. In Campeche more generally it is known from the sites of Edzná (Forsyth 1983:17–20), where it is classified as Chatel Orange-red, but should probably be considered a variety of Juventud Red, Constitución (Ancona et al. 2009a:237), Cerro de los Muertos (Ancona et al. 2009b:1103), Playa Esmeralda (Ancona et al. 2010), Tixchel (Ball 1978:122; Ancona et al. 2010), Villamar (Ancona et al. 2010:261), and Los Guarixés (Ancona et al. 2010:261). The type is widespread and present at many other sites throughout the Maya Lowlands

Comment: Although an occasional sherd of Juventud Red was identified from the excavations in Group 1, Structure 1 in Champotón, there is relatively little evidence from our excavations there for this type or time period. The best evidence for it comes from the other side of the Champotón River at Moquel, in the deepest level at the northern base of the large platform of Group 1 (see Folan et al. 2003:67, fig. 4). As stated above, this material is very late in the Mamom horizon and suggests that the earliest occupation for the area that we have is likely the transition from Mamom to Chicanel.

Guitarra Incised: Variety Unspecified (Figure 2.1, f–m)

Frequency: 19 sherds (27%; 12%)

Established: Smith and Gifford (1966:170) as Guitara Incised (see Forsyth 1993:34 for an explanation of the name change).

Description:

Principal Identifying Attributes: (1) red to red-orange slip; (2) waxy, lustrous vessel surfaces; (3) round-section, preslip incisions; (4) frequent placement of one to two parallel incised lines on everted rims or encircling the rim on everted or slightly restricted direct rim vessel forms; (5) dishes or bowls with flaring walls and wide to moderate, horizontal or downturned everted rims.

Paste, Firing, and Temper: The same as Juventud Red: Variety Unspecified.

Surface Finish and Decoration: Surface finish is like that of Juventud Red. The only decoration consists of fine (<1 mm) [rare] to medium-line (1–2 mm) shallow incisions encircling vessels on everted rims or encircling the exterior body of restricted vessel forms. Incision was invariably executed prior to the application of the slip and generally consists of from one to two lines encircling the vessel. Spacing between the incised lines varies considerably. Occasionally, a single incised line encircles the vessel on top of the everted rim. These incisions are much narrower and very different in cross-section from the grooves frequently found on the everted rims of Chicanel horizon vessels. A single example had a circle with an enclosed dot or punctate on top of an everted rim. No examples of more complex incised designs were noted in this small collection

Forms:

1. Everted rim dish or bowl with wide horizontal or downturned rims and flaring walls (Figure 2.1, f–j).
2. Thin-walled, restricted round-sided vessels (Figure 2.1, k–l).

3. Direct rim vase with straight sidewalls (Figure 2.1, m).

Intrasite Locations and Contexts: Same as Juventud Red.

Intersite Locations and Contexts: The type occurs at many other sites throughout the Maya Lowlands and is well referenced, so that all of the sites at which it occurs in one variety or another would make a very long and tedious list.

Comment: see Juventud Red above.

Desvario Chamfered: Variety Unspecified (Figure 2.1, n–o)

Frequency: 2 sherds (3%; 1%)

Established: Smith and Gifford (1966:170)

Description:

Principal Idenfying attributes: (1) red to red-orange slip; (2) waxy lustrous vessel surfaces; (3) raised chamfer on exterior body near rim; (4) deep bowls with slightly flaring rim

Paste, Firing, and Temper: Same as Juventud Red: Variety Unspecified.

Surface Finish and Decoration: Surface finish is like that of Juventud Red. Decoration is in the form of true chamfers—raised bands 2–2.5 cm in width encircling the vessel on the exterior body within 1.5–5 cm of the lip of the vessel.

Forms:

1. Deep bowl with slightly flaring rims. The form is rare, and none are complete. They may simply be flat-bottomed vessels (cf. Smith 1955:fig. 14b7, 9; Rice 1979:fig. 7dd, ee). This is the only form known (Figure 2.1, n–o).

Intrasite Locations and Contexts: Same as Juventud Red.

Intersite Locations and Contexts: The type occurs at many other sites throughout a large portion of the Maya Lowlands, so that all of the sites at which it occurs in one variety or another would make a very long and tedious list.

Comment: This is a rare type at most of the sites where it has been recovered. But it does serve as an excellent Mamom horizon marker since chamfering of the raised band type only very rarely occurs in later times.

Chunhinta Ceramic Group (45)

Chunhinta Black: Variety Unspecified (Figure 2.1, p–r)

Frequency: 33 sherds (73%; 20%)

Established: Smith and Gifford (1966:170)

Description:

Principal Indentifying Attributes: (1) dark gray to black slip; (2) lustrous vessel surfaces; (3) dishes or bowls with flaring walls and everted rims; (4) tecomates.

Paste, Firing, and Temper: The paste is medium to fine textured. Paste color is generally dark gray to black (2.5YR 2.5–3/0; 5YR 2.5/1), suggesting that during the final stages of firing the pottery was subjected to a reducing atmosphere. One sherd, however, has light red paste (10R 5/6), indicating that the vessel may have first been exposed to an oxidizing atmosphere, and then later to a reducing one, which produced the black color on the surface. Temper consisted of white to gray calcite. Some sherds, at least, also clearly show crushed sherd temper. These often appear as red specks in an otherwise dark gray to black paste.

Surface Finish and Decoration: Slipped surfaces are a black to dark gray color (2.5YR 2.5/0, 3/0–2; 5YR 2.5/1). The slip was applied to both interior and exterior surfaces on unrestricted vessels, while restricted forms, such as tecomates, were generally unslipped on the interior.

Forms:

1. Bowls or dishes with flaring walls and direct or everted rims (Figure 2.1, p–q).
2. Thin-walled tecomates (Figure 2.1r).

Intrasite Locations and Contexts: Same as Juventud Red, although an occasional sherd of Chunhinta Black was recovered from Group 1, Structure 1.

Intersite Locations and Contexts: The type occurs at many sites throughout the Maya Lowlands.

Desprecio Incised: Variety Unspecified (Figure 2.1, s–t)

Frequency: 9 sherds (20%; 5%)

Established: Smith and Gifford (1966:170) as Deprecio Incised (see Forsyth 1993 for an explanation of the name change).

Description:

Principal Identifying Attributes: (1) dark gray to black slip; (2) lustrous vessel surfaces; (3) medium-line, round-section preslip incision; (4) thin-walled tecomates.

Paste, Firing, and Temper: Same as Chunhinta Black: Variety Unspecified.

Surface Finish and Decoration: Surface finish is like that on Chunhinta Black. Decoration consists of medium-line preslip incision on vessel exteriors. In most cases it consists of two circumferential parallel incisions encircling near the rim on thin-walled tecomate forms.

Forms:

1. Thin-walled tecomates (Figure 2.1, s–t). This is the only form known.

Intrasite Locations and Contexts: Same as Juventud Red.

Intersite Locations and Contexts: The type occurs at many sites throughout the Maya Lowlands.

Pital Ceramic Group (37)

Pital Cream: Variety Unspecified (No illustration)

Frequency: 25 sherds (68%; 15%)

Established: Smith and Gifford (1966:170)

Description:

Principal Identifying Attributes: (1) beige-colored slip; (2) lustrous vessel surfaces; (3) flaring-walled shallow dishes.

Paste, Firing, and Temper: The paste is medium textured and dense. Temper consists of white to gray-colored calcite, but some examples suggest there may be sherd temper as well. Paste color ranges generally a strong to weak red color (10R 4–5/8, 10 R 4/6; 2.5YR 4–5/6–8); however, two sherds have slightly darkened cores, and some sherds have a light gray core or area (5YR 6/2; 10YR 6/3). Temper consists of white and gray calcite. At least some examples also have sherd temper.

Surface Finish and Decoration: The surface color of the slip is a creamy tan or beige (2.5YR 5/4; 4/4; 5YR 6/4). Two sherds from the same vessel were smudged black on the interior, although it is not clear if this was due to the original firing or something that happened later. The surface color was clearly obtained through some sort of firing process, as it differs decidedly from the paste color in most instances.

Forms:

1. Flaring-walled shallow dish with direct, rarely everted, rim (no illustration). Bases were presumably flat.

Intrasite Locations and Contexts: Most of these sherds came from Moquel, Group 3, P2, 2-60-3.00.

Intersite Locations and Contexts: The type occurs at many sites throughout the Maya Lowlands.

Paso Danto Incised: Variety Unspecified (Figure 2.1, u–y).

Frequency: 12 sherds (32%; 7%)

Established: Smith and Gifford (1966:170)

Description:

Principal Identifying Attributes: (1) beige-colored slip; (2) lustrous vessel surfaces; (3) medium-line incisions, generally circumferential; (4) sharp incurved rim vessels.

Paste, Firing, and Temper: Same as Pital Cream.

Surface Finish and Decoration: Same as Pital Cream with the addition of medium-line incisions. The only design in these incisions was one example of a "bouncing line" motif (Adams 1971:82). Otherwise, they are all circumferential. Usually there are two such lines near the rim, and parallel to one another. One sherd, however, had two such lines on the downturned everted rim and two others encircling the body of the vessel. Incisions were always executed prior to the application of the slip.

Forms:

1. Bowl with sharply incurved rim (Figure 2.1, u–w). Base form is unknown.
2. Dish or bowl with everted, downturned rim (Figure 2.1x).
3. Deep bowl with direct rim (Figure 2.1y)

Intrasite Locations and Contexts: Most of these sherds came from Moquel, particularly Trench A, Qu. 3–4 and Group 3, P2, 2–60–3.00. One sherd was recovered from Group 1, Structure 1 however.

Intersite Locations and Contexts: The type is widespread in the Maya Lowlands, although not in large quantities.

Muxanal Ceramic Group (7)

Muxanal Red-on-cream: Variety Unspecified (Figures 2.1, z–bb)

Frequency: 6 sherds (86%; 4%)

Established: Smith and Gifford (1966:170)

Description:

Principal Identifying Attributes: (1) cream-colored slip on interiors, red slip on exteriors or vice versa; (2) lustrous vessel surfaces; (3) flaring-walled dishes or bowls.

Paste, Firing, and Temper: The paste is medium to fine textured, and dense. Paste color is similar to Juventud Red. In fact, the paste is generally a strong red. Two examples, however, have a gray core (10YR 5/1; 5/3). The temper is also like Juventud Red. It is clear that some sherds contain sherd temper as well.

Surface Finish and Decoration: This type is a combination of Juventud Red and Pital Cream. The colors are differentially placed on vessel interiors and exteriors. The more general pattern is for the interior to be slipped red, carrying over onto the top of the rim. Then the exterior would be slipped cream. Nonetheless, variations occur in which there is a red band on either side of the rim and on the top of the rim, and cream slip on both the exterior and interior. In addition, one example has painted parallel hatches in red on the exterior cream slip.

Forms:

1. Flaring-walled dishes or bowls with direct rim (Figure 2.1z).
2. Deep bowls with slightly flaring neck (Figure 2.1aa).
3. Tecomate (Figure 2.1bb).

Intrasite Locations and Contexts: This type is rare, but occurs with other Middle Preclassic types at Moquel in Group 3, P2, 2–6002.00. An occasional sherd has been recovered from Group 1, Structure 1.

Intersite Locations and Contexts: The type occurs at many sites throughout the Maya Lowlands.

Ajal Ceramic Group (5)

Ajal Resist: Variety Unspecified (Figure 2.2, a–c)

Frequency: 5 sherds (100%; 3%)

Established: This type was defined at Nakbé by Forsyth (1993) and originally designated as Tierra Mojada Resist. Subsequent observation indicated that it is a distinct type from Tierra Mojada Resist.

Description:

Principal Identifying Attributes: (1) reddish orange to cream slip color; (2) lustrous vessel surfaces; (3) red-orange or greenish brown blotches.

Paste, Firing, and Temper: The paste is medium textured and appears to be the same as Juventud Red. In fact, the paste is generally a strong red. The temper is also like Juventud Red.

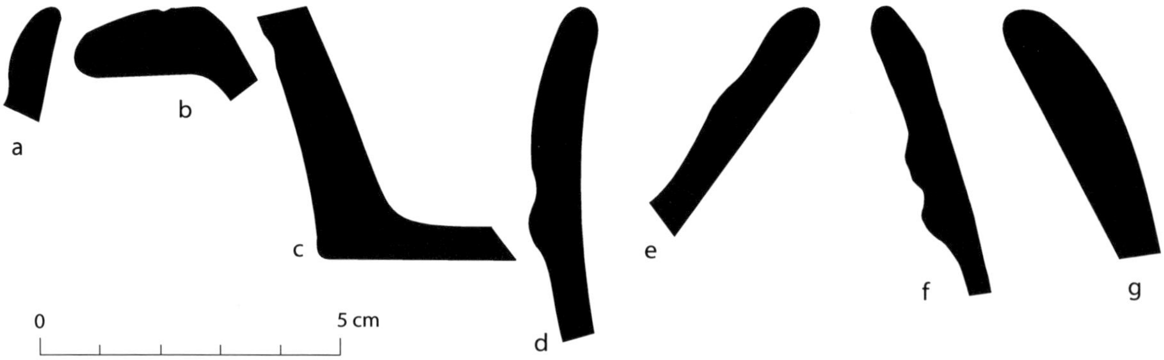

Figure 2.2. Juventud, Chunhintal, and Muxanal Ceramic Groups profile drawings—a–c. Ajal Resist, d. other Juventud Group: Fluted, e. possible Centenario Fluted, f. other Chunhinta Group: Chamfered and Fluted, g. Other Muxanal Group: Loche Incised-dichrome.

Surface Finish and Decoration: The surfaces of this type are marked by what is clearly intentional blotching. One form has a reddish orange slip (10R 5.5/8), lighter in hue than the generally deeper red of Juventud Red, combined with greenish brown/tan blotches (10YR 6/6). On another example, the slip is a creamy brown, like Pital Cream (7.5YR 6.5/4), with reddish orange blotches (10R 5.5/8). These examples might at first appear to be firing errors, but the blotches on Ajal Resist sometimes actually form simple designs, indicating that the effect was intentional rather than produced by mistake.

Forms:

1. Tecomate or near tecomate form (Figure 2.2a).
2. Everted rim dish or bowl with wide downcurved rims and flaring walls (Figure 2.2b).
3. Flaring-walled vessel of some sort with a flat bottom (Figure 2.2c).

Intrasite Locations and Contexts: This type is very rare and occurs at Moquel; however, most examples were from a surface collection.

Intersite Locations and Contexts: This type is known from Nakbé in the Peten (Forsyth 1993). It is probably more widespread, although not recognized as Juventud or other red-slipped types. It probably should be considered a provisional type for the time being.

Other Juventud Group: Fluted

A single sherd of Juventud Red with exterior, horizontal flutes was recovered from Moquel, G3, P2, 2–60–3.00. The vessel is a restricted bowl slipped on both the interior and exterior (Figure 2.2d).

Other Chunhinta Group: Pink Stucco

A single sherd bore traces of a covering of pink-colored stucco adhering to the black surface of the vessel. This pattern of painted stucco is known from the site of Nakbé.

Other Chunthinta Group: Fluted

A single thin-walled tecomate sherd bore wide, horizontal flutes. This is perhaps an example of Centenario Fluted (Figure 2.2e).

Other Chunhinta Group: Chamfered and Fluted

A single sherd of Chunhinta Black with an exterior chamfer, which was in turn fluted with a single flute (Figure 2.2f) was recovered from Group 1, Structure 1, I15, C5. The vessel appears to be a flaring-walled dish with a direct rim.

Other Muxanal Group: Loche Incised-dichrome (Ball 1977:83)

A single sherd of Muxanal Red-on-cream with two parallel, circumferential preslip lines about 2–3 cm below the rim of a flaring-walled slightly thickened rim dish or bowl was recovered from Moquel, Structure 1, Trench L, Qu. 4 (Figure 2.2g).

Table 2.1. Middle Preclassic: The La Mantilla Ceramic Complex type count.

PASO CABALLO WAXY WARE (Forsyth 1989:7)	**164**
Juventud Ceramic Group	**70**
Juventud Red: Variety Unspecified	48
Guitarra Incised: Variety Unspecified	19
Desvario Chamfered: Variety Unspecified	2
Other Juventud Group	1
Chunhinta Ceramic Group	**45**
Chunhinta Black: Variety Unspecified	33
Desprecio Incised: Variety Unspecified	9
Other Chunhinta Group	3
Pital Ceramic Group	**37**
Pital Cream: Variety Unspecified	25
Paso Danto Incised: Variety Unspecified	12
Muxanal Ceramic Group	**7**
Muxanal Red-on-cream: Variety Unspecified	6
Other Muxanal Group	1
Ajal Ceramic Group	**5**
Ajal Resist: Variety Unspecified	5

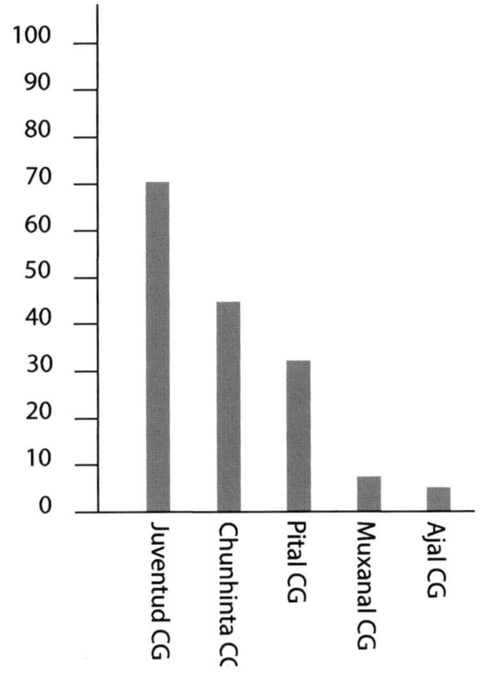

Figure 2.3. Frequency distribution of the Middle Preclassic period ceramic groups recovered from Champotón, Campeche, México.

THE PETENTUN CERAMIC COMPLEX

The Petentun complex pertains to the Late Preclassic period at Champotón (Chicanel horizon). Ceramics from this period have been recovered in considerable quantities from Group 1, Structurel 1. It represented one of the major occupational periods of that locality. It was also present in significant amounts at Moquel but quite rare in the Pozo del Monte-Las Mercedes area (see Folan et al. 2004).

The complex includes the following types and varieties:

Paso Caballo Waxy Ware

Sierra Ceramic Group

Sierra Red: Chon Variety
Ciego Composite: Ciego Variety
Repasto Black-on-red: Repasto Variety
Hongo Composite: Hongo Variety
Alta Mira Fluted: Alta Mira Variety
Laguna Verde Incised: Variety Unspecified

Polvero Ceramic Group

Polvero Black: Polvero Variety

Flor Ceramic Group

Flor Cream: Flor Variety

Uaxactun Unslipped Ware

Sapote Ceramic Group

Sapote Striated: Sapote Variety
Achiotes Unslipped: Variety Unspecified

PASO CABALLO WAXY WARE [3252]

Sierra Ceramic Group (2703)

Sierra Red: Chon Variety (Figures 2.4–2.8)

Frequency: 2582 sherds (96%; 69%)

Established: Smith and Gifford (1966:170). The Chon Variety was established by Forsyth (1983:33–37) at Edzná.

Description:

Principal Identifying Attributes: (1) red slip; (2) lustrous, waxy vessel surfaces; (3) labial, medial, and lateral flanges or ridges; (4) wavy rims or flanges; (5) everted rims; (6) grooving on everted rims; (7) rim protuberances.

Paste, Firing, and Temper: The paste is medium textured and dense. Paste color ranges from red to light red. Other colors occasionally occur, but the color of this type is consistently red to one degree or another. The principal paste color ranges around 10R 4–5/8, but other colors are 10R 4–6/6, 2.5YR 4–5/6–8; lighter colors are 2.5YR 6/4–6. Most sherds are oxidized throughout, but dark cores are sometimes present; these range from olive gray (5Y 5/2) to black (2.5YR 2.5/0. Temper is generally white to gray limestone. Sherd temper also seems to be present in most examples. The pieces of sherd sometimes incorporate temper particles from the sherds from which they were made.

Surface Finish and Decoration: Vessel surfaces were very well smoothed prior to the application of the slip. The slip is thick and adherent. Unless badly weathered it has a waxy feel to the surface. Bonding between slip and paste surface is excellent such that the surfaces of this type do not erode as readily as those of other slipped wares from later time periods. The slip color varies from 10R 4–5/6–8; 2.5YR 6/8 to 7.5R 4/6–8. Black to dark gray fire-clouding does occur, as do occasional cream-colored clouds. The slip was generally highly polished giving a lustrous appearance to the vessels. On unrestricted forms both the interior and exterior were generally slipped. Exterior bases were generally unslipped. On highly restricted forms only the exteriors were slipped.

Decoration occurs in the form of preslip grooving on the interior everted rim. This is the only location were such rim grooving is found on Sierra Red vessels. Such spaced, circumferential grooves usually number anywhere from one to three. This characteristic is a virtual diagnostic for the type, and is extremely common. Other forms of decoration consist of spaced, vertical notches cut into labial, medial, or lateral flanges. Although much rarer than rim grooving, it is also diagnostic of the type. Both rims and flanges occasionally bear protuberances or scallops.

Figure 2.4. Sierra Red: Chon Variety ceramics.

Forms:

1. Everted rim dish or bowl (Figures 2.5, 2.6, a–g) Bases are flat.
2. Lateral flange or ridge dish or bowl (Figure 2.6, h–u). The silhouette is composite.
3. Lateral angle dish or bowl (Figures 2.6, v–x; 2.7, a–e). Bases were flat.
4. Medial flange or ridge dish or bowl (Figure 2.7, f–k). Bases were flat.
5. Labial flange dish or bowl (Figure 2.7, l–r). Bases were flat.
6. Flaring-walled dish or bowl (Figures 2.7, s–y; 2.8, a–e). Bases were flat
7. Incurved rim bowl (Figure 2.8, f–h). Bases were flat.
8. Short to medium-necked jar (Figure 2.8, i–l). Bases were presumably flat.
9. Restricted orifice small-shouldered jar (Figure 2.8m). Base form is unknown.
10. Miscellaneous vessel forms (Figure 2.8, n–x).

The variety of vessel shapes, and minor variations on these is large, such that a listing

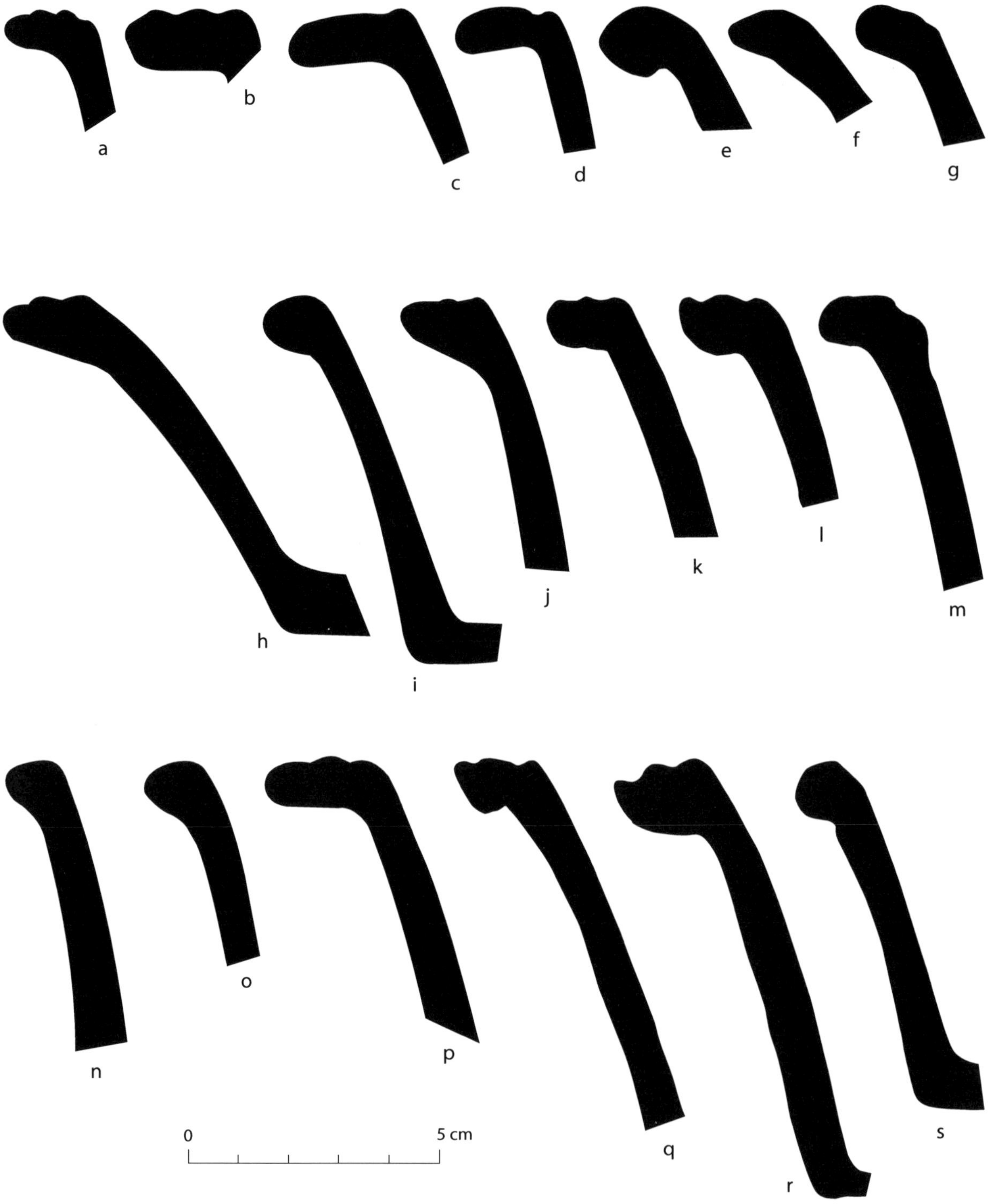

Figure 2.5. Sierra Ceramic Group profile drawings—Sierra Red: Chon Variety.

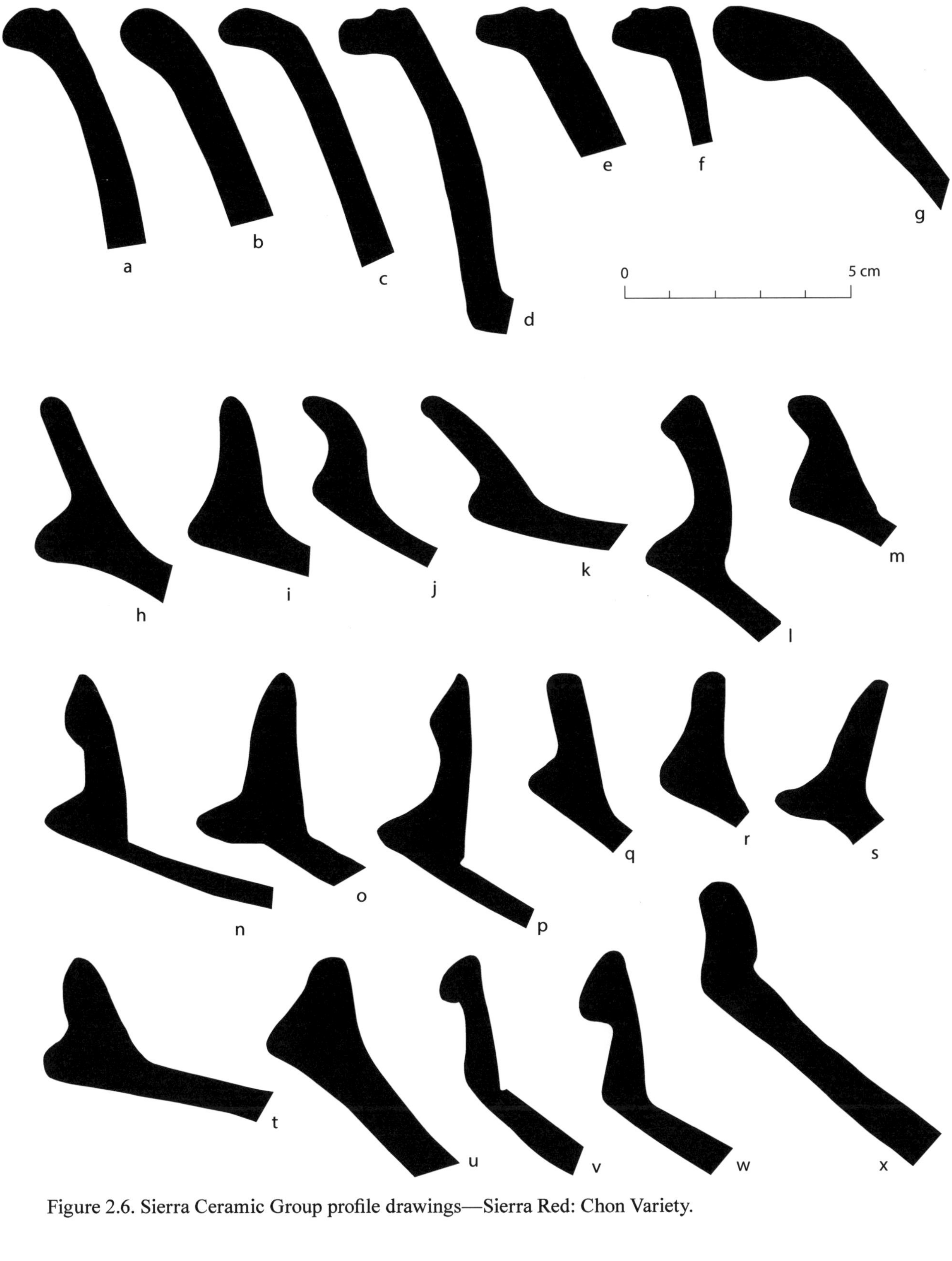

Figure 2.6. Sierra Ceramic Group profile drawings—Sierra Red: Chon Variety.

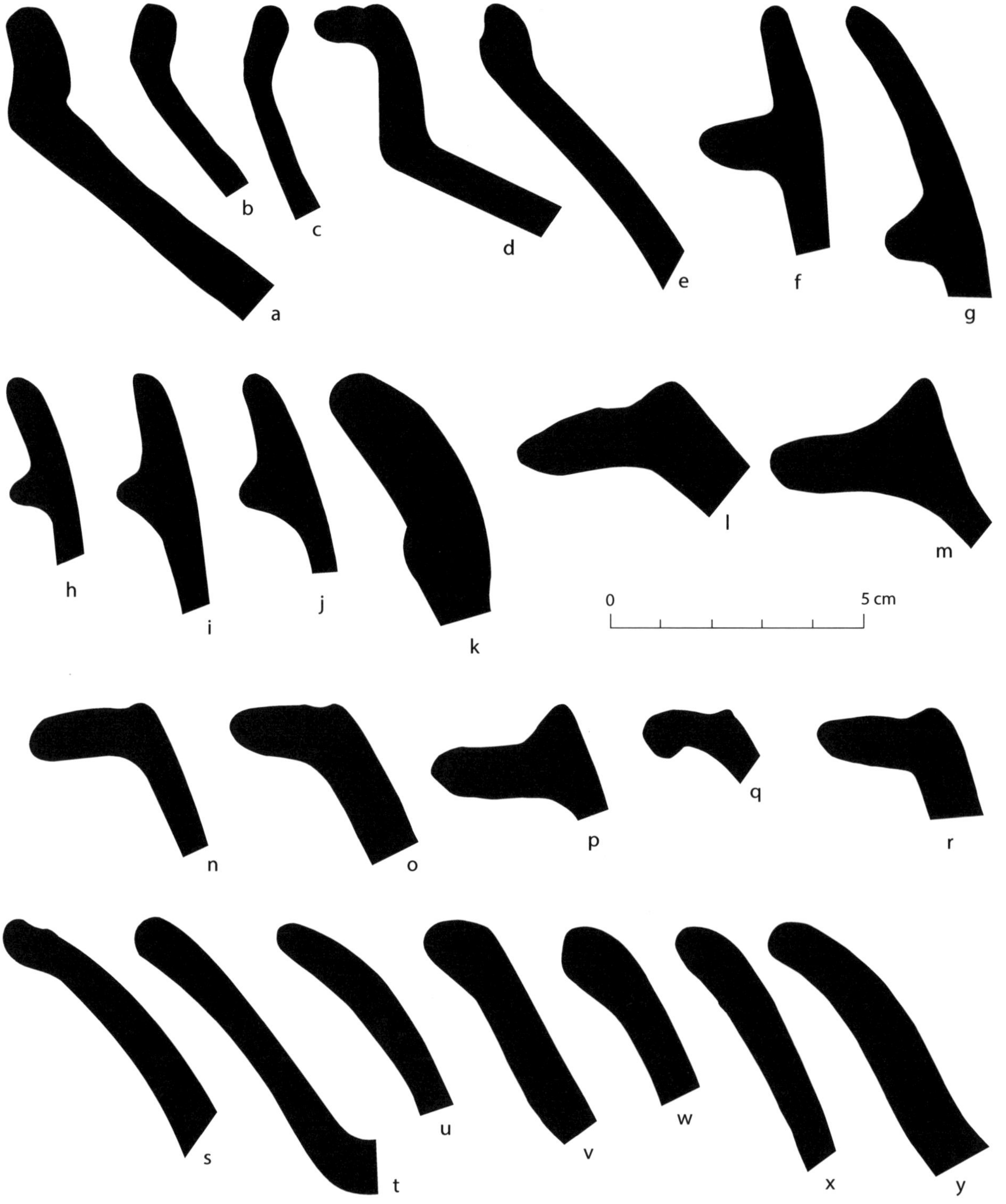

Figure 2.7. Sierra Ceramic Group profile drawings—Sierra Red: Chon Variety.

Figure 2.8. Sierra Ceramic Group profile drawings—Sierra Red: Chon Variety.

of forms cannot adequately describe the range of variation in vessel and rim form during this era. This pattern is duplicated all over the Maya Lowlands where the Sierra Ceramic Group is found (cf. Forsyth 1983:37).

Bases and Supports: The overwhelmingly dominant base form is flat. They were usually, but not invariably, unslipped on the exterior. All other kinds of bases are very rare. Occasionally solid teat pod supports also occur, but these appear to occur late in the ceramic complex.

Appendages: Protuberances on rims or flanges occur rarely. Handles are extremely rare.

Intrasite Locations and Contexts: Sierra Red was recovered from many contexts on Structure 1 of Group 1, but was significantly concentrated along the entire southern half of the east side of the Preclassic platform in excavation area I, Units 18–28, particularly in Units 23–28. In Group 3, Structure 1 at Moquel, across the Champotón River from the city of Champotón proper, Sierra Red also occurred in several contexts, but was heavily concentrated in Trench L.

Intersite Locations and Contexts: Sierra Red is the dominant Late Preclassic slipped type throughout most of the Maya Lowlands, and Champotón is no exception. Sierra Red from Champotón is more similar to that described for Edzná (Forsyth 1983:33–37) than to any other site described to date. Ek (2015) lists the type as present in several sites in the Champotón region; however, he does not provide frequency by type, but rather by ceramic group. Still, the Sierra Ceramic Group is listed as present at all of the sites in the area around Champotón that he investigated (Ek 2015:435). The Chon Variety is also present at the site of Villa Madero, about 6 miles north of Champotón (personal observation, INAH Ceramoteca, Mérida, Yucatan).

Ciego Composite: Ciego Variety (Figure 2.9)

Frequency: 42 sherds (1%; 1%)

Established: Type established by Ball (1977:114) at Becán.

Description:

Principal Identifying Attributes: (1) red slip; (2) lustrous, waxy interor surfaces; (3) vessel exteriors unslipped and striated.

Paste, Firing, and Temper: Same as Sierra Red.

Surface Finish and Decoration: Surface finish is the same as Sierra Red on the interior of the vessels. The red-firing slip was applied to the lip and/or everted rim; however, the slip does not continue down onto the exterior of the vessel. It is left unslipped, presenting a surface that consists only of the paste. This unslipped surface was then striated, usually in a vertical or diagonal pattern (see Forsyth 1983:43–44 for a more detailed account of this type).

Forms:

1. Everted-rim dish or bowl (Figure 2.9, a–i). Bases are flat.
2. Labial flange dish or bowl (Figure 2.9j). Bases were flat.
3. Flaring-walled dish or bowl (Figure 2.9k). Bases were flat.

Intrasite Locations and Contexts: Same as Sierra Red.

Intersite Locations and Contexts: Although a minor type, it usually occurs wherever significant deposits of Sierra Red are found in the Northern Lowlands. It is not common in the Southern Lowlands. Thus, it seems to have a more northernly distribution. Ek (2015:435) lists the type as present in several sites in the Champotón region, although he does not provide frequency by type. It has been found at Becán (Ball 1977:114), Edzná (Forsyth 1983:43–45), Villa Madero (personal observation, INAH Ceramoteca, Mérida, Yucatan), Yaxuná (Johnstone 2001:51) and, perhaps, Balamkú (Pierrebourg 2003:337). It is probably more widespread than this listing indicates.

Figure 2.9. Sierra Ceramic Group profile drawings—Ciego Composite: Ciego Variety.

Repasto Black-on-red: Repasto Variety (Figure 2.10, a–g)

Frequency: 31 sherds (1%; <1%)

Established: Smith and Gifford (1966:161,170) at Uaxactún.

Description:

Principal Identifying Attributes: (1) red slip; (2) lustrous, waxy vessel surfaces; (3) black paint over red slip applied in blotchy resist or parallel line fashion.

Paste, Firing, and Temper: The same as Sierra Red: Chon Variety.

Surface Finish and Decoration: The surfaces were finished like those of Sierra Red. Decoration was effected by applying a black paint to vessel surfaces over the red slip. The most common form of black paint was applied so as to create wide (ca. 1 cm.) parallel black lines placed on vessel exteriors or interiors or both. One example, nevertheless, has a series of thin (2mm) lines that form a larger design pattern. Here, the visual effect was clearly that of positive painting. In other cases, however, the black paint was applied over a large portion of the vessel in a resist-like pattern that left irregular areas of the surface in red. This created an overall visual impression of negative painting. Both kinds of decoration were, in fact, produced by positive painting—that is, the black paint was applied over the slipped surface. The red slip color is similar to that for Sierra Red. The color of the black paint ranges from a deep black (2.5YR 2/0; 5YR 2/0) to a washed-out gray (10R 4/2).

Forms:

1. Everted rim dish or bowl (Figure 2.10, a–c). Bases are flat.
2. Flaring-walled dish or bowl (Figure 2.10, d–e).
3. Incurved rim bowl (Figure 2.10, f–g).
4. Deep bowls with slightly flaring sides (no illustration).

Intrasite Locations and Contexts: Same as Sierra Red.

Intersite Locations and Contexts: This type occurs in relatively small quantities at most sites where Sierra Ceramic Group pottery is present. Ek (2015:435) lists the type as present in several sites in the Champotón region; however, he does not provide frequency by type, but rather by ceramic group. It is present at Villa Madero (personal observation, INAH Ceramoteca, Mérida, Yucatan).

Hongo Composite: Hongo Variety (Figures 2.10, h–n)

Frequency: 31 sherds (1%; <1%).

Established: Type and variety established by Ball (1977:114).

Description:

Principal Identifying Attributes: (1) red slip; (2) lustrous, waxy vessel surfaces; (3) mushroom stand form; (4) unslipped and fingernail impressed upper surfaces.

Surface Finish and Decoration: Surface finish is like that of Sierra Red except for the upper exterior surface and interior of the mushroom stand form. The upper surface was left unslipped, smoothed, and lightly impressed with the fingernail or, perhaps, a crescent-shaped object. This resulted in a series of small, shallow, arc-shaped impressions (see Adams 1971:fig. 19b).

Forms:

1. Mushroom stand (Figure 2.10, h–n are bases). This is the only form known for this type.

Intrasite Locations and Contexts: Same as Sierra Red.

Intersite Locations and Contexts: This type is found in association with other members of the Sierra Ceramic Group over a wide area of the Maya Lowlands. Although it never occurs in large quantities, it does appear consistently at most sites where there is a Chicanel occupation. Ek (2015:435) lists the type as present in several sites in the Champotón region; however, he does not provide frequency by type, but rather by ceramic group. It is present at Villa Madero (personal observation, INAH Ceramoteca,

Figure 2.10. Sierra Ceramic Group profile drawings—a–g. Repasto Black-on-red: Repasto Variety, h–n. Hongo Composite: Hongo Variety, o–q. Alta Mira Fluted: Alta Mira Variety, r–s. Laguna Verde Incised.

Mérida, Yucatan). Sites where it is known to occur include Becán (Ball 1977:195–196), Edzná (Forsyth 1983:45), Yaxuná, Maní, and the northern Yucatan coast (Ball 1978:111; see also Brainerd 1958:fig. 17e1, 18), and Dzibilnocac (personal observation, Instituto Yucateco de Antropología e Historia, Mérida, Mexico) in the Northern Lowlands. Because it is often not distinguished as a separate type by many analysts, albeit included in the Sierra Red category, it often does not appear in type descriptions. It is widespread throughout complexes of the Chicanel Ceramic Sphere and occurs consistently, although in relatively small numbers, as to be a virtual marker for that sphere.

Alta Mira Fluted: Alta Mira Variety (Figures 2.10, o–q, 2.11)

Frequency: 8 sherds (<1%; <1%)

Established: Smith and Gifford (1966:170).

Description:

Principal Identifying Attributes: (1) red slip; (2) lustrous, waxy vessel surfaces; (3) vertical and/or horizontal fluting on vessel exteriors; (4) restricted barrel-shaped vessels.

Paste, Firing, and Temper: Same as Sierra Red.

Surface Finish and Decoration: The surface finish is like that found on Sierra Red. Decoration consists primarily of vertical fluting on the exteriors of vessel bodies. The flutes are generally rounded, forming a smooth, undulating surface made up of alternating round-section troughs and crests. A few examples have horizontal circumferential flutes on the exterior. On barrel-shaped vessels, the vertical flutes run the length of the body from near the rim to near the basal break. On other forms they generally begin a ways below the rim of the vessel.

Forms:

1. Slightly restricted barrel-shaped vessels (Figure 2.10o; cf. Forsyth 1983:fig. 11B–F).

Figure 2.11. Alta Mira Fluted: Alta Mira Variety ceramics.

2. Deep bowls with slightly flaring sides (Figure 2.10, p–q).

Intrasite Locations and Contexts: Same as Sierra Red.

Intersite Locations and Contexts: Although a minor type, it consistently occurs wherever significant deposits of Sierra Red are found. Ek (2015:435) lists the type as present in several sites in the Champotón region; however, he does not provide frequency by type, but rather by ceramic group. It is present at Villa Madero (personal observation, INAH Ceramoteca, Mérida, Yucatan)

Laguna Verde Incised: Variety Unspecified (Figure 2.10, r–s)

Frequency: 7 sherds (<1%; <1%)

Established: Type established by Smith and Gifford (1966:170).

Description:

Principal Identifying Attributes: (1) red slip; (2) lustrous, waxy vessel surfaces; (3) incised designs in simple linear patterns; (4) labial flange bowls or dishes.

Paste, Firing, and Temper: Same as Sierra Red.

Surface Finish and Decoration: Surface finish is the same as Sierra Red. Decoration takes the form of incised geometric lines on the tops of labial flanges. The incisions were executed prior to the application of the slip. Some examples are merely circumferential, but others form simple geometric designs, especially, a series of semi-circles or diagonal parallel incisions.

Forms:

1. Labial flange dish or bowl (Figure 2.10r). Bases were presumably flat
2. Flaring-walled dish or bowl with direct rim. (Figure 2.10s).

Intrasite Locations and Contexts: Same as Sierra Red. This is a rare type at Champotón.

Intersite Locations and Contexts: Although a minor type, it usually occurs wherever significant deposits of Sierra Red are found. Ek (2015:435) lists the type as present in several sites in the Champotón region; however, he does not provide frequency by type, but rather by ceramic group. It is present at Villa Madero (personal observation, INAH Ceramoteca, Mérida, Yucatan).

Polvero Ceramic Group (437)

Polvero Black: Polvero Variety (Figures 2.12–2.13)

Frequency: 426 sherds (97%; 11%)

Established: Type and variety established by Smith and Gifford (1966:161, 170)

Description:

Principal Identifying Attributes: (1) black slip; (2) lustrous, waxy vessel surfaces; (3) labial and lateral flanges or ridges; (4) wavy rims or flanges; (5) everted rims; (6) lateral flange or ridge dishes or bowls.

Paste, Firing, and Temper: The paste is medium textured on most examples with paste color ranging from red (2.5YR 4–5/6–8) to light red (2.5YR 6/6) indicating that the black color of the surface was accomplished by smudging of the surfaces, probably late in the firing process. On the other hand, some pieces have dark paste the color of which ranges from dark brown (5YR 3/2) to black (5YR 2.5/1). Red paste seems to be common, although dark pastes are not rare. Dark cores do not seem to occur frequently, although several examples exhibit dark paste on one side of a sherd (from 1/3 to 1/2 of the cross-section), while the other side shows oxidation. Dark yellowish brown paste appears occasionally (10YR 4–5/6). Temper is similar to that of Sierra Red with white to gray calcite particles; however, it is clear that crushed sherd was also used as an aplastic. These pieces of crushed sherd are especially noticeable in the dark paste examples.

Surface Finish and Decoration: Surfaces were well smoothed. A slip, which fired to a black color (2.5YR 2.5/0; 5YR 2.5–3/1) to dark gray (2.5YR 3/0) through a dusky red color (10R 2.5–3/1; 2.5YR 3/1–2), was applied. Surface mottling to a reddish brown (10R 3–4/2; 5YR 4/4) or weak red (10R 4/4) color on portions of the vessel surface is not uncommon. The slip was polished to create a lustrous, shiny surface. As on types of the Sierra Ceramic Group, decoration occurs in the form of multiple parallel preslip grooving on everted rims. This decorative technique does not seem to be as common, however, on Polvero Black vessels as it is on Sierra Red examples. Flanges, particularly labial and lateral flanges, are common. These were sometimes wavy or notched, but this is relatively rare, as are rim protuberances.

Forms:

1. Lateral flange dish or bowl (Figure 2.12, b–e). The silhouette is composite. Bases were flat.
2. Medial flange bowl (Figure 2.12, f–g). Bases were flat
3. Dish or bowl with flaring walls (Figure 2.12, h–k).
4. Everted rim dish or bowl (Figure 2.12, l–w). Bases were flat.
5. Labial flange dish or bowl (Figure 2.12, a, x–y). Bases were flat.

Intrasite Locations and Contexts: Same as Sierra Red.

Intersite Locations and Contexts: This type is a widespread and common type throughout both the Southern and Northern Lowlands.

Figure 2.12. Polvero Ceramic Group profile drawings—Polvero Black: Polvero Variety.

Figure 2.13. Polvero Black: Polvero Variety ceramics.

Ek (2015:435) lists the type as present in several sites in the Champotón region; however, he does not provide frequency by type, but rather by ceramic group. It is present at Villa Madero (personal observation, INAH Ceramoteca, Mérida, Yucatan).

Comment: Although Polvero Black is a smudged variant of Sierra Red, occurring in most of the same forms and with the same decorative treatments, there seems to be a tendency for Polvero Black to emphasize flanged vessels to a considerably greater degree than Sierra Red. Labial, medial, and lateral flange vessels make up a greater proportion of the form classes than Sierra Red. This pattern not only occurs at Champotón, but at most (many?) sites where Chicanel ceramics are found. At Champotón Polvero Black is much less common than Sierra Red.

Flor Ceramic Group (112)

Flor Cream: Flor Variety (Figures 2.14–2.15)

Frequency: 106 sherds (95%; 3%)

Established: Smith and Gifford (1966:158,170)

Description:

Principal Identifying Attributes: (1) cream slip; (2) lustrous, waxy vessel surfaces; (3) labial and lateral flanges or ridges; (4) wavy rims or flanges; (5) dish or bowl forms.

Paste, Firing, and Temper: The paste is generally medium textured. Paste color tends to range from red or light red (2.5YR 5/6–8; 6/6) to a dark to pale brown color (7.5YR 3–4/4; 10YR 7/3–4), although dark paste also occurs occasionally (7.5YR 3/0; 10YR 2/1). The temper is the same as Sierra Red and Polvero Black—a

Figure 2.14. Flor Cream: Flor Variety ceramics.

mixture of calcite and sherd; but other particles may be present as well.

Surface Finish and Decoration: Vessel surfaces were well smoothed before slipping. As with other members of Paso Caballo Waxy Ware, the slipped surfaces were well polished. The slip ranges in color from white or gray to very pale brown (10YR 7/0–48/1–3), pinkish gray (7.5YR 7–8/2) to pinkish white (5YR 8/2) are also common. Black or dark gray fire-clouding also occur. The only decoration noted takes the form of rim grooving on the upper surfaces of everted rims in a manner similar to that found on Sierra Red. In addition, ridge and flange notching also occurs.

Forms:

1. Labial flange dish or bowl (Figure 2.15, f–h, j–p). Bases were flat.
2. Lateral flange or ridge dish or bowl (Figure 2.15i). Bases were flat.
3. Everted rim dish or bowl (Figure 2.15, a–e). Bases were flat.
4. Restricted orifice small-shouldered jar (Figure 2.15q). Base form is unknown.
5. Miscellaneous vessesl forms (Figure 5.15, r–s).

Bases and Supports: Bases are apparently generally flat. Solid, circular nubbin pods occur rarely.

Intrasite Locations and Contexts: Same as Sierra Red

Intersite Locations and Contexts: This is a well-known type found at a wide variety of sites in both the Southern and Northern Lowlands. It generally is found wherever

Figure 2.15. Flor Ceramic Group profile drawings—Flor Cream: Flor Variety.

Sierra Ceramic Group vessels are found as an important component of the ceramic complex. Ek (2015:435) lists the type as present in several sites in the Champotón region; however, he does not provide frequency by type, but rather by ceramic group.

Comment: Like Polvero Black, Flor Cream tends to occur more frequently in labial and lateral flange vessels than in the Sierra Red type. Just why this should be so is not clear, but it is a pattern observed at many sites in the Maya Lowlands. It is also clear, as a result of fire-clouding found on various vessels, that the differences between Sierra, Polvero, and Flor vessel surfaces is due to firing. Otherwise, the vessels seem to be made from the same paste and the same slip.

Figure 2.16. Sapote Striated: Sapote Variety ceramics.

UAXACTUN UNSLIPPED WARE [192]

Sapote Ceramic Group (192)

Sapote Striated: Sapote Variety (Figures 2.16–2.17, a–h)

Frequency: 116 sherds (60%; 3%).

Established: Type and variety established by Smith and Gifford (1966:162, 170).

Description:

Principal Identifying Attributes: (1) unslipped vessel surfaces; (2) fine to medium-line striations on vessel exteriors; (3) short-necked jar forms.

Paste, Firing, and Temper: The texture of the paste of this ware ranges from medium coarse to coarse. Paste colors range from red to light red (10R 5/6–8; 2.5YR 6/4–6) to reddish brown (5YR 6–7/4), light brown (7.5YR 6/4) to dark reddish brown (5YR 3/2); however, paste color varies considerably. Even though vessel surfaces may be gray to dark gray, they often have reddish paste, although others have dark paste as well. Temper is crushed limestone of one form or another. In both size (0.1–0.3 mm) and proportion, it is significantly larger than in the Paso Caballo pottery, thus giving the pottery its coarse texture.

Surface Finish and Decoration: Surfaces are often gray to light gray (5YR 5–8/1), but darker hues also occur (5YR 2.5–3/1). Light red surfaces are also found, however (2.5YR 6/4–6), as well as beige surfaces (7.5YR 8/4). In fact, although there is a strong tendency for gray to light red surfaces to predominate, surface color is quite variable even on a given vessel. Exteriors were roughly smoothed or finished and then striated. Striations normally occur only on the exterior body with the exterior neck

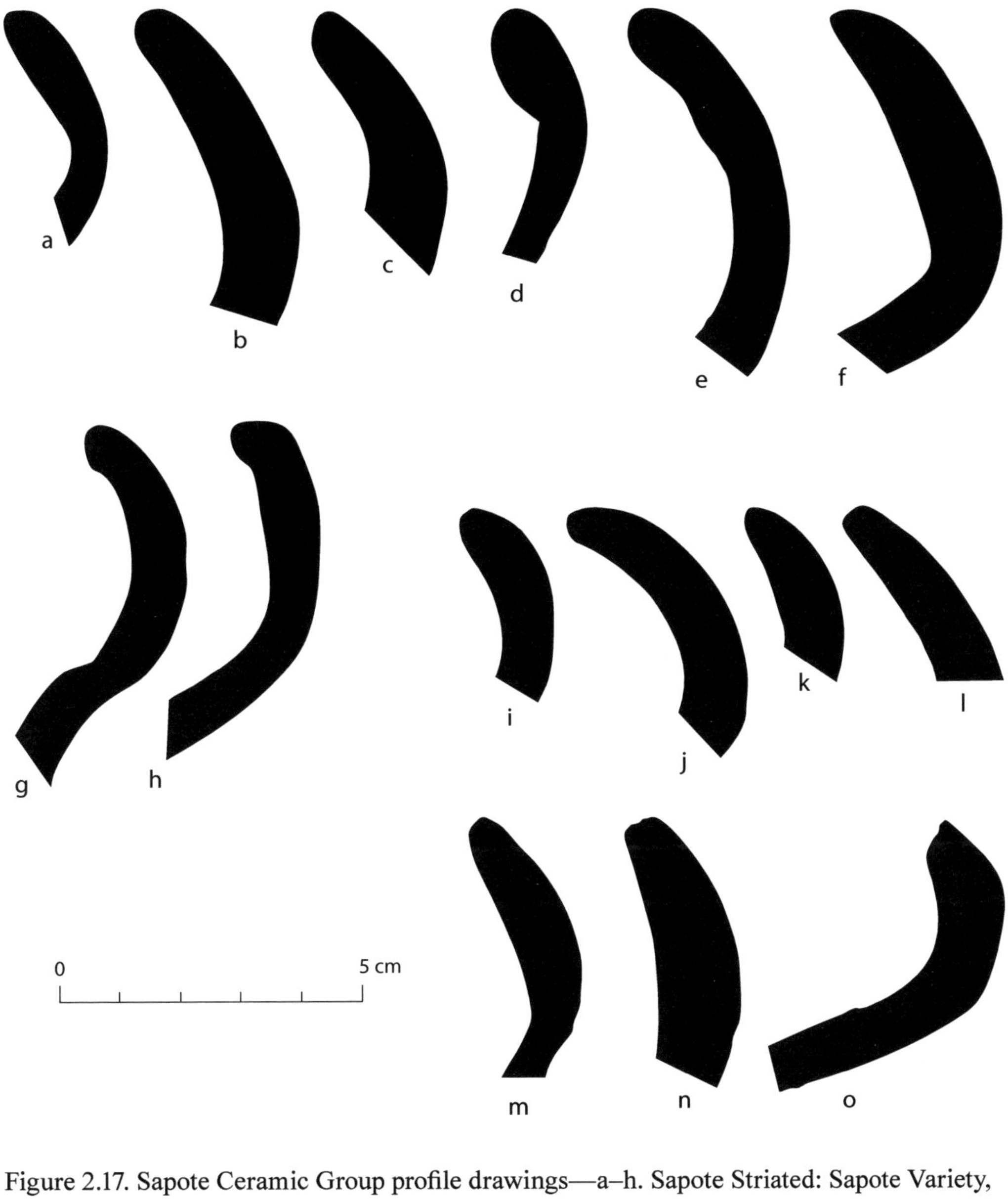

Figure 2.17. Sapote Ceramic Group profile drawings—a–h. Sapote Striated: Sapote Variety, i–o. Achiotes Unslipped: Variety Unspecified.

left unstriated, although a few examples bear striations right up to near the rim of the vessel. Notably, on some examples there are horizontal striations on the interior neck, although this is not common. Striations are characteristically narrow (0.25–0.60 mm) and usually closely spaced (1–3 mm). Striations can be horizontal, vertical or diagonal, although it appears that all of these variations might be used on different sections of the exterior.

Forms:

1. Short-necked jar (Figure 2.17, a–h).

Intrasite Locations and Contexts: Same as Sierra Red. The type was also found in some quantity at Group 1, Structure 1 B-32.

Intersite Locations and Contexts: This is the dominant unslipped type throughout much of the Southern Lowlands, and much of the Northern Lowlands as well. Ek (2015:435) lists the type as present in several sites in the Champotón region; however, he does not provide frequency by type, but rather by ceramic group. It is present at Villa Madero (personal observation, INAH Ceramoteca, Mérida, Yucatan).

Comment: Sapote Striated usually makes up a third or more of Late Preclassic complexes; nonetheless, at Champotón it is relatively scarce compared to Paso Caballo Ware. Just why this should be so is not clear.

Achiotes Unslipped: Variety Unspecified (Figure 2.17, i–o)

Frequency: 76 sherds (40%; 2%)

Established: Type established by Smith and Gifford (1966:154,170) as a Mamom horizon type. Established as a Chicanel horizon type by Adams (1971:18) and Culbert (n.d.:ch. 21; Ca9; Ci12). They have defined this type essentially to include both the Mamom horizon and Chicanel horizon (Paila Unslipped) unslipped plain pottery, see Forsyth (1989:49).

Description:

Principal Identifying Attributes: (1) unslipped vessel surfaces; (2) smooth to rough vessel exteriors and interiors; (3) short to medium-necked jar forms.

Paste, Firing, and Temper: Same as Sapote Striated: Sapote Variety.

Surface Finish and Decoration: Surface colors are similar in range of variation to Sapote Striated. Achiotes Unslipped differs from Sapote Striated in that vessel exteriors were left plain rather than striated.

Forms:

1. Short-necked jars (Figure 2.17, i–o). This is the overwhelmingly dominant form.

Intrasite Locations and Contexts: Same as Sierra Red.

Intersite Locations and Contexts: This type is widespread in both the Northern and Southern Maya Lowlands. Ek (2015:435) lists the type as present in several sites in the Champotón region; however, he does not provide frequency by type, but rather by ceramic group. It is present at Villa Madero (personal observation, INAH Ceramoteca, Mérida, Yucatan).

Comment: Achiotes Unslipped is less common than Sapote Striated at Champotón but is proportionally more common relative to that type than is usually the case in many Late Preclassic ceramic complexes.

Other Sierra Group: Alta Mira Fluted with black painting

A single sherd of a flaring-walled, everted rim dish bore vertical exterior fluting with black splotches near the exterior rim. It seems a kind of combination of Alta Mira Fluted and Repasto Black-on-red (See Figure 2.18a).

Other Sierra Group: Correlo Incised-dichrome.

A single example of Correlo Incised-dichrome was recovered from Group 1, Structure 1, I-21a. It bears a series of incised parallel lines cut through the slip to reveal the paste underneath on the interior rim of a lateral-flange bowl (see Figure 2.18b).

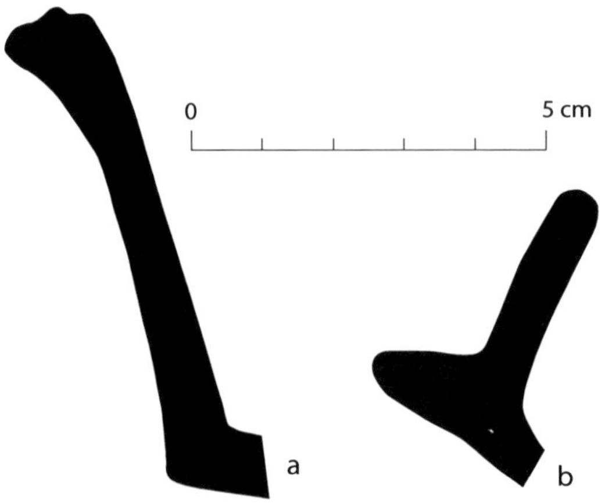

Figure 2.18. Profile drawings—a. Alta Mira Fluted with black painting, b. Correlo Incised-dichrome.

Other Polvero Group: Unnamed reed-impressed & incised

Four rims, one body, and one base from a deep bowl with a slightly bolstered rim bore reed impressions combined with incisions. These may well be from the same vessel, but only two of the rims fit together. The effect was to produce areas with multiple reed impressions within lightly incised lines; however, some of these incised zones bore many reed impressions, while others only one or two. The reed impressions seem to have been executed after the application of the slip but before firing. This piece may represent a very late facet of the Late Preclassic.

Other Polvero Group: Unnamed incised

Two examples of what may be Lechugal Incised were recovered from unknown proveniences. One consists of preslip incising in a hatched pattern on the exterior wall of a vessel. Another has parallel diagonal incisions that reach to near the base of a vessel with small teat supports. A third example is a deep bowl that was slipped on the exterior from the rim down about 3 cm, and then left unslipped below that. In the unslipped area were executed deep parallel diagonal incised lines.

Other Polvero Group: Mushroom Stand

Two sherds from what appear to be a Polvero Black mushroom stand were recovered from Group 1, Structure 1 I–28a.

Other Polvero Group: Koben Composite

A single sherd of Koben Composite was recovered from Group 1, Structure 1, I–11a (see Forsyth 1983:48–49 for a description of Koben Composite).

Other Flor Group: Accordion Incised

Five rim sherds bearing horizontal preslip medium-width incisions were recovered—two from Group 1, Structure 1, and three from Moquel.

Other Flor Group: Fluted

A single body sherd belonging to the Flor Ceramic Group bore horizontal flutes on the exterior. Vessel form is unknown.

The Terminal Preclassic

Near the end of the Late Preclassic, new decorative and form modes appear that are unequivocally different from the previous Late Preclassic pattern, some of which presage the succeeding Early Classic pattern. Still, many of the old Late Preclassic forms continue to be manufactured. Among the new modes that appear at this time are an increase in exteriorly bolstered or folded rims, raised "hooked" rims or variants thereof, mammiform supports, as well as the appearance of orange-slipped monochromes, dichromes, and even trichromes. This period is not well represented at Champotón—and is not altogether completely clear. Below, I outline the types and varieties that pertain to this period, but the typology is certainly incomplete and is often difficult to distinguish from the Late Preclassic proper. I therefore treat it as a subdivision of the Late Preclassic period, although this may turn out to be a mistaken decision when more data are available.

Sierra Red: Variety Unspecified (Figure 2.19)

Frequency: Not counted apart from the Late Preclassic sherds.

Established: Smith and Gifford (1966:170).

Description:

Principal Identifying Attributes: (1) red slip; (2) lustrous, waxy vessel surfaces; (3) rounded-bottom vessels with "hooked rim;" (4) basal angle dish or bowl with triangular rim bolster.

Paste, Firing, and Temper: The paste is the same as the Chon Variety.

Surface Finish and Decoration: Essentially the same as the Chon Variety; however, the preslip grooving on the interior everted rim, so characteristic of the Chon and Sierra Varieties, is much less common on the Unspecified variety.

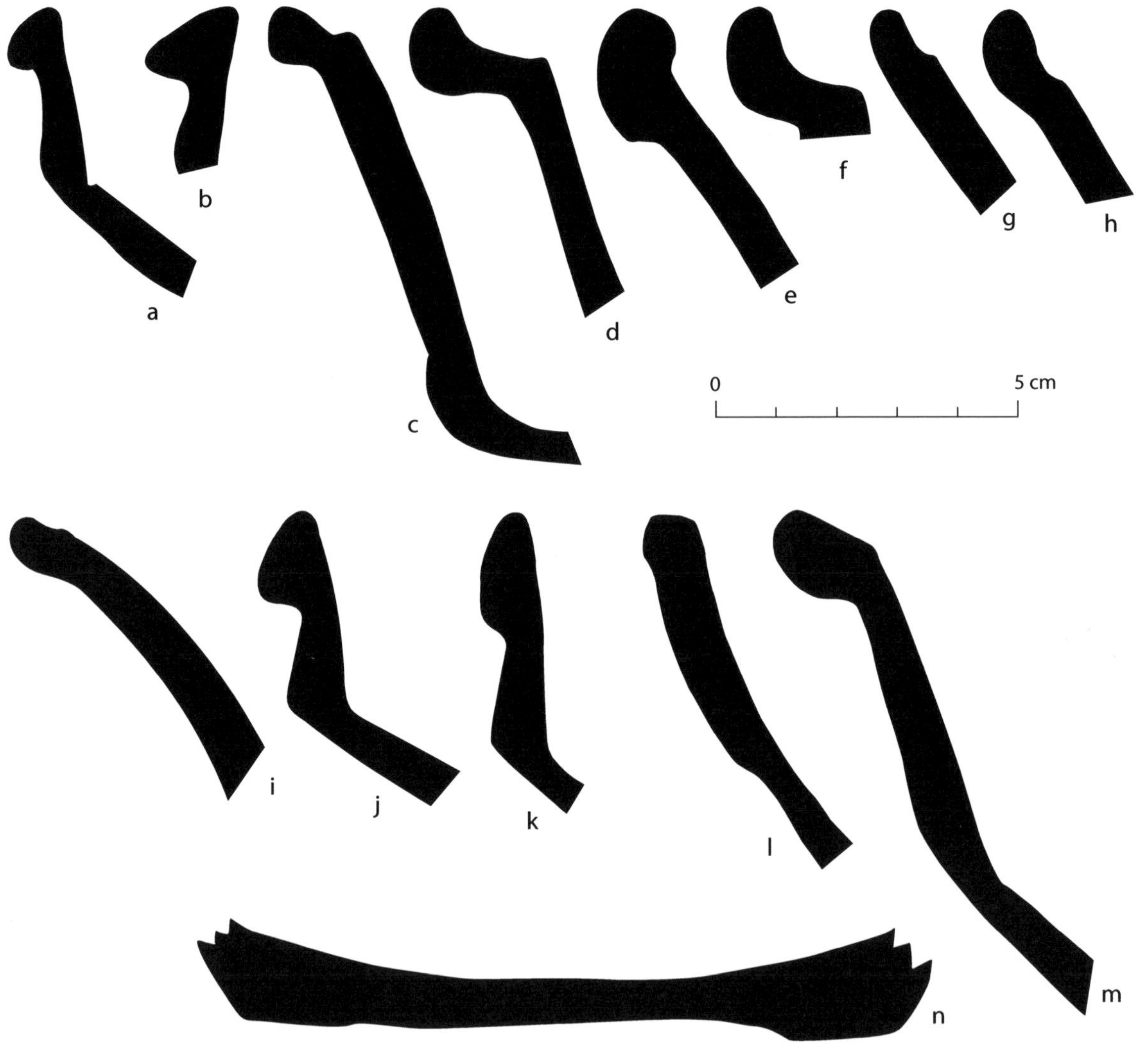

Figure 2.19. Sierra Ceramic Group profile drawings—Sierra Red: Variety Unspecified.

Forms:

1. Rounded-bottom vessels with "hooked rim" (Figure 2.19, c–i). Bases probably had tetrapod teat supports.
2. Basal angle dish or bowl with triangular rim bolster (Figure 2.19, a–b, j–k). Base form is unknown.
3. Miscellaneous vessel forms (Figure 2.19, l–n).

Bases and Supports: Although no complete bases were recovered, evidence from other areas where this type is present (e.g., Nakbé, El Mirador) suggests that vessels with hooked rims probably bore solid tetrapod teat supports (see Figure 2.19n). Other vessels may have had flat bottoms.

Intrasite Locations and Contexts: This variety was recovered from many of the same contexts as the Chon Variety but in much smaller amounts. There was no apparent stratigraphic separation between the two varieties, but most of this material was probably in secondary context in any event. The Unspecified variety was very rare, but present, at Moquel.

Intersite Locations and Contexts: The production of Sierra Red vessels continues into the Terminal Preclassic period at a number of sites. It clearly does so in the Mirador Basin (Forsyth n.d. b:450; personal observation), and almost certainly at other sites as well (see Brady et al. 1998:22)

Comment: Sierra Red continued to be manufactured during the Terminal Preclassic at the time that new slip and paste types (a new ware) were being introduced into the ceramic inventory. Evidence of this is provided by the fact that new forms accompanied the new slip and paste types, and Sierra Red (and other Paso Caballo Waxy Ware types) was manufactured in these new forms. Hooked rim vessels with very different bases and supports from standard Late Preclassic ones, as well as basal angle dishes or bowls with triangular rim bolsters, were diagnostic of new Terminal Preclassic pottery that was introduced into the Maya Lowlands, including Champotón. These new forms were duplicated in Paso Caballo Waxy ware vessels. Moreover, new rim and vessel forms, which were apparently not associated with the newly introduced ware, also occur in some frequency in Sierra Red and Polvero Black (and probably Flor Cream as well). Nevertheless, more traditional forms, such as lateral flange and angle dishes or bowls, continue to be manufactured. Since there is no change in the paste or surface characteristics of this pottery, it is only changes in form that the Unspecified variety can be identified as Terminal Preclassic

Polvero Ceramic Group

Polvero Black: Variety Unspecified (Figure 2.20, a–b)

Frequency: Not counted apart from the Late Preclassic sherds.

Established: Type and variety established by Smith and Gifford (1966:161,170).

Description:

Principal Identifying Attributes: (1) black slip; (2) lustrous, waxy vessel surfaces; (3) rounded-bottom vessels with "hooked rim;" (4) Basal angle dish or bowl with triangular rim bolster.

Paste, Firing, and Temper: Same as the Polvero Variety.

Surface Finish and Decoration: Same as the Polvero Variety.

Forms:

1. Rounded-bottom vessels with "hooked rim" (Figure 2.20a). Bases probably had tetrapod teat supports.
2. Basal angle dish or bowl with triangular rim bolster. Base form is unknown (no illustration).
3. Miscellaneous vessel forms (Figure 2.20b).

Intrasite Locations and Contexts: Same as Sierra Red: Variety Unspecified.

Intersite Locations and Contexts: The production of Polvero Black vessels continues into the Terminal Preclassic period at a number of sites. It clearly does so in the Mirador Basin (Forsyth 2006:450; personal observation), and almost certainly at other sites as well (see Brady et al. 1998:22).

Comment: See comment section under Sierra Red: Variety Unspecified. The same pattern obtains for Polvero Black: Variety Unspecified.

Flor Ceramic Group?

Mateo Red-on-cream: Variety Unspecified (Figure 2.20, c–l)

Frequency: Not counted apart from the Late Preclassic sherds.

Established: Smith and Gifford (1966:170).

Description:

Principal Identifying Attributes: (1) red slip on interiors, cream slip on exteriors or vice versa, or the above with red designs, usually in the form of multiple parallel lines on the cream base slip; (2) lustrous, waxy surface finish.

Paste, Firing, and Temper: Paste is generally like that of Sierra Red suggesting that these

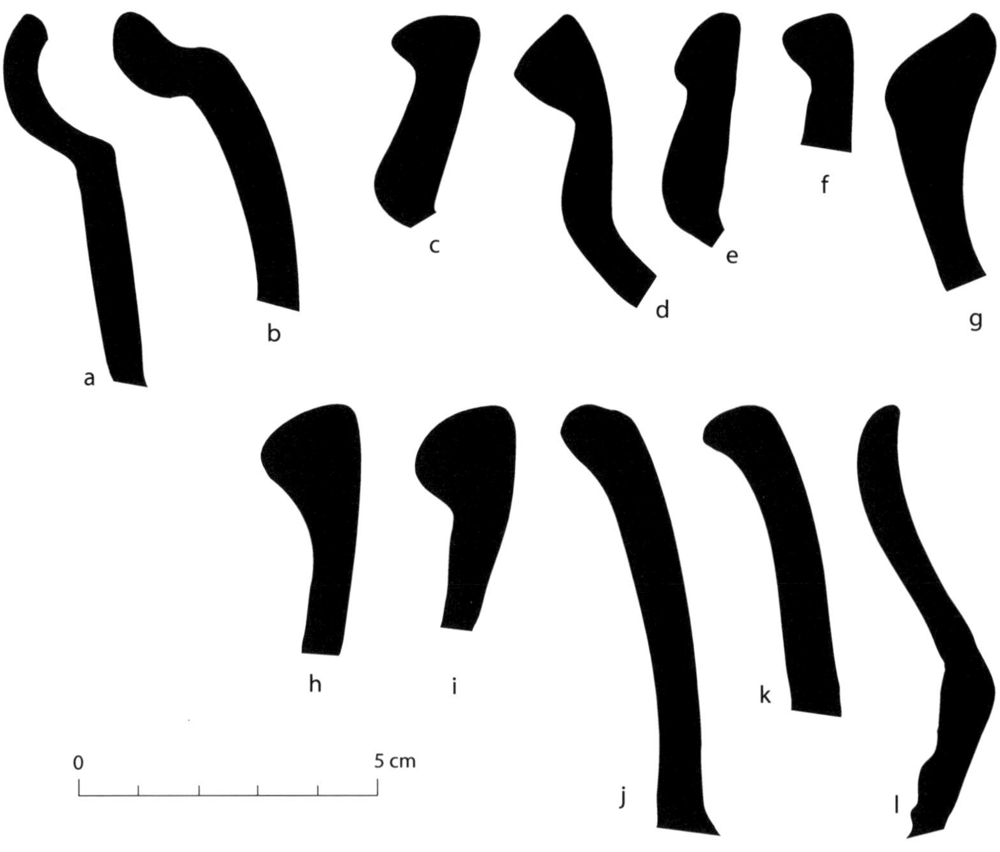

Figure 2.20. Polvero and Flor Ceramic Groups profile drawings—a–b. Polvero Black: Variety Unspecified, c–l. Mateo Red-on-cream: Variety Unspecified.

vessels were essentially manufactured like Sierra Red but with the differential slip color purposely achieved.

Surface Finish and Decoration: Interiors were slipped with a red-firing slip identical to that found on Sierra Red. Vessel exteriors were slipped cream like that found on Flor Cream. Sometimes the field colors were reversed. On one vessel both the interior and exterior were slipped cream and bore a red band near the rim. It is not clear how this differential effect was achieved. In some cases, the cream slip was applied first over most of the vessel, and the red slip applied over this. In other cases, it is not clear that this was so. On most examples the effect is merely differential colors with the red on one side, usually on the rim, and cream on the other. In a few examples, however, the cream area bears multiple vertical parallel red or red-orange lines running down the interior of the vessel.

Forms:

1. Basal angle dish or bowl with triangular rim bolster (Figure 2.20, c–f).
2. Slightly everted rim dish or bowl (Figure 2.20, j–k).
3. Composite silhouette vessel (Figure 2.20l).
4. Miscellaneous forms (Figure 2.20, g–i).

Intrasite Locations and Contexts: Same as Sierra Red.

Intersite Locations and Contexts: This type is widespread, although not usually very numerous, in the Maya Lowlands in a Terminal Preclassic context.

Comment: Mateo Red-on-cream is primarily a Terminal Preclassic type. Both in its principal shape, the basal angle dish or bowl with triangular rim bolster, and in its decorative elements, multiple parallel lines, it is similar to Caramba Red-on-red-orange, Escobal Red-on-buff, and other types of the Terminal Preclassic (ca. AD 1–150). Smith and Gifford (1966:170) classified it as part of the Flor Ceramic Group, and most other analysts have followed them (see Forsyth 1983:51–52), but perhaps it should be considered as a separate ceramic group. It is possible that it begins earlier in the Late Preclassic period, but most of the examples are, for the reasons given above, clearly late.

PETEN GLOSS WARE [36]

Iberia Ceramic Group (36)

Iberia Orange: Iberia Variety (Figure 2.21, a–i)

Frequency: 34 sherds (95%; not calculated).

Established: Established as Iberia Orange: Iberia Variety by Sabloff (1975:90) at Seibal [Ceibal].

Description:

Principal Identifying Attributes: (1) creamy orange slip; (2) light-colored underslip; (3) red to orange-colored paste; (4) mammiform supports; (5) hooked rim mode.

Paste, Firing, and Temper: The paste is medium textured, dense, and strong. Paste color ranges from pink (10R 6/4–6; 2.5YR 6/4; 5YR 7/4) through orange (light red) colors, although red paste is also common (2.5YR 4–5/8). Firing was carried out in an oxidizing atmosphere and was generally quite thorough and complete; only rarely are there darkened areas where the paste was not oxidized. Temper consists of crushed calcite; thus, the paste is carbonate.

Surface Finish and Decoration: Surfaces were apparently well smoothed prior to slipping; however, many of these sherds are badly weathered and surfaces are pitted. Surfaces were slipped, apparently using a double-slipping technique in which a white to cream (10YR 8/1) colored underslip was first applied. Then an orange-firing reddish yellow (5YR 6–7/4–8; 7.5YR 7/6), or light red (2.5YR 6/6–8) slip was applied. In some cases the underslip may not have been applied. It is sometimes difficult to determine because of the weathered nature of the surfaces. In other cases, the cream underslip is clearly visible with smaller pieces of orange slip on top. Both slips are poorly bonded to the vessel surface and weather easily, such that it is rare to find an example with the slip intact.

Forms:

1. Flaring-walled dish or bowl with interior hooked rim and rounded bottom. (Figure 2.21, a–f). This is by far the most common form. At least some of these vessels almost certainly bore tetrapod supports, either of the solid teat or hollow mammiform categories.
2. Basal angle dish or bowl with rounded rim bolster (Figure 2.21, g–i). Base form is presumably similar to Form 1.

Supports: A single basal sherd of Iberia Orange bore the partial remains of a large, probably mammiform, foot pod. We thus have little direct evidence of mammiform or teat supports for Iberia Orange at Champotón. Still, given that in all other respects, Iberia Orange is identical to that type found in other areas of the Maya Lowlands, it follows logically that they did have these kinds of supports. See Forsyth (1989:53–55) for a fuller discussion and illustration of the supports for this type.

Intrasite Locations and Contexts: This type is not common at Champotón but was found in larger numbers in Group 1, Structure 1, Areas D and I.

Intersite Locations and Contexts: This is actually a fairly widespread type in both the Northern and Southern Lowlands, although it never seems to be especially numerous. While it was defined at Seibal [Ceibal] (Sabloff 1975:90, 94), it has not been readily recognized by other analysts until recently (Brady et al.

Table 2.2. Late Preclassic: the Petentun Ceramic Complex type count.

PASO CABALLO WAXY WARE	3252
Sierra Ceramic Group	**2703**
Sierra Red: Chon Variety	2582
Ciego Composite: Ciego Variety	42
Repasto Black-on-red: Repasto Variety	31
Hongo Composite: Hongo Variety	31
Alta Mira Fluted: Alta Mira Variety	8
Laguna Verde Incised: Variety Unspecified	7
Other Sierra Group	1
Correlo Inicised-dichrome	1
Polvero Ceramic Group	**437**
Polvero Black: Polvero Variety	426
Other Polvero Group	11
Flor Ceramic Group	**112**
Flor Cream: Flor Variety	106
Other Flor Group	6
UAXACTUN UNSLIPPED WARE	192
Sapote Ceramic Group	**192**
Sapote Striated: Sapote Variety	116
Achiotes Unslipped: Variety Unspecified	76
Total	3444

1998:31–32). See also Forsyth 1989:53–55 for further discussion of the type.

Comment: This type is a diagnostic marker for the Terminal Preclassic (or Protoclassic 1 in the Brady et al. [1998] terminology). In addition to Champotón, I have noted its presence at Santa Rosa Xtampak as well (personal observation).

Other Terminal Preclassic: Caramba Red-on-red-orange

A single sherd of Caramba Red-on-red-orange was recovered from Group 1, Structure 1, I–18a. This is a typical Caramba basal angle dish with triangular rim bolster vessel (Figure 2.21j).

Other Terminal Preclassic: Sacluc Black-on-orange

Two sherds of Sacluc Black-on-orange were recovered from Group 1, Structure 1.

Other Terminal Preclassic: Escobal Red-on-buff

Three sherds, two from Moquel, and one from area K of Group 1, Structure 1 are in our sample.

Other Terminal Preclassic: Usulutan

One body and two rim sherds of what appear to be Usulutan imports were recovered from area I of Group 1, Structure 1 (Figure 2.21, k–l).

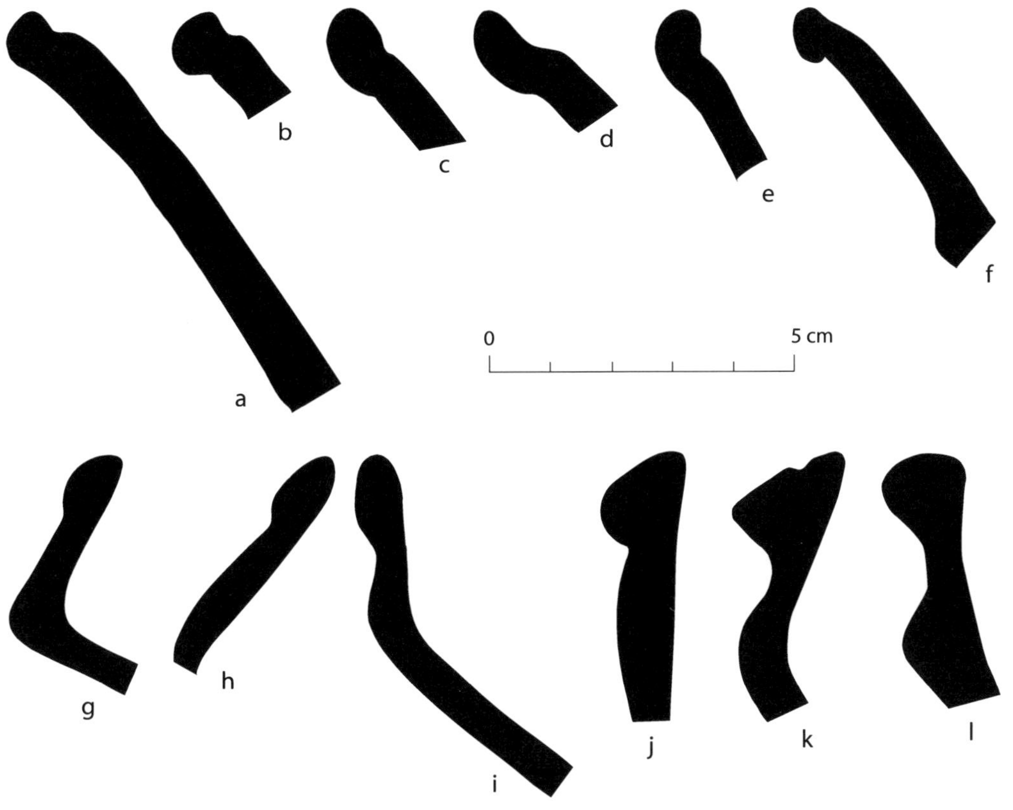

Figure 2.21. Iberia Ceramic Group profile drawings—a–i. Iberia Orange: Iberia Variety, j. Other Terminal Preclassic: Caramba Red-on-red-orange, k–l. Other Terminal Preclassic: Usulutan.

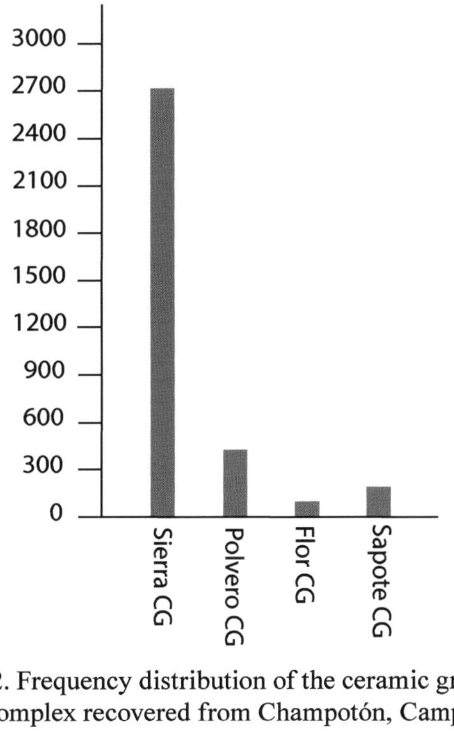

Figure 2.22. Frequency distribution of the ceramic groups of the Petentun Ceramic Complex recovered from Champotón, Campeche, México

CHAPTER 3

CERMIC TYPE DESCRIPTIONS, CLASSIC PERIOD

EARLY CLASSIC

Early Classic ceramics in the Champotón Project's collections are very rare. Based on excavations carried out by the project, there is evidence of presence, but not much else. The total number of recognizable sherds from this period barely exceeds 100. Given this, I have declined to define a ceramic complex. It may well be that there was a significant occupation at Champotón during Early Classic times, but it is not evident in the ceramic data.

Peten Gloss Ware

Aguila Ceramic Group

Aguila Orange: Aguila Variety
San Blas Red-on-orange: San Blas Variety
Dos Arroyos Orange-polychrome: Dos Arroyos Variety

PETEN GLOSS WARE [106]

Aguila Ceramic Group (97)

Aguila Orange: Aguila Variety (Figures 3.1–3.2)

Frequency: 57 sherds (59%; 53%)

Established: Type and variety established by Smith and Gifford (1966:154, 171)

Description:

Principal Identifying Attributes: (1) orange slip color; (2) glossy surface finish; (3) cylindrical neck jar; (4) rounded Z-angle bowl; (5) annular bases.

Paste, Firing, and Temper: The paste is medium textured. Vessels were fired in an oxidizing atmosphere resulting in light red to red (2.5YR 5–6/6; 4/6) but more pinkish gray paste colors also occur (7.5YR 7/4). Temper is normally a medium-sized (average size: 0.3–0.4 mm) gray calcite. One unusual sherd has a much higher number of white calcite particles as temper, which are, however, smaller than the usual size (average: 0.2 mm).

Surface Finish and Decoration: Vessel surfaces were well smoothed prior to slipping. The application of the slip often involved the application of a cream to pinkish underslip, although not all sherds necessarily received this cream underslip. An orange-firing slip was applied to the surface(s) and polished to a high gloss. The most common color is a strong light red (2.5YR 5–6/8) although reddish yellow occurs rarely 5YR 7/8). The majority of examples, however, tend toward the light red end of the spectrum. The slip was applied to vessel interiors, exteriors, or both depending on vessel shape.

Forms:

1. Cylindrical neck jar (Figure 3.2, e–j). This is the most common form. Only vessel exteriors, and occasionally the interior neck, were slipped. Base form is unknown, but presumably flat or annular.
2. Rounded Z-angle bowl (Figure 3.2a). Bases are almost certainly annular.
3. Sharp Z-angle bowl (not illustrated). This form is not common in the Champotón collection.
4. Basal-angle dish or bowl (Figure 3.2b). This is not a common form; it was slipped on both the exterior and interior. Presumably bases were annular.

Bases and Supports: Several annular bases are associated with most forms of this type (Figure 3.2, c–d).

Figure 3.1. Aguila Orange: Aguila Variety ceramics.

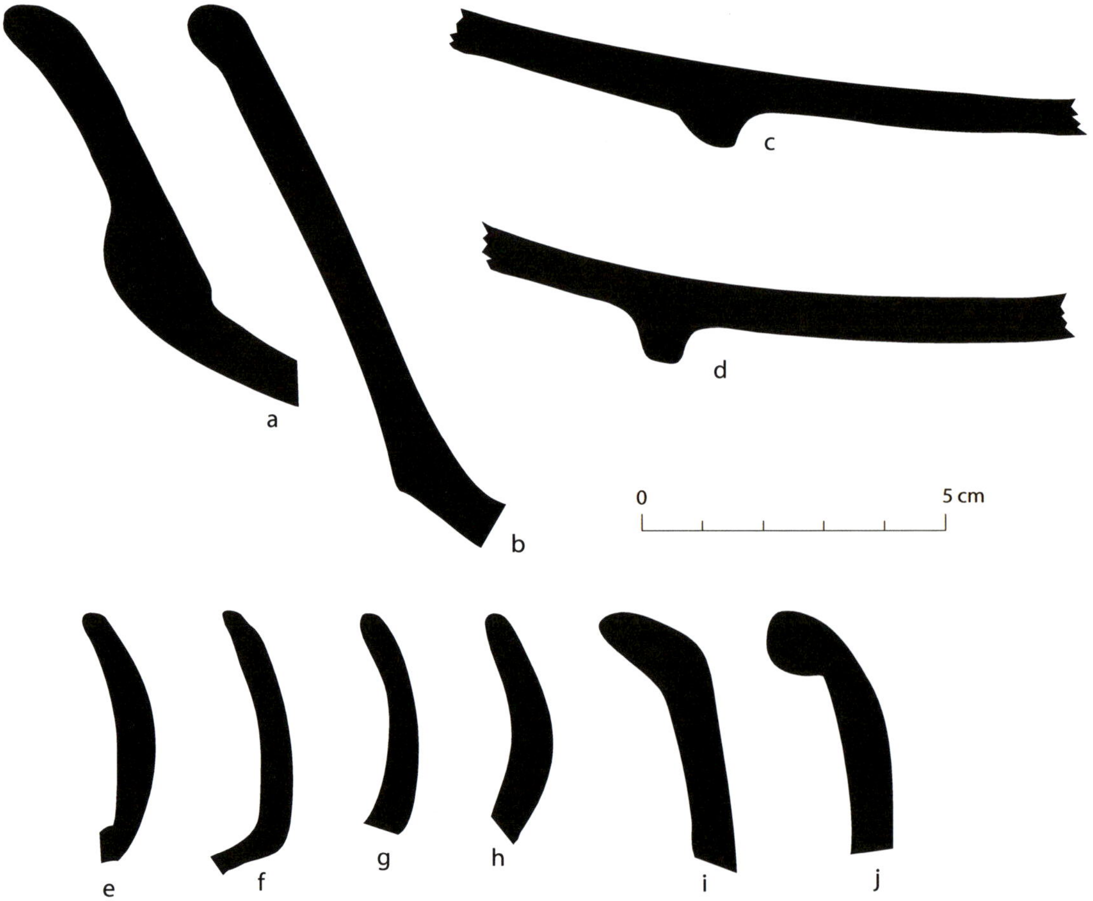

Figure 3.2. Aguila Ceramic Group profile drawings—Aguila Orange: Aguila Variety.

Intrasite Locations and Contexts: Aguila Orange, like other Early Classic types, is not common at Champotón. It was recovered primarily from Group 1, Structure 1 (Guadalupe), particularly in Areas D and I. It was also found in very small quantities at Moquel.

Intersite Locations and Contexts: This is a widespread and well-represented type throughout the Lowlands. Ek (2015:448) lists the type as present in some sites in the Champotón region; however, he does not provide frequency by type, but rather by ceramic group. It is present at Villa Madero (personal observation, INAH Ceramoteca, Mérida, Yucatan); compare this to the Tampak Variety from Edzná (Forsyth 1983:67–68).

Comment: Aguila Orange is rare in the Champotón region. It is also fairly unusual in that there are few examples of clear rounded Z-angle bowls, so common in other areas where this type is present. This may, however, simply be a function of sampling given the relative weakness of the Early Classic occupation at the site—at least based on what we have recovered to date.

San Blas Red-on-orange: San Blas Variety (Figure 3.3, a–d)

Frequency: 10 sherds (10%; 9%)

Established: Type and variety established by Smith and Gifford (1966:162, 171) at Uaxactún.

Description:

Principal Identifying Attributes: (1) orange slip color; (2) glossy surface finish; (3) double-slipping technique; (4) red paint applied over orange slip.

Paste, Firing, and Temper: Same as Aguila Orange.

Surface Finish and Decoration: The same as Aguila Orange. Red paint (10R 4/8; 2.5YR 4–5/8) was added to vessel rims covering the top of the lip and about 1 cm on the interior or exterior or both. In fact, a red lip band occurs on most examples of this type. On one sherd an additional red band, about 1 cm wide, was added near the basal break. The relatively few sherds of this type do not permit a more detailed analysis of the decorative technique.

Forms:

1. Rounded Z-angle bowl (Figure 3.3a).
2. Flaring-walled dish or bowl (Figure 3.3b).
3. Miscellaneous forms (Figure 3.3, c–d).

Intrasite Locations and Contexts: This type is rare in our collections. It is known to occur at both Group 1, Structure 1 and Moquel.

Intersite Locations and Contexts: Although rarely numerically significant, it tends to occur wherever there is Aguila Ceramic Group pottery. Ek (2015:448) lists the type as present in some sites in the Champotón region; however, he does not provide frequency by type, but rather by ceramic group; compare this to the Halal Variety from Edzná (Forsyth 1983:68–69).

Dos Arroyos Orange-polychrome: Dos Arroyos Variety (Figure 3.3, e–i)

Frequency: 25 sherds (26%; 23%)

Established: Type and variety established by Smith and Gifford (1966:157, 171) at Uaxactún.

Description:

Principal Identifying Attributes: (1) orange slip color; (2) glossy surface finish; (3) double-slipping technique; (4) polychrome painted in black and red over orange slip; (5) Z-angle bowl; (6) annular base.

Paste, Firing, and Temper: Same as Aguila Orange.

Surface Finish and Decoration: Prior to slipping, vessel surfaces were well smoothed. The cream underslip is usually present on Dos Arroyos vessels. The orange-firing overslip, like that applied to all Aguila Ceramic Group vessels, was then applied over the underslip. This slip was applied to vessel interiors and exteriors on unrestricted forms. Decoration was executed in the form of integrated polychrome painting consisting of geometric designs painted in red (10R 4–5/6–8; 2.5YR 4–5/8) and black

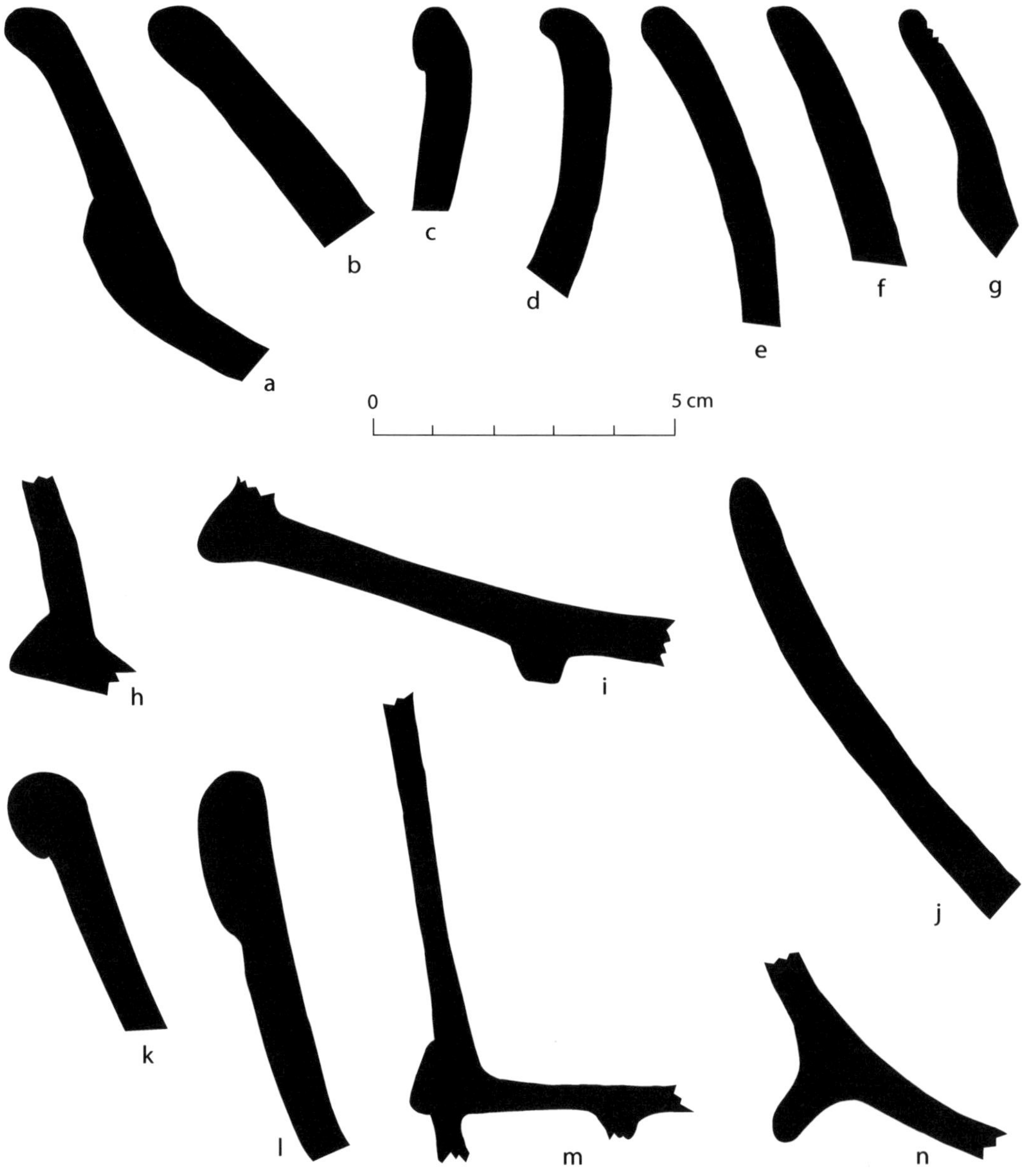

Figure 3.3. Aguila Ceramic Group profile drawings—a–d.San Blas Red-on-orange: San Blas Variety, e–i. Dos Arroyos Orange-polychrome: Dos Arroyos Variety; Other Early Classic Specials: j. Aguila Orange-unslipped exterior, k. Nitan Composite, l. San Blas Red-on-orange-unslipped exterior, m. Lucha Incised, n. Yaloche Cream-polychrome.

(5YR 2–3/0–2), the latter grading into dark brown. No abstract or naturalistic designs were noted, but the sample is very small. A near universal characteristic of the design pattern is the use of alternating circumferential lines or bands in red and black, often separated by a narrow band in the orange slip color. These are usually found near the rim on either the exterior or interior or both. On sharp Z-angle bowls the zone from the point of the Z-angle down to the base is apparently unslipped.

Forms:

1. Sharp Z-angle bowl (Figure 3.3, e–i).
2. Basal-break bowl (not illustrated).

Bases and Supports: As with other members of the Aguila Ceramic Group the annular base is overwhelmingly the dominant form.

Intrasite Locations and Contexts: It was found primarily in two excavation areas in Group 1, Structure 1: B569 and I4a. Twenty of the known 25 sherds were recovered in these two areas, although a few were also found at Moquel.

Intersite Locations and Contexts: This is a widespread type during Early Classic times in the Lowlands. Ek (2015:435, 438) lists the type as present in some sites in the Champotón region; however, he does not provide frequency by type, but rather by ceramic group. It is present at Villa Madero (personal observation, INAH Ceramoteca, Mérida, Yucatan); compare this to the Unspecified Variety from Edzná (Forsyth 1983:71, 73).

Other Aguila Ceramic Group: Aguila Orange-unslipped exterior

One rim and two body sherds, all from the same vessel, bear the orange slip of Aguila Orange on the interior and up onto the top of the rim but were left unslipped on the exterior (Figure 3.3j). The form of the vessel is a large, shallow bowl or small basin with a direct rim. It is, in pattern and general shape, reminiscent of Nitan Composite (Forsyth 1983:73, 75) but lacks the exterior striations that characterize that type.

Other Aguila Ceramic Group: Nitan Composite

A single sherd in Group 3, Structure 1 is a bolstered rim basin that bore orange slip on the interior and was unslipped on the exterior (Figure 3.3k). The unslipped exterior bears horizontal striations. It is essentially identical to Nitan Composite (Forsyth 1983:73, 75). Ek (2015:448) lists the type as present in some sites in the Champotón region.

Other Aguila Ceramic Group: San Blas Red-on-orange-unslipped exterior

A single rim sherd of a bolstered rim bowl or basin with Aguila Orange slip on the interior and a red-painted rim band at the lip, and an unslipped exterior was recovered from Group 1, Structure 1, I–24a (Figure 3.3l). It is much like the type Chivic Composite (Forsyth 1983:75), except that it lacks the exterior striations; compare with Ek (2015).

Other Balanza Ceramic Group: Balanza Black

Four body and one rim of what are clearly basal flange or sharp Z-angle bowls were recovered from Champotón and Moquel. Balanza Ceramic Group vessels were extremely rare in the collections recovered by the Proyecto Champotón.

Other Balanza Ceramic Group: Lucha Incised

One rim and two body sherds from Lucha Incised cylinder tripods were recovered from area I at Group 1, Structure 1 (Figure 3.3m). The two body sherds are from the same vessel, which is significantly weathered. However, it bore fine-line hatched designs on its exterior. The rim sherd is a very badly weathered, small cylinder tripod with only traces of black slip and with at least one circumferential incised line near the base of the vessel.

Other Peten Gloss Ware: Yaloche Cream-polychrome

A single body sherd from a basal flange bowl bears an orange slip on the interior but a cream slip on the exterior. Simple designs in red and black were painted on the cream slip (Figure 3.3n).

UAXACTUN UNSLIPPED WARE

Quintal Unslipped

A single rim sherd of a tall-necked jar, found in Group 1, Structure 1, D-38a–39c, is Quintal Unslipped. Another body sherd from area I-24a bears a typical Early Classic screw-head button appliqué.

Small numbers of completely weathered basal flange sherds were also recovered from Champotón, as well as a couple from Moquel. Other than that, they pertain to the Early Classic period and little else can be determined about them.

Table 3.1. Early Classic type count.

PETEN GLOSS WARE	106
Aguila Ceramic Group	**97**
Aguila Orange: Aguila Variety	57
San Blas Red-on-orange: San Blas Variety	10
Dos Arroyos Orange-polychrome: Dos Arroyos Variety	25
Other Aguila Ceramic Group	5
Balanza Ceramic Group	**8**
Other Peten Gloss Ware	**1**
UAXACTUN UNSLIPPED WARE	1
Quintal Unslipped	**1**

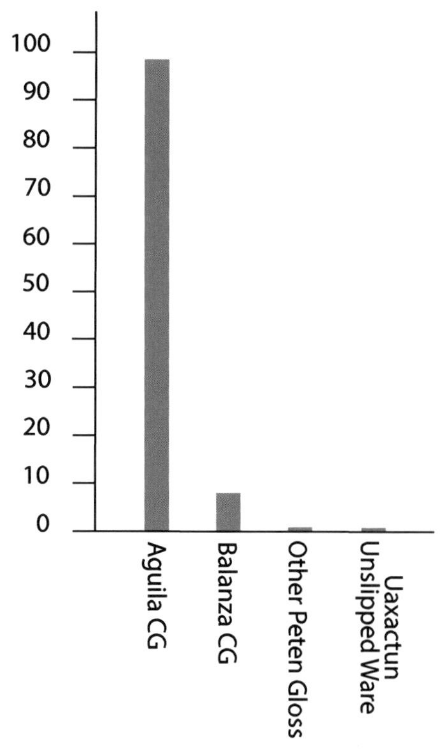

Figure 3.4. Frequency distribution of the Early Classic period ceramic groups recovered from Champotón, Campeche, México

CHAPTER 4

CERMIC TYPE DESCRIPTIONS, LATE/TERMINAL CLASSIC PERIODS

THE LATE/TERMINAL CLASSIC CERAMICS

While the Champotón Project recovered ceramics from the Late and Terminal Classic periods in the region, they have presented considerable difficulty in making sense of them. Given the primarily architectural context of much of the ceramic material recovered from the site, it has not been possible to separate these, and I have therefore treated them as a single ceramic unit, although that is probably not the case. It is possible, however, that future work at the site may make it possible to divide this material into two or more complexes. Ek (2015; 2016) has attempted to do so based on stratigraphic excavations from sites and locations outside of Champotón proper, and his interpretations may have considerable merit. Nevertheless, the Champotón Project materials cannot be readily differentiated based on our data.

Celestún Red Ware

Baca Ceramic Group

Baca Red: Baca Variety

Nimun Ceramic Group

Nimun Brown: Nimun Variety

Unspecified Ware

Unspecified Ceramic Group

Carpizo Red: Carpizo Variety
Carpizo Red: Chenvega Variety

Fine Gray Ware

Chablekal Ceramic Group

Chablekal Gray: Chablekal Variety
Chicxulub Incised: Chicxulub Variety
Cholul Fluted: Cholul Variety
Telchac Compsoite: Telchac Variety
Chekubul Impressed: Chekubul Variety
Dimar Composite: Dimar Variety
Chamblas Composite: Chamblas Variety
Other Chablekal Ceramic Group

Tsibul Ceramic Group

Tsicul Black: Variety Unspecified
Xuxac Incised: Variety Unspecified

Campeche Gloss Ware

Charote Ceramic Group

Charote Red: Charote Variety
Pixoyal Incised: Pixoyal Variety
Ulumal Fluted: Ulumal Variety
Sihochac Dark-red-on-red: Sihochac Variety

Simochac Ceramic Group

Simochac Orange-polychrome: Simochac Variety

Cui Ceramic Group

Cui Orange-polychrome: Cui Variety

Chukul Ceramic Group

Chukul Orange-polychrome: Chukul Variety

Undesignated Ceramic Group

Undesignated Cream-polychrome

Hoxa Unslipped Ware

Chencan Ceramic Group

Chencan Brown-on-orange: Chamizal Variety
Keste Incised: Keste Variety

Undesignated Unslipped Ware

Neza Ceramic Group

Neza Unslipped: Neza Variety

Puuc Unslipped Ware

Acapulquito Ceramic Group

Acapulquito Unslipped: Variety Unspecified
Yakatzib Striated: Yakatzib Variety

Moxa Gray Ware

Hontun Ceramic Group

Chumpic Incised: Variety Unspecified

Isla Fina Fine Buff Ware

Dzitbalché Ceramic Group

Dzitbalché Fine Buff
Cerro de Caracoles Red-on-white

Fine Orange Ware

Altar Ceramic Group

Altar Orange: Altar Variety
Tumba Black-on-orange: Tumba Variety
Trapiche Incised: Trapiche Variety

Balancán Ceramic Group

Provincia Plano-relief: Provinica Variety

Silhó Ceramic Group

Silhó Orange: Silhó Variety
Yalton Black-on-orange: Yalton Variety

Puuc Slate Ware

Muna Ceramic Group

Muna Slate: Muna Variety

Undesignated Wares

Undesignated Ceramic Groups

Tajonal Unslipped: Tajonal Variety
Undesignated Brown/Buff type
Undesignated Black

CELESTÚN RED WARE [1593]

This ware was tentatively defined by Simmons (n.d.) in an unpublished manuscript. Within the ware, Simmons defined two distinct ceramic groups: (1) a red paste group he named Baca, and (2) a brown paste group he called Nimun.

Baca Ceramic Group (1530)

Baca Red: Baca Variety (Figures 4.1–4.2)

Frequency: 1509 sherds (99%; 33%).

Established: Simmons (n.d.:3). Alberto Ruz (1969:144–145, 160) first described the pottery of this ceramic group from Jaina and Campeche under the label "Cerámica rojiza con baño crema." Piña Chán (1968:57, figs. 8p–f) subdivided this pottery into two categories: "Cerámica Rojiza con baño crema" and "Cerámica Rojiza con baño blanco" (1968:figs. 9a–f). Ball (1978:94) elaborated somewhat on it as well without defining it in type-variety terms. It was Simmons (n.d.:3–5) who established the type as Baca Red as a result of his studies of Dzibilchaltún ceramics. Jiménez (2002:23–30) added important distributional and other data to the type description.

Description:

Principal Identifying Attributes: (1) red paste; (2) cream wash on one or both surfaces; (3) flaring-walled tripod dishes or bowls; (4) milky surface finish.

Paste, Firing, and Temper: The paste is dense and strong, resisting breakage under hand pressure. It is medium textured. It is generally a very strong, intense red (2.5YR 4/8; 10R 4–5/8), but sometimes ranges to light red (10R 6/6). The intensity of the paste color is quite distinctive and is usually, though not invariably, visibly different from the paste of other oxidized types whose colors overlap. The temper appears to be calcite and crushed sherd, another factor that differentiates the paste from other oxidized types. The sherd temper is usually lighter in color than the strong red of the paste. The distinctive paste makes this pottery relatively easy to identify even when the surfaces are badly weathered. Almost all examples are completely oxidized throughout the cross-section of the vessel.

Surface Finish and Decoration: Ruz (1969: 144, 160) described the surfaces of this ceramic group as polished on the interior and rough or smoothed on the exterior. This is indeed often the case, but sometimes both surfaces are reasonably well smoothed. Because this ware tends to weather readily, intact surfaces are not common. In the best examples, however, the interiors of the overwhelmingly dominant form are well finished and the exteriors much less so. The interior surface of tripod dishes and bowls was covered with a cream wash, or in some cases, slip. Ruz (1969:144, 160) again calls it a slip. Nonetheless, most of the examples from Champotón only have vestiges of the cream slip and give the appearance of having only received a thin, cream-firing wash, if that. This may be misleading due to the strong tendency for the surfaces of these vessels to erode easily. Only a few examples were recovered that bear a thick, strongly adherent cream slip. Given this thinness of the slip, and its tendency to weather, most vessel surfaces have a milky pink appearance (5YR 6–7/2–3; 2.5YR 6/4–6) due to the fact that the strong red paste below affects the visual impression. Although exteriors often did not receive this wash or slip, the surface color is usually lighter than the paste deeper into the vessel wall.

Forms:

1. Flaring-walled tripod dish or bowl (Figures 4.1; 4.2, a–o). This is overwhelmingly the dominant form known for this type. Rims are direct or slightly everted. As indicated by Ruz (1969:144), the bases may be flat and marked by a basal break, or may be slightly rounded or convex. In any case they invariably have tripod supports of one form or another.
2. Thickened rim bowls or basins (Figure 4.2, p–r). This is a very rare form. Base form is unknown.
3. Short-necked jar (Figure 4.2, t–u). This is an extremely rare form.
4. Jar with everted downturned chamfered rim (not illustrated). This is a rare form.
5. Flaring-necked jar with thick vessel walls (not illustrated). This is a rare form.

Bases and supports: Bases for the dominant form are flat or slightly convex (rounded). The supports on this form are extremely varied. Both hollow and solid supports are found, and in various shapes, from oven-shaped to conical spikes. An interesting common form of foot found only on pottery of this ceramic group, and the related Fine Buff, consists of solid or hollow feet with 2, or sometimes 3, little knobs of clay applied near the bottom, perhaps mimicking the effect of clawed feet (see Ruz 1969:160). An illustration of some of the varied support forms can be seen in Ruz (1969:fig. LI: 58–69).

Intrasite Locations and Contexts: Widespread in Group 1, Struture 1 but particularly numerous in Areas A–D, I. It also occurs significantly in Trench L at Moquel.

Intersite Locations and Contexts: This type was first recognized in coastal Campeche at the sites of Campeche and Jaina (Ruz 1969; Piña Chán 1968:57), where it was called Cerámica Rojizo con baño crema. However, it has subsequently been recognized as occurring over a wide area of the coast of northwestern Yucatan and Campeche, as well as in the interior in the Chenes region (Williams-Beck 1999:69–72). It appears to be a significant member of the Canbalam Sphere (Ball 1978:134ff) and may extend down the coast as far as Los Guarixés (Ruz 1969), if not beyond, but it was not encountered at El Aguacatal (Ruz 1969; Matheny 1970). See Ball (1978:94) and Jiménez (2002:25) for a list of sites where this pottery is known to occur. The type is common in the Champotón region (Ek 2015:461, 474). It is present at Villa Madero (personal observation, INAH Ceramoteca, Mérida, Yucatan).

Comment: The vast majority of the sherds recovered from Champotón are weathered, and thus the cream slip is mostly eroded and therefore not readily visible. Some examples that still had the cream slip adhering to them do occur in the collections.

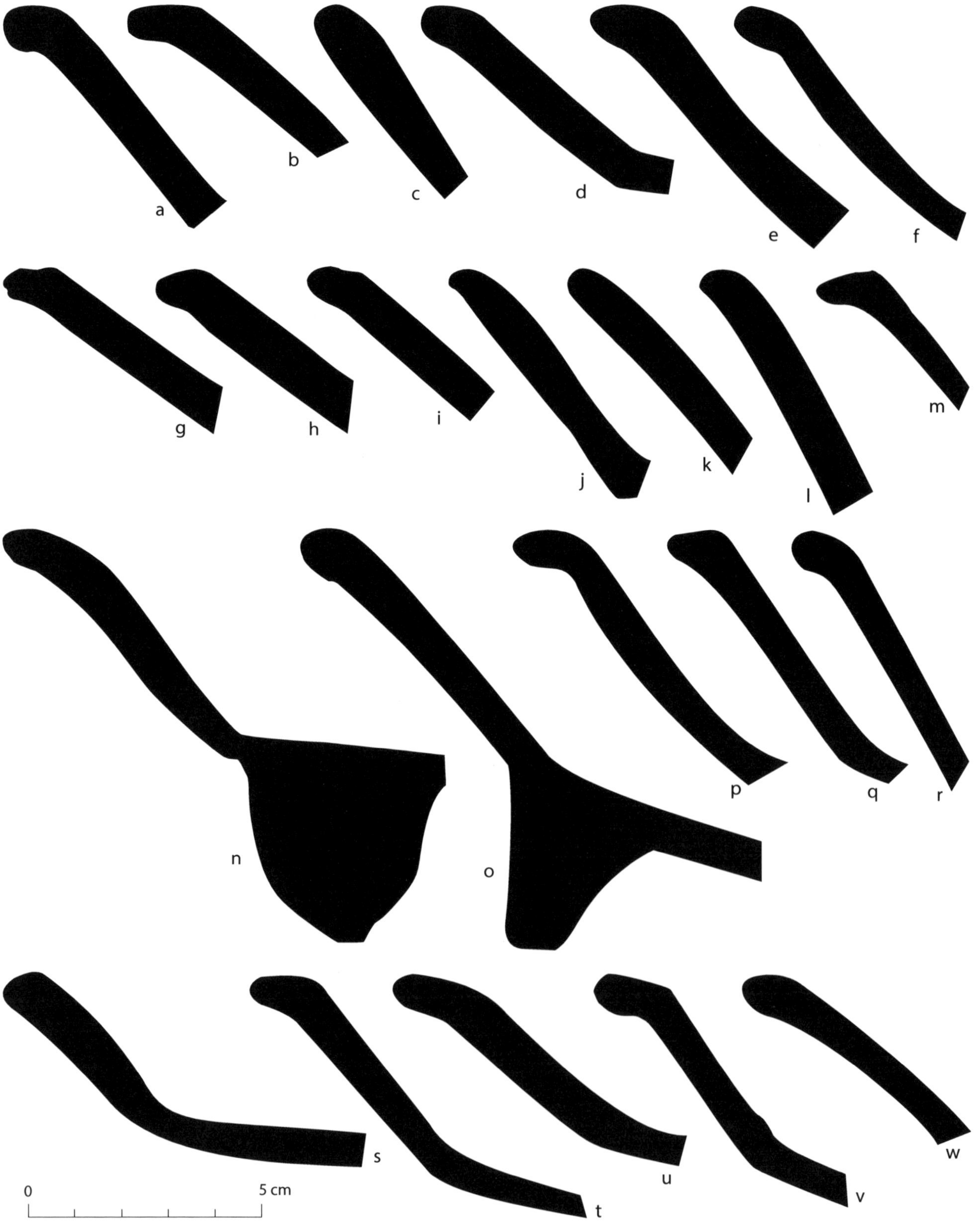

Figure 4.1. Baca Ceramic Group profile drawings—Baca Red: Baca Variety.

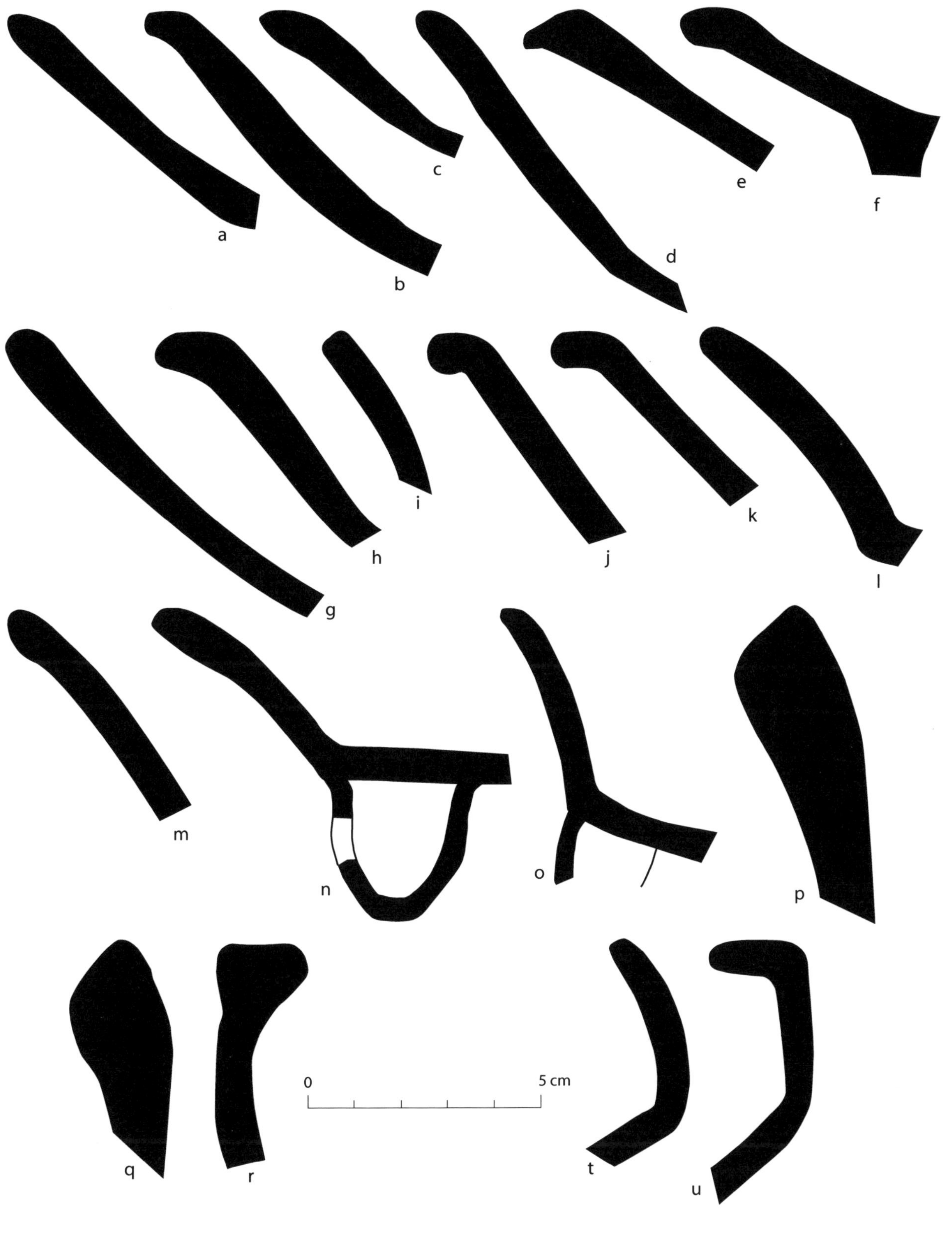

Figure 4.2. Baca Ceramic Group profile drawings—Baca Red: Baca Variety.

Other Baca Group: Chavihau Specular Red?

Two sherds with red paint on the rim, and two others with very weathered evidence of such paint, were recovered from Group 1, Structure 1. According to Ruz (1969:144, 160) the painting of such red bands was not infrequent on this pottery. We did not find any examples of more complex designs, such as those illustrated by Ruz (1969:fig. LI:1–14), however. Jiménez (2002:26), following Simmons (n.d.:5), has described a bichrome type, Chavihau Specular Red, which seems from her description, to be similar to these sherds. She describes painted designs on the interiors of the vessels, however, which to date have not been found at Champotón.

Other Baca Group: Black-on-cream (San Pablito Negative?)

On one rim and one body of the black-painted type of this groups were found in Group 1, Structure 1. According to Ruz (1969:160) these designs were negative-painted, but the Champotón examples do not have a negative-painted effect. The black paint is a weak, faint paint that does not contrast strongly with the background and actually has a light gray color because of its faintness. This may be what has led others to call it a negative-painted effect. Jiménez (2002:27) has named the type San Pablito Negative, and these two sherds are probably that type. It is a fairly widely distributed type along the coastal regions of the peninsula. It is rare at Champotón, although this may be because most Baca ceramics at Champotón are badly weathered, lacking much of the wash or slip. I have seen examples of these in Piña Chán's type collection in the Museo Nacional de Antropología e Historia in Mexico City (see Piña Chán 1968:57), and the far superior examples there likewise bear the weak, faded black paint, although a few have a more vivid black color.

Other Baca Group: Red Slip

At least six rims, two bodies and two other sherds of this pottery that bore a red slip, rather than the usual cream wash, were recovered from Group 1, Structure 1. In most cases this red slip was badly eroded. It is possible, therefore, that a few of the sherds classified as Baca Red that were often badly eroded, may belong to this category also. Nonetheless, the red-slipped examples do not appear to have been very common at Champotón, and they occur in the same dominant form as Baca Red.

Other Baca Group: Impressed-appliqué

One rim sherd from excavation Unit A12a and a body sherd from G1, E1, very much like the ones identified by Ruz (1969:160, figs. LI:70; LII:3) at Jaina, bear an appliquéd band just above the basal break on the exterior. This band was then thumb- or finger-impressed. Jiménez (2002:26) defined an impressed type at Xcambó that she named Sinanche Impressed that may incorporate these sherds. At least she references the same illustrations in Ruz that I provide here. Her description, however, of the basal band differs from how the Champotón, Campeche, and Jaina examples were manufactured. These latter were finger-impressed. Jiménez describes the impression on Sinanche as consisting of "parallel vertical lines that were impressed with a cutting instrument." Her illustration of the type shows a crenelated basal ridge. This is not how the impressed bands found at Champotón were decorated. So it is not clear if there are different manners of impressing the appliquéd band, or whether I have misinterpreted what she wrote.

Other Baca Group Appliqué

A single body sherd of otherwise weathered Baca Red bore an appliquéd spike. The sherd is too small to be able to determine if the vessel bore only a single spike or several.

Other Baca Group: Striated

Two body sherds of this type bore striation on the external body.

Nimun Ceramic Group (63)

Nimun Brown: Nimun Variety (Figures 4.3–4.4)

Frequency: 63 sherds (100%; 1%).

Established: Established by Simmons (n.d.: 9–10). Ruz (1969:143–144; fig. XLVII:16, 18–21, 23–24; XLVIII:16–18, 20–24, 26–28; 155–156; fig. LI:4–8) first described the pottery of this ceramic group from Campeche and Jaina under the label Cerámica café o ladrillo, although his designation clearly incorporates a much wider range of types than the current one. Piña Chán (1968:59; fig. 9j–ñ, q–v) classified this material as "Tipo Pizarra-Café Rojizo. Ball (1978:94) called this pottery "Undesignated Unslipped-smoothed." It was Simmons (n.d.:8–10), however, who established the ware, ceramic group, and type within the type-variety system. Jiménez (2002:36ff) provides additional information based on a large collection from Xcambó.

Description:

Principal Identifying Attributes: (1) dull surfaces; (2) pink to reddish brown surface color; (3) matte surface finish; (4) highly everted rim jar.

Paste, Firing, and Temper: The paste is medium textured. The vessels were generally fired in an oxidizing atmosphere, which produced a red to reddish yellow paste. The most common colors are 2.5YR 5–6/8 and 5YR 5–6/8. Some sherds, however, have a brown-colored paste (5YR 4–5/4) or pale gray (10YR 6/3). Most examples were oxidized throughout the cross-section of the vessel wall, but there are sometimes unoxidized or partially oxidized cores that range from gray to brownish gray (10YR 6/1–3). Occasionally this pattern is reversed, and the pale to brownish gray color is found on the outside of the cross-section and the core is red or reddish yellow. Temper appears to be calcite.

Surface Finish and Decoration: Ruz (1969: 143, 155) described the surfaces of this ceramic group as smoothed, while Piña Chán (1968:59) and Jiménez (2002:36) describe them as slipped. In the original definition offered by Simmons (n.d.:8), however, he notes the following for the Nimun Ceramic Group:

> A "slate-like" translucent slip the same color as the underlying surface is occasionally present, or sometimes just a weak brown wash, but the majority of sherds appear to be unslipped. The weak cream-colored slip common in Baca Red was never noted.

Simmons (n.d. 9) also notes that one of the principal identifying attributes of Nimun Brown has a "(g)enerally unslipped or weakly slipped brown surface." At Champotón the surfaces were indeed smoothed, and the surface paste strongly compacted; however, although highly smoothed, they are completely non-lustrous, but instead are consistently and unmistakably matte. This is the case on both interiors and exteriors. As a result of this smoothing and compaction, surface colors differ somewhat from paste colors, although there is no indication of the application of anything to the surface that would give it a different hue. More than likely, it is the rise of smaller particles to the surface from the smoothing and compacting itself that produced the color difference. Still, some examples from Jaina (personal observation, Museo Nacional de Antropología e Historia) do appear to bear brownish wash or slip. At Champotón surface colors range from pink (5YR 7/3–4) to reddish brown (5YR 6/3–4), although some examples can take on a more grayish color (5YR 5–6/2). Some examples of body sherds bear dark brown blotches (see Piña Chán 1968:lam. 9p for an example of a sherd with this kind of blotching) identical in execution and decorative effect as those found on Chencan Brown-on-orange (Forsyth 1983:121–123; also see in this volume). Nonetheless, these are not very common on this type at Champotón. This pattern is also known from Jaina (Piña Chán 1968:lam. 9p; personal observation, Museo Nacional de Antropología e Historia). Sherds with this kind of surface addition should perhaps be considered a different type, but they are rare at Champotón.

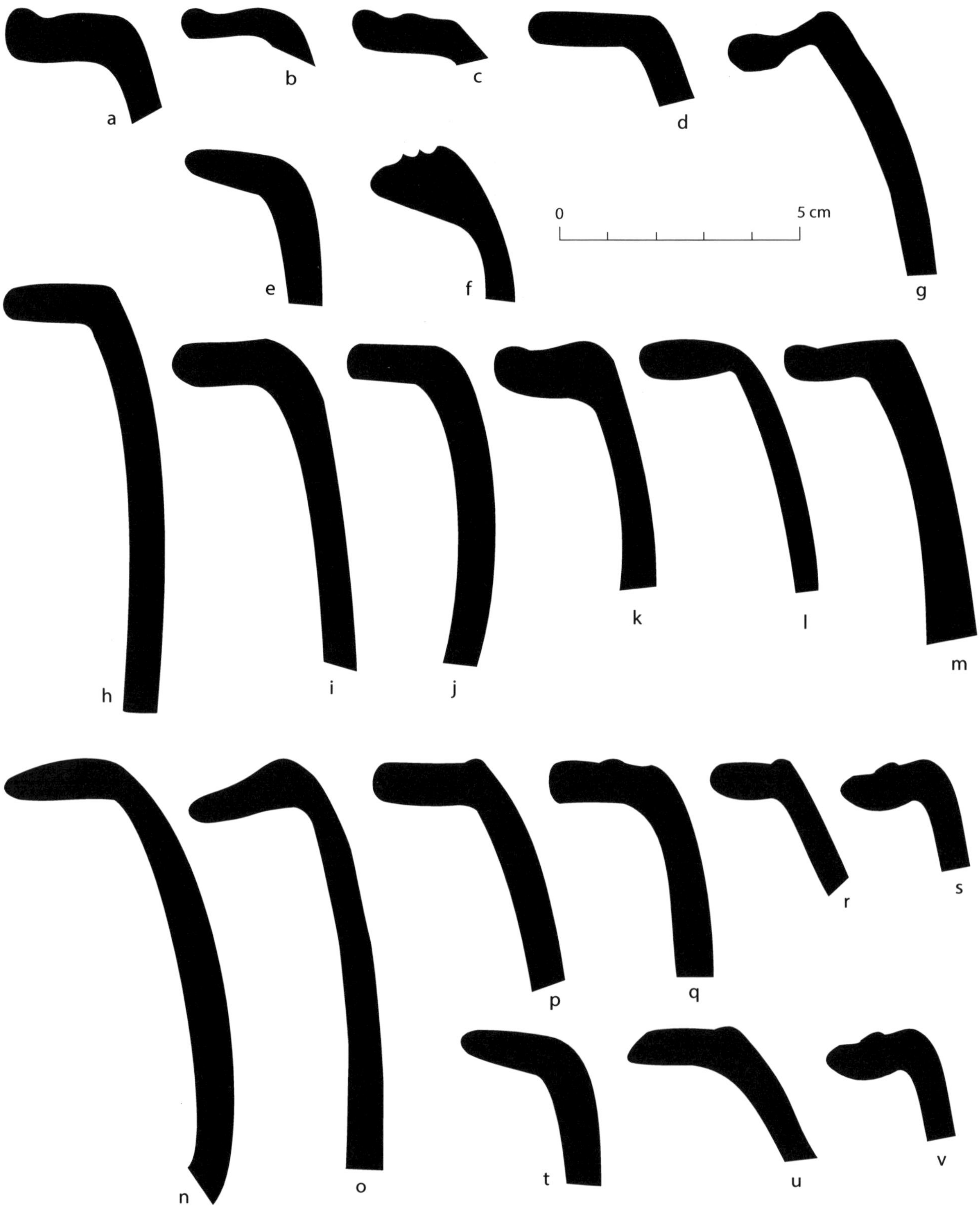

Figure 4.3. Nimun Ceramic Group profile drawings—Nimun Brown: Nimun Variety.

Figure 4.4. Nimun Brown: Nimun Variety ceramics.

Forms:

1. Tall cylindrical to slightly flaring-necked jar with strongly everted rim (Figure 4.3, a–e, g–v). This is overwhelmingly the dominant form known for this type. The rims are so highly everted that they are actually horizontal or even slightly downward angling. Usually they are plain, but sometimes have from one to three circumferential grooves (see Comment section below). Others actually have a rounded, upturned ridge at the exterior of the everted rim (Figure 4.3, a–e). Body and base forms are not certain, but bodies were presumably globular.

2. Jar with everted downturned chamfered rim (Figure 4.3f). Although rare, this rim form may also occur on more unrestricted vessels (cf. Ruz 1969:fig. XLVII, 17, 22, 25–27).

3. Short flaring-necked jar with everted rim (no illustration). Bodies are presumably globular.

Intrasite Locations and Contexts: In various deposits on Structure 1, Group 1 in Areas C, D, and particularly I. It also occured at Moquel.

Intersite Locations and Contexts: This type was first recognized in coastal Campeche at the sites of Campeche and Jaina, first by Ruz (1969:143; fig. XLVII:16–27; 155; fig. LI:4–8), and later at Jaina by Piña Chán 1968:59). However, both there and elsewhere it is part of a larger ceramic group that is apparently widespread along the coast of Campeche and northwestern Yucatán. Nimun Brown group was provisionally defined at Dzibilchaltún by Simmons (n.d.:9). Ball (1978:96) references some other types of this ware along the coast under the heading "Undesignated Unslipped-striated Types," but does not deal with the present type. Jiménez (2002:36–37) reports large quantities of the type from Xcambó. The type is common in the Champotón region (Ek 2015:461, 474). It is present at Villa Madero (personal observation, INAH Ceramoteca, Mérida, Yucatan).

Comment: I have examined the collection of pottery recovered by Piña Chán (1968) from Jaina, now stored in the basement of the Museo Nacional de Antropología e Historia, and observed this type as present. It occurs in a far greater range of shapes and decoration than the Champotón examples. This type and ware is not numerous at Champotón. Nevertheless, it is strange that other types of this ware do not show up here.

With respect to Form 1, I have chosen to treat the grooved upper rims as part of the Nimun type in a manner analogous to Sierra Red. Simmons (n.d.:11) classified these particular vessels as Tixkokob Incised: Broad-groove variety, but suggesting that it was a provisional category. Jiménez (2002:38) follows the pattern suggested by Simmons. Apart from issues of the appropriate classificatory approach, the crucial point is that Champotón shares this particular attribute with pottery from other sites on the peninsula.

UNSPECIFIED WARE [43]

Unspecified Ceramic Group (43)

Carpizo Red: Carpizo Variety (Figures 4.5–4.6)

Frequency: 35 sherds (90%; <1%)

Established: Type and variety established at Edzná by Forsyth (1983:95).

Description:

Principal Identifying Attributes: (1) polished red slip; (2) glossy surface finish; (3) unslipped exteriors; (4) interiorly bolstered rim basins.

Paste, Firing, and Temper: The paste is dense and strong, resisting breakage under hand pressure. It is medium textured. Paste color is red (10R 5/6–8; 4/4–6) to reddish yellow (5YR 6/4–6). Most examples were oxidized throughout the vessel wall. Few dark cores occur, but some examples were not thoroughly oxidized, resulting in darker paste colors (10R 4/4). Nevertheless, oxidation was significantly thorough on most examples of this type from Champotón. The temper is white to gray calcite. The particle size is larger on average than is the case for Charote Ceramic Group vessels, reflecting the larger size of Carpizo vessels. While there is a large range in particle size, large particles, some as much as 1 mm in diameter, are not uncommon.

Surface Finish and Decoration: Surfaces were well smoothed on the interior and rim of Carpizo vessels and more cursorily smoothed on vessel exteriors. Vessel interiors received a red-firing slip (10R 5/8; 2.5YR 4–5/8) that covered the interior and the top of the rim, usually as far as the edge of the rim or slight bolster. Below the break or edge, the vessel exterior was left unslipped and plain. The color of the red slip is variable, however, and can vary from light red (2.5YR 5.5/8) to a stronger red (10R 4–5/8). The unslipped exteriors have a more yellowish hue, ranging from 5YR 5–6/4 to 2.5YR 6–7/4.

Forms:

1. Incurved rim basin (Figures 4.5, a–m). This is overwhelmingly the dominant form for this type. Bases were flat.
2. Basin with thickened rim (Figure 4.5, n–p). Bases are flat.

Intrasite Locations and Contexts: In general, Late to Terminal Classic refuse in Group 1, Structure 1, as well as at Moquel.

Intersite Locations and Contexts: It was first recognized and defined at Edzná (Forsyth 1983:95). See the references there for other locations. The type is common in the Champotón region (Ek 2015:448, 458). It is present at Villa Madero (personal observation, INAH Ceramoteca, Mérida, Yucatan).

Comment: This type is the Campeche analog of the ubiquitous incurved rim basins and bowls that are found throughout the Maya area and beyond during the Late and Terminal Classic. It does not appear to be as frequent a vessel form in the Campeche collections as in other regions of the Maya area. Williams-Beck (1999:97) suggests that she and Boucher consider Carpizo Red to actually be part of the Chenes Slate Ware that Williams-Beck defined for that area.

Figure 4.5. Unspecified Ceramic Group profile drawings—Carpizo Red: Carpizo Variety.

Figure 4.6. Carpizo Red ceramics.

Whatever the larger issue about the nature of central Campeche slate wares, Carpizo Red is not in any form a member of the slate category. As indicated above, it is consistently red-slipped and has a non-slate surface finish and feel. A few of the Edzná sherds did have gray mottling (Forsyth 1983:95), but these are not the characteristic surfaces of the type, which is overwhelmingly a strong red, and definitely not related to slate wares in any way except in being restricted to heavily rim bolstered basins.

Carpizo Red: Chenvega Variety (Figure 4.7)

Frequency: 4 sherds (10%; <1%)

Established: Type established at Edzná by Forsyth (1983:95). Variety established in current study.

Description:

Principal Identifying Attributes: (1) polished red slip; (2) glossy surface finish; (3) light red paste; (4) round-sectioned handles, often large.

Paste, Firing, and Temper: The paste is like that of the Carpizo Variety except there is a tendency for the Chenvega Variety to have paste colors more towards lighter reddish hues (5YR 6–7/4–6).

Surface Finish and Decoration: Surfaces were well smoothed except for the interiors of restricted vessels, such as jars. Vessel surfaces received a red-firing slip (10R 5/8; 2.5YR 4–5/8) that covered the exterior and interior of unrestricted vessels. Restricted vessels, such as necked jars, were slipped on the exterior, and sometimes on the interior neck of the jar. One particular form, a necked jar with a highly everted rim bore slip on the exterior and on the interior (that is, upper) portion of the everted rim, but not on the interior neck. This gives the effect of having a red band running around the vessel on the upper surface of the everted rim, but in other cases the interior neck was not slipped. The color of the red slip is variable, however, and can range from light red (2.5YR 5.5/8) to a stronger red (10R 4–5/8). Unslipped portions of restricted vessel are generally lighter in color (5YR 7/6 to 2.5YR 5–6/8).

Forms:

1. Flaring-walled dish with direct or slightly everted rim (Figure 4.7, a–i).
2. Flaring-walled dish with direct or slightly everted rim and exterior basal ridge in the form of a sharp Z-angle (Figure 4.7, j–k).
3. Jars with outflaring necks. (Figure 4.7, l–m).
4. Jars with highly everted rims. (Figure 4.7, n–o).
5. Thin-walled hemispherical dishes or bowls (Figure 4.7p).
6. Miscellaneous forms (not illustrated).

Bases and Appendages: Base form is not known for any of the forms. Jar forms apparently often bore large to small round-section handles. Some of these are very large, but a small one was also noted. These round-section handles were made in an unusual way. They appear to have been manufactured in two stages: (1) a round-section handle, smaller in diameter than the final version of the handle, was manufactured; (2) then another layer of clay was added on top of this original handle, making it a larger, thicker handle. This is apparent when the handle has broken off the vessel; one readily observes the smaller, earlier stage version inside the later stage one in the cross-section of the handle.

Intrasite Locations and Contexts: In general Late to Terminal Classic refuse in Group 1, Structure 1, as well as at Moquel.

Intersite Locations and Contexts: The type was first recognized and defined at Edzná (Forsyth 1983:95), but the Chenvega Variety was not found there, although it is possible that it was present is small quantities, and simply not recognized. This variety is defined here for the first time. The type is found in the Champotón region (Ek 2015:448, 458).

Comment: The Chenvega Variety differs from the Carpizo Variety in terms of shape and the related feature of slip placement. The Carpizo Variety consists solely of basins with unslipped exteriors. In this sense it parallels the

Figure 4.7. Unspecified Ceramic Group profile drawings—Carpizo Red: Chenvega Variety.

distinction between Tinaja Red: Tinaja Variety and Tinaja Red: Subín Variety as defined by Foias (1996:478–481). Otherwise, there are few differences between the two varieties. The Chenvega Variety can be confused with Charote Red in that both have red paste and red slip; however, the Charote Ceramic Group slip is much more highly polished and brilliant than the Carpizo Ceramic Group slip, and the paste is different both in color and temper. Nevertheless, when working with sherds, many of which have been weathered or suffered other post-depositional modifications, they can be confused, and are not always easy to separate. In some ways the Chenvega Variety is a kind of residual category of red-slipped vessels that occur in modest quantities at Champotón.

Other Carpizo Ceramic Group: Incised

Four sherds with one to several simple preslip incisions were recovered from Group 1, Structure 1.

FINE GRAY WARE [919]

Chablekal Ceramic Group (852)

This ceramic group is highly variable at Champotón, and apparently other coastal sites. The standard types listed by Smith based on Mayapan examples do not adequately reflect the range of variation in this group. This is because most Chablekal Group pottery that has been recognized previously at non-coastal sites is the result of small numbers of vessels traded into those sites. These trade vessels apparently represent pieces intended for display or which were highly desirable, and thus traded over long distances; however, they represent only a portion of the wider range of Chablekal materials that were used, not only as special pieces, but also as quotidian functional vessels. This wider set of vessels is found primarily in the littoral from Tabasco to Yucatan and appears to form an integral component of the ceramic complexes at coastal sites. Piña Chán's (1968) excavation at Jaina illustrates the large variability in Fine Gray pottery, as well as subsequent work at Jaina, Champotón and Xcambó.

Chablekal Gray: Chablekal Variety (Figures 4.8–4.9)

Frequency: 584 sherds (69%; 13%)

Established: Type and variety established by Smith (1971:18, 134) at Mayapan, but see Smith and Gifford (1966:521). Smith did not provide a detailed type-variety description of each of the types, but instead only a ware description and a listing of the types with some data. Subsequent analysts have provided type descriptions of various sorts (see Ball 1978:116; Forsyth 1983:117–118; Jiménez 2002:222ff, Piña Chán 1968:41, 43, 45; Ruz 1969:145–146, 163–164; Simmons n.d.:51).

Description:

Principal Identifying Attributes: (1) gray surface color; (2) matte surfaces (3) fine temperless paste; (4) flaring-walled dish; (5) composite silhouette bowls.

Paste, Firing, and Temper: The paste is fine textured, lacking temper. Like other examples of Chablekal Group pottery, the sherds have a distinctive ring when they are dropped on a hard surface or against other sherds. Firing took place in a non-oxidizing or reducing firing atmosphere, which resulted in the gray surface and paste colors (2.5YR 5–6/0; 7.5YR 4–6/0; 5Y 6/0). The color of the paste does not generally differ from the surface; however, black cores do occur. Small flecks of what may be mica occasionally show in the paste, but they are not common.

Surface Finish and Decoration: Surfaces were well smoothed and compacted and are very smooth to the touch when not eroded. Generally, the surfaces are matte, lacking any luster. This is a well-established characteristic of this ware, although some examples do attain a very light luster, and a small minority a noticeable luster. Jiménez (2002:222) states that this type, and others in the ceramic group, bear a slip of the same clay as the paste. Whether or not a slip was actually applied, or whether the fine smoothing of the vessel surfaces merely brought the finer and smaller clay particles in the paste to the surface, thus creating the appearance of a slip, is a matter not clear to me.

Forms:

1. Flaring-walled dish (Figure 4.9, a–e). The rims may be direct, slightly everted or slightly everted and thickened. Sometimes the rim is strongly everted. Bases are flat or slightly convex (cf. Piña Chán 1968:lam. 1x–a'). At least some examples bore hollow tripod supports, and this may have been the case in most examples.
2. Composite silhouette bowl (Figure 4.6, f–h). The most common form generally has a sharp break (corner point) with the area below the break curving toward

Figure 4.8. Chablekal Ceramic Group ceramics.

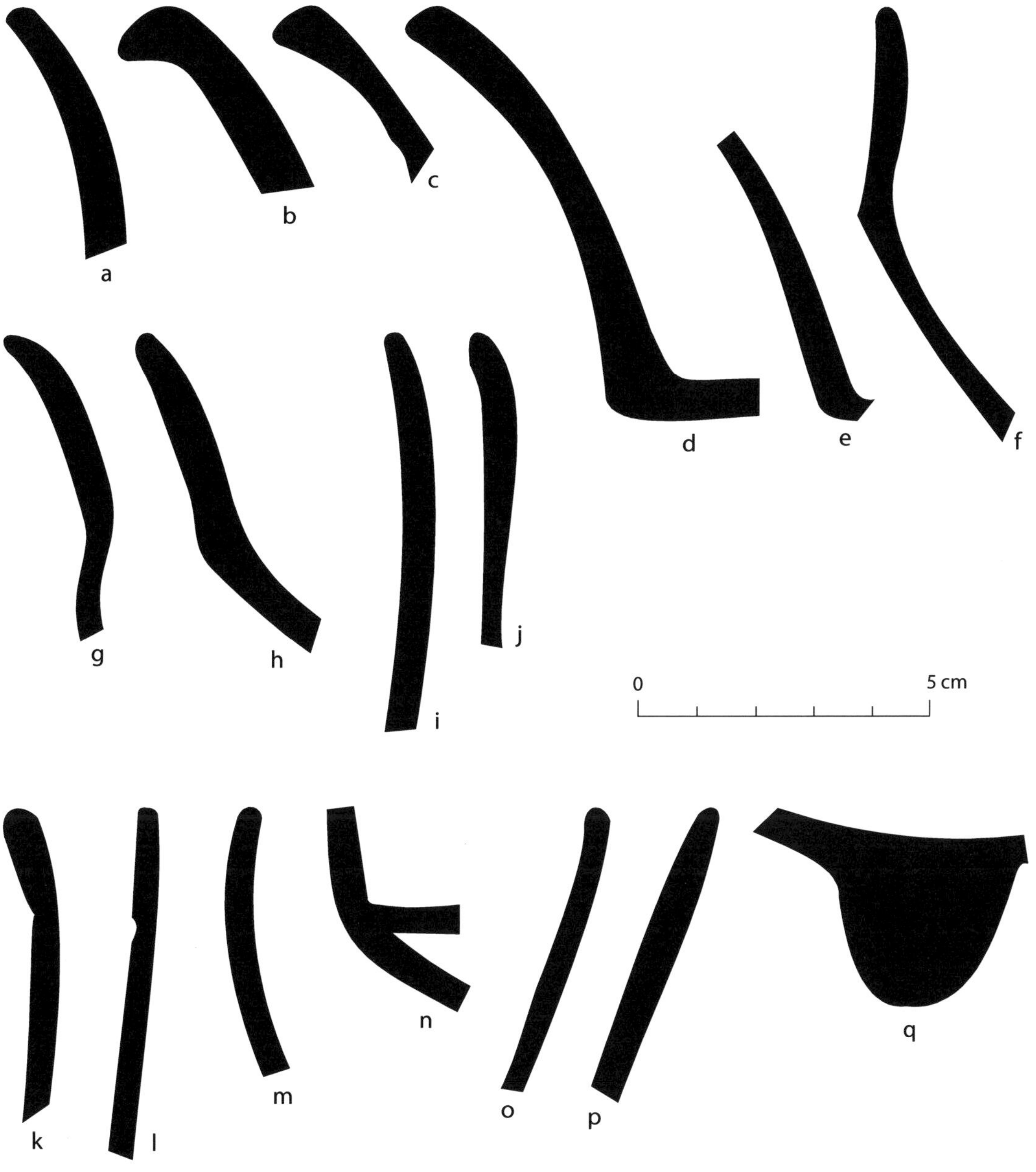

Figure 4.9. Chablekal Ceramic Group profile drawings—Chablekal Gray: Chablekal Variety.

the base. In other examples the change in contour is less sharp. In addition, there are several variants of orifice restriction, some with unrestricted, and others with restricted, orifices (cf. Piña Chan 1968:lam. 1l–m and n–t). Bases are presumably flat.

3. Unrestricted or slightly restricted vase (Figure 4.9, i–l). These are deep vessels with flat bottoms. Some examples are cylindrical or have a slight eversion at the rim. Other examples angle slightly inward. Occasional examples have a slightly thickened rim about 1.5–2.0 cm wide (cf. Piña Chán 1968:lam. 2g', k', n').

4. Hemispherical bowl (Figure 4.9m). Base form is unknown.
5. Small jar (no illustration). The neck of the jar is usually slightly outflaring (cf. Piña Chán 1968:lam. 1a–f). Base form is unknown.
6. Flaring-walled bowl with double base (Figure 4.9n; cf. Berlin 1956:fig. 4i, m; Brainerd 1958:fig. 36b; Forsyth 1983: fig. 32cc). The base was presumably flat; however, in other known examples of this form, there are often tripod teat or round hollow supports. No evidence for supports on this form was found at Champotón, though.
7. Miscellaneous forms (Figure 4.9, o–q).

Bases and supports: Bases were generally flat or concave, but there were significant numbers of oven-shaped to hemispherical hollow and occasionally solid, supports. These are known to occur on flaring-walled dishes, but whether they occur on other forms is not known.

Intrasite Locations and Contexts: It occurs in a number of different excavation units in Group 1, Structure 1, but seems to be most frequent in Areas A–C, F, and I. It is also found at Moquel, particularly in Trench L.

Intersite Locations and Contexts: This type is a well-established and well-known one. It occurs in small quantities at numerous sites in both the Northern and Southern Lowlands as a result of trade into those sites. It is along the Campeche and Yucatecan coasts that it occurs in much greater quantity. It is particularly common at Jaina (Piña Chán 1968:43–45; Ruz 1969:163–164; personal observation, Museo Nacional de Antropología e Historia), Campeche (Ruz 1969:145–146), and Xcambó (Jiménez 2002:222–224). Ball (1978:109) also mentions Uaymil, Isla Piedras Isla Cerritos, Holkotun, Emal, and Canbalam and also indicates its presence in some quantity at Dzibilchaltún (see Simmons n.d.: 51). It also occurs at Jonuta and Tecolpan in Tabasco (Berlin 1956:118–120). The Fine Gray material from Huimango (Berlin 1956:fig. 5n–v, ff–oo, qq–ccc) seems somewhat varied from standard Chablekal. Jiménez (2002:224) indicates its presence at Villa Madero, between Campeche and Champotón, as well as at Chunchucmil and Oxkintok. It is definitely present at Villa Madero (personal observation, INAH Ceramoteca, Mérida, Yucatan). The type is common in the Champotón region (Ek 2015:461, 474–475, 479).

Chicxulub Incised: Chicxulub Variety (Figure 4.10)

Frequency: 210 sherds (25%; 5%)

Established: Type and variety established by Smith (1971:18, 134) at Mayapan. Smith did not provide a detailed type-variety description of each of the types, but instead only a ware description and a listing of the types with some data. Subsequent analysts have provided type descriptions of various sorts (see Piña Chán 1968:41, 43, 45; Ruz 1969:145–146, 163–164); Ball 1978:109–110; Forsyth 1983:119; Jiménez 2002:224; Simmons n.d.:55).

Description:

Principal Identifying Attributes: (1) gray surface color; (2) matte surfaces; (3) fine temperless paste; (4) incision on exterior vessel walls; (5) composite silhouette bowls.

Paste, Firing, and Temper: Same as Chablekal Gray.

Surface Finish and Decoration: Surfaces were treated in the same fashion as Chablekal Gray with the exception of exterior incision on vessel walls. Incised decoration occurs in the form of V- or U-shaped incisions. These may consist of from one to four circumferential lines near the rim (three is common), or a combination of vertical and horizontal lines that zone off rectangular or stepped areas, or as sets of vertical or diagonal lines. These zoned areas are then diagonally hatched by means of parallel incisions, or in some cases cross-hatching. Usually these lines are well executed, but sometimes hatched lines go beyond the outlined area or the outlining lines do not meet exactly. The width and depth of the incisions varies, sometimes on the same vessel. Sometimes the V- and U-shaped incision are combined on the same vessel, but when this happens, the two

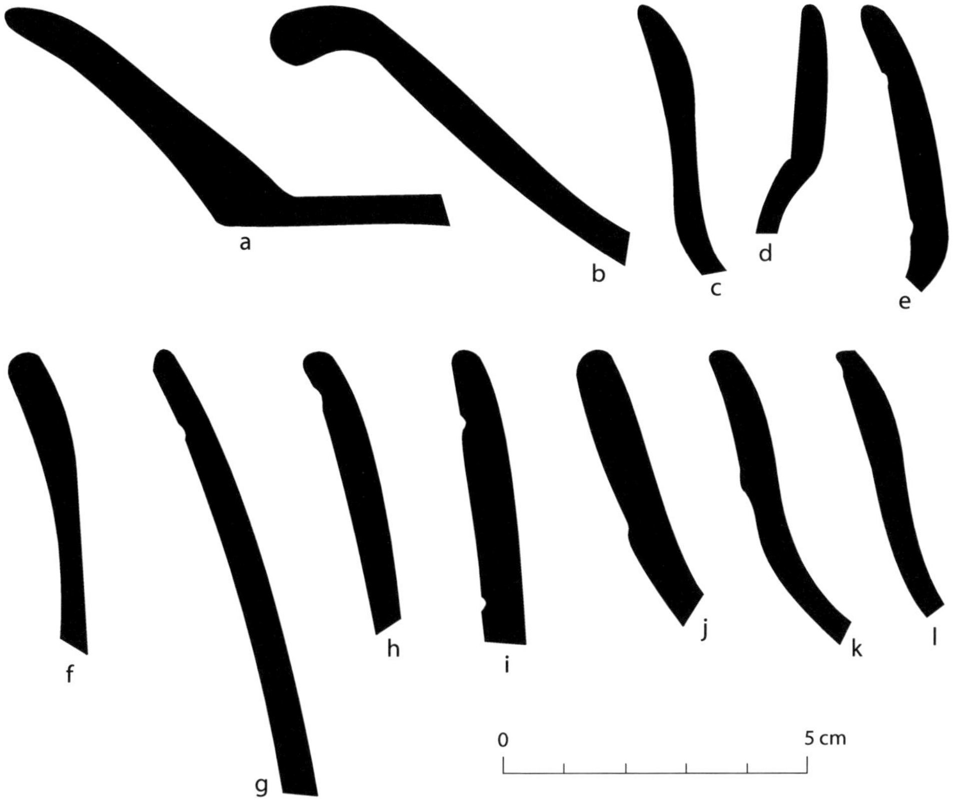

Figure 4.10. Chablekal Ceramic Group profile drawings—Chicxulub Incised: Chicxulub Variety.

kinds of incision tend to occur in different areas of the vessel exterior. On composite vessel forms, different kinds of incising sometimes occurs on different portions of the vessel. For example, the rim area may have zoned-hatched decoration, while the body area has parallel vertical lines or some other combination. Occasionally there are hatched triangles on the tops of everted rims, although this is not common. In a few cases unusual incised designs occur. In several examples there are incised diagonal lines with perpendicular lines incised within the areas outlined by the diagonal lines, but not crossing them. Another example has groups of three curved lines. Generally speaking, the incised designs are rather simple and geometric; however, occasionally more curvilinear designs appear. In one case a row of what might be highly abstracted bird heads encircle a vessel near the rim; rarely, an incised monkey occurs. Piña Chán's (1968:lam. 1–2) drawings illustrate the range of variation in the incising, although not all of his drawings represent Chicxulub Incised. There is considerable variation in the incised designs found on this pottery.

Forms:

1. Flaring-walled dish (Figure 4.10, a–b). The rims may be direct, slightly everted, and thickened. Bases are flat or slightly convex (cf. Piña Chán 1968:lam. 1x–a'). At least some examples bore hollow tripod supports, and this may have been the case for most.

2. Composite silhouette dish or bowl (Figure 4.10, c–e). The most common form generally has a sharp break (corner point) with the area below the break curving toward the base. In other examples the change in contour is less sharp. And in still others, there is a slight projection at the break. In addition, there are several variants of orifice restriction, some with

unrestricted, and others with restricted, orifices (cf. Piña Chán 1968:lam. 1l–m and n–t). Bases are presumably flat. Occasional examples have a slightly thickened rim about 2–3 cm wide (cf. Piña Chán 1968:lam. 2g', k', n').

3. Unrestricted or slightly restricted vase (Figure 4.10, f–i). These are deep vessels with flat bottoms.
4. Hemispherical bowl (Figure 4.10, j–l). Some examples have exterior changes in contour. Base form is unknown.
5. Small jar (no illustration). The neck of the jar is usually slightly outflaring (cf. Piña Chan 1968:lam. 1a–f). Base form is unknown.

Intrasite Locations and Contexts: In general refuse from Structure 1, Group 1, but most common in Areas A, C, F, and I. It is also found at Moquel, particularly in Trench L.

Intersite Locations and Contexts: This type, along with other members of the Chablekal Ceramic Group, is a well-established and well-known one. It occurs in small quantities at a large number of sites in both the Northern and Southern Lowlands as a result of trade into those sites. It is along the Campeche and Yucatecan coasts that it occurs in much greater quantity. It is particularly common at Jaina (Piña Chán 1968:43–45; Ruz 1969:163–164; personal observation, Museo Nacional de Antropología e Historia), Campeche (Ruz 1969:145–146), and Xcambó (Jiménez 2002:224–225). Ball (1978:109) also mentions Uaymil, Isla Piedras, Tambo, Emal, and Dzibilchaltún. Jiménez (2002:225) adds Villa-Madero, Canbalam, La Providencia, as well as Edzná, and Chunchucmil. It is definitely present at Villa Madero (personal observation, INAH Ceramoteca, Mérida, Yucatan). The type is also found in the Champotón region (Ek 2015: 461, 474–475, 479). It also occurs at Jonuta and Tecolpan in Tabasco (Berlin 1956:118–120).

Comment: There is a wide range of incison encompassed in this type. It might be possible with more careful analysis to divide the type into varieties based on variation in the kind of incision employed. It could be argued that there might be a continuum of incision into fluting—from the narrow V-shaped incision to the broader U-shaped variant, but such an analysis remains to be done. Jiménez (2002:224) does provide a list of design patterns in Chicxulub pottery.

Cholul Fluted: Cholul Variety (Figure 4.11)

Frequency: 34 sherds (4%; <1%)

Established: Type and variety established by Smith (1971:18, 134) at Mayapan, although Smith did not provide a detailed type-variety description of each of the types, instead just a ware description and a listing of the types with some data. Subsequent analysts have provided type descriptions of various sorts (see Piña Chán 1968:41, 43, 45; Ruz 1969:145–146, 163–164); Ball 1978:99; Forsyth 1983:119–120; Jiménez 2002:225).

Description:

Principal Identifying Attributes: (1) gray surface color; (2) matte surfaces; (3) fine temperless paste; (4) circumferential or vertical fluting on exterior vessel walls; (5) composite silhouette bowls.

Paste, Firing, and Temper: Same as Chablekal Gray.

Surface Finish and Decoration: Surfaces were treated in the same fashion as Chablekal Gray with the exception of exterior fluting on vessel walls. Fluted decoration occurs in two forms. One consists of flutes that run vertically, or occasionally diagonally, down the vessel exterior. These may start near the rim and cover the entire exterior, although on composite forms, they may begin below the change in contour or break. The other form consists of horizontal or circumferential flutes that encircle the vessel. These tend to occur on flaring-walled dishes or bowls. Flute width varies from about 5–10 mm. The flutes also take different forms. Some have sharp peaks separating them, like the flutes found on Greek columns. Others have wider crests. The horizontal flutes tend to be more undulating or wavy, while there is greater variation in the vertical fluting.

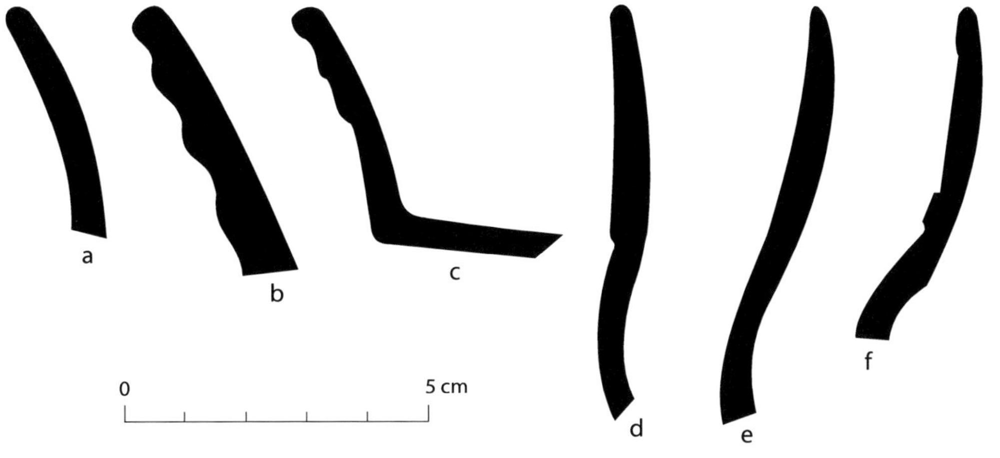

Figure 4.11. Chablekal Ceramic Group profile drawings—Cholul Fluted: Cholul Variety.

Forms:

1. Flaring-walled dish or bowl (Figure 4.11, a–c). The rims may be direct, slightly everted or slightly everted and thickened. Bases are flat or slightly convex (cf. Piña Chán 1968:lam. 1x–a').
2. Composite silhouette dish or bowl (Figure 4.11, d–f). These may take the form of a sharp break (corner point) with the area below the break curving toward the base, while in other examples the change in contour is less sharp. Bases are presumably flat.

Intrasite Locations and Contexts: This type is rare, most common in Area I. It is also found at Moquel, particularly in Structure 1, Trench L.

Intersite Locations and Contexts: This type, along with other members of the Chablekal Ceramic Group, is a well-established and well-known one. It occurs in small quantities at numerous sites in both the Northern and Southern Lowlands as a result of trade into those sites. It is along the Campeche and Yucatecan coasts that it occurs in greater quantity. It occurs at Jaina (Piña Chán 1968:43–45; Ruz 1969:163–164; personal observation, Museo Nacional de Antropología e Historia), Campeche (Ruz 1969:145–146), and Xcambó (Jiménez 2002:225). Ball (1978:99) also mentions Isla Piedras, Uxmal, Dzibilchaltún (see Simmons n.d.:58), Dzebtun, Dzibilchaltun, as well as Huimango and Tamulté in Tabasco. It was also recovered from Edzná, but in very small quantities. The type is also found in the Champotón region (Ek 2015:461, 474–475, 479). It is also present at Villa Madero (personal observation, INAH Ceramoteca, Mérida, Yucatan).

Telchac Composite: Telchac Variety (Figure 4.12a)

Frequency: 5 sherds (<1%; <1%)

Established: Type and variety established by Smith (1971:18, 134) at Mayapan, although Smith did not provide a detailed type-variety description of each of the types, instead just a ware description and a listing of the types with some data. Subsequent analysts have provided type descriptions of various sorts (see Piña Chán 1968:41, 43, 45; Ruz 1969:145–146, 163–164; Ball 1978:99; Forsyth 1983:120; Simmons n.d.:62).

Description:

Principal Identifying Attributes: (1) gray surface color; (2) matte surfaces; (3) fine temperless paste; (4) incision on vessel exteriors; (5) small, dentate-like punctuation.

Paste, Firing, and Temper: Same as Chablekal Gray.

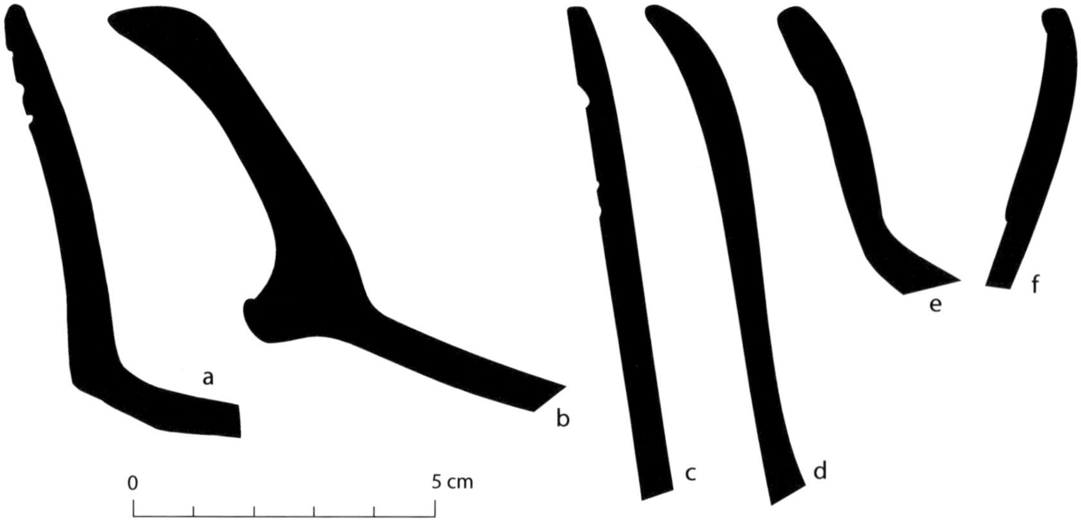

Figure 4.12. Chablekal Ceramic Group profile drawings—a. Telchac Composite: Telchac Variety, b. Chekubul Impressed: Chekubul Variety, c. Dimar Composite: Dimar Variety, d. Chamblas Composite: Chamblas Variety, e–f. Other Chablekal Ceramic Group.

Surface Finish and Decoration: Surfaces were treated in the same fashion as Chicxulub Incised except that shallow dentate-like punctuations were placed within the areas outlined by incisions. In short, this type is a combination of incision and dentate punctuation. Most of the designs are simple geometric ones, but one example of what is an incised monkey bears dentate punctations around the monkey figure, although within the larger area outlined by incised lines (cf. Brainerd 1958:fig. 36b, d, g).

Forms:

1. Unrestricted vase (no illustration).These are relatively deep vessels with flat bottoms.

2. Flaring-walled bowl with double base (no illustration; cf. Berlin 1956:fig. 4i, m; Forsyth 1983:fig. 32cc; Brainerd 1958:fig. 36b). The base was presumably flat.

3. Small bowl with rounded bottom (Figure 4.12a). Probably had round tripod supports.

Intrasite Locations and Contexts: This type is extremely rare in the Champotón collections. Four of the sherds are from Structure 1, Group 1, and only one is from Moquel.

Intersite Locations and Contexts: This type, along with other members of the Chablekal Ceramic Group, is a well-established and well-known one. Telchac was widely traded, as most of the so-called Fine Gray "monkey pots" belong to this type. It seems to have been widely traded in small quantites, occurring as a rare type at many sites in both the Northern and Southern Lowlands. It is along the Campeche and Yucatecan coasts that it occurs in greater, but still not significant, quantities. It occurs at Jaina (Piña Chán 1968:43–45; Ruz 1969:163–164, Campeche (Ruz 1969:145–146). Ball (1978:99) also mentions Uaymil, Isla Piedras, and Dzibilchaltún (see Simmons n.d.:62). A single example was found in the Edzná ceramic collection (Forsyth 1983:120). It also occurs at Jonuta and Tecolpan (Berlin 1956:118–120, fig. 4i). It is found in the Champotón region (Ek 2015: 461, 474–475, 479). It is also present at Villa Madero (personal observation, INAH Ceramoteca, Mérida, Yucatan).

Figure 4.13. Chekubul Impressed ceramics.

Chekubul Impressed: Chekubul Variety (Figures 4.12b, 4.13)

Frequency: 4 sherds (<1%; <1%)

Established: Established in the present study

Description:

Principal Identifying Attributes: (1) gray surface color; (2) matte surfaces; (3) fine temperless paste; (4) thumb impression on basal flange or at basal break; (5) flaring-walled dish or bowl with everted rim.

Paste, Firing, and Temper: Same as Chablekal Gray.

Surface Finish and Decoration: Surfaces were treated in the same fashion as Chablekal Gray, although on three of the sherds there is a basal flange or heavy ridge that was then thumb impressed all the way around the vessel. On one example there is no flange or ridge, but the sharp basal break was thumb impressed. The impressions were made by pressing the thumb or finger directly into the plastic clay. On the examples we have noted so far the drag technique of impressing the thumb and dragging the clay ahead of the thumb or finger was not used.

Forms:

1. Flaring-walled dish or bowl with everted rim (Figure 4.12b). Bases are flat or slightly convex (cf. Piña Chán 1968:lam. 3h'–j', m'–n'). At least one example of this type seems to have a small portion of a scar where a support was attached. In other types of this ceramic group that do not bear impressed designs, tripod supports are known to occur on this form.

2. Unknown form with flaring wall and a flat base (not illustrated). This vessel does not have a flange, but does have a small, hollow support attached to what appears to be a flat bottom.

Intrasite Locations and Contexts: This type is extremely rare in the Champotón collections, but the fact that more than one vessel is represented, and in different excavation units, suggests that it is an intentional product and not just a fluke. In fact, Piña Chán (1968:lam. 3j', m') shows sherds that are similar in form and appear to also have been impressed. Four of the sherds are from Structure 1, Group 1, and only one is from Moquel.

Figure 4.14. Dimar Composite ceramics.

Intersite Locations and Contexts: Other than the possible examples listed for Jaina, this type has not been reported from other sites; however, Berlin (1956:fig. 4ff) does illustrate a similar black ware vessel.

Comment: Although this type at Champotón is based on a small number of sherds, it is clear that it is an intentional product that was not limited to Champotón. Therefore, it was part of the ceramic inventory of the Chablekal Group and was produced consistently albeit rarely.

Dimar Composite: Dimar Variety (Figures 4.12c, 4.14)

Frequency: 2 sherds (<1%; <1%)

Established: Established in the present study.

Description:

Principal Identifying Attributes: (1) gray surface color; (2) matte surfaces; (3) fine temperless paste; (4) vertical fluting on vessel exteriors; (5) gouge-incision in the area near the rim above the vessel flutes; (6) vase form.

Paste, Firing, and Temper: Same as Chablekal Gray.

Surface Finish and Decoration: Surfaces were treated in the same fashion as Chablekal Gray. Decoration takes the form of a band of circumferential designs about 1–1.5 cm below the rim of the vessel. These designs were created by a combination of gouging and incising. The decorated zone is separated by a narrow plain zone; below this, a parallel series of vertical flutes run down the vessel exterior. Piña Chán (1968:fig. 4g) illustrates an example of this type. The Champotón examples do not bear glyphs in the rim band, just a series of simple repetitive symbols.

Forms:

1. Cylindrical vase (Figure 4.12c). These are deep vessels, probably with flat bottoms. This is the only form known for this type.

Intrasite Locations and Contexts: The two examples from Champotón were found in Structure 1, Group 1 in Areas D-56 and D-549.

Intersite Locations and Contexts: As indicated above, Piña Chán (1968:lam. 4g) illustrates an example of this type from Jaina. Berlin (1956:fig. 4rr) illustrates an example from Huimango that is vaguely similar, although it may not be identical to Dimar Composite. At Xcambó, Jiménez (2002:225-226) describes two types, Petenes Gouged and Cacalchén Carved, the latter taken from Simmons (n.d.:66), which have some comparative decorative elements but not this particular combination of

Figure 4.15. Chamblas Composite ceramics.

gouge-incising and fluting. Note the range of variation and decorative techniques, singly and in combination, that the makers of Fine Gray pottery used, even if infrequently.

Comment: Although this type at Champotón is based on a small number of sherds, it is clear that it is an intentional product that was not limited to Champotón. Therefore, it was part of the ceramic inventory of the Chablekal Group and was produced consistently albeit rarely.

Chamblas Composite: Chamblas Variety (Figures 4.12d, 4.15)

Frequency: 5 sherds (<1%; <1%)

Established: Established in the present study.

Description:

Principal Identifying Attributes: (1) gray surface color; (2) matte surfaces; (3) fine temperless paste; (4) incision on exterior vessel walls; (5) finger-gouged impression in zoned areas.

Paste, Firing, and Temper: Same as Chablekal Gray.

Surface Finish and Decoration: Surfaces were treated in the same fashion as Chablekal Gray. Decoration takes the form of vertical, horizontal, or diagonal incision in forms similar to that of Chicxulub Incised. This can take the form of parallel vertical lines or zoned areas with hatching, using medium or wide-line incision. Added to the incision, however, are finger-gouged impressions that occur on areas of the vessel not bearing incised designs, or within areas outlined by incised designs. On small jar forms, for example, the incised line(s) is (are) placed near the rim, while the finger impressions are located on the rounded body of the vessel. The impressions were made by pressing the finger or thumb into the plastic clay and then dragging the clay a short distance. Because the impressions are relatively deep, ridges of clay were pushed up in front of the finger as it moved, forming raised edges at the end of the stroke that formed the impression. This appears to have been done intentionally. On the "wavy rim" form the finger impressions are zoned in vertical columns zoned by broad U-shaped incisions.

Forms:

1. Small jar form with vertical neck and globular body (no illustration; cf. Piña Chán 1968:lam. 2a–j for the form only and lam. 3d, which bears the finger

impressions). These jars are relatively small, and were certainly not used to store or carry large quantities of whatever they held.

2. Unknown "wavy rim" vessel (Figure 4.12d). These are very unusual vessels which, when seen from above looking down into the vessel, have a wavy rim profile. At first I thought this was a rounded vessel with an appended flat, or nearly flat flange or wing, such as is sometimes found on Classic period censers, but examining the interior of the vessel calls this interpretation into question. It is not clear what the exact shape of these two different vessels actually is; given that there are two of them from different vessels (and found in different excavation units) indicates that they were being made for some particular purpose.

Intrasite Locations and Contexts: Three of the five examples from Champotón come from area I of Structure 1, Group 1, while the other two sherds come from Areas C and D respectively.

Intersite Locations and Contexts: Piña Chán (1968:lam. 3d) illustrates an example of this type from Jaina. Not reported from any other sites as far as I know.

Comment: Although this type at Champotón is based on a small number of sherds, it is clear that it is an intentional product that was not limited to Champotón. Therefore, it was part of the ceramic inventory of the Chablekal Group, and was produced consistently albeit rarely.

Other Chablekal Ceramic Group

Two sherds from cylindrical vase forms bear a horizontal raised band chamfer encircling the vessels similar to the band chamfers found on Desvario Chamfered vessels. The bands occur within 1.5 to 3.0 cm of the rim. Otherwise they appear to be without further surface manipulation. One sherd bears clapboard chamfering near the base of a flaring-walled flat-bottomed tripod dish, and a single rim bears clapboard-like chamfering as well. Two examples of composite silhouette vessels bear carved or gouged designs combined with incision—a carved-incised type—perhaps Cacalchén Carved (Simmons n.d.:66; Jiménez 2002:225-226). Still another sherd from a composite silhouette vessel is gadrooned (Figure 4.12e). Finally, a single restricted orifice vessel bore extremely fine incised geometric designs (Figure 4.12f).

Tsicul Ceramic Group (67)

This pottery was originally defined by Robert E. Smith (1971:17) as Fine Black Ware on the basis of a small collection of sherds recovered from Mayapan. Simmons examined a significant amount of this pottery recovered from Dzibilchaltún and argued that: "In the large sample present in these Dzibilchaltún collections, it was apparent that Fine Black was only Fine Gray with a black slip added" (Simmons n.d.:49). As a result, and because the black slip is often badly eroded, Simmons made no effort to separate the two in the Dzibilchaltún collection, classifying them all as Fine Gray using the types established for the latter (Chablekal Ceramic Group). Subsequently, Socorro Jiménez (2002:230–232; Ancona and Jiménez 2005:215), working with fine black pottery from Xcambó, defined a separate ceramic group for the black-slipped fine paste ceramics called Tsicul. She likewise defined a number of types within the ceramic group that are roughly analogous to some previously defined for Fine Gray pottery of the Chablekal Group.

Tsicul Fine Black: Variety Unspecified (Figure 4.16, a–d, 4.17, c–h)

Frequency: 43 sherds (63%; 1%). This pottery does not seem to be as common at Champotón as it does at more northern coastal sites, such as Campeche and Jaina.

Established: Established by Socorro Jiménez (2002:230–231) at Xcambó, Yucatan. See the discussion above for the complicated classificatory issues surrounding fine black pottery, see also Ancona and Jiménez (2005).

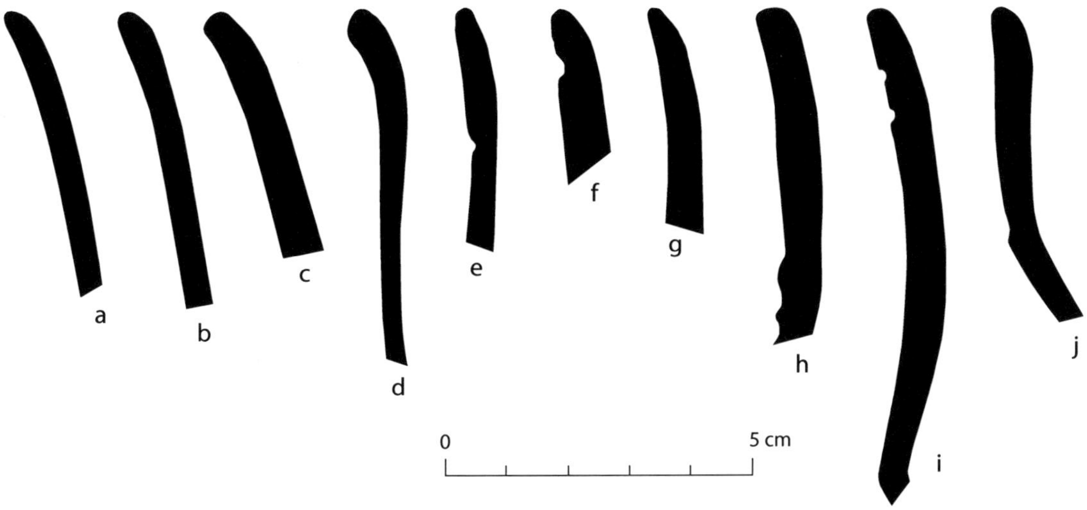

Figure 4.16. Tsicul Ceramic Group profile drawings—a–d. Tsicul Fine Black: Variety Unspecified, e–h. Xuxac Incised: Variety Unspecified, i. Other Tsicul Ceramic Group: Composite, j. Other Tsicul Ceramic Group: Gouge-incised.

Description:

Principal Identifying Attributes: (1) black, readily weathered slip; (2) polished surfaces (3) fine temperless paste; (4) thin-walled vase form; (5) flaring-walled dish.

Paste, Firing, and Temper: The paste is fine textured, lacking temper. Firing took place in a non-oxidizing or reducing firing atmosphere, which resulted in the gray to brownish gray paste surface colors (2.5YR 5–6/0–2; 7.5YR 4–6/0; 5Y 6/0), although some sherds were reduced all the way through the cross-section, resulting in a dark black core and surface color (Gley 1 2.5/N; 2.5YR 2.5–3/0). There is usually a distinct difference, however, between the dark black core making up the bulk of the cross-section of the sherd, and a very thin band immediately under the surface that is gray. Nevertheless, an occasional sherd has an oxidized core (10R 5/6) beneath black to gray surfaces.

Surface Finish and Decoration: Surfaces were well smoothed and compacted, and are very smooth to the touch when not eroded. Generally, the surfaces appear matte, lacking any luster, but this is probably due to weathering of the slip. On those examples on which the slip is strongly adherent they bear a low luster. A black-firing slip was applied to some or all of the vessel surfaces, depending on form. This slip typically fires a strong black to very dark gray color (2.5YR 2.5–3/0), although some fine black sherds overlap with the darkest Chablekal surface colors (2.5YR 4/0). The black slip is quite thin and tends to weather readily. For this reason many sherds that bore a black slip originally were probably classified as Chablekal Gray given that the underlying surfaces, once the slip has eroded away, usually appears similar to Chablekal Ceramic Group surfaces. This complicates sorting issues since the forms and decorative techniques applied to fine paste, black-slipped pottery are similar to those of the Chablekal Group.

Forms:

1. Deep vase with slightly flaring walls with direct or slightly everted rim (Figure 4.16, a–d). Rim diameter is unknown. Bases were flat. Vessel interiors of vases were sometimes only slipped part way down the interior wall.

2. Flaring-walled dish (no illustration). The rims of the few examples are direct. The base of a single example is flat. It bore a

Figure 4.17. Tsicul Ceramic Group: a–b. Xuxac Incised; c–h. Tsicul Fine Black.

basal ridge or skirt and exhibited a hollow support, almost certainly indicating tripod supports. This form seems to be an analog of Form 1 of Chablekal Gray.

Intrasite Locations and Contexts: It occurs in a number of different excavation units in Group 1, Structure 1 but seems to be most frequent in Areas A–C, and I. It is also found at Moquel, particularly in Trench L. This distribution is similar to that for Chablekal Gray and might suggest that they were used in similar contexts; however, since much of the Champotón pottery is from structural fill, this is not certain.

Intersite Locations and Contexts: This type has a significant distribution along the coast of Yucatan and Campeche. Ek (2015:461) has reported it for the Champotón region. This particular pottery is known from Xcambó (Jiménez 2002:230ff.), where it was given the current typological classification, but it has been known from other sites for some time. It is particularly well represented at Jaina. Piña Chán (1968:45, 48) called it Tipo Negro, although this designation included all members of the Tsicul Ceramic Group, not just Tsicul Fine Black. Nevertheless, I have seen examples of Tsicul Fine Black in the collections from Jaina stored in the Museo Nacional de Antropología e Historia in Mexico City. Ruz (1969:163) lumped the black-slipped fine paste ceramics together with the gray surface pottery (Tsicul and Chablekal) but noted the presence of black-slipped examples. He did the same at Campeche (Ruz 1969:145). Ancona and Jiménez (2005:215) add Uaymil and Los Guarixés to the list.

Xuxac Incised: Variety Unspecified (Figure 4.16, e–h, 4.17, a–b)

Frequency: 14 sherds (21%; <1%).

Established: Type established by Jiménez (2002:231) at Xcambó, Yucatan. Also see Ancona and Jiménez (2005).

Description:

Principal Identifying Attributes: (1) black, readily weathered slip; (2) polished surfaces; (3) fine temperless paste; (4) incision on exterior vessel walls.

Paste, Firing, and Temper: Same as Tsicul Fine Black

Surface Finish and Decoration: Similar to Tsicul Fine Black with the addition of incision on the exterior body of the vessel. Incised decoration occurs in the form of V- and/ or U-shaped incisions. These may consist of several circumferential lines near the rim or in combination with other vertical and horizontal lines. Zoned-hatched areas also occur. Due to the small sample, the overall design patterns are not clear, but this type seems to be a black-slipped analog to Chicxulub Incised. The black slip, as is the case for Tsicul Fine Black, tends to weather readily and is often only present in some areas, or may have worn away altogether. One example has a zoned area outlined and hatched by deep, wide incisions, with lighter incisions running horizontally on the parallelograms thus formed.

Forms:

1. Deep vase with slightly flaring walls with direct rim (Figure 4.16, e–h). Rim diameter is unknown. Bases were apparently flat.
2. Composite silhouette bowl (no illustration).

Intrasite Locations and Contexts: Most examples from Champotón come from Group 1, Structure 1, Areas D, I, or N. Two sherds were recovered from Moquel Trench L.

Intersite Locations and Contexts: Ek (2015:462) reports it from the Champotón area. This type occurs at Jaina (Piña Chán 1968:45, 48) and Xcambó (Jiménez 2002: 231). It probably occurs at other sites where Tsicul Fine Black is found.

Other Tsicul Ceramic Group: Composite

Three rim sherds and one body sherd, plus two rims and one body from the same vessel, have incision similar to Xuxac Incised creating zoned rectangular or stepped areas. Inside the zones outlined by incision are shallow dentate-like punctuations in horizontal or diagonal lines (Figure 4.16i). Thus, it is analogous to Telchac Composite, but within the Tsicul Ceramic Group.

Other Tsicul Ceramic Group: Fluted

Two body sherds of what is probably Coloradas Fluted (Jiménez 2002:231) were recovered from Champotón.

Other Tsicul Ceramic Group: Gouge-incised

A single sherd from a composite silhouette bowl bore gouge-incised decoration on the upper portion of the exterior above the break. No form of decoration was noted below the break, but the sherd is quite narrow (Figure 4.16j). Compare El Cuyo Composite at Xcambó (Jiménez 2002:231).

CAMPECHE GLOSS WARE [487]

Charote Ceramic Group (221)

Charote Red: Charote Variety (Figures 4.18–4.19)

Frequency: 179 sherds (81%; 4%)

Established: Type and variety established by Forsyth (1983:91, 93) at Edzná.

Description:

Principal Identifying Attributes: (1) red slip color; (2) highly glossy surface finish; (3) flaring-walled dishes; (4) round-sided bowls.

Paste, Firing, and Temper: The paste is thin to medium textured depending on the vessel. It is red in color (10R 5/6–8; 4/8; 2.5YR 5/6–8), but some examples are light red (2.5YR 6/4–6). The vast majority of vessels are oxidized throughout the vessel cross-section; however, occasionally

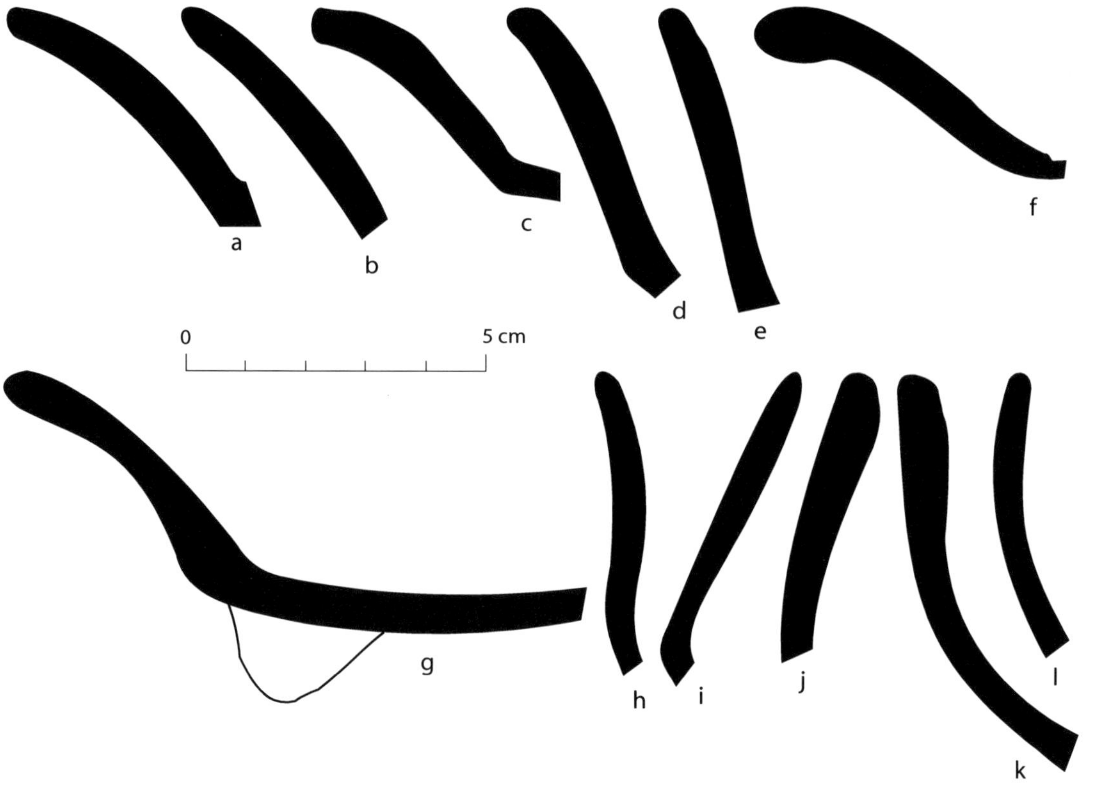

Figure 4.18. Charote Ceramic Group profile drawings—Charote Red: Charote Variety.

there is a pale brown core (10YR 7/3). Temper consists of white to gray calcite.

Surface Finish and Decoration: Surfaces were smoothed before the application of the slip. A highly polished red-firing slip was applied to both vessel surfaces. The red slip ranges from 10R 4–5/8 to 2.5 YR 4–5/8. Occasionally a cream-colored primary slip was applied to the vessel before the red-firing slip, but this is not the usual pattern.

Forms:

1. Flaring-walled dish or bowl with direct or slightly everted rim (Figure 4.18, a–g). Bases are flat or slightly rounded. Most of these vessels seem to have solid oven-shaped or slab tripod supports. One example has a scalloped solid slab foot. Presumably, these were tripod supports but are very large in relation to vessel size.
2. Composite silhouette bowl (Figure 4.18, h–j). Several examples have restricted orifices but not all of them do. Base form is unknown.
3. Round-sided bowl (Figure 4.18, k–l). Base form is presumably flat.

Intrasite Locations and Contexts: At Champotón it occurs in the greatest quantity in Areas C, D, and I of Group 1, Structure 1. It is also found in some quantity at Moquel in Structure 1.

Intersite Locations and Contexts: This type was defined at Edzná and it, or members of the Charote Ceramic Group, was present in several sites in Campeche (e.g., Jaina, Santa Rosa Xtampak, Dzibilnocac). Examples of the ceramic group also occur at Huaymil and apparently at Dzibilchaltún (see Forsyth 1983:94). In addition to Champotón and Moquel, Ek (2015:461, 471) has recovered this type from sites in the region around Champotón, including especially Ulumal and San Dimas.

Figure 4.19. Charote Ceramic Group ceramics.

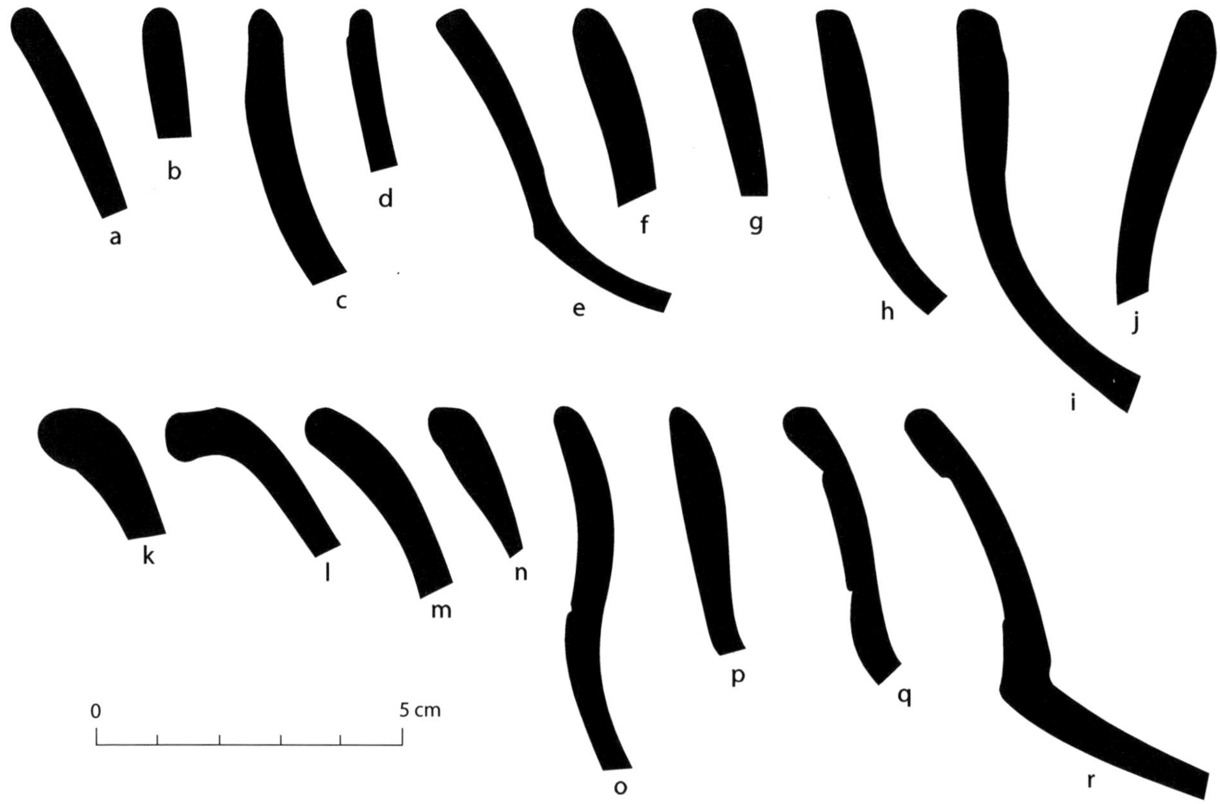

Figure 4.20. Charote Ceramic Group profile drawings— a–d. Pixoyal Incised: Pixoyal Variety, e–j. Ulumal Fluted: Ulumal Variety, k–n. Sihochac Dark-red-on-red: Sihochac Variety, o–p. Other Charote Ceramic Group: Incised and fluted, q. Other Charote Group: Chamfered and Fluted, r. Other Charote Group: Chamfered, Incised, and Fluted.

Comment: Although this is not a major type at Champotón, it is much more common here, and at sites directly inland from Champotón like Ulumal and San Dimas (Ek 2015:471), than at any other location heretofore observed in the Maya Lowlands. It may well have been manufactured in the region around Champotón, but we have no secure evidence of that. Its relative rarity and very high gloss finish may indicate that it was a special category of ceramic not readily available to most consumers of ceramic vessels, although this is purely speculation.

Pixoyal Incised: Pixoyal Variety (Figure 4.20, a–d)

Frequency: 15 sherds (7%; <1%)

Established: Type and variety established by Forsyth (1983:93) at Edzná.

Description:

Principal Identifying Attributes: (1) red slip color; (2) highly glossy surface finish; (3) medium-line preslip incising; (4) round-sided bowls.

Paste, Firing, and Temper: Same as Charote Red.

Surface Finish and Decoration: Surface finish is the same as Charote Red; however, the vessel exteriors were incised. They occur as shallow preslip lines place vertically or circumferentially. Occasionally, more complex designs occur. One example has fine-line cross-hatching, and another has a bouncing line motif. Another has short vertical incisions placed in a circumferential manner right at the wall base break—a kind of incised notching.

Forms:

1. Flaring-walled dish or bowl with direct or slightly everted rim (Figure 4.20, a–b). Base form is unknown but may be the same as for Charote Red.
2. Round-sided bowl (Figure 4.20, c–d). Base form is presumably flat.

Intrasite Locations and Contexts: Same as Charote Red.

Intersite Locations and Contexts: See Charote Red.

Ulumal Fluted: Ulumal Variety (Figure 4.20, e–j)

Frequency: 11 sherds (5%; <1%)

Established: Type and variety established by Forsyth (1983:93–94) at Edzná.

Description:

Principal Identifying Attributes: (1) red slip color; (2) highly glossy surface finish; (3) shallow, contiguous fluting on vessel exteriors.

Paste, Firing, and Temper: Same as Charote Red.

Surface Finish and Decoration: Surface finish is the same as Charote Red; however, the vessel exteriors were fluted. The flutes are very shallow and narrow (3–7 mm) and run contiguously around the vessel exterior. They generally run vertically all the way to the base of the vessel. These flutes are executed so lightly and finely that they are sometimes only discernible by rotating the sherd in the light and running one's finger horizontally across the flutes. On flaring-walled vessels with rounded bases, the flutes are often only found on the rounded basal section.

Forms:

1. Flaring-walled dish or bowl with direct or slightly everted rim (Figure 4.20, e–g). Base form is unknown but some vessels have a rounded basal section.
2. Round-sided bowl (Figure 4.20, h–j). Bases are flat or slightly indented.

Intrasite Locations and Contexts: Same as Charote Red.

Intersite Locations and Contexts: See Charote Red.

Sihochac Dark-red-on-red: Sihochac Variety (Figure 4.20, k–n)

Frequency: 5 sherds (2%; <1%)

Established: Type and variety established by Forsyth (1983:94–95) at Edzná.

Description:

Principal Identifying Attributes: (1) red slip color; (2) highly glossy surface finish; (3) dark red paint and lip bands over the red slip.

Paste, Firing, and Temper: Same as Charote Red.

Surface Finish and Decoration: Surface finish is the same as Charote Red. Decoration consists of dark red paint (7.5 R 3/8, 4/6; 10R 3/6, 4/8) applied as a band to the lip of the vessel.

Forms:

1. Flaring-walled dish or bowl with direct or slightly everted rim (Figure 4.20, k–n). Base form is unknown but may be the same as for Charote Red.

Intrasite Locations and Contexts: Same as Charote Red.

Intersite Locations and Contexts: See Charote Red.

Other Charote Ceramic Group: Incised and fluted

Three sherds of the Charote Ceramic Group bear incising like that on Pixoyal Incised and fluting like that on Ulumal Fluted. This composite type was also noted at Edzná, although it was not named (Forsyth 1983:97, Agua Potable Special: Charote Ceramic Group-Unnamed Composite) see Figure 4.20, o–p.

Other Charote Ceramic Group: Gadrooned

Two body sherds with preslip gadrooning were also recovered from Champotón.

Other Charote Group: Chamfered

Four rim sherds, three from the same vessel, bear chamfering on the exterior of the vessel. Three of the sherds appear to have a darker red paint or slip on the chamfered area.

Other Charote Group: Chamfered and Fluted

One rim sherd bears a wide chamfer on the upper portion of a flaring-walled vessel and vertical flutes below the chamfer along the curving base, see Figure 4.20q.

Other Charote Group: Chamfered, Incised, and Fluted

A single rim sherd bears circumferential preslip incisions and chamfering on the vessel exterior. Below the basal break, the curving lower portion of the vessel bears the typical flutes of Ulumal Fluted on the exterior, see Figure 4.20r.

Comment: The evidence from both Edzná and Champotón indicate that it was not uncommon for the makers of Charote Ceramic Group vessels to combine various forms of decorative techniques on a single vessel. Based on present evidence they appear not to have been numerous, but the pattern does appear to be consistent.

Simochac Ceramic Group (227)

Simochac Orange-polychrome: Simochac Variety (Figures 4.21, 4.22, a–r, u–v)

Frequency: 185 sherds (81%; 4%)

Established: Established in the present study. It will probably be possible to break this type into varieties, and perhaps distinct types, when a better preserved sample of Champotón Late Classic polychromes are recovered.

Description:

Principal Identifying Attributes: (1) orange slip color; (2) glossy surface finish; (3) red and black paint applied over orange slip; (4) tripod plates or dishes with flat bases and everted rims; (5) hemispherical bowls; (6) tall vases.

Paste, Firing, and Temper: The paste is medium textured and well mixed. Vessels were fired in an oxidizing atmosphere. Paste color ranges from reddish yellow (5YR 6/6, 7.5YR5–6/6–8) to light red (10R 4/3, 5–6/4). Some examples bear a cream to pink-firing underslip, but this is often not present. The temper is cloudy gray calcite.

Surface Finish and Decoration: Vessels were very well smoothed prior to slipping. Vessels were covered with an orange-firing slip (2.5YR 6/8; 5YR 6–7/6–8), usually on both surfaces, although a significant number of tripod dishes were unslipped on the exterior. This seems to be a common, though hardly universal, characteristic of the Campeche region. On other forms, on the other hand, the principal decoration is on the exterior, and the interior is slipped a monochrome orange except for the rim band. Decoration consists of naturalistic conventionalized, geometric and, occasionally, glyphic designs in red (7.5R 3–4/6–8; 10R 4–5/6–8) and black (2.5/N; 7.5R 2/0; 10R 2.5 /1–2; 3/1–2) paint on the orange slip. Glyphic elements of design are usually limited to bands just below the rim on the exteriors of unrestricted vessels. Because the sherds are small and badly weathered, it is not possible to determine the general pattern of element arrangement. Among those design elements that do occur are: brackets, triangles, circles, solid disks, the dress shirt, solid ovoids, and sausages. There are undoubtedly many others. Vessels almost invariably have a rim band painted red, but sometimes black. In a number of cases, red and black alternate on the rim band. This band is often separated by a narrow area bearing the orange slip and then bears a circumferential line or band, or two, below the narrow orange area. If the rim band is black, the low line or band tends to be red, and vice versa. This pattern is not as common, however, as it is in the southern polychromes such as Palmar Orange-polychrome. Another characteristic of rim-painting on these vessels, usually on tripod dishes with thickened or bolstered rims,

Figure 4.21. Simochac Orange-polychrome ceramics.

is the formation of solid triangles or outlined squares with a dot in the middle. The latter are not anywhere near universal, but constitute an excellent marker for the Campeche polychromes. They occur, however, on a number of types in addition to Simochac vessels (e.g., Cui Orange-polychrome [see below] and Makat Orange-polychrome, Boucher and Palomo 1989:510).

Forms:

1. Flaring-walled tripod plate or dish with flat or slightly rounded base. Rims are often thickened and bolstered and slightly everted (Figures 4.22, a–h; u–v). Supports may be solid or hollow and are usually short rather than the tall supports so popular in the Southern Lowlands. Vessel exteriors are often unslipped, but there are many examples that bear an orange slip on the exterior as well; however, these virtually never bear any form of decoration on the exteriors other than the orange slip. Vessel exteriors occasionally have a raised band or ridge at the body-base juncture (see Figure 4.22, u–v).
2. Hemispherical bowls with flat bottom with direct or slightly beveled rim (Figure 4.22, i–m).
3. Tall vase (Figure 4.22, n–o). Vessel walls are straight, slightly incurved, or slightly outcurved. Vessel height is not known but is high relative to vessel diameter. Bases were flat
4. Round-sided plates or dishes with direct or slightly beveled/everted rims (Figure 4.22, p–r). Bases were presumably flat. Exteriors were often, though not invariably, unslipped.
5. Barrel-shaped vessels (cf. Smith 1955: fig. 33) (no illustration). Vessel orifices are slightly restricted.
6. Unknown jar form (not illustrated).

Bases and appendages: Bases on most forms are flat. Tripod dishes have low solid or hollow supports. No handles or other appendages were noted.

Intrasite Locations and Contexts: In general Late Classic desposits are particularly well represented in Structure 1 Group 1, Areas D and I. At Moquel they occur mostly in Structure 1 excavations.

Intersite Locations and Contexts: It is not possible to provide exact correlations to this type, as it is newly defined here; however, many of the sherds illustrated by Piña Chán (1968:lam. 5a–o; lam. 6y–z) at Jaina would fall within the Simochac category at Champotón. Probably some of the polychromes reported by Ruz (1969:fig. L) belong to this type, but other types are also represented in Ruz's illustrations.

Comment: Simochac Orange-polychrome is a local analogue of Palmar Orange-polychrome in the Southern Lowlands. The two areas were clearly sharing the same ideas about polychrome pottery manufacture and decoration, but the Campeche area differs somewhat with respect to form, motif emphasis, and decorative elements, although there is sufficient overlap to make separation difficult, particularly when dealing with sherds—and ones that are often weathered at that. That is, some examples of Campeche polychromes are relatively easy to distinguish because of distinctive features that they often bear, while others, lacking such distinctive features, at least on the parts of the sherds under analysis, are much harder to differentiate. As indicated above, it will probably be possible to divide this material into a number of distinct varieties or types when a fuller body of vessels and sherd collections are available. In fact, Simochac should be considered a tentative type, rather than one that is tightly defined. It may well be that it will fit within other already established types. It is not known to what extent this type may or may not be related to what Ball (1978:98) called Hool Orange Polychrome because it was never described or illustrated. Boucher and Palomo (1989) have defined several orange-polychrome types for the Campeche area on the basis of museum pieces, but only small quantities of these have been recognizable in the Champotón collections. Still, it is possible that a larger number of Champotón orange-polychrome sherds may pertain to one or more of them, but were not recognizable because

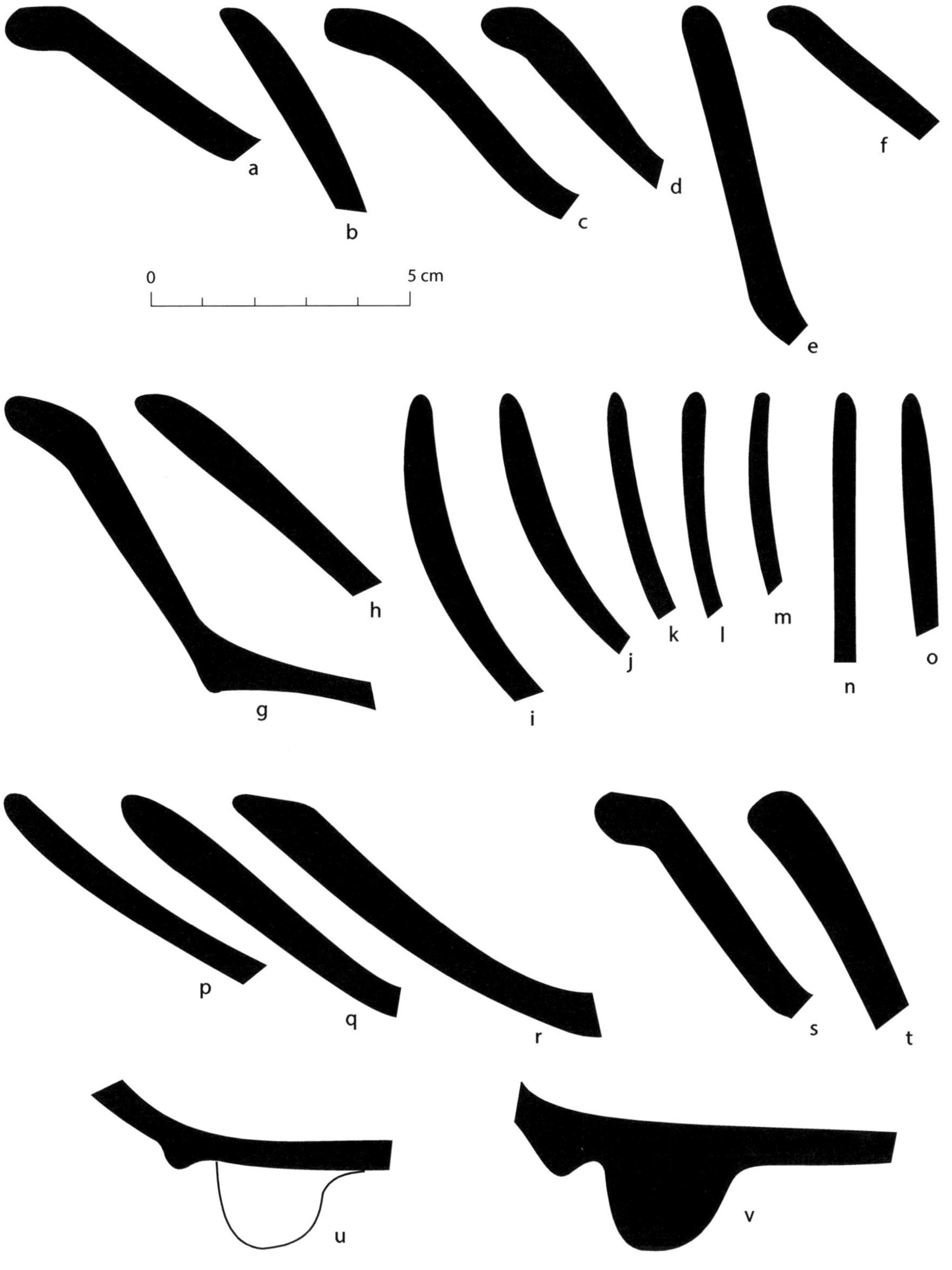

Figure 4.22. Profile drawings: a–r, u–v. Simochac Ceramic Group, Simochac Orange-polychrome: Simochac Variety; s–t. Cui Ceramic Group, Cui Orange-polychrome: Cui Variety.

of the small size of the sherds. Of the types described by them, Makat Orange-polychrome seems the most similar to the bulk of the Champotón Orange-polychromes, although this is not clear given that the Champotón examples vary in exterior treatment and include a wider range of vessel forms. This is not surprising given the small size of the museum collection from which they derived their classification. Jiménez (2002:56–57; see also 182–189) has also described a number of orange-polychrome types, which may or may not relate to what I am here calling Simochac. Similarly, it was not possible to differentiate subdivisions of the Late Classic polychromes. Given the nature of the contexts, there was insufficient evidence for chronological distinctions, such as those between Tepeu 1 and 2 in the Southern Lowlands although a few forms seem to conform to Tepeu 1 patterns in the south. There are examples of vessel forms that tend to occur in Tepeu 1 in the south but no evidence that they can yet be temporally differentiated at Champotón. Polychrome ceramics of the Campeche area require more analytical work before an effective type-variety classification will be of much use to analysts. Whether my designation of the Champotón orange-polychromes as Simochac Orange-polychrome will be part of that clarification, or merely confuse the issue more, remains to be seen.

Other Simochac Group: Orange Monochrome

A total of ten rims and 26 bodies bearing an orange slip like that found on Simochac Orange-polychrome were recovered from Champotón (one from Moquel). I have not designated these as a type because most are small and probably represent unpainted areas of Simochac Orange-polychrome vessels.

Other Simochac Group: Red-on-orange

A small number of sherds bearing an orange slip like that on Simochac vessels bore a red-painted band at the rim. Two sherds are small thin-walled bowls bearing the red band on both the interior and exterior of the rim. Two other sherds, from the same vessel, represent everted rim dishes or bowls. It is the everted upper surface of the rim that bears the red paint. These two are unusual, however, in that they also bear lightly executed vertical preslip flutes on the interior of the diverging vessel wall. The exterior is slipped orange, as is the interior. Another sherd bears red designs on an orange ground. It may be part of an orange-polychrome vessel or merely a red-on-orange one.

Other Simochac Ceramic Group

A single sherd from an everted rim dish or bowl bore an all over orange slip with a red rim band. The interior of the vessel bore multiple parallel vertical flutes. Presumably, a series of vertical flutes ran all the way around the interior of the vessel. This is a unique piece.

Cui Ceramic Group (6)

Cui Orange-polychrome: Cui Variety (Figures 4.22, s–t, 4.23)

Frequency: 6 sherds (100%; <1%)

Established: Established by Ball (1975:34); see also Forsyth (1983:89–90).

Description:

Principal Identifying Attributes: (1) orange slip color; (2) glossy surface finish; (3) red and black paint applied over orange slip; (4) "turkey vulture" motif; (5) tripod plates or dishes with flat bases and everted rims; (6) unslipped exteriors.

Paste, Firing, and Temper: The paste is medium textured and well mixed. Vessels were fired in an oxidizing atmosphere. Paste color ranges from light to dark red (2.5YR 5–6/6–8; 10R 5–6/8). The temper is calcite.

Surface Finish and Decoration: Vessels were very well smoothed prior to slipping. Vessels interiors were covered with an orange-firing slip (2.5YR 6/8; 5YR 7/6–8). Decoration consists of naturalistic and geometric designs in red (7.5R 3–4/6–8; 10R 4–5/6–8) and black (2.5N/; 7.5R 2/0; 10R 2.5/1–2; 3/1–2) paint on the orange slip. No glyphic elements occur on this type as far as is known. Among the design elements

Figure 4.23. Cui Orange-polychrome ceramic.

that do occur are: arches, elongated ellipses, sausage-like elements, solid painted circles, dress shirt design, open circles with dots in the middle, cell-like squares or rectangles, triangles, scrolls, and others. The decoration is found on vessel interiors, with the principal design on the interior floor of the vessel. This invariably consists of an elaborately executed "turkey vulture" or cui owl (see Forsyth 1983:89–90 for a detailed description of the iconography and design). Exteriors are generally unslipped; however, a couple of examples do bear a thin, yellow-firing slip (10YR 7–8/3–4).

Forms:

1. Flaring-walled tripod plate or dish (Figure 4.22, s–t). Vessel exteriors commonly bear a raised band or ridge at the basal break. Bases are flat or slightly convex. This is the only form known for this type and invariably bears solid or hollow tripod supports.

Intrasite Locations and Contexts: This type is very rare, but five sherds were found in Structure 1 Group 1, Areas D and I. One sherd was recovered from Moquel.

Intersite Locations and Contexts: This type has been found widely in Campeche and western Yucatan (see Ball [1975] for a list of known sites; see also Forsyth [1983:90] and Jiménez [2002:56] for additional sites). Ball (1978:98) also lists Campeche (Ruz 1969:fig. L23–31, 41–44; of these figs. L25–26 and 43 are almost certainly Cui) and Jaina (Ruz 1969:fig. LIV36–49; Piña Chán 1968:lam. 6s–z; 6t–v, x are clearly Cui; the other may or may not be Simochac). Given that it is clear there are numerous orange-polychrome types featuring flaring-walled tripod dishes, it is unclear whether all of the examples referenced by Ball are necessarily Cui Orange-polychrome. For Campeche, Ruz's figs. L25–26, 43 clearly are; others may be as well, but may belong to other orange-polychrome types. For Jaina, it is possible that some of the sherds illustrated in Ruz's fig. LIV36–39 may be Cui, but none of them are unequivocably so. Piña Chán's illustrations in lam. 6 t–v, x are almost certainly of this type. Sherds illustrated in lam. 6s, w, y–z may or may not be Cui. Cui vessels have been found as far south as Calakmul (personal communication, William Folan 2010). They have also been found in other sites as well such as Xcambó (Jiménez 2002:56). Likewise, Cui Orange-polychrome occurs in the Chenes region (Williams-Beck 1999:122–124), see also Ek (2015:448)

Comment: This is a well-established type in the Campeche area; however, it is distinguished from other similar vessels on the basis of its distinctive iconography. Some sherds can easily be confused with Simochac Orange-polychrome, as well as Makat Orange-polychrome (Boucher and Palomo 1989:510) given that vessel form and many design elements, rather than the overall motifs, are shared on these types. Ball (1975) argued that Cui functioned primarily as a part of burial assemblages and was manufactured for that purpose.

Chukul Ceramic Group (6)

Chukul Orange-polychrome: Chukul Variety (no illustration)

Frequency: 6 sherds (100%; <1%)

Established: Established by Boucher and Palomo (1989:499–502).

Description:

Principal Identifying Attributes: (1) orange slip color; (2) glossy surface finish; (3) red and black paint applied over orange slip; (4) seated human figure as the central motif on the interior bottom of the dish; (5) large "bracket" designs on interior wall; (6) tripod plates or dishes with flat bases.

Paste, Firing, and Temper: Same as Sihochac Orange-polychrome.

Surface Finish and Decoration: Both interior and exterior surfaces are slipped. Vessels were very well smoothed prior to slipping. Complex motifs were painted in red and black on the orange base and other designs were placed on the interior side wall. Exteriors are slipped but not painted. There is always a rim band, usually red. See Boucher and Palomo (1989:499–502) for a fuller description of the design that characterizes this type. This type can be confused with Simochac Orange-polychrome when examining sherds. The "bracket" (*corchetes* in Spanish) design on the interior wall is a diagnostic for this type, and the type can often be picked out of a bunch of orange-polychrome sherds because this element seems to be unique to Chukul.

Forms:

1. Flaring-walled tripod plate or dish (no illustration). Vessel exteriors commonly bear a raised band or ridge at the basal break. Bases are flat or slightly convex. This is the only form known for this type.

Intrasite Locations and Contexts: This type is very rare at Champotón. Four of the six sherds were recovered from Moquel.

Intersite Locations and Contexts: According to Boucher and Palomo (1989) this type is known to occur at Jaina (Piña Chán 1968:lam. 5r–s; Ruz 1969:fig. LIV26–27; fig. LXXIII). They also report it as present at Dzibilnocac and at a number of sites in Yucatan, including Maní and Providencia. Jiménez (2002:61–63) reports its presence at Xcambó, as well as at Villa Madero.

Undesignated Ceramic Group (18)

Undesignated Cream-polychrome (no illustration)

Frequency: 18 sherds (100%; <1%).

Established: Not established.

Description:

Principal Identifying Attributes: (1) dull cream slip color on exterior; (2) glossy orange slip on interior; (3) red and black paint applied over cream slip.

Paste, Firing, and Temper: Same as Sihochac Orange-polychrome. This is somewhat surprising given the cream color of the exterior surface, but the interiors are a strong orange.

Surface Finish and Decoration: Both interior and exterior surfaces are slipped. Vessels were very well smoothed prior to slipping. The exterior was slipped with cream to pinkish-firing slip (5R 8/2; 5YR 8/2–4), while the interiors bear a strong orange slip (2.5YR 6/8). Designs in red and black were painted over the dull cream slip. The sherds are too small to determine the overall motifs, but at least some of them are complex. No decoration of any kind appears to have been added to the vessel interiors. In this aspect, the type is similar to a pattern often seen on Zacatal (Zacatel) Cream-polychrome in the Southern Lowlands—cream-polychrome on the exterior with orange-slipped interiors. A similar pattern also occurs on Sagú Cream-polychrome (Forsyth 1983:90–91; Boucher and Palomo 1989:490–495), but Sagú bears an alternating red and orange pattern not found on Champotón vessels.

Forms: Vessel forms are not known. The body sherds seem to indicate some sort of rounded vessel. Two rim sherd suggest a vase form.

Intrasite Locations and Contexts: This type is very rare at Champotón, but examples have been recovered from both Champotón and Moquel.

Intersite Locations and Contexts: This material may be a variety or variant of Sagú Cream-polychrome, but that is not clear. No comparative information is available for this type.

Other Campeche Gloss Ware-Chimbote Ceramic Group

Five sherds of Chimbote Cream-polychrome (Ball 1977:77–78; Forsyth 1983:80–81; Williams-Beck 1999:127–128) were recovered from Champotón. In addition, two sherds of Moro Orange-polychrome (Ball 1977:74; Forsyth 1989:81–83; Williams-Beck 1999:127–128) were also found. Given how numerous these types were at Becán and Edzná, it is surprising that they are so rare at Champotón. It may well be they are inland types and were not part of the coastal complexes, since coastal and interior regions exhibited separate ceramic complexes during the Late and Terminal Classic periods. Nonetheless, both Chimbote and Moro were recovered at Xcambó on the Yucatecan coast (Jiménez 2002:64–68).

Other Campeche Gloss Ware-Sayan Red-on-cream

One rim and one body sherd of Sayan Red-on-cream were recovered from Structure 1 of Group 1.

Other Campeche Gloss Ware-Black-on-cream

One rim sherd and two body sherds of a black-on-cream type occurred at Champotón. The rim sherd is from a deep vase. The paste is a reddish color, but the surfaces are dark. The exterior was covered with a dull cream slip that seems to weather easily. A black rim band and painting in black was applied on the exterior cream surface. Interiors are unslipped and gray to black.

HOXA UNSLIPPED WARE [181]

Chencan Ceramic Group (181)

Chencan Brown-on-orange: Chamizal Variety (Figures 4.24–4.25)

Frequency: 136 sherds (76%; 3%).

Established: Ware, group, and type defined by Forsyth (1983:121–123) at Edzná. The Chamizal Variety is defined here.

Description:

Principal Identifying Attributes: (1) unslipped vessel surfaces; (2) orange to pink surface colors; (3) medium-textured paste; (4) decoration by means of brown blotches; (5) incurved rim basins.

Paste, Firing, and Temper: The paste is medium textured. It is generally strong and varies considerably in color from light red (orange) (10R 6/8; 2.5YR 6/8) to red (2.5YR 5/8; 10R 5/8) to brown (7.5YR 5–6/4). There is generally only slight contrast between the surface and interior paste colors, probably due to compaction of particles on the surface. Firing was carried out in an oxidizing atmosphere, which usually resulted in complete oxidation of the core; however, sometimes there is a gray to light brown core (10YR 6/1–2). The temper is variable. Most examples have calcite temper mixed with what appears to be crushed sherd temper, although some examples have only calcite.

Surface Finish and Decoration: Vessel surfaces were reasonably smoothed but not burnished. On basin forms the interior was more carefully smoothed than on the exterior. The opposite is true of jars. The surfaces have a matte, brick-like appearance. The only decoration consists of dark brown (2.5YR 2–4/2) blotches, stripes, and splatter-like drops on the unslipped vessel surface. The decoration is essentially the same as on the Chencan Variety; however, the Champotón examples exhibit fewer variants of decoration than the Chencan Variety, perhaps due to sample size.

Forms:

1. Incurved rim basin with thickened rim (Figure 4.24, a–d). This seems to be the primary form at Champotón. Bases were presumably flat.
2. Everted rim jar (Figure 4.24e).
3. Round-sided dish or bowl (Figure 4.24f). This is a rare form.

Intrasite Locations and Contexts: In Champotón itself it was found only in Group 1, Str. 1, but most numerous in Areas C and I. It also occurs at Moquel, particularly in Trench L.

Intersite Locations and Contexts: This type was first recognized and defined at Edzná (Forsyth 1983:121), when I noted a probable

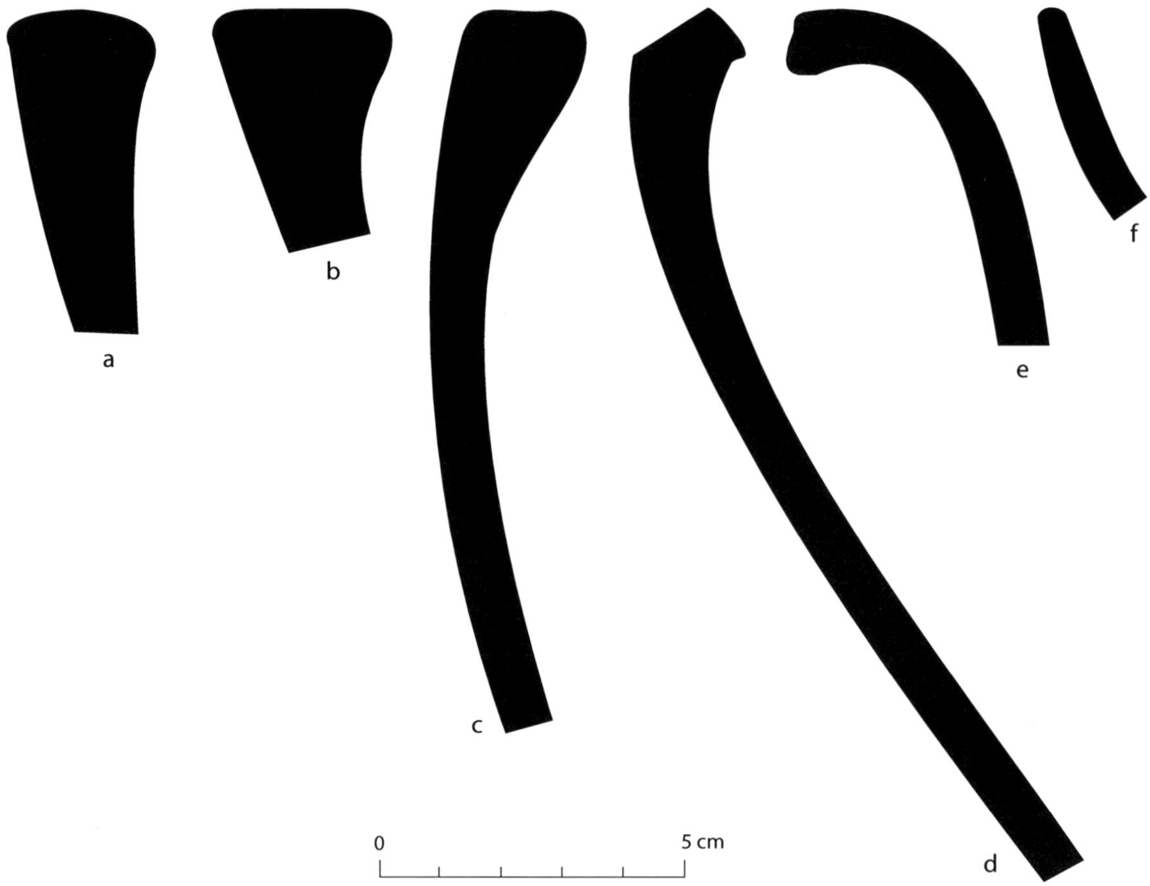

Figure 4.24. Chencan Ceramic Group profile drawings—Chencan Brown-on-orange: Chamizal Variety.

example illustrated by Piña Chán (1968:fig. 10u). Subsequently, I reviewed Piña Chán's type collection from Jaina in the Museo Nacional de Antropología e Historia, but no examples of the type appeared in that collection, which suggests that it was not a common type there. In fact, the illustrated sherd may be a Nimun Brown sherd, as that type both occurs at Jaina and bears a similar kind of blotched and spattered decoration. At Calakmul, Boucher and Dzul (2006:595, 608) report this type as present in small quantities. To date the type appears in quantity only at Edzná, but it may have a wider distribution in the area of coastal Campeche, although that remains to be seen, see Ek (2015:461, 474).

Comment: The Chamizal Variety differs from the Chencan Variety in subtle ways, primarily in slight differences in paste color and especially in vessel form. The distinctive forms noted at Edzná do not occur commonly at Champotón. Further work is needed on this pottery, as it seems to be restricted in distribution.

Keste Incised: Keste Variety (Figures 4.26–4.27) (previously called Kaymuch Unslipped as a preliminary designation)

Frequency: 40 sherds (22%; <1%)

Established: Present study.

Description:

Principal Identifying Attributes: (1) Unslipped vessel surfaces; (2) pink to reddish yellow surface color; (3) matte surface finish; (4) vertical, parallel incised to striated lines

Figure 4.25. Chencan ceramics.

encircling the vessel near the rim; (5) lower portion of vessel not incised; (6) large bowls or drums.

Paste, Firing, and Temper: The paste is thin to medium textured. It is quite dense and, given its general thickness, has relatively few and small aplastics, although this tends to be somewhat variable. This gives the sherds a heavy, dense feel to them. The most common paste color is yellowish red (5YR 5/8) but grades into reddish yellow (5YR 6/8), although sometimes it is a strong red (2.5YR 4–5/8; 10R 4.5/6). Some sherds, however, have a brown-colored paste (7.5YR 5–6/4). Many examples were oxidized throughout the cross-section of the vessel wall, but given the general thickness of these vessels, there are often unoxidized or partially oxidized cores. These darker cores tend toward a light brownish gray color (2.5YR 5–7/2) although occasionally they are darker (2.5Y 4/2). Temper seems to be variable. Some examples seem to have sherd temper, others very small white particles (0.1–0.2 mm) that may be calcite, and others may have volcanic ash as well. This issue could be addressed with high magnification on the paste.

Surface Finish and Decoration: Surfaces were smoothed but not highly burnished. In fact they have a dull, matte appearance to them. Non-incised areas vary from smooth and reasonably well finished to uneven and not very well finished. The latter, however, is rare. Vessel surfaces are a pink to reddish yellow surface color (5YR 7/4–8), although occasional examples are more brown colored (7.5YR 6/4). Beginning at or near the rim of the vessel, a series of vertical (occasionally diagonal), parallel incisions, which on some vessels can grade into striations, encircle the exterior of the vessel. These incisions can vary from 1–8 mm apart. The average seems to be about 3 mm. The closer ones grade into striation and tend not to be as deep as the more widely space ones. The more striated-like examples tend to not penetrate very deeply into the surface, whereas the more widely spaced ones are generally much more deeply cut into the surface of the vessel (as much as 3 mm). The heavily incised lines are usually not very well executed, resulting in varying widths between incisions. That is, there is not a consistent distance between the vertical incisions. It is possible that the striated end of the continuum could be separated out as a different variety, but there is a gradation here that suggests they really are the same type. Although the overall form of these vessels is unknown, there are enough body sherds to indicate that the incisions/striations did not continue all the way down the vessel exterior. Instead, they stop at some point. In several examples they stop at a chamfer-like rise in the vessel wall (see Figure 4.26, m–o); the surface is plain below this point.

Forms:

1. Large jar or basin (Figures 4.26, a–l). The exact shape of this vessel is unknown, as mostly rim and body sherds have been recovered.
2. Exterior offset basin (Figure 4.26, m–o). Base form is unknown but presumably flat.
3. Necked jar (Figure 4.26, p–s). Base form is unknown.

Intrasite Locations and Contexts: Group 1, Structure 1, Areas A and C.

Intersite Locations and Contexts: This type is not known from any other site as yet. It is defined here for the first time.

Comment: Although I know of no other examples of this type from anywhere else in the Maya Lowlands, the pattern of spaced incisions at or near the unslipped rim does occur in other wares and types. Brainerd (1958) reported vertical incisions or grooves on unslipped necks of jar or drum forms in various wares dating to the Florescent (Cehpech), Early Mexican (Sotuta), and Late Mexican (Tases) periods (Brainerd 1958:fig. 25a; 40e2, 20; 72k4–20; see also fig. 42g7); see also Smith (1971:fig. 39). I have seen Chenes Slate Ware (Williams-Beck (1999:210) jars from Santa Rosa Xtampak that have an unslipped area near the neck with similar incisions (personal observation, 2008); however, none of these have the same paste or appearance as Keste Incised. Moreover, these other examples were slipped below the area of

Figure 4.26. Chencan Ceramic Group profile drawings: Keste Incised: Keste Variety.

Figure 4.27. Keste Incised: Keste Variety ceramics.

incisions or striations, whereas we have little evidence of that for Keste. Only two or three sherds bore a small area of what might have been the remnants of a red slip, one over the incised area, and the other two below it, but it is not clear that these vessels were regularly slipped, although the lack of the basal portion of them makes this assertion somewhat equivocal. It is also possible that some examples from Champotón are pedestal bases rather than rims, although this cannot be demonstrated.

Other Chencan Group: Black-on-brown

Two body sherds, which might be from the same vessel, of what otherwise would be Keste Incised bear wide, vertical black-painted lines spaced about 2.8 cm apart. The rim of the vessel is incised like normal Keste Incised. Below the vertical incisions the vessel wall juts outward a little less than 4 mm to form the body, thus forming a sharp break between the incised portion of the vessel and the rest of the body surface. Although weathered, the lines are clearly positive painted.

UNDESIGNATED UNSLIPPED WARE

Neza Ceramic Group (132)

Neza Unslipped: Neza Variety (Figures 4.28–4.29)

Frequency: 132 sherds (100%; 3%). Body sherds that should pertain to this type may have been counted with other unslipped types.

Established: Present study.

Description:

Principal Identifying Attributes: (1) unslipped vessel surfaces; (2) bolstered-rim basins.

Paste, Firing, and Temper: The paste is generally coarse textured. Paste color varies from red (10R 4/6–8; 2.5YR 4/6–8; 5/8) to grayish brown (10YR 51.5) to light grayish brown (2.5Y 6/2 to black (7.5R3/0). The vast majority of vessels lack a dark core, but a few examples have areas that were not oxidized

Figure 4.28. Neza Unslipped: Neza Variety cermaics.

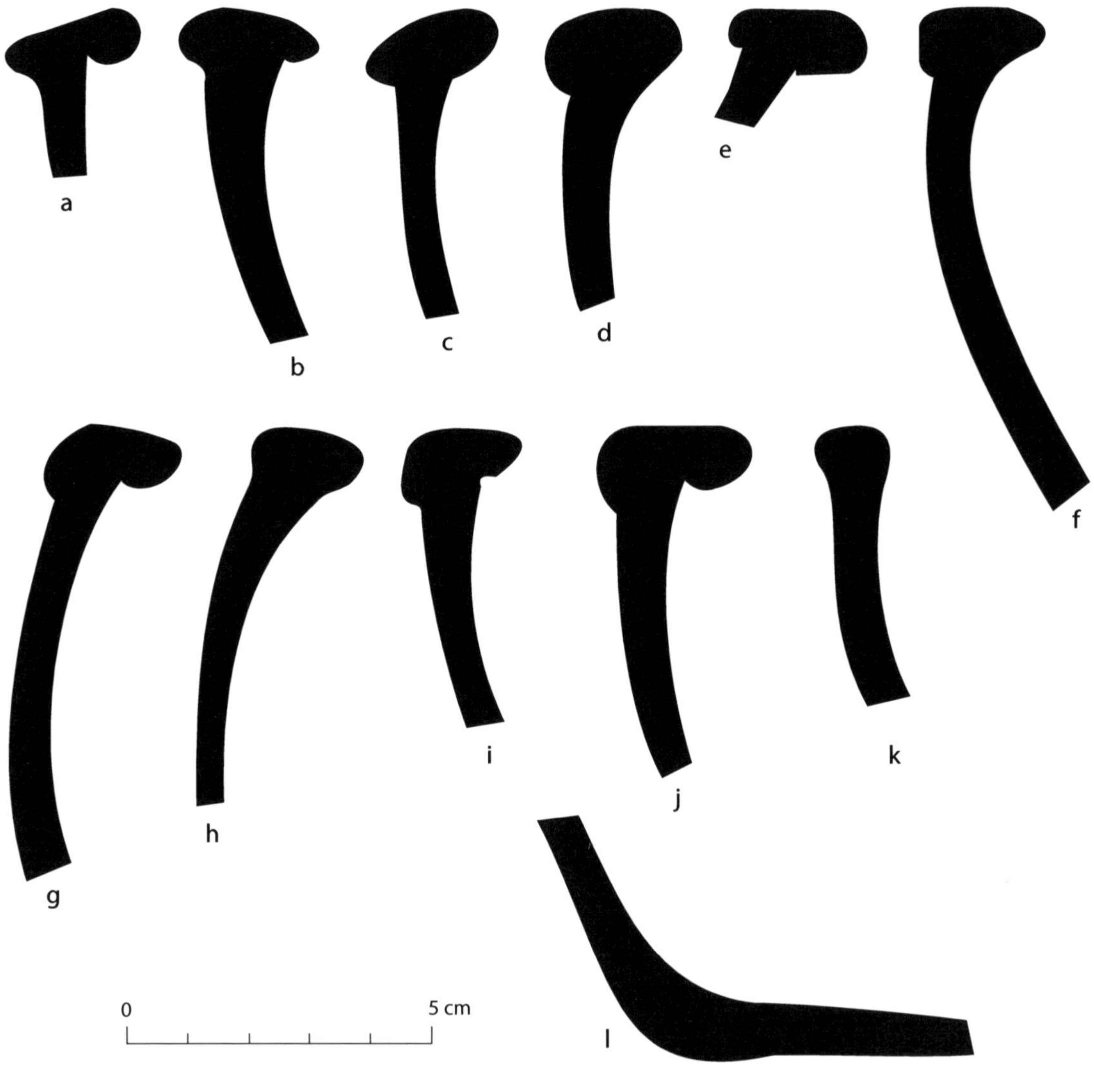

Figure 4.29. Neza Ceramic Group profile drawings: Neza Unslipped: Neza Variety.

throughout the whole vessel cross-section. Temper consists of white to gray calcite in heavy concentrations, although the latter varies somewhat. A few sherds may also have some sherd temper, but this is not the general pattern. The paste is similar to that of Carpizo Red: Carpizo Variety and may simply be an unslipped version of that same ceramic.

Surface Finish and Decoration: Surfaces were smoothed but not generally polished. Vessel interiors seem to have been better finished than vessel exteriors. Smoothing tends to bring finer particles to the surface, resulting in surfaces that vary in color somewhat from the paste. Surface colors tend to a light brownish gray (7.5YR 7/2; 10YR 6.5/1–2) to a pinkish red (7.5YR 7/4); however, the surfaces are often mottled to one degree or another, so that colors are rarely consistent on the vessel surface. Gray to dark gray (7.5YR 4–5/0) clouding occurs on some vessels.

Forms:

1. Incurved rim basin (Figure 4.29, a–j). Lip form varies from folded to triangular to T-shaped. This is overwhelmingly the dominant form for this type. Bases are flat (Figure 4.29l).
2. Basin with thickened rim (Figure 4.29k). Bases are flat.

Intrasite Locations and Contexts: It is found in different excavation units in Group 1, Structure 1, but seems to be most frequent in Area A. It is also found at Moquel in Structure 1.

Intersite Locations and Contexts: I am aware of no other sites with ceramics of this specific type; however, Neza vessel shapes are very similar, if not identical, to some of those reported for the site of Campeche (Ruz 1969:XLVIII, 8–31) and for Jaina (Ruz 1969:LI, 41,43–53; Piña Chán 1968:lam. 9j–p, see also lam. 9 c'–l' for a similar form but on slipped and trickled vessels). Despite the similarity in form, however, they are different types.

Comment: Many of the Campeche and Jaina examples are typically striated on the exterior, although many are not, which is definitely not the case with Neza Unslipped. Moreover, Ball (1978:96) indicates that the Campeche and Jaina examples are part of what he called Nimun Brown Ware, which Simmons (n.d.:8) designated as part of Celestún Red Ware, Nimun Ceramic Group. Neza Unslipped is definitely not Nimun Brown. Neza appears to be an unslipped version of Carpizo Red that has the same, or very similar, vessel and rim forms as some of the Nimun Brown ware from Campeche, Jaina, and Huaymil. There seems to be parallelism between Champotón and the more northern coastal sites in that Champotón shares vessel and rim shapes, but they are not the same wares. Neza is neither Baca Red nor Nimun Brown. Nonetheless, the principal vessel form appears to be very similar to what Jiménez (2002:20; fig. 9a–g) named Providencia alisado at Xcambó. Ek (2015:476) appears to have classified what herein I call Neza Unslipped as Acapulquito Unslipped (see below).

PUUC UNSLIPPED WARE [645]

Acapulquito Ceramic Group (645)

Acapulquito Unslipped: Variety Unspecified (Figures 4.30–4.32)

Frequency: 198 sherds (30%; 4%)

Established: Type established by Forsyth (1983:125) at Edzná.

Description:

Principal Identifying Attributes: (1) unslipped vessel surfaces; (2) coarse paste with temper particles often protruding; (3) wide, flaring necks; (4) bolstered or thickened rims; (5) jar forms.

Paste, Firing, and Temper: The paste is almost always coarse textured. Paste color ranges from red (10R 5/6–8; 6/6; 5YR 6/6; 5YR 4–5/6) to brown (5YR 4/3; 5/4; 7.5YR 5/4). The vast majority of vessels are oxidized throughout the vessel cross-section, but occasional dark cores do occur (7.5R3/0). The temper consists of white to gray calcite; temper particles average 0.5–1.0 mm, although occasional particles are as large as 3 mm.

Surface Finish and Decoration: The surfaces were smoothed but not to a high finish. They are only relatively smooth to the touch. Temper consists of white to gray calcite in heavy concentrations. It is readily visible macroscopically, often showing in the weathered surfaces of the vessels. Although no slip was applied to these surfaces, the smoothing brought finer particles of clay to the surface, accounting, in part, for the subtle difference between paste color and surface color. The latter tends to be somewhat more grayish (10R 5–6/1; 5YR 6/1) to brownish (7.5YR 7/2–4) than the underlying paste, which is often, but not invariably, a somewhat reddish tone (10R 4–5/6–8).

Forms:

1. Everted rim jar with hyperboloid neck and thickened or folded rim (Figure 4.31). Bases are flat or slightly concave.

Figure 4.30. Acapulquito Unslipped: Variety Unspecified ceramics.

2. Flaring-neck jar with direct rim (Figure 4.32, q–r). Bases are flat or slightly concave.

3. Strongly incurved-rim basin (Figure 4.32, a–o). There is a sharp angle or ridge at the corner point (Shepard 1968:226) where the rim breaks inward from the general contour of the basin. Rim diameter is not known, but based on examples from Edzná (Forsyth 1983:125) they were usually in the 35–50 cm range. This seems likely at Champotón also, as the basins are large. The lip can be either direct (rare), thickened, or folded. Base form is unknown; compare Forsyth (1983:fig. 34W–ee). This is a rare form

4. T-rim basin (Figure 4.32p). There is likewise a sharp angular corner point as in Form 1 above. This attribute is characteristic of the type in general. Rim diameter is unknown. The lip of this form, rather than being thickened, forms a nearly T-shaped angle. Base form is unknown; compare Forsyth (1983:fig. 34Q–v). This is a rare form.

Intrasite Locations and Contexts: It occurs in widespread excavation units in Group 1, Structure 1, but seems to be most frequent in Area I. It is also found at Moquel. The type was defined at Edzná (Forsyth 1983:125; refer there for similarities to other sites), where it is very common. Ek (2015:474, 476) reports the type from around the Champotón area.

Intersite Locations and Contexts: This is apparently a widespread type throughout central Campeche. It was defined by Forsyth (1983:125) at Edzná. It is analogous to Cambio Unslipped in the Southern Lowlands and Acapulquito should perhaps be considered a variety of Cambio.

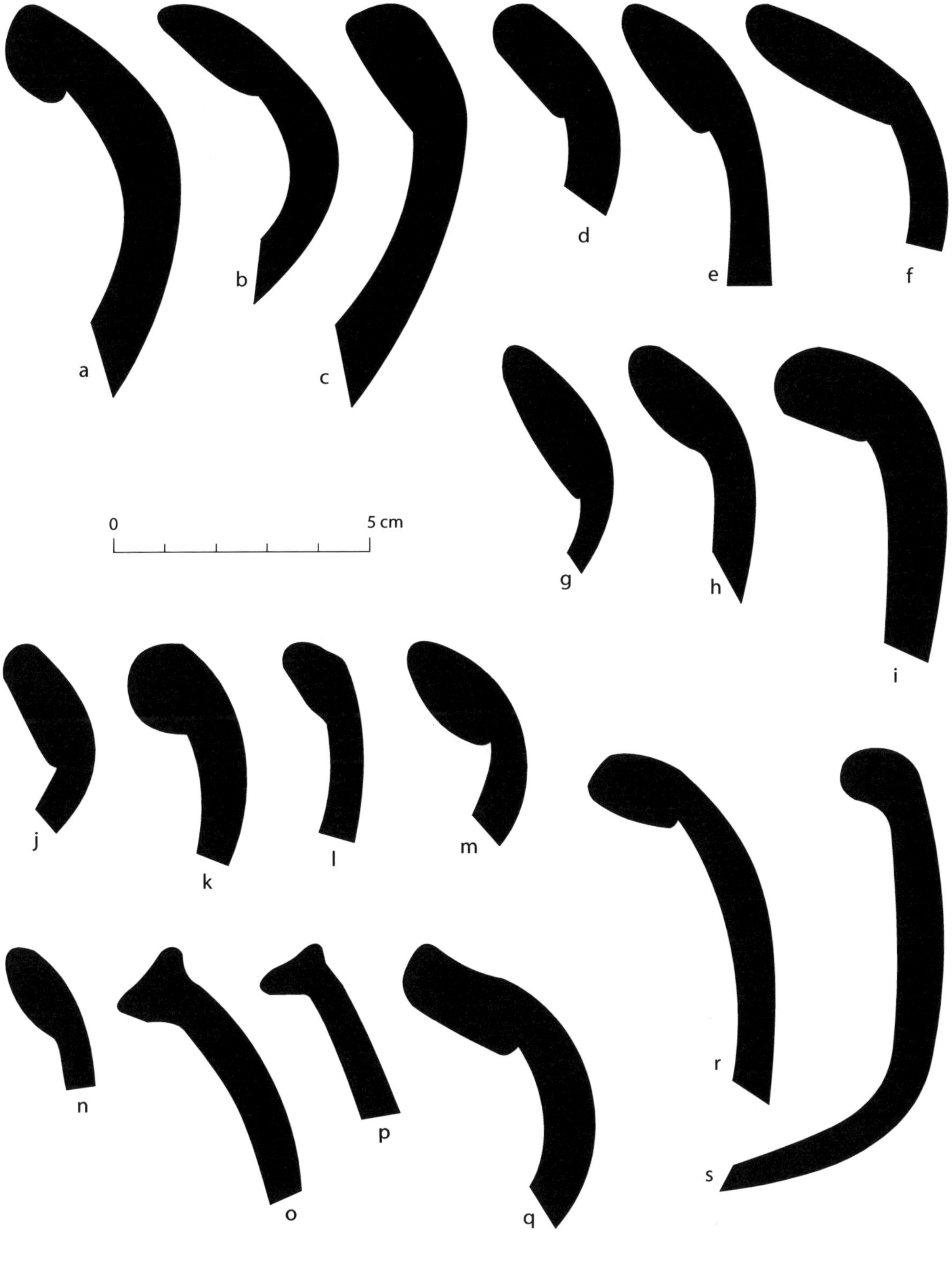

Figure 4.31. Acapulquito Ceramic Group profile drawings—Acapulquito Unslipped: Variety Unspecified.

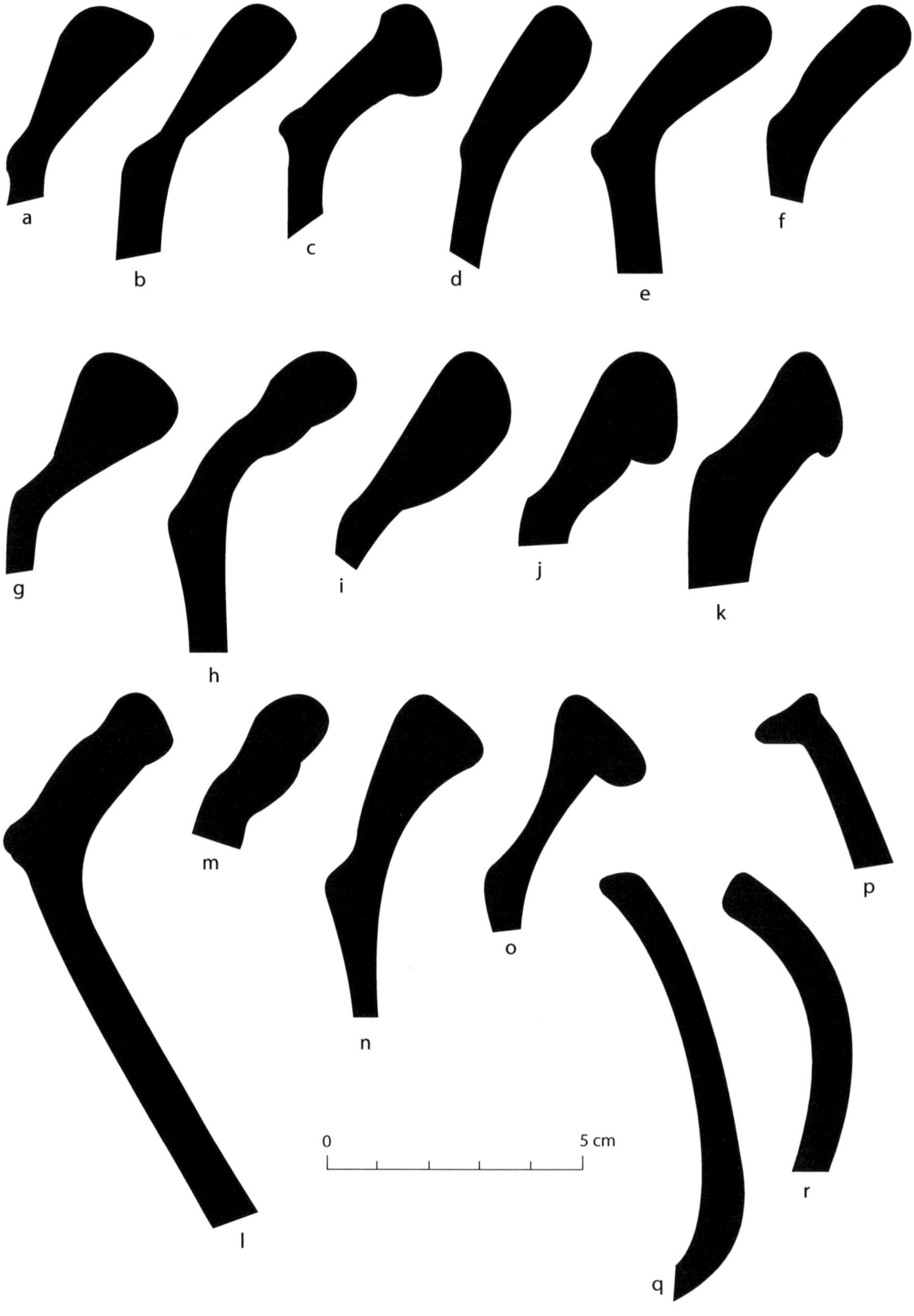

Figure 4.32. Acapulquito Ceramic Group profile drawings—Acapulquito Unslipped: Variety Unspecified.

See Intersite Locations and Contexts below for Yakatzib Striated for more on this issue.

Comments: Williams-Beck (1999:84–85) has argued that what I have called Acapulquito Unslipped originally carried a brown-colored "slip" ("engobe aguado") that readily erodes and can thus give the appearance of being an unslipped type. She therefore renamed the type Acapulquisimo Brown. It is not clear to me that this is necessarily the case for most of the examples in the Champotón collection, or the Edzná one for that matter. As noted above, however, the compaction of the vessel surfaces during formation sometimes does present a surface that can give the appearance of a slip, due to the finer smoothing of the vessel bringing smaller clay particles to the surface. This compaction occurs most frequently on the interior of the basins. And it is precisely on the interior and up onto and over the rim a short distance—a common pattern of slipping during Late and Terminal Classic times in the Maya Lowlands and beyond. Still, basins are a rare form in this type; the overwhelming majority are jars. On most of the examples in the Champotón collection, it is impossible to argue for a slip or wash. On the other hand, there are a few examples in which this, indeed, may be the case; however, this does not appear to be the case at Champotón. Willams-Beck (1999:84) places this pottery in Chenes Slate Ware without specifying why it fits into that category. It is clearly not a slate ware in the traditional use of that term.

Yakatzib Striated: Yakatzib Variety (Figures 4.33–4.34)

Frequency: 447 sherds (69%; 10%).

Established: Yakatzib Striated: Yakatzib Variety was established as a separate type at Edzná by Forsyth (1983:125–126).

Description:

Principal Identifying Attributes: (1) unslipped vessel surfaces; (2) coarse paste with temper particles often protruding; (3) wide, flaring necks; (4) bolstered or thickened rims; (5) jar forms.

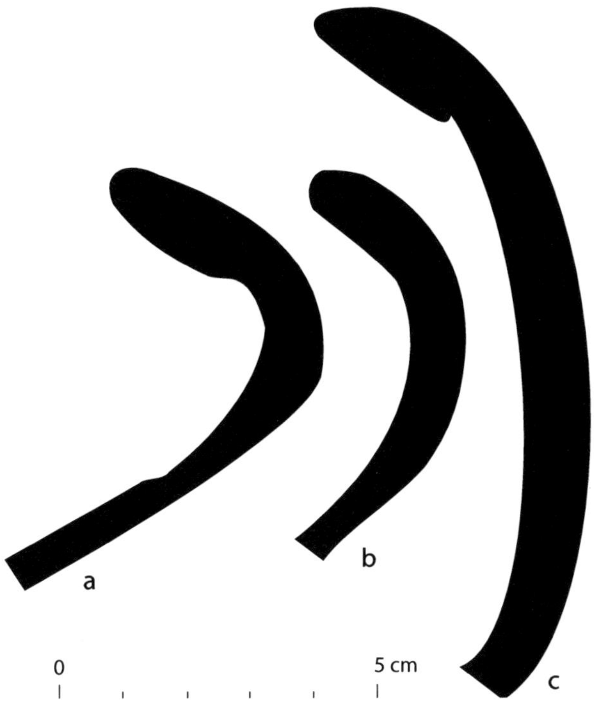

Figure 4.33. Acapulquito Ceramic Group profile drawings: Yakatzib Striated: Yakatzib Variety.

Paste, Firing, and Temper: Same as Acapulquito Unslipped.

Surface Finish and Decoration: Surface finish is the same as Acapulquito Unslipped with the exception that vessel bodies were striated on their exteriors. The striation is generally heavy in execution. The striation begins on the exterior at or near the neck-body juncture and covers the whole exterior of the jar down to the basal break. The exterior bottoms of the vessels are not striated. The striations tend to run vertically, horizontally, or diagonally, and sometimes in more complicated patterns, but it tends not to be uniform, with different sections of the vessels' exterior having striations in different directions.

Forms:

1. Everted rim jar with hyperboloid neck and thickened or folded rim (Figure 4.33, a, c). Bases are flat or slightly concave.
2. Flaring-neck jar with direct rim (Figure 4.33b). Bases are flat or slightly concave.

Figure 4.34. Yakatzib Striated: Yakatzib Variety ceramics.

Intrasite Locations and Contexts: It occurs in widespread excavation units in Group 1, Structure 1, but seems to be most frequent in Area I. It is also found at Moquel but is rare there.

Intersite Locations and Contexts: This type is one of the most widespread in the Maya Lowlands. It dominates most ceramic complexes in central Campeche (see Comment section below). It is very similar to Encanto Striated in the Southern Lowlands. It varies slightly from region to region, but the essential nature of these vessels remains the same.

Comment: Yakatzib Striated is very similar to Encanto Striated in the Southern Lowlands. Many of the rim forms of Yakatzib Striated are virtually identical to those found on Encanto Striated rims I have handled in the thousands from the Mirador Basin in northern Guatemala. Perhaps Yakatzib should be considered a variety of Encanto Striated. I have maintained the Yakatzib name here, but the fact is that many of these vessels would be difficult to distinguish macroscopically from those found much farther south. Others have actually designated similar materials as Encanto (Jiménez, Ceballos et al. 2006:354), but there remains considerable confusion with respect to the classification of the unslipped striated vessels in the Yucatan Peninsula (Yokat, Yakatazib, Encanto). Because the striation on Yakatzib vessels begins only at the juncture of the tall neck and the globular body, thus leaving the tall neck unstriated, many of the rim sherds classified as Acapulquito Unslipped may very well be the rim portion of Yakatzib vessels. The rim forms of Yakatzib Striated are identical to those for Acapulquito Unslipped with the addition of striation on the globular body.

MOXA GRAY WARE [26]

A small number of sherds (26) were recovered in the Group 1 Structure 1 excavations that mimic the Chablekal Ceramic Group pottery, but which are not fine paste ceramics. In terms of form and, when present, decorative technique, they are clearly imitations of the Chablekal Group. The most distinctive of this small group of sherds is the incised pottery because, even in relatively small sherds, it is possible to recognize the distinctive style of incising used on Chicxulub vessels. The undecorated examples of this pottery are not as clearly demarcated, as the rim sherds are small, and thus form is far less clear. For this reason, I have designated a type for this pottery only for the incised examples. Designation of the plain type (Hontun Gray?; see Forsyth 1983:113), and those with other decorative techniques, if there are any, will have to await a larger sample.

Hontun Ceramic Group (26)

Chumpic Incised: Variety Unspecified (no illustration)

Frequency: 14 sherds (54%; <1%)

Established: Type established at Edzná (Forsyth 1983:115). The Champotón material is left as an unspecified variety.

Description:

Principal Identifying Attributes: (1) unslipped, matte vessel surfaces; (2) thin paste; (3) thin vessel walls; (4) incision on exterior vessel walls; (5) composite silhouette bowls.

Paste, Firing, and Temper: The paste is thin textured. It is quite a dense paste and bears tiny fragments of temper particles barely visible in cross-section with a magnifying glass, but they are extremely small in most cases. Paste color varies considerably from pink (5YR 7/4) to reddish brown (5YR 6/3), pinkish gray (5YR 6/2) to light or brownish gray (10 YR 5–7/2). One example has a deep black paste color (7.5 YR 2/0). Black to grayish cores occur on a number of sherds. Although not technically a fine-paste pottery, the thin texture appears to be an attempt to mimic fine-paste ceramics. Temper consists of very small particles of what appears to be calcite, but the exact composition of the temper remains to be determined.

Surface Finish and Decoration: Surfaces were smoothed and compacted. They do not appear to be slipped, but smoothing and polishing may sometimes give the appearance of a slip of the same clay used for the paste as finer particles are brought to the surface. Suface colors, like the paste, vary considerably, ranging from pale to reddish brown (10YR 6/3; 7.5 YR 6/3) to various shades of gray and brownish gray (10YR 7/1; 7.5YR 4.5/0; 7.5YR 6/2). The exterior surfaces bear incised designs consisting primarily of an area outlined by incising—that is zoned regions that bear interior hatching or cross-hatching. Although the zoned regions are usually rectilinear, forming simple, step- or fret-like areas, on two examples the incised outlines form rounded areas. The style of incision is identical to that found on Chicxulub Incised, and this pottery appears to be an attempt to copy that pottery in a non-fine paste ware. All examples have a circumferential incised line or groove running about 0.5 cm below the lip, although on one example is about 1.5 cm below the lip. The zoned areas tend to occur below this circumferential line, and, in fact, the line often serves as the upper boundary for the zoned areas of incision.

Forms:

1. Composite silhouette dish or bowl (no illustration). This form generally has a sharp break or shoulder with the area below the break curving toward the base. In other examples, the change in contour is less sharp. This is the only known example for which there is clear evidence, but others probably occur.

Intrasite Locations and Contexts: This is a very rare type, but examples were recovered from various excavation units in Group 1, Structure 1, particularly Areas I and F.

Intersite Locations and Contexts: The type occurs at Edzná; see Forsyth (1983:115) for information on its distribution. Ek (2015:475, 477) has recovered this type, as well as others from the same ceramic group, from sites around Champotón.

Comment: Hontun Ceramic Group pottery is very rare at Champotón, and it is not clear how important its manufacture and use at the site may have been. In addition to the Chumpic Incised sherds, ten plain sherds were recovered, as well as one gouged-incised example, and one incised and punctuated example. Both of these were body sherds.

ISLA FINA FINE BUFF WARE [184]

Dzitbalché Ceramic Group (184)

Dzitbalché Fine Buff: Dzitbalché Variety (Figure 4.35, a–f)

Frequency: 150 sherds (82%; 3%).

Established: Type and variety established by Ball (1977:42–43) at Becán as Dzitbalché Orange Buff; however, the pottery was first reported from Jaina as "Cerámica anaranjada-Tipo I" by Ruz (1969:156–157) in his MA Thesis in 1945, which was not published in book form until 1969 by INAH. Subsequently, Piña Chán (1968:53–55; lam. 7) also described it as part of the Jaina ceramics. Jiménez, Belamar et al. (2006:502) gave it the ware name of Isla Fina Ware. Ek (2015) calls this material Isla Fina/Dzitbalché, but in his recent publication (2016:533), he uses Isla Fina for the ceramic group and type name.

Description:

Principal Identifying Attributes: (1) fine paste; (2) matte vessel surfaces; (3) dull cream to buff slip; (4) hollow 'jaguar claw' supports.

Paste, Firing, and Temper: The paste is fine textured. There are extremely small particles of temper, but as Ruz (1969:156) pointed out "(t)he granulation of the clay is as fine as that of Fine Orange despite containing temper." Paste color varies considerably but generally has lower chroma than Fine Orange sherds. As Ruz (1969:156) again put it "...to the naked eye it is distinguished from said Fine Orange by its always more pallid color." Common paste colors are reddish brown to reddish yellow (5YR 6/4–8) to pink (5YR 7/3–4; 7.5 YR 7/4). Most examples are oxidized throughout the cross-section of the sherd, but darker cores are not uncommon. The color of these cores varies from very pale brown (10YR 7/3) to gray (10YR 7/2; 6/1).

Surface Finish and Decoration: Surfaces were smoothed and compacted, interiors more so than exteriors. They appear to have received a weak wash that sometimes fires to weak white to pale gray to pale brown color (10YR 7–8/2–3), but others are more pink (5YR 7/3; 7.5YR 7/3), and an occasional sherd has a more gray color (5YR 7/1). For the most part the surface colors are pallid, thus the buff designation, ranging through pink. Perhaps as a result of the wash, surfaces are generally more pallid than the underlying paste.

Forms:

1. Dish with rounded walls and enlarged, everted rim (Figure 4.35, a–e). This is by far the most common form. Some may be sufficiently deep to be considered bowls (cf. Piña Chán 1968:lam. 7k–m), but most are more shallow. A few examples bear a basal flange or skirt often decorated by spaced groups of crenelations. Others have a raised offset near the base on the exterior near the wall base junction (cf. Piña Chán 1968:lam. 7y, j'–l'; Ruz 1969:fig. LII, 15, 17). Tripod supports take various forms, including tall, hollow rectangular examples (cf. Ruz 1969:fig. LII, 17, 39–41). Others, and virtually diagnostic for this ware, are round to almost quadrangular and bear three extensions that mimic the appearance of a 'jaguar claw'. Some round supports are also known to occur. Bases were slightly concave, but some examples have flat bottoms.

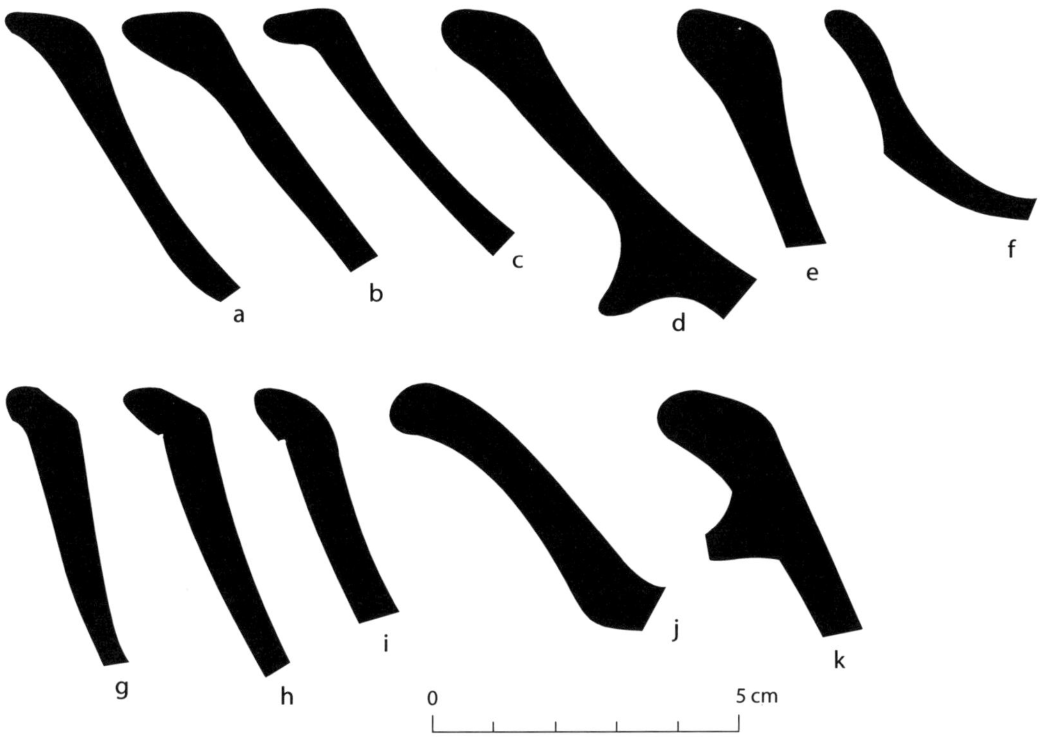

Figure 4.35. Dzitbalché Ceramic Group profile drawings: a–f. Dzitbalché Fine Buff: Dzitbalché Variety, g–k. Cerro de Caracoles Red-on-white: Cerro de Caracoles Variety.

Bases and appendages: Supports are very common in this type (see Form 1 description for the kinds of tripod supports found on these vessels). A few pedestal supports have also been recovered, but it is not clear in our collections what the vessel form associated with them is (cf. Ruz 1969:fig. LII, 18).

Intrasite Locations and Contexts: It occurs in Areas A–D, H–I, and N–P of Group 1, Structure 1, but is especially concentrated in Area I. Twenty-one sherds came from Moquel.

Intersite Locations and Contexts: The pottery of this kind was first recognized at Jaina by Ruz (1969:fig. LII, 15–45) and later at the same site by Piña Chán (1968:lam. 7) as described above. It is also found at Becán (Ball 1977:42–43), where it was first described in type-variety terms. It apparently occurs at numerous sites along the Campeche and north Yucatecan coasts. Jiménez (2002:44–45) mentions many sites including Isla Piedras, Villa Madero, Uaymil, Petenes de Xlabaroo, La Providencia, Paso Holuntún, as well as Dzibilchaltún, Oxkintok, and Comalcalco. Ek (2015:461, 468–469) also encountered it at sites in the Champotón region.

Comment: A few sherds classified as Dzitbalché would probably fall under the category of Lerma Dichrome (Jiménez 2002:45).

Cerro de Caracoles Red-on-white: Cerro de Caracoles Variety (Figure 4.35, g–k)

Frequency: 12 sherds (7%; <1%).

Established: Type and variety established by Jiménez (2002:46) at Xcambó; however, see the corresponding entry under Dzitbalché Fine Buff for examples that were described in non-type-variety terms by Ruz (1969) and Piña Chán (1968) at Jaina.

Description:

Principal Identifying Attributes: (1) fine paste; (2) matte vessel surfaces; (3) strong cream slip; (4) red paint applied to upper surface of rim.

Paste, Firing, and Temper: Same as Dzitbalché Fine Buff.

Surface Finish and Decoration: The initial preparation of the surface was identical to that for Dzitbalché Fine Buff; however, both surfaces were then covered with a white- to cream-firing slip that contrasts with the buff surfaces below. The slip is fairly adherent, although it does weather on some occasions. It may be that on the occasional vessel the slip was applied only on the interior of the vessel, but on most of the small sample from Champotón, both the interior and exterior are slipped white/cream (10YR 8/1–2; 7.5YR 8/1–2). A red to cherry-colored (10R 4–5/6–8) paint was applied to the upper surface of the slightly enlarged, everted rim, forming a circumferential band on the rim. This is the only location where red paint is found on the examples from Champotón. No examples of red bands, such as those described by Piña Chán (1968:54; lam. 7, f–m) as "Anaranjada con banda roja," were recovered from Champotón. Given the small sample size though, this is perhaps not particularly significant.

Forms:

1. Dish with rounded walls and enlarged, everted rim (Figure 4.35, g–i); compare Ruz (1969:fig. LII, 17–22) for this form. One example bears an appliquéd element on the exterior just below the rim, but it is broken off, so its exact form is unknown. Presumably, tripod supports like those described for Dzitbalché Fine Buff occur on these vessels, but no examples of such were found attached to the small number of sherds recovered in our investigations.

2. Basal-break dish with direct slightly everted rim (Figure 4.35j). This is not a common form.

3. Flaring-wall bowl with everted rim (Figure 4.35k). Unlike Form 1, this bowl is deeper and does not have the rounded or curved walls. It does not seem to be a major form at Champotón.

Intrasite Locations and Contexts: It occurs in very small quantities in Areas A, C–D, and F of Group 1, Structure 1. Only three sherds of this type were recovered from Moquel.

Intersite Locations and Contexts: This type is reported from relatively few sites but likely because it has only been defined relatively recently. It is Jiménez (2002:46), working on collections from Xcambó, Yucatan, who has brought some type-variety classificatory order to the many variants of Fine Buff pottery. In addition to Jaina and Xcambó, Jiménez (2002:46) lists Isla Piedras, Villa Madero, and Uaymil as sites where this type has been recognized. I suspect that it is distributed more widely along the Campeche coast. Ek (2015:461) lists it as present in some of the sites around Champotón.

Other Dzitbalché Group: El Remate Red-on-buff

Two rim sherds of what Jiménez (2002:45) described as El Remate Red-on-buff were recovered in the Champotón collections. The decoration is similar to that on Cerro de Caracoles Red-on-cream except that the body of the vessels lacked the white to cream slip, leaving the buff color of the surfaces intact and red paint covering the upper surface of the rim. On one sherd the red paint extends down the interior of the vessel for an undetermined distance from the rim

Other Dzitbalché Group: Jaina Composite ?

Three examples of the rather diagnostic modeled animal heads that were attached to some of the Fine Buff vessels were recovered from Champotón, although not attached to a vessel (cf. Piña Chán 1968:lam. 7n'–ñ'; Ruz 1969:fig. LX–D; see Jiménez 2002:47 for a description and fig. 13a). Whether or not these were attached to a vessel with a red-painted band is therefore not determinable, but it seems likely that they do pertain to the Jaina Composite type.

Other Dzitbalché Group: Chamfered

One rim and one base from an otherwise Dzitbalché Fine Buff vessel bear exterior clapboard chamfering. Both were found in the same excavation lot and almost certainly are from the same vessel. The exterior base bears a remnant of a hollow support.

Other Dzitbalché Group: Red slip

Four sherds bearing a red slip on both the interior and exterior were also found. One is a portion of a pedestal base. Three also have indications of simple incising (cf. Piña Chán 1968:55; lam. 7a"–c").

Other Dzitbalché Group: White slip

One rim and two bodies of sherds bearing the white slip characteristic of Cerro de Caracoles Red-on-cream were also recovered. In the case of body sherds, they may simply be portions of Cerro de Caracoles or other types in the areas where the red paint is not found.

Other Dzitbalché Group: Incised

At least six sherds that bear incised designs on the exterior of the vessel have been recovered. To the extent the designs can be discerned, they seem to mimic designs found on Fine Gray vessels.

Other Dzitbalché Group: Impressed

Two sherds bear finger-impressed-like designs. One sherd has them at the basal break, while the other consists of a band of small impressions as a circumferential band on the exterior wall of a small vessel.

FINE ORANGE WARE [214]

Altar Ceramic Group (83)

Previously known as Y Fine Orange (Smith 1958:151, 153)

Altar Orange: Altar Variety (Figures 4.36, a–i, 4.37)

Frequency: 57 sherds (69%; 1%) Altar Orange; Altar Fine Orange.

Established: Type and variety established by Smith and Gifford (1966:173) at Uaxactún; see also Smith (1971:19), but also see Adams (1971:30) and Sabloff (1975:189–206) for fuller descriptive accounts of the type.

Description: Given the widespread and well-known nature of Fine Orange Ceramics, it is not necessary to repeat all of the descriptive data for every site where the ceramics were found, especially since they are the result of production in limited regions of the Maya area (see Ball 1978:77).

Principal Identifying Attributes: (1) fine orange-colored paste; (2) orange- to red-firing slip of the same clay as the paste; (3) round-sided bowl.

Paste, Firing, and Temper: The paste of the Altar Ceramic Group of Fine Orange Ware has been defined by a number of analysts (see Smith 1955:28–29; 1958:151–153; Smith and Gifford 1966:165; Adams 1971:30; Sabloff 1975:189–206; Bishop and Rands 1982).

Surface Finish and Decoration: See Smith and Gifford (1966:165) for a description of the surfaces of the Altar Ceramic Group. See Sabloff (1975:189) for a description of the surface finish of the Altar Orange type. There is considerable Altar Ceramic Group material in Berlin's Z-Fine Orange category (personal observation, ceramoteca, INAH-Yucatan); this was noted by Adams (1971:27) as well.

Forms:

1. Bowl with rounded walls (Figure 4.36, a–g). This is a typical form for Altar Ceramic Group range (cf. Berlin 1956:fig. 3a; Smith 1958:fig. 2a–b; Smith 1971:fig. 9a, c; Sabloff 1975:fig. 371l–o). The Altar Orange examples from Champotón lack any of the decoration seen in the above illustrations.
2. Flaring-walled dish or bowl with bulbous hollow supports (Figure 4.36h). This is a rare form at Champotón (cf. Berlin 1956:fig. 3dd; Adams 1971:fig. 66k, chart 11, 3a)
3. Deep everted rim bowl (Figure 4.36i). This is a rare form at Champotón (cf. Ruz 1969:fig. XXX, 1–12; Berlin 1956:fig.

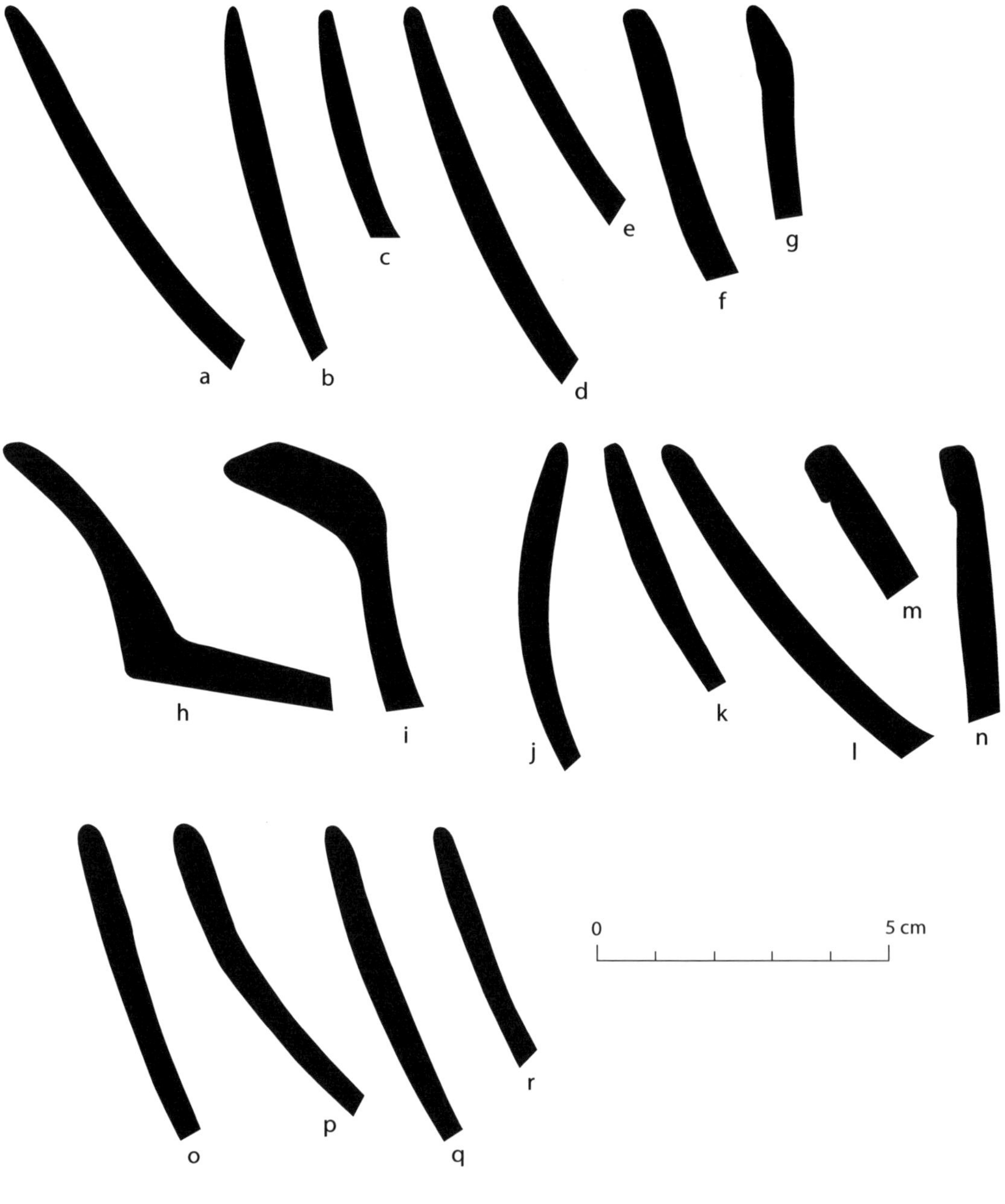

Figure 4.36. Altar Ceramic Group profile drawings: a–i. Altar Orange: Altar Variety; j–n. Tumba Black-on-orange: Tumba Variety; o–r. Trapiche Incised: Variety Unspecified.

3mm–ss; Adams 1971:fig. 66b–c, chart 11, 2a–b). It is especially common at Los Guarixés on the Isla del Carmen, so much so that Ball (1978:82), following Brainerd (1958:54), suggested that it may have been manufactured there, or, alternatively, it was imported in great abundance.

Intrasite Locations and Contexts: Twenty-nine of the Altar Orange sherds come from Area C of Group 1, Structure 1, while five more come from Area D. Eight sherds of this type were recovered from Moquel.

Figure 4.37. Altar Orange: Altar Variety ceramics.

Intersite Locations and Contexts: Altar Orange, like other members of the Altar Ceramic Group, was produced in the Usumacinta drainage with an emphasis in the upper Usumacinta (Bishop et al. 2005:179). It is present in larger quantities at sites in this region, such as Altar de Sacrificios (Adams 1971:27) and Seibal [Ceibal] (Sabloff 1975:189, 192). It also occurs, apparently in some quantity, at Yaxchilan (López 1989:141–142) in this same region. However, as noted above, it also occurs in great quantity at Los Guarixés, along the Campeche coast. It may be that Los Guarixés was a shipping point for this material along the Campeche and Yucatecan littoral and into the interior. As noted above, it occurs in quantity in Berlin's collections from Tecolpan/Jonuta, although he lumped it in with Z Fine Orange (now Balancán Ceramic Group). Although it is restricted in distribution in large quantity, it is an extremely widespread type, along with other members of its ceramic group. It has been found in small quantities over much of the Maya Lowlands during the Terminal Classic period; see also Ball (1978:81–82) for a list of known sites. Ek (2015:461, 466) reports it from some sites around the Champotón area.

Tumba Black-on-orange: Tumba Variety (Figure 4.36, j–n)

Frequency: 14 sherds (17%; <1%).

Established: Type and variety established by Smith and Gifford (1966:173) at Uaxactún; see also Smith (1971:19), but see Adams (1971:27) and Sabloff (1975:189, 182) for fuller descriptive accounts of the type.

Description: Given the widespread and well-known nature of Fine Orange Ceramics, it is not necessary to repeat all of the descriptive data for every site where the ceramics were found, especially since they are the result of production in limited regions of the Maya area (see Ball 1978:77).

Principal Identifying Attributes: (1) fine orange-colored paste; (2) orange-firing slip of the same clay as the paste; (3) black paint applied near the rim on exteriors and/or interiors; (4) round-sided bowl.

Paste, Firing, and Temper: Same as Altar Orange.

Surface Finish and Decoration: See Smith and Gifford (1966:165) for a description of the surfaces of the Altar Ceramic Group. See Sabloff (1975:206–207) for a description of the surface finish of the Tumba type. One of the interesting characteristics of this type, at least on the bowls with round-sided walls, is that there is often a circumferential area on the interior of the rim that is a darker color than the rest of the vessel interior. It is not a well-executed band, but often has a streaky effect. The color varies from a deep orange, to a light brown, to even gray in some instances (see, for example, Figure 4.37 lower right sherd). I have noted this pattern on examples from many sites, including from Tecolpan/Jonuta (Berlin 1956:fig. 3b, s; personal observation, ceramoteca, INAH-Yucatan).

Forms:

1. Bowl with round-sided walls (Figure 4.36, j–l). This is a typical form for Tumba Black-on-orange (cf. Sabloff 1975:fig. 399, 401; Forsyth 1989:fig. 50C–D.)
2. Flaring-walled vessel with small rim offset (Figure 4.36, m–n). Only two examples of this form are known, and they differ slightly from one another.

Intrasite Locations and Contexts: It occurs in very small quantities in Areas A and D of Group 1, Structure 1. Only one sherd of this type was recovered from Moquel.

Intersite Locations and Contexts: Tumba Black-on-orange was, like other members of the Altar Ceramic Group, produced in the Usumacinta region (Bishop 2003). It is present in larger quantities at sites in the region of Altar de Sacrificios (Adams 1971:30) and Seibal [Ceibal] (Sabloff 1975:204, 206). It also occurs, apparently in some quantity, at Yaxchilan (López 1989:29) in this same region. It occurs at Los Guarixés (Ruz 1969:90ff; fig. XXX, 54–57) on Isla de Carmen at the mouth of the Laguna de Términos. It is an extremely widespread type, along with other members of its ceramic group, which was widely traded. It has been found in small quantities over much of the Maya Lowlands during the Terminal Classic period. See Ball (1978:86) for other sites where it is known to occur; see also Ek (2015:461).

Trapiche Incised: Variety Unspecified (Figure 4.36, o–r)

Frequency: 12 sherds (14%; <1%).

Established: Type and variety established by Smith and Gifford (1966:173) at Uaxactún; see also Smith (1971:19) but see Adams (1971:45) and Sabloff (1975:192, 194) for fuller descriptive accounts of the type.

Description: Given the widespread and well-known nature of Fine Orange Ceramics, it is not necessary to repeat all of the descriptive data for every site where the ceramics were found, especially since they are the result of production in limited regions of the Maya area (see Ball 1978:77). See Smith (1971:19) for a description of Fine Orange Ware and an outline of the Altar Ceramic Group to which Trapiche Incised belongs.

Principal Identifying Attributes: (1) fine orange-colored paste; (2) orange to red-firing slip; (3) fine- to medium-line circumferential incisions near the rim; (4) round-sided bowl.

Paste, Firing, and Temper: Fine Orange paste has been described in some detail by Smith (1955:28–29; 1971:19) and by Smith and Gifford (1966:166).

Surface Finish and Decoration: See Smith and Gifford (1966:165) for a description of the surfaces of the Altar Ceramic Group. See also Sabloff (1975:192) for a description of the surface. Most of the sherds in the Champotón collection are badly weathered, so there is little evidence of slip on most of them; however, both red (2.5YR 4/8; 5/6) and probably dark brown slip are found on some sherds. Decoration consists of from two (the most common) to three circumferential fine, occasionally medium, incised lines near the rim in a manner similar to that often found on Tumba Black-on-orange sherds (cf. Smith 1958:fig. 1b). In fact, it is possible that one or more of the sherds I have called Trapiche may be badly weathered Tumba. On a couple of sherds, however, the incisions appear to have been placed lower on the body of the only form known for this type at Champotón.

Forms:

1. Bowl with round-sided walls (Figure 4.36, o–r). This is a typical form for the Altar groups (cf. Smith 1958:fig. 1b).

Intrasite Locations and Contexts: It occurs in very small quantities in Areas A, D, and F of Group 1, Structure 1. None were recovered from Moquel.

Intersite Locations and Contexts: Trapiche Incised was, like other members of the Altar Ceramic Group, produced in the Usumacinta region (Bishop 2003). It is present in larger quantities at sites such as Altar de Sacrificios (Adams 1971:27) and Seibal [Ceibal] (Sabloff 1975:192, 194). It also occurs, apparently in some quantity, at Yaxchilan (López 1989:173) in this same region. No examples of the Ixpayac Variety (Adams 1971:27) were noted. This is a rare, although widespread, type along with other members of its ceramic group; it was traded extensively; see also Ek (2015:461).

Balancán Ceramic Group (20)

Also known as Z Fine Orange (Smith 1958:151).

Provincia Plano-relief: Provincia Variety (Figure 4.38, a–d)

Frequency: 13 sherds (76%; <1%).

Established: Type and variety established by Smith and Gifford (1966:173) at Uaxactún, but not described. Smith (1971:19) likewise referenced it, but did not provide a description, but see Adams (1971:52), Sabloff (1975:208–209), and Forsyth (1989:120) for fuller descriptive accounts of the type.

Description: Given the widespread and well-known nature of Fine Orange Ceramics, it is not necessary to repeat all of the descriptive data for every site where the ceramics were found, especially since they are the result of production in limited regions of the Maya area (see Ball 1978:77). See Smith and Gifford (1966:166) and Smith (1971:19) for a description of Fine Orange Ware and an outline of the Balancán Ceramic Group to which Provincia Plano-relief belongs.

Principal Identifying Attributes: (1) fine orange-colored paste; (2) orange-slipped interiors; (3) usually white, but sometimes black or both, slip applied to exterior or portions of the exterior; (4) plano-relief decoration accompanied by incision; (5) round-sided bowl.

Paste, Firing, and Temper: Fine Orange paste has been described in some detail by Smith (1955:28–29; 1971:19). Bishop et al. (2005:25–26) have argued, based on chemical composition, that the Balancán Ceramic Group was manufactured in the lower Usumacinta drainage.

Surface Finish and Decoration: See Smith and Gifford (1966:166) for a description of the surfaces of the Balancán Ceramic Group. See Sabloff (1975:208–209) for a description of the surface finish of the Provincia type. All Champotón examples bear a thick white slip on the exterior of the vessels, although it is known from other sites, that some vessels had a black slip (e.g., Smith 1971:fig. 9g; 58i). In fact, it may be that one sherd that I have tentatively classified as Palizada Black-on-orange is really Provincia, but the black-slipped area covers only a very small portion of the sherd and bears fine-line incision—hence the Palizada classification. The slip on Provincia sherds at Champotón covers the whole vessel exterior as far as can be discerned from broken pieces. Complex plano-relief designs were cut through the white slip allowing the underlying paste color to show through. See Sabloff (1975:209) for a description of design elements. Included in the plano-relief carving is the use of simple incision through the white slip to add details. Vessel interiors on the Champotón sherds were slipped white or orange. Two orange-slipped interiors bear black-painted scallops at the rim (cf. Smith 1971:fig. 9d; Berlin 1956:fig. 3c–d).

Forms:

1. Bowl with round-sided walls (Figure 4.38, a–c). This is the principal form for this type.
2. Bowl or vase with slightly incurved side (Figure 4.38d). Only one example of this form is known.
3. Cylindrical vase? (no illustration). Only one example of a basal fragment is in the Champotón collection. The cylindrical vase form is thus a supposition, as no upper portion of the vessel is known (cf. Smith [1971:fig. 9m] and Berlin [1956:fig. 3z–aa] as examples of the form).

Intrasite Locations and Contexts: It occurs in very small quantities in Areas A and D of Group 1, Structure 1. Two body sherds were recovered from Moquel.

Intersite Locations and Contexts: Provincia Plano-relief was, according to Bishop et al. (2005:178), like other members of the Balancán Ceramic Group produced in the lower Usumacinta. Its main area of distribution is along the Campeche and Yucatecan coasts and in the Northern Lowlands. Nevertheless, like the middle Usumacinta Altar group, it is not limited to those areas, but, in small quantities, is found in the Southern Lowlands as well. See Ball (1978:88) for a list of known sites where

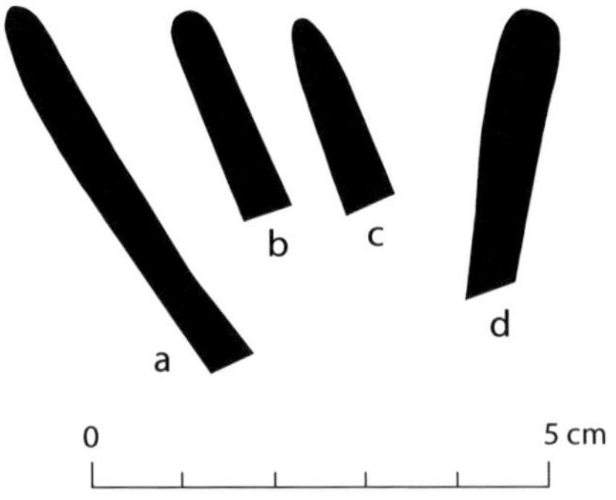

Figure 4.38. Balancán Ceramic Group profile drawings—Provincia Plano-relief: Provincia Variety.

Provincia Plano-relief occurs. Thus, while Balancán and Altar groups have different areas where they seem to be concentrated, examples of both groups can be found in both the Northern and Southern Lowlands. This is especially so for the finely decorated types, such as Provincia Plano-relief. It occurs in quantity at Los Guarixés (Ruz 1969:fig. XXXI, 13, 18–28, 30, 33–37, 39–40) on Isla de Carmen at the mouth of the Laguna de Términos. It is an extremely widespread type that was widely traded and has been found in small quantities throughout much of the Maya Lowlands during the Terminal Classic period; see also Ek (2015:461).

Other Balancán Group: Balancán Orange?

One rim, four bodies and one base of what is probably Balancán Orange were recovered from Champotón. All are covered by a thick white slip on the exterior and orange on the interior.

Other Balancán Group: Palizada Black-on-orange?

A single body sherd of what may be Palizada Black-on-orange was recovered from Area C at Champotón.

Other Fine Orange: Altar/Balancán Orange

One rim, nine bodies, and two bases are from small sherds that are too small or weathered to determine type, but by their form and thinness are almost certainly members of either the Altar or Balancán Ceramic Groups.

Silhó Ceramic Group (99)

Also known as X Fine Orange (Smith 1958:153ff)

Silhó Orange: Silhó Variety (Figure 4.39, a–i)

Frequency: 55 sherds (56%; 1%).

Established: Type and variety established by Smith and Gifford (1966:173) at Uaxactún, but not described. Smith (1971:21) likewise referenced it, but did not provide a full description. See Smith (1957) for a detailed description of Silhó Ceramic Group whole vessels. See Ball (1978:102–103) for a substantial discussion on the state of the interpretation of the pottery; a more recent treatment can be found in Sauri et al. (2005:229–243).

Description: Given the widespread and well-known nature of Fine Orange Ceramics, it is not necessary to repeat all of the descriptive data for every site where the ceramics were found, especially since they are the result of production in limited regions of the Maya area (see Ball 1978:77). See the publications listed under the Established heading for a more thorough description of this pottery.

Principal Identifying Attributes: (1) fine orange-colored paste; (2) red slip color; (3) hollow tripod supports, often bulbous; (4) pedestal bases.

Paste, Firing, and Temper: Fine Orange paste has been described in some detail by Smith (1955:28–30; 1971:21) ; see also Smith and Gifford (1966:166). Bishop et al. (2005:26) have argued, based on chemical characteristics, that the Silhó Ceramic Group was manufactured in the lower Usumacinta drainage.

Surface Finish and Decoration: See Smith and Gifford (1966:166) for a description of the surfaces of the Silhó Ceramic Group; see also Smith (1957:135–136) for a more detailed description of these vessels. Many Champotón examples are badly weathered and thus present only the color of the paste on their surfaces. Those examples which still bear slip have a red to red-brown (7.5R 4–5.5/6–88; 10R 5–6/8) slip that was applied to vessel interiors and exteriors on unrestricted forms and on exteriors on restricted ones. Only one example bore an exterior white slip (10YR 8/1). An occasional piece presents portions of the vessel that are gray to dark brown, probably due to poor control during firing.

Forms:

1. Small jar (Figure 4.39, a–c); compare with Smith (1971:fig. 22d, f).
2. Pyriform vessel (Figures 4.39, d–e); compare with Smith (1957:fig. 1b; 1971:fig. 22g; Berlin 1956:fig. ee).
3. Dish with flaring walls and flat bottom (Figures 4.39, f–g); compare with Smith (1957:fig. 1e; 1971:fig. 22r–u).
4. Restricted orifice bowl (Figure 4.39h); compare with Smith (1957:11d5–6).

Intrasite Locations and Contexts: It occurs in very small quantities in Areas A, C, and I, but especially in C, of Group 1, Structure 1. Seven sherds were recovered from Moquel.

Intersite Locations and Contexts: This type has a wide distribution. It is especially common in the Tabasco region around Jonuta/Tecolpan, and was, according to Bishop et al. (2005:26), manufactured in that region in the area between Jonuta and the delta. It is also found at a numerous sites along the Campeche and Yucatecan coasts, as well as at sites in the northern interior of Yucatan; see Ball (1978:102) for a list of known sites for this type. See also Sauri et al. (2005:233) for many additional sites with Silhó Orange. Neither of these is probably exhaustive of the distribution. Notably, a Campeche coast/northern Yucatan concentration is evident even though it occurs in other regions in modest quantities.

Comment: Silhó Orange and other members of the Silhó Ceramic Group have long been utilized as a marker for the Early Postclassic in

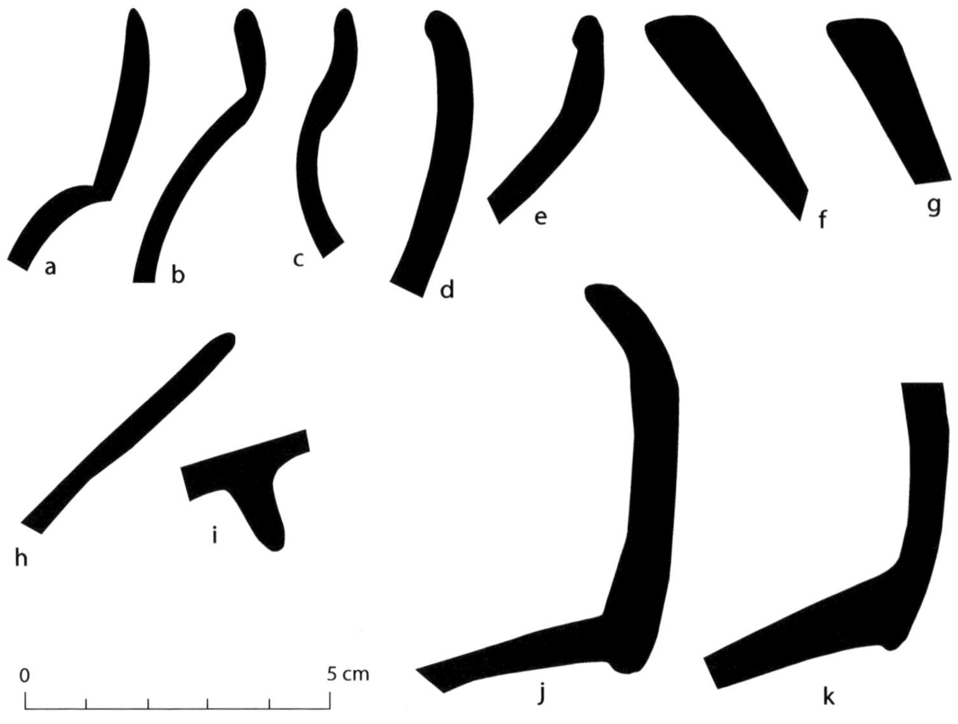

Figure 4.39. Silhó Ceramic Group profile drawings: a–i. Silhó Orange: Silhó Variety; j–k. Yalton Black-on-orange: Yalton Variety.

the Maya region, (Brainerd 1941; 1958:56; Smith 1971:15, 182–184, however, authors have begun to question the long-accepted chronology and have argued that there was a period of overlap between the Terminal Classic Fine Orange types and the Silhó Ceramic Group (see Sauri et al. 2005:231 for a more recent discussion of this issue). According to this argument, the manufacture of Silhó Orange and other members of the ceramic group would have begun in the mid-eighth century and lasted until about the beginning of the twelfth century. Thus, I am treating it as a Terminal Classic manifestation at Champotón, although some, or all, of it may have been manufactured after AD 1000. Ek (2015:500, 503) considers the Silhó group ceramics he recovered in some sites around Champotón as part of the Postclassic period.

Yalton Black-on-orange: Yalton Variety (Figure 4.39, j–k)

Frequency: 38 sherds (38%; <1%).

Established: Type and variety established by Smith and Gifford (1966:164, 173) at Uaxactún, but not described. Smith (1971:21–22) likewise referenced it, but did not provide a full description; however, see Smith (1957) for a detailed description of Silhó Ceramic Group whole vessels. See Ball (1978:106) for a brief description of the type. A more recent treatment can be found in Sauri et al. (2005:233).

Description: Given the widespread and well-known nature of Fine Orange Ceramics, it is not necessary to repeat all of the descriptive data for every site where the ceramics were found, especially since they are the result of production in limited regions of the Maya area (see Ball 1978:77). See the publications listed under

Figure 4.40. Yalton Black-on-orange: Yalton Variety ceramics.

the Established heading for a more thorough description of this pottery

Principal Identifying Attributes: (1) fine orange-colored paste; (2) red slip color; (3) black paint applied to exterior surfaces, especially jar shoulders and bodies; (4) necked jars.

Paste, Firing, and Temper: Fine Orange paste has been described in some detail by Smith (1955:28–30; 1971:21). See also see Smith and Gifford (1966:166) and Sauri et al. (2005:230). Bishop et al. (2005:26) have argued, based on chemical characteristics, that the Silhó Ceramic Group was manufactured in the lower Usumacinta drainage.

Surface Finish and Decoration: Surface and slip are the same as Silhó Orange. Yalton differs in having painted designs on vessel exteriors. For design elements see Brainerd (1958:fig. 76a, c, f–g, i, k–m; 77r–w; 78f, i–x; 79n, q) and Smith (1971:fig. 22b, f–h, l, n, t–v) for examples of the black-painted designs.

Forms:

1. Necked jar (Figure 4.39, j–k). Most are large, but some are considerably smaller; compare Smith (1957:fig. 1A1–2, 4) and Brainerd (1958:fig. 76a-d).
2. Jar with outcurving sides (no illustration). This is a large vessel; compare Smith (1957:fig. d9; Brainerd 1958:fig. 76h–i, j1–4, l, o).
3. Pyriform vessel (no illustration); compare Smith (1957:fig. b5; Brainerd 1958:fig. 77dd, gg, jj).

Intrasite Locations and Contexts: The type is about evenly distributed in small quantities in Areas A, C, and D of Group 1, Structure 1. No examples were recovered from Moquel.

Intersite Locations and Contexts: This type has a wide distribution. It is especially common in the Tabasco region around Jonuta/Tecolpan, and was, according to Bishop et al. (2005:26), manufactured in that region in the area between Jonuta and the delta. It is it also found at numerous sites along the Campeche and Yucatecan coasts, as well as at sites in the northern interior of Yucatan. See Ball (1978:106) for a partial list of known sites for this type. See also Sauri et al. (2005:233) for many additional sites with Silhó Orange. Neither of these is probably exhaustive of the distribution. Notably, a Campeche coast/northern Yucatan concentration is evident even though it occurs in other regions in modest quantities. Ek (2015:500, 503) considers the Silhó group ceramics he recovered in some sites around Champotón as part of the Postclassic period.

Other Silhó Ceramic Group: Pocboc Gouged-incised

One rim and body sherd of Pocboc Gouged-incised were recovered from Group 1, Structure 1.

Other Silhó Ceramic Group: Cumpich Incised

Three rim sherds of Cumpich Incised were recovered from Group 1, Structure 1. Two of them are from pyriform vessels. A single partial vessel of Cumpich Incised was also recovered from Champotón.

Other Silhó Ceramic Group: Pomuch Polychrome?

A single body sherd of what may be Pomuch Polychrome was recovered from Group 1, Structure 1, Lot C22.

Fine Orange Ware

Fine Orange Ware pottery was much more common than the above type descriptions would lead one to believe; however, because most of it was weathered, such that surfaces were eroded away, it was usually impossible to assign many sherds to a specific type or ceramic group. Although it is impossible to be certain, most of the unidentified sherds are likely not to be Matillas group examples. This latter pottery is abundant at Champotón and has certain characteristics that often make it possible to distinguish from the earlier Fine Oranges, although there are, of course, exceptions. This suggests that the unidentified Fine Orange fragments from the site (525 sherds), pertain to either the Altar, Balancán, or Silhó groups. The 67 rim sherds tend to suggest this as well. These sherds were not counted in the final counts for the Champotón types.

Imitation Fine Orange

A total of 17 sherds were recovered which, in their surface appearance, or decorative techniques, imitated Fine Orange paste ceramics, but had paste that was not Fine Orange. I have simply designated these as Imitation Fine Orange.These sherds were not counted in the final counts for the Champotón types.

PUUC SLATE WARE [59]

Muna Ceramic Group (59)

Muna Slate: Muna Variety (Figure 4.41)

Frequency: 42 sherds (69%; <1%)

Established: Type and variety established by Smith (1971:27–28) at Mayapan, but not described in detail. See also see Ball (1978:103), Forsyth (1983:99–101), and Jiménez (2002:83–85). Also known as Florescent Medium Slateware (Brainerd 1958:52–53).

Description: Given the widespread and well-known nature of Puuc Slate Ware, it is not necessary to repeat all of the descriptive data for every site where the ceramics were found (see Ball 1978:77). See the publications listed under the Established heading for a more thorough description of this pottery.

Principal Identifying Attributes: (1) translucent gray to buff slip color; (2) waxy surface finish; (3) medium to thick vessel walls; (4) bolstered rim basins.

Paste, Firing, and Temper: See Brainerd (1958:53), Smith (1971:28), and Forsyth (1983:99). See also Chung et al. (1998) for a discussion of the aplastics in Puuc Slate Ware.

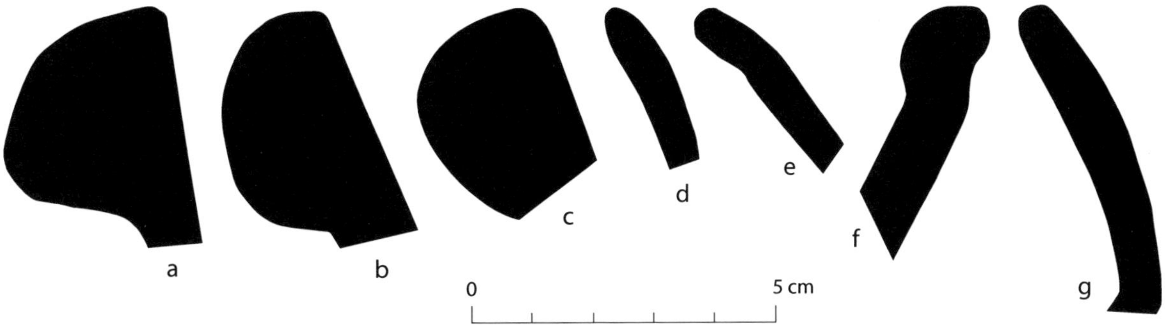

Figure 4.41. Muna Ceramic Group profile drawings—Muna Slate: Muna Variety.

Surface Finish and Decoration: Surfaces were smoothed prior to the application of the slip, which has a soapy or waxy feel and achieves a strong translucent luster on unweathered sherds. Slip color varies from gray to pale brown (10YR 6–8/1; 7/2–3) to brownish gray (10YR 6/2).

Forms:

1. Basin with exteriorly thickened rim bolster (Figure 4.41, a–c). These are large examples of a well-known form; compare Brainerd (1958:fig. 44b1–14), Smith (1971:fig. 4a–c, g), and Forsyth (1983:fig. 26m–o).
2. Flaring-walled basal-break dish (Figure 4.41, d–e); compare Brainerd (1958:fig. 46a–c), Smith (1971:fig. 6a–d, f–g), and Forsyth (1983:fig. 26a–f).
3. Restricted orifice jar (Figure 4.41f); compare Smith (1971:fig. 5b) and Brainerd (1958:fig. 41a45–46; b7–10).
4. Outflaring necked jar (Figure 4.41g); compare Brainerd (1958:fig. 40d2, 15, 17–18; e2).

Intrasite Locations and Contexts: The type is about evenly distributed in small quantities in Areas A, C, D and I of Group 1, Structure 1. Eight examples were recovered from Moquel.

Intersite Locations and Contexts: This has a wide distribution in Yucatan and in the interior of Campeche and Quintana Roo. See Brainerd (1958:figs. 40–49), Ball (1978:103), Jiménez 2002:85–86), and Williams-Beck (1999:153) for further information on its distribution.

Comment: Muna Slate, as well as all of the members of the Muna Ceramic Group, are extremely rare in the collections from Champotón. This accords well with Ruz's observation (1969:208) that the slate wares are not common on the coast but rather seem to be an inland phenomenon. It likewise accords with Ek's (2015:474–475, 477) findings in sites near Champton According to Ball (1978:103) it occurs with more frequency from Jaina northward along the coast. In fact, with perhaps the exception of Fine Orange Ware, the whole Cehpech complex is rare at Champotón. It occurs also at Villa Madero (personal observation, INAH, Yucatan).

Other Muna Ceramic Group: Sacalum Black-on-slate

Two rims and six bodies of what appears to be Sacalum Black-on-slate were recovered from Champotón, and only two of the bodies were from Moquel.

Other Muna Ceramic Group: Chumayel Red-on-slate

Four rims and four bodies of what may be Chumayel Red-on-slate were found at Champotón. No examples were recovered from Moquel.

Other Muna Ceramic Group: Xaya Gouged-incised

One rim of Xaya Gouged-incised was recovered from Group 1, Structure 1. It bears two separated circumferential bands of gouged and incised lines forming what appear to be stepped frets or rectangular volutes.

Thin Slate Ware

Three rims and five bodies of Ticul Thin Slate were recovered, three of which came from Moquel. A single untyped sherd of the Ticul Ceramic Group also was found.

Puuc Red Ware

Four rims and four bodies of Teabo Red occurred in our collections. Only one of these, a body, was from Moquel.

Cahuich Coarse Cream Ware

Two body sherds of Holactun Black-on-cream occurred in Lot A11a and C20a respectively in Group 1, Structure 1.

Dzitas Slate Ware

One rim and six bodies of what may be Dzitas Slate came from Group 1, Structure 1 at Champotón. In addition, three bodies of what may be Balam Canché Red-on-slate were also found.

UNDESIGNATED WARES [99]

Undesignated Ceramic Groups (19)

Tajonal Unslipped: Tajonal Variety (Figure 4.42, a–g)

Frequency: 19 sherds (100%; <1%)

Established: Present Study

Description:

Principal Identifying Attributes: (1) unslipped surfaces; (2) flat or nearly flat plate; (3) circular form; (4) generally thick vessel walls.

Paste, Firing, and Temper: The paste is medium textured. There is considerable variation in color, but the tendency is toward red (10R 5.6) to pale brown (7.5YR 6–7/4) to brownish gray (10YR 6.2) paste. Some sherds were oxidized throughout the cross-section of the vessel, while others have a dark core with the red penetrating both surfaces. Despite the variability there is a tendency towards reddish color. Temper particles are not generally large. What seem to be micaceous particles appear commonly.

Surface Finish and Decoration: Surfaces were coarsely smoothed but not burnished. Upper surfaces are sometimes better smoothed than bottom surfaces, but this is not regularly the case. Overall, the surfaces are coarse. Some of this may be due to weathering, but it seems that coarse surfaces were the norm for this pottery. Surface colors vary from red (2.5YR 6/6) through buff (10YR 7–8/3–4) to light gray (10YR 7/2), but the red to buff tone is the most common. Three sherds, two from the same excavation unit, bore a red slip. It cannot be discounted that these vessels were all slipped; however, if that was the case, it is a particularly fugitive one, as the overwhelming majority of the vessels exhibit no evidence of slipping at all.

Forms:

1. Extremely shallow circular plate (Figure 4.42, a–g). All but two sherds are rims. Judging by the differences in the rims or edges, there is considerable variation in the overall size of the plates. Rims (edges) vary considerably. Some are direct and rounded; others have what looks like an incision on the top of the edge. Still others have a groove. Some rims are squared rather than rounded. The vessel is flat or very slightly concave on its upper surface. Occasional rims have a slight ridge on the upper surface, but it is not certain this was intentional. This is the only form known for the type.

Intrasite Locations and Contexts: This is not a common type, most of the sherds came from Areas D and I, with a few from Area N of Group 1, Structure 1. No examples were recovered from Moquel.

Intersite Locations and Contexts: It is not apparent that it occurs at any other known site.

Comment: These vessels appear to be what are known as comales, which were used in more recent times for making tortillas. Whether that was the function of these particular vessels in the past cannot be determined. Three sherds of this form bear a weathered red slip. Whether a red-slipped version of this form was common at Champotón is not clear. Some of these vessels may be made from the same paste as Baca Red.

Undesignated Brown/Buff Type (Figure 4.42, h–q)

Frequency: 38 sherds (100%; <1%).

Established: Present Study.

Description:

Principal Identifying Attributes: (1) unslipped surfaces; (2) bolstered or thickened rims; (3) lightweight paste; (4) brown to gray surface color.

Paste, Firing, and Temper: Although the vessel walls are relatively thick, the paste is thin-textured with fine white temper particles. Despite the thickness of the walls and the thickened and bolstered rims, this pottery is remarkably light in weight, as if it has air pockets in it. No such pockets are visible, however, and the lightweight feel of the sherds must be due to some characteristic of the paste. Paste color varies from grayish brown (2.5YR 6–7/2; 10YR 6/2–3) to red (10R 5/8) to reddish yellow (5YR 6/8). Sometimes the paste is red all the way through the cross-section, but in many sherds the cores are grayish brown and the paste closer to the surface is red or reddish yellow.

Surface Finish and Decoration: Surfaces were smoothed but are not particularly smooth to the touch. Some vessels were better smoothed than others, and it is not unusual for surface to have pitting in the surfaces, although this is not invariably the case. Surface color is generally a light to yellowish brown (7.5YR 7–8/3; 10YR 7–8/3–4, although there is some variability. A few sherds have a more reddish surface (2.5YR 6/6). One has a gray surface (7.5YR 7/2).

Forms:

1. Bowl with exteriorly folded bolster (Figure 4.42, h–m). Only rims are known, so the exact size and base form is not clear.
2. Restricted orifice bowl or basin with exterior offset (Figure 4.42, n–q). The offset occurs on the exterior body anywhere from 0.8–1.6 cm below the rim. It consists of a generally sharp change in the contour that produces a raised ridge where the vessel wall extends out abruptly about 1–2 mm. On one vessel, the offset is less pronounced and creates a smoother contour.

Intrasite Locations and Contexts: This is not a common type, but 15 of the sherds came from Areas C and D of Group 1, Structure 1. No examples were recovered from Moquel.

Intersite Locations and Contexts: It is not apparent that it occurs at any other known site.

Comment: One large rim sherd of this pottery bore spaced vertical incision on the exterior, starting at the lip and continuing down the outside of the vessel for an unknown distance. This is the same effect that was used on Keste Incised.

Unspecified Black (Figure 4.42, r–w)

Frequency: 42 sherds (100%; <1%)

Established: Not positively established

Description:

Principal Identifying Attributes: (1) black-firing slip; (2) thin vessel walls; (3) thin to medium paste; (4) orangish fire-clouding.

Paste, Firing, and Temper: The paste is dense and well compacted. It is thin to medium textured. Paste color ranges from black (2.5YR 2.5/0) through gray (10YR 6/2) to reddish brown (5YR 4–5/4), depending on the degree of oxidation during firing. The temper size is small, but apparently does include some sherd temper.

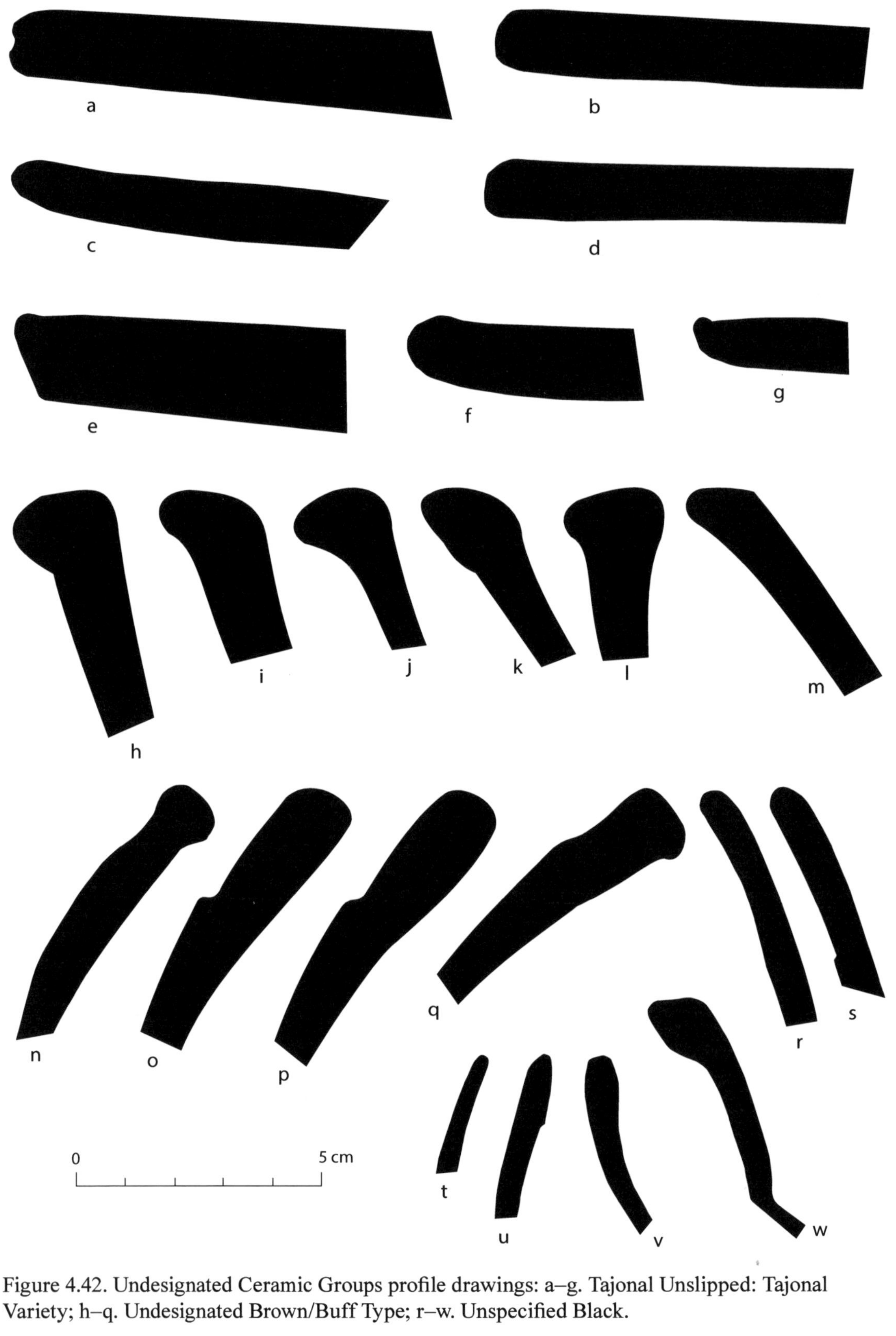

Figure 4.42. Undesignated Ceramic Groups profile drawings: a–g. Tajonal Unslipped: Tajonal Variety; h–q. Undesignated Brown/Buff Type; r–w. Unspecified Black.

Surface Finish and Decoration: Surfaces were well smoothed and compacted. A black-firing slip was applied to both interior and exterior surfaces on unrestricted vessels but limited to the exterior of restricted ones. The black slip ranges from 2.5YR 2.5–3/0 to reddish black (10R 2.5/1). As is common on black-fired ceramics, some sherds bear brownish/orangish fire-clouding that give the surface a mottled or spotted effect.

Forms:

1. Flaring-wall bowl with direct rim (Figure 4.42, r–s).
2. Small, restricted orifice bowl (Figure 4.42, t–u).
3. Small sub-hemisperical bowl (Figure 4.42v).
4. Bolstered rim dish or bowl (Figure 4.42w).

Intrasite Locations and Contexts: Found mostly in Areas C, D and I of Group 1, Structure 1. No examples were recovered from Moquel.

Intersite Locations and Contexts: The few examples from Champotón are reminiscent of Infierno Black in southern Campeche and northern Guatemala and of Tonanche Black (Forsyth 1983:85–86). It is possible that what I have here designated Unspecified Black is in fact Tonanche Black (cf. Ek 2015:448).

Other Undesignated Black: Incised

Two rims and four body sherds of vessels that are of the same paste and surface finish as Undesignated Black bear postslip incised designs on the exterior surface. All examples bear one or more circumferential lines near the rim, or in one case the base, within which geometric designs are incised. These sherds are reminiscent of Carmelita Incised in southern Campeche and northern Guatemala (cf. Forsyth 1989:figs. 41C–D, L; 42A–B, H, W). They are also reminiscent of the fine-line incising on Pajaral Gouged-incised (Forsyth 1983:86) but without the gouge-incising (see Ek 2015:448).

Other Undesignated Black: Basal impressed

Two sherds bearing finger impressions at the basal break were noted. The raised band at the break bears circumferential impressions. The impressions appear to have been produced by using a finger or thumb. These examples are very similar to Bilak Impressed from the region around El Mirador (cf. Forsyth 1989: fig. 44, N, Q-R).

The Champotón excavations produced a number of miscellaneous materials that do not seem to fit a nice, neat classificatory profile. Thus, a number of sherds that were analyzed and recorded are not represented in the typology presented here. This is especially true for the Classic period materials. Since most of them came from mixed architectural fill, some doubt remains as to where some of these materials fit in the overall scheme of the Classic period at Champotón. One such category consisted of a special kind of deep striation or combing on the exterior of unslipped vessels. The striations are so regularly spaced that it seems they were made with an instrument. This differs significantly from the standard form of striation found on unslipped vessels; however, there is considerable variation among these combed examples, such that they do not seem to present a coherent set that could be counted as a type. I have chosen to highlight that a "combed" unslipped pattern occurs at Champotón (over 70 sherds) but have not attempted to define one or more specific types. Suffice it to say that this type of combed striation is not limited to necked jars.

Table 4.1. Late and Terminal Classic ceramic type count.

CELESTÚN RED WARE	1593
Baca Ceramic Group	**1530**
Baca Red: Baca Variety	1509
Other Baca Group: Chavihau Specular Red?	4
Other Baca Group: Black-on-cream (San Pablito Negative?)	2
Other Baca Group: Red Slip	10
Other Baca Group: Impressed-appliqué	2
Other Baca Group: Appliqué	1
Other Baca Group: Striated	2
Nimun Ceramic Group	**63**
Nimun Brown: Nimun Variety	63
UNSPECIFIED WARE	43
Unspecified Ceramic Group	**43**
Carpizo Red: Carpizo Variety	35
Carpizo Red: Chanvega Variety	4
Other Carpizo Ceramic Group: Incised	4
FINE GRAY WARE	919
Chablekal Ceramic Group	**852**
Chablekal Gray: Chablekal Variety	584
Chicxulub Incised: Chicxulub Variety	210
Cholul Fluted: Cholul Variety	34
Telchac Compsoite: Telchac Variety	5
Chekubul Impressed: Chekubul Variety	4
Dimar Composite: Dimar Variety	2
Chamblas Composite: Chamblas Variety	5
Other Chablekal Ceramic Group	8
Tsicul Ceramic Group	**67**
Tsicul Fine Black: Variety Unspecified	43
Xuxac Incised: Variety Unspecified	14
Other Tsicul Ceramic Group: Composite	7
Other Tsicul Ceramic Group: Fluted	2
Other Tsicul Ceramic Group: Gouge-incised	1

CAMPECHE GLOSS WARE	487
Charote Ceramic Group	**221**
Charote Red: Charote Variety	179
Pixoyal Incised: Pixoyal Variety	15
Ulumal Fluted: Ulumal Variety	11
Sihochac Dark-red-on-red: Sihochac Variety	5
Other Charote Ceramic Group: Incised and fluted	3
Other Charote Ceramic Group: Gadrooned	2
Other Charote Group: Chamfered	4
Other Charote Group: Chamfered and Fluted	1
Other Charote Group: Chamfered, Incised, and Fluted	1
Simochach Ceramic Group	**227**
Simochac Orange-polychrome: Simochac Variety	185
Other Simochac Group: Orange Monochrome	36
Other Simochac Group: Red-on-orange	5
Other Simochac Ceramic Group	1
Cui Ceramic Group	**6**
Cui Orange-polychrome: Cui Variety	6
Chukul Ceramic Group	**6**
Chukul Orange-polychrome: Chukul Variety	6
Undesignated Ceramic Group	**18**
Undesignated Cream-polychrome	18
Other Campeche Gloss Ware-Chimbote Ceramic Group	**7**
Other Campeche Gloss Ware-Sayan Red-on-cream	**2**
HOXA UNSLIPPED WARE	181
Chencan Ceramic Group	**181**
Chencan Brown-on-orange: Chamizal Variety	136
Keste Incised: Keste Variety	40
Other Chencan Group: Black-on-brown	2
Other Campeche Gloss Ware-Black-on-cream	3
UNDESIGNATED UNSLIPPED WARE	132
Neza Ceramic Group	**132**
Neza Unslipped: Neza Variety	132

PUUC UNSLIPPED WARE	645
Acapulquito Ceramic Group	**645**
Acapulquito Unslipped: Variety Unspecified	198
Yakatzib Striated: Yakatzib Variety	447
MOXA GRAY WARE	26
Hontun Ceramic Group	**26**
Chumpic Incised: Variety Unspecified	14
Other Hontun Ceramic Group	12
ISLA FINE BUFF WARE	184
Dzitbalché Ceramic Group	**184**
Dzitbalché Fine Buff	150
Cerro de Caracoles Red-on-white	12
Other Dzitbalché Group: El Remate Red-on-buff	2
Other Dzitbalché Group: Jaina Composite ?	3
Other Dzitbalché Group: Chamfered	2
Other Dzitbalché Group: Red slip	4
Other Dzitbalché Group: White slip	3
Other Dzitbalché Group: Incised	6
Other Dzitbalché Group: Impressed	2
FINE ORANGE WARE	214
Altar Ceramic Group	**83**
Altar Orange: Altar Variety	57
Tumba Black-on-orange: Tumba Variety	14
Trapiche Incised: Trapiche Variety	12
Balancán Ceramic Group	**20**
Provincia Plano-relief: Provinica Variety	13
Other Balancán Group: Balancán Orange ?	6
Other Balancán Group: Palizada Black-on-orange	1
Other Fine Orange: Altar/Balancán Orange	**12**
Silhó Ceramic Group	**99**
Silhó Orange: Silhó Variety	55
Yalton Black-on-orange: Yalton Variety	38
Other Silhó Ceramic Group: Pocboc Gouged-incised	2
Other Silhó Ceramic Group: Cumpich Incised	3
Other Silhó Ceramic Group: Pomuch Polychrome ?	1

PUUC SLATE WARE	59
Muna Ceramic Group	**59**
Muna Slate: Muna Variety	42
Other Muna Ceramic Group: Sacalum Black-on-slate	8
Other Muna Ceramic Group: Chumayel Red-on-slate	8
Other Muna Ceramic Group: Xaya Gouged-incised	1
TICUL SLATE WARE	9
Ticul Thin Slate: Ticul Variety	8
Ticul Ceramic Group	1
PUUC RED WARE	8
Teabo Red: Teabo Variety	8
CAHUICH COARSE CREAM WARE	2
Holactun Black-on-cream	2
DZITAS SLATE WARE	10
Dzitas Slate	7
Balam Canche Red-on-slate?	3
UNDESIGNATED WARES	99
Undesignated Ceramic Group	**19**
Tajonal Unslipped: Tajonal Variety	19
Undesignated Brown/Buff type	**38**
Undesignated Black (consider Tonanche similarity)	**42**
Total	4611

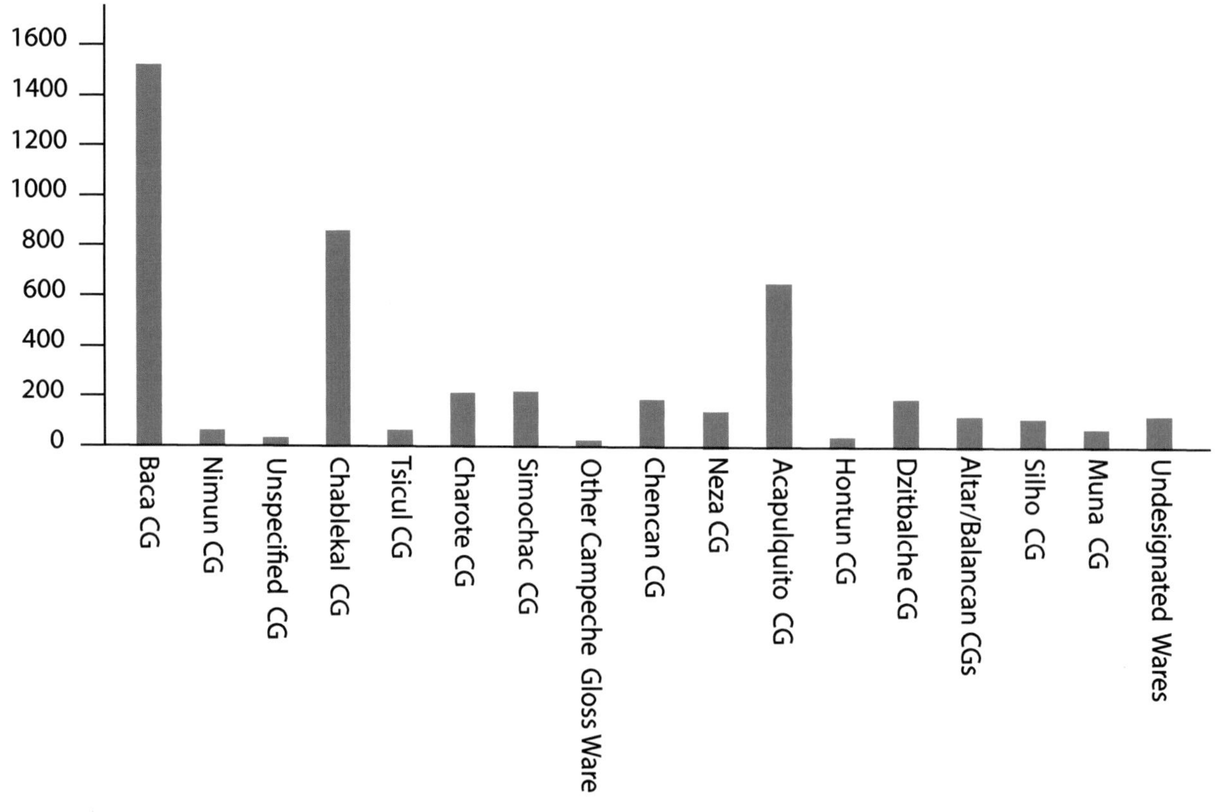

Figure 4.43. Frequency distribution of the various Late/Terminal Classic period ceramic groups recovered from Champotón, Campeche, México

CHAPTER 5

CERMIC TYPE DESCRIPTIONS, LATE POSTCLASSIC PERIODS

THE PABOX CERAMIC COMPLEX

The Late Postclassic period is the most heavily represented one at the site of Champotón. Group 1, Structure 1, but particularly the Pozo del Monte-Las Mercedes area were heavy in Pabox ceramics.

Champotón Unslipped Ware

Imí Ceramic Group

Imí Unslipped: Imí Variety
Imí Unslipped: Kaymuch Variety
Chento Painted: Chento Variety
San Patricio Incised: San Patricio Variety
Couoh Appliqué: Couoh Variety Appliqué
Pozo del Monte Composite: Pozo del Monte Variety Appliqué
Chen Pec Modeled: Chen Pec Variety
Cherna Incised: Cherna Variety
Cherna Incised: Red-rim Variety

Almendros Ceramic Group

Almendros Mottled: Almendros Variety
Arrocera Brushed: Arrocera Variety

Bomal Red Ware

Moquel Ceramic Group

Moquel Red: Moquel Variety
Moquel Red: Unslipped-exterior Variety
Tajonal Incised: Tajonal Variety

Peto Cream Ware

Kukula Ceramic Group

Xcanchakan Black-on-cream

Fine Orange Ware

Matillas Ceramic Group

Matillas Orange: Matillas Variety
Matillas Orange: Red-slipped Variety
Villahermosa Incised: Villahermosa Variety
Nacajuca Black-on-orange: Nacajuca Variety
Sayula Polychrome: Sayula Variety
Chilapa Gouged-incised: Chilapa Variety
Salto Composite: Salto Variety
Grijalva Incised Polychrome: Grijalva Variety

CHAMPOTÓN UNSLIPPED WARE [30,878]

Imí Ceramic Group [28,675]

Imí Unslipped: Imí Variety (Figures 5.1–5.5)

Frequency: 19,860 sherds (69%; 48%).

Established: Type and variety established in current study from Champotón; however, this pottery corresponds to Ruz's (1969:117–118) "Cerámica café" and "Cerámica grisácea." In fact, there is little difference between these two categories other than minor variations in color tone. A brief look at Ruz's color designations for them shows the similarity. I first attempted to separate them but abandoned it fairly quickly when I realized that the differences represented the ranges of variation in a single class of pottery. Ruz's description of this pottery, although he did not use type names, is quite good, and I have in most instances found that our collections match his findings closely. Where there are differences, I note them in the description. Navulá Unslipped (Smith 1971:24, 135) is perhaps an analog to Imí Unslipped, and

Figure 5.1. Imí Ceramic Group.

some might prefer to see Imí as a variant of that type. I perceive sufficient differences between the two to define a new type and group. There are, nevertheless, general similarities between the Northern Lowlands and Champotón that others might consider compelling.

Description:

Principle Identifying Attributes: (1) unslipped, unpolished vessel surfaces; (2) cream- to buff- to gray-colored paste; (3) cream to buff vessel surfaces, (4) rough surface finish; (5) tall-necked jars with thickened, folded and/or grooved lips.

Paste, Firing, and Temper: The paste is medium to coarse textured. Paste color ranges from tan or buff to a slightly more reddish buff to brown (10YR 6–8/3–4; 2.5Y 7–8/2–3; 7.5YR 6–7/4). The paste appears to have been fired in an oxidizing atmosphere, given that some sherds have dark to gray cores where firing did not reach all the way through the pottery. The oxidizing atmosphere rarely resulted in strongly red paste and surfaces, but rather in a cream to buff to pinkish cream color. The actual variation in paste color is relatively minimal in this type. Champotón Postclassic unslipped pottery is characterized by this paste. Clearly similar vessels to the north at Seibaplaya (personal observation, INAH, Campeche, 2005) have a much more oxidized paste. Indeed, all Postclassic types in the UAC collections, with the exception of Fine Orange Ware, are made

Figure 5.2. Imí Unslipped: Imí Variety ceramics.

from this same paste. The temper is invariably calcite in considerable quantity, although occasional inclusions of other materials also occur. Particle size ranges from 0.2 mm to 0.9 mm, but the primary size range appears to be between 0.6 to 0.9 mm.

Surface Finish and Decoration: The surfaces are unslipped. They were reasonably well smoothed, but not polished. Surfaces are generally slightly uneven, and temper particles can be seen protruding from the vessel surface. Some examples are better smoothed than others. Surface colors are typically quite close to the paste colors. They do sometimes seem a slightly lighter shade of buff, perhaps due to the smoothing effect, which brought finer particles to the surface, but surface colors cover the same range as the paste (see above). Some examples have the remains of stucco applied to one or both surfaces. This is rarely intact, however, and the overall configuration of the stucco is not usually apparent. It is a not an uncommon occurrence on sherds of this type and other members of the same ceramic group. The overall color of the surfaces contrasts with the earlier unslipped ceramics that tend much more to gray hues rather than the more whitish or creamish color of the Imí pottery. Ruz (1969:117, 118) talks of a light wash applied to the surface of this pottery, but this is not really the case. What does occur sometimes is that the smoothing process was sufficient to bring the smaller, finer clay particles to the surface. This sometimes makes for a slight difference in color between the surface and the paste, and it does not appear that anything was added to the surface of these vessels.

Forms:

1. Tall-necked jar [olla] (Figure 5.3). Jar neck height varies, but the tall-necked jars measure from around 6 cm to as high as 19 cm, although the majority are between 6–8 cm. The necks flare out from the body-neck juncture, and some even have a slight recurve to them. Occasionally, there is a neck that is cylindrical rather than outflaring. Although direct rims occur, most of the jar necks have rims that are thickened, folded, or flattened, and often beveled toward the interior. The beveled lip also typically has a groove or depression on the top of the lip that runs all the way around the mouth of the vessel. This gives the interior lip a look of having an interior ridge. Some beveled lips do not have the groove, but do have an interior ridge, although many have no ridge at all. The folded rims are usually folded to the exterior, but there is considerable variability and complexity to the folded and thickened rims of these jars (see Figure 5.3). This form makes up the tall-necked portion of what Ruz (1969:117, 118) called "ollas" and "ollas sin decoración," respectively. I have separated the tall-necked jars from the medium-necked ones, although there is, of course, some overlap in characteristics. The bodies are globular, and many, if not most, probably had strap handles placed horizontally on the body, although similar strap handles also occur in other forms. These handles are common in the Imí type. Base forms were either flat or slightly indented; compare with Ruz 1969:figs. XXXVI/1–5, 17, 19, 21 and XL/1, 3–4).
2. Medium-necked jar [olla] (Figures 5.4, a–f.). This form is similar to Form 1 above, except that the jar necks are considerably shorter and lack some of the more exotic lip forms, but the beveled and grooved, or beveled with an interior ridge, rims are frequent. Direct rims seem, however, to be more frequent in this form than in the tall-necked variant. Jar neck height varies, but is generally less than 6 cm. Rims are similar to those in the tall-necked jars except that folded and thickened rims, especially those with complex form, are much less common. Direct, flattened, and interiorly beveled rims are the most common, some with either the circumferential groove or small interior ridge mentioned above. These necks tend to be outflaring, but straight, lacking the slight recurve that sometimes occurs on the higher necked jars. These jars also had horizontal strap handles,

Figure 5.3. Imí Ceramic Group profile drawings—Imí Unslipped: Imí Variety.

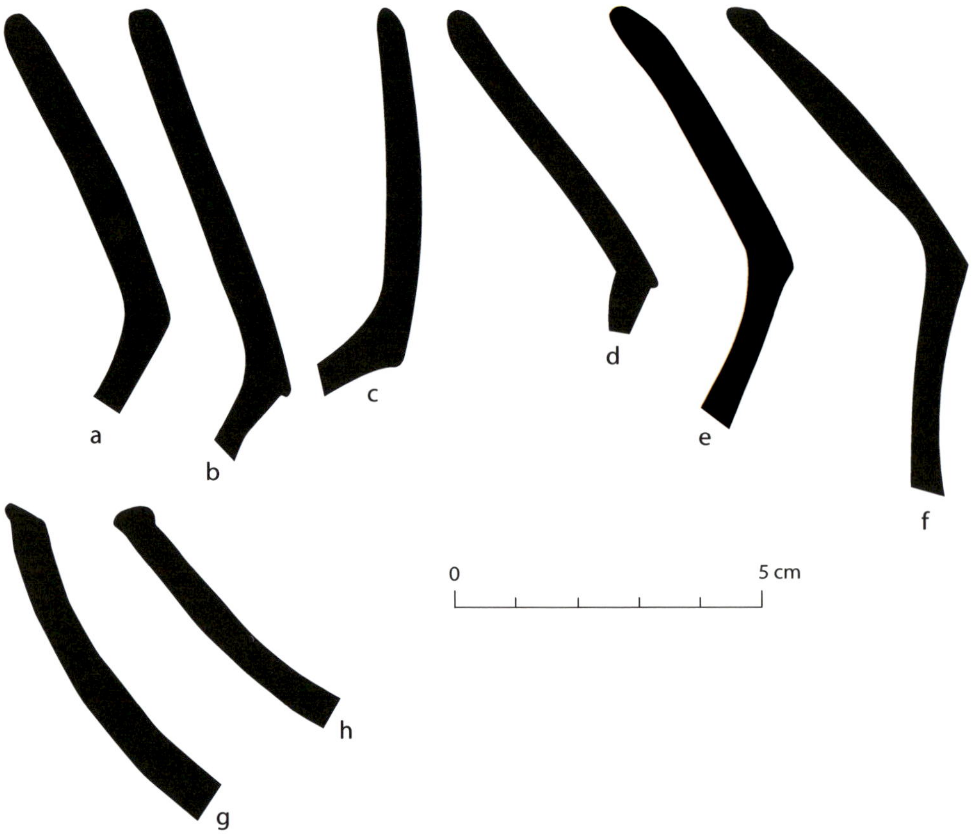

Figure 5.4. Imí Ceramic Group profile drawings—Imí Unslipped: Imí Variety.

proportional to the size of the jar. Base forms were similar to Form 1. This form comprised the medium-necked portion of what Ruz (1969:117, 118) called "ollas" and "ollas sin decoración" respectively; compare with Ruz (1969:figs. XXXVI/6–8; XL/5–6).

3. Small sub-hemispherical dish (rarely bowl) with tripod supports (Figures 5.4, g–h; 5.5, a–g). This form has a rounded bottom, usually with tripod supports. These supports may be solid, in which case they are often cone-shaped, or hollow. The hollow supports are quite variable; compare the foot forms illustrated by Ruz (1969:fig. XL/65–75). All of these hollow forms occur in this and other vessels, as well as the hollow bulbous type. Because of the rounded nature of the base, these supports are asymmetrical in shape so as to present a level vessel when resting on the supports. These vessels are generally small with rim diameters 25 cm or less, although occasionally larger examples do occur. These vessels may have small to large flanges about 1/3 of the way down the vessel from the lip, which project outward and downward from the curving vessel wall. They are usually crenellated. Flanges are relatively rare, however. Rims may be direct but usually are beveled and grooved or ridged; compare with Ruz (1969:figs. XXXVI/32; XL/21–24).

4. Dish or bowl with rounded or flaring sides and flat bottom (Figure 5.5, h–j). Rims may be direct, beveled, and grooved or ridged, folded, or thickened. Some of these vessels are quite large, with rim diameters exceeding 30cm, while others are much smaller. This is a large form category encompassing considerable

Figure 5.5. Imí Ceramic Group profile drawings —Imí Unslipped: Imí Variety.

variation. Bases are flat; compare with Ruz (1969:fig. XL/9–10, 12–20).

5. Incurved rim bowl with or without a exteriorly bolstered rim (Figure 5.5, k–m). This form is not common, but does occur consistently. At least one example has a vertically placed strap handle; compare with Ruz (1969:figs. XXXVI/25–28; XL/11).

6. Miscellaneous forms. (Figure 5.5n)

Hollow tripod supports are frequent on dish or bowl forms (Figure 5.5o). In addition, a number of pedestal bases occur in this material (Figure 5.5, p–r). It is likely they are segments of Couoh Appliqué. It is also possible that some of the above forms occasionally had pedestal bases as well.

Intrasite Locations and Contexts: Imí materials are found in almost all deposits recovered from the site of Champotón. Notably, it is found in pure deposits in a number of operations. All of the material recovered from the Pozo de Monte-Mercedes barrios of Champotón pertains to this complex (with the exception of the occasional earlier sherd incorporated into Postclassic materials). In addition, it occurs in pure contexts associated with the Postclassic Structure 1-G of Group 1 (Barrio de Guadalupe), as well as in mixed structural deposits from and around Structure 1.

Intersite Locations and Contexts: Imí Unslipped is presently known only from Champotón and its immediate environs. It may turn out to be more widely distributed than currently indicated when greater knowledge of the Postclassic occupation of the surrounding areas is undertaken. However, settlement survey by Ek (2015:503, 516) in the region around Champotón indicates that this ware does not extend very far from Champotón itself. It is roughly analoguous to Navulá/Panaba Unslipped at Mayapán (Smith 1971) as a Hocabá and Tases period type. Navulá/Panaba is a widespread type in the northern plains area.

Comment: The Imí Unslipped differs from the Navulá Unslipped in a number of ways. Vessel forms, for both jars and tripod vessels, are quite different. Likewise, not surprisingly, paste characteristics are also different. The Champotón paste is so far unique to the site, and neutron activation on clays recovered from the savanna near Champotón indicate that the Imí Ceramic Group materials were manufactured from it. Rim treatment is also unique to Champotón and differentiates the Imí type from Navulá. Some might wish to consider it a regional variant of Navulá Unsliped

It should be noted here that this type-variety constitutes the overwhelmingly dominant pottery of the Late Postclassic at Champotón—nearly 40% of the total sherds recovered from the site. No other class of pottery is close to it. On the other hand, striated pottery (Arrocera Brushed) is much less common (around one-tenth the quantity of Imí pottery, and the latter occurs essentially in a single form). This is exactly the opposite of the case at Mayapán and most other Late Postclassic complexes in the north, where striated pottery dominates the plain, unslipped vessels. In short, Imí Unslipped pottery has a horizon-level resemblance to the Panaba/Navulá materials at Mayapan, and lumpers might be inclined to place Imí Unslipped into that category. Nevertheless, a detailed inspection of the Mayapan collection in the ceramoteca of Centro INAH-Yucatan convinces me otherwise; it is probably an analog to the Mayapan Late Postclassic unslipped plain ceramics. Shared characteristics include some overlap in foot forms, handles and other characteristics.

Imí Unslipped: Kaymuch Variety (Figures 5.6–5.7)

Frequency: 72 sherds (<1%; <1%). Some examples of this variety may have been lumped with the Imí Variety before it was decided to separate them out as a separate variety.

Established: Type and variety established in current study from Champotón. This variety corresponds to Ruz's (1969:119) form category of "sahumadores" in his "Cerámica grisácea." I have separated out this form as a distinct variety due to its unique shape and function. In all other characteristics, however, it is the same as the Imí Variety. This variety may be considered as analogous to the ladle censers of Navulá Unslipped (see Smith 1971:24, 135), but there are some differences as noted below.

Description:

Principal Identifying Attributes: (1) unslipped, unpolished vessel surfaces; (2) cream to buff to gray paste; (3) cream to buff vessel surfaces; (4) rough surface finish; (5) handled censers (*sahumadores*).

Figure 5.6. Imí Unslipped: Kaymuch Variety ceramics.

Paste, Firing, and Temper: The same as the Imí Unslipped: Imí Variety.

Surface Finish and Decoration: The same as the Imí Unslipped: Imí Variety

Forms:

1. Ladle Censer (Figure 5.7). This is the only form for this variety. The bowl part of the censer is generally small, normally between 12 and 18 cm, although larger sizes occur rarely. The handle is almost invariably hollow and attaches to the bowl slightly below the rim of the bowl. The bowl is hemispherical to sub-hemispherical with a round bottom. Rims may be direct but usually are beveled and grooved or beveled and ridged. All handles are circular/cylindrical, and most are hollow at both ends, as indicated by Ruz (1969:119). Some examples, however, have the proximal end of the hollow handle closed off. That is, the end closest to the holder is not open but closed; these are in the minority, however. The vast majority are open at both ends. Handles tend to measure 10–12 cm in length, and widen and curve as they approach contact with the bowl. These censers are not uncommon in the unslipped pottery and do not seem to be restricted to particular contexts, suggesting that they were widely used among the inhabitants of the site; compare with Ruz (1969:fig. XL, 48–49).

Intrasite Locations and Contexts: The same as the Imí Variety.

Intersite Locations and Contexts: This variety is known so far only from Champotón and small sites immediately in its vicinity (Ek 2015:502). The Kaymuch Variety has a horizon-level resemblance to similar handled censers from around the Maya area and beyond. This kind of censer is widely distributed in the Northern

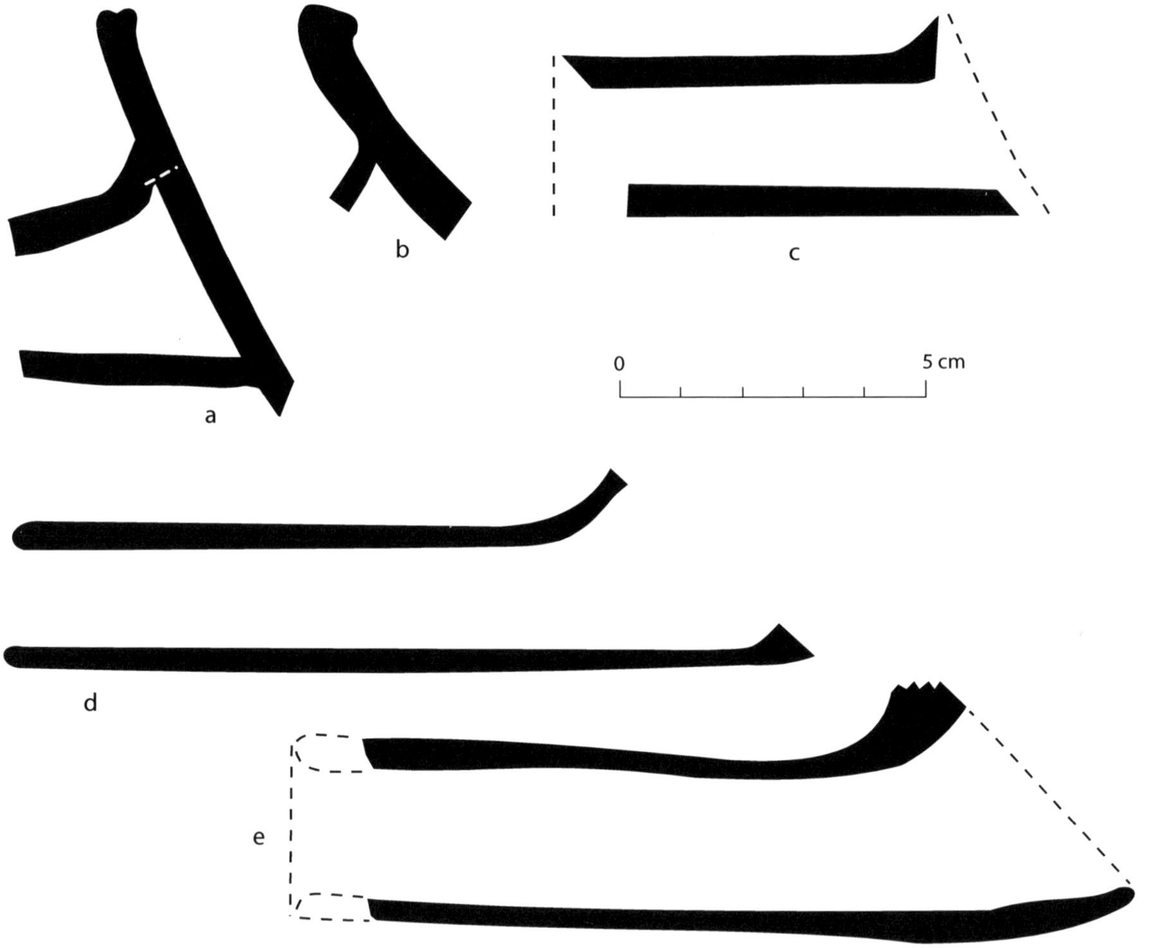

Figure 5.7. Imí Ceramic Group profile drawings—Imí Unslipped: Kaymuch Variety.

Lowlands. It is usually just classified as part of the Navulá Variety (cf. Smith 1971:fig.33a–e); however, although the Mayapan ladle censers are similar in shape to the Champotón ones, an inspection of examples in the Centro INAH-Yucatan ceramoteca suggests that the former are considerably larger in general than are the Champotón examples. Lip form also differs somewhat. Except for the specialized rim form, similar ladle censers have been recovered from Flores Island in Guatemala (Forsyth n.d.a; personal observation).

Comment: The hollow handle sometimes carries through into the censer bowl, leaving a hole in the wall of the bowl where the handle attaches. Sometimes the hole is closed off by the wall of the bowl, leaving no hole in the bowl itself. Apart from the handle, the censer bowl was not perforated.

Chento Painted: Chento Variety (Figures 5.8–5.9)

Frequency: 277 sherds (1%; <1%)

Established: Type and variety defined in the present study. Perhaps an analog of Acansip Painted at Mayapán (Smith 1971:24, 136).

Description:

Principal Identifying Attributes: (1) unslipped, unpolished vessel surfaces; (2) cream to buff to gray paste; (3) cream to buff vessel surfaces;

Figure 5.8. Chento Painted: Chento Variety ceramics.

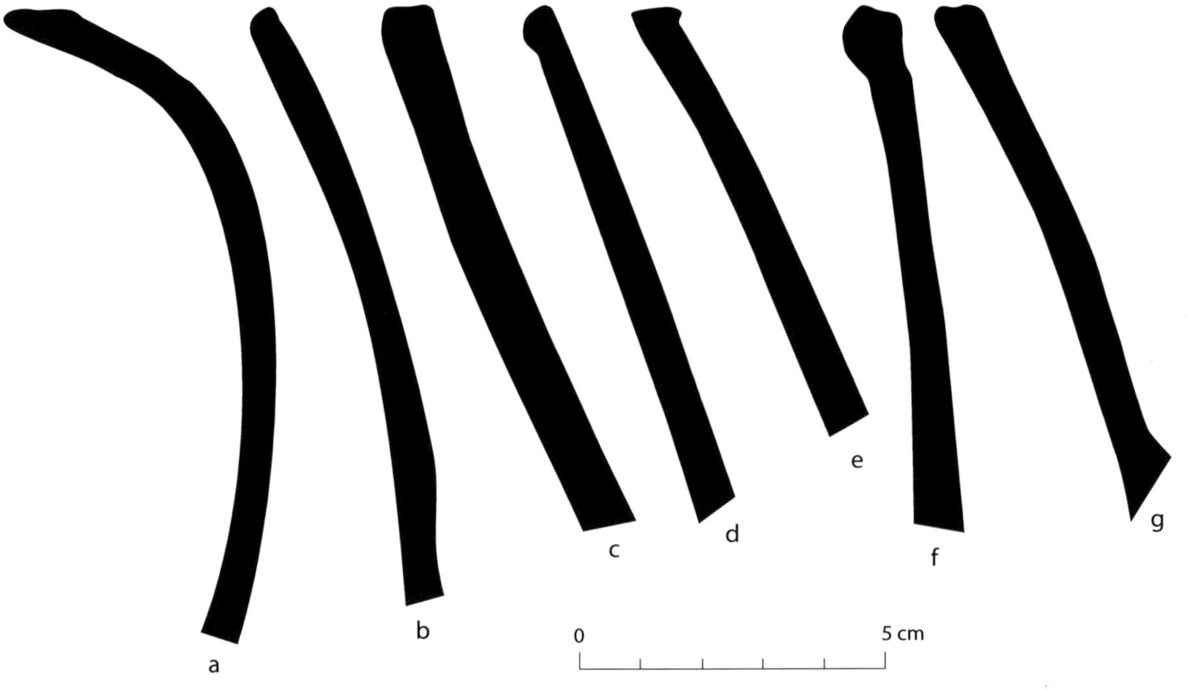

Figure 5.9. Imí Ceramic Group profile drawings—Chento Painted: Chento Variety.

(4) rough surface finish; (5) paint added to the unslipped surface of the vessel(s).

Paste, Firing, and Temper: The same as the Imí Unslipped: Imí Variety.

Surface Finish and Decoration: The same as the Imí Unslipped: Imí Variety, except that paint was added to all or part of the vessel surface after firing. Red and blue are the two most common colors, but occasionally other tones occur, including green and brown, and even white. Red to brown bands of varying widths sometimes encircle a vessel. In other cases the paint may adhere to a thin layer of stucco that may have covered all or part of the vessel. Because the paint was applied after firing, it is often fugitive and wears away easily. Frequently it is seen in crevices or other protected areas, having weathered away elsewhere. In other cases, the entire surface retains the painted surface. Given the lack of whole vessels and large fragments, it was not possible to determine any overall design for the painting, but it appears to often have been placed on large areas of the surface. The paint is rarely strong or thick on our examples and tends to be fragile, although this may be a function of erosion. The colors are pastel-like.

Forms:

1. Globular jars with tall outflaring necks and direct or thickened rims (see Imí Variety Form 1) (Figure 5.9, a–e).
2. Globular jars with tall outflaring necks and grooved rim tops (see Imí Variety Form 1) (Figure 5.9, f–g). Painting probably occurs on other forms as well.

Intrasite Locations and Contexts: The same as the Imí Unslipped: Imí Variety.

Intersite Locations and Contexts: The same as Imí Unslipped: Imí Variety. This type may parallel to some extent with Acansip Painted at Mayapán (see above). See Ek (2015:502) for other sites near Champotón.

Comment: Painted pottery at Champotón was not common, unless much of the paint has weathered away, but it does form a small percentage of the recovered Late Postclassic ceramics. A number of pedestal bases bearing postfire paint have been recovered. Whether they belong to Chento Painted or Pozo del Monte Composite (see below) cannot be determined with certainty.

San Patricio Incised: San Patricio Variety (Figures 5.10–5.12)

Frequency: 247 sherds (<1%; <1%)

Established: Type and variety defined in the present study.

Description:

Principal Identifying Attributes: (1) unslipped, unpolished vessel surfaces; (2) cream to buff to gray paste; (3) cream to buff vessel surfaces; (4) rough surface finish; (5) medium-line incisions in simple patterns incised into the surface of the vessel.

Paste, Firing, and Temper: The same as the Imí Unslipped: Imí Variety.

Surface Finish and Decoration: The same as the Imí Unslipped: Imí Variety, except that medium-line incisions were cut in the vessel surface. Usually these are moderately shallow but occasionally they are deep. Often there are from one to three spaced circumferential lines around the vessel. Other times they run vertically. Sometimes perpendicular lines, singly or in pairs, intersect with the circumferential ones at spaced locations around the vessel, although such incised lines rarely cover much of the vessel surface. They are almost never found on rims, and instead are limited, for the most part, to exterior bodies. It has not been possible to discern the overall pattern of the designs, but it is clear that they are indeed simple and probably do not form any complex motifs. Like other forms of decoration, incising is not particularly common on Imí Ceramic Group vessels.

Forms:

1. Exteriorly bolstered or grooved rim deep vases (Figure 5.10).
2. Restricted, inflaring-walled bowls with exteriorly-bolstered rims (no illustration).
3. Medium-necked jar with direct rim (Figure 5.11).

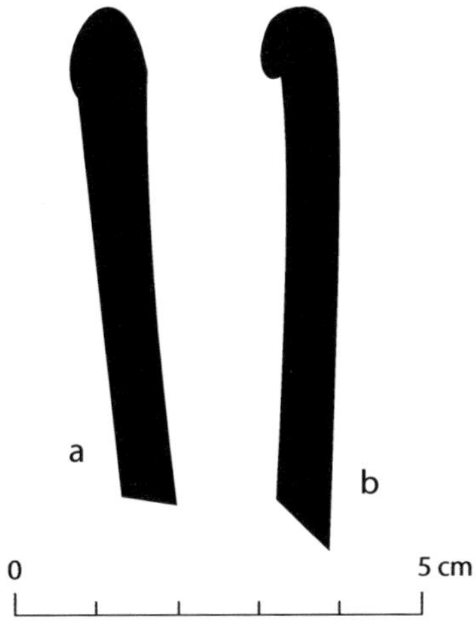

Figure 5.10. Imí Ceramic Group profile drawings—San Patricio Incised: San Patricio Variety.

Figure 5.11. San Patricio Incised Vessel.

Incising probably occurs on other forms as well, but most sherds with incising are body sherds, and vessel form is not readily discernible.

Intrasite Locations and Contexts: The same as the Imí Unslipped: Imí Variety.

Intersite Locations and Contexts: The same as Imí Unslipped: Imí Variety.

Figure 5.12. San Patricio Incised: San Patricio Variety ceramics.

Comment: This type probably does not have an analog at Mayapan. It is definitely not an analog to Chenkeken Incised. Although Chenkeken Incised was not described by Smith (1971), and was practically unillustrated, detailed examination of the Mayapan type collection housed in the ceramoteca of Centro INAH-Yucatan shows that Chento Incised is radically different from Chenkeken. The latter is characterized to a considerable extent by dishes or bowls, or other forms, with one to three, but usually two, broad, parallel incised circumferential lines placed just below the rim on the interior, or by incisions in the bottom of grater bowls. Only a single example of incised lines near the rim exists at Champotón, and the grater bowls at Champotón are quite different from Mayapan examples.

Couoh Appliqué: Couoh Variety (Figures 5.13–5.18)

Frequency: 3837 sherds (13%; 9%)

Established: Type and variety defined in the present study. Perhaps this is an analog of Hunacti/Thul Appliqué at Mayapan (Smith 1971:24, 135). Ruz (1969: 119) describes this type under the category "Braseros" of his "Cerámica grisácea." The description of the Couoh Appliqué vessels, however, includes only the "Braseros" section in the left-hand column of Ruz's publication. See Ruz (1969:fig. XL 43–47, 50–56) for illustrations of this type recovered from Champotón.

Description:

Principal Identifying Attributes: (1) unslipped, unpolished vessel surfaces; (2) cream- to buff- to gray-colored paste; (3) cream to buff vessel surfaces; (4) rough surface finish; (5) appliqué elements added to the surface; (6) basal skirts or flanges; (7) pedestal bases; (8) censers.

Paste, Firing, and Temper: The same as the Imí Unslipped: Imí Variety.

Surface Finish and Decoration: The same as the Imí Unslipped: Imí Variety, except that vessel surfaces received various forms of appliqué decoration singly or in combination. The most common form of appliquéd element seems to have been the raised, thumb-impressed band, usually, although not invariably, placed just below or just above a break in the countour of the vessel, depending on whether it was near the top or the bottom of the vessel (cf. Brainerd 1958:fig. 97a–c; Smith 1971:figs. 30g–i, k, u; 31b–d, r, t, bb). This form of appliqué, which began as a decorative element in the Classic period, is widespread on Postclassic censers. A second form of appliqué is a set of ceramic spikes (cone-shaped elements with the point jutting outward) that were usually applied in spaced, vertical rows (cf. Ball 1977:fig. 43; Smith 1971:fig. 30v; 31b). Sometimes the points of the spikes do no project straight out, as would the point of a cone, but instead the point droops or curves downward. A third form of appliqué consists of round, button-like elements that were placed on the vessel exterior. Sometimes they are simple round disks, but in other cases they are a more complex series of concentric elements placed one atop the other (cf. Smith 1971:fig. 31c–d). There are other elements that occur, but the above three are overwhelmingly the dominant ones. Any of these appliqué forms may occur in isolation, but usually decoration consists of two, or all three, of them on the same vessel. In this sense, Cuouh vessels show a similar pattern to other such censers found throughout the Maya Lowlands during the Postclassic period. The appliquéd decoration is very similar to that found on Mayapan censers (Smith 1971:figs. 30g, u; 31a, c–e, bb); however, the appliqué buttons on Couoh Appliqué are often more elaborate than the simple ones seen on the Cehac-Hunacti vessels. Whether it should be considered a characteristic of surface finish or not, a marker for Cuouh Appliqué is the regular presence of moderate- to large-sized, down-curving ridges, flanges, or skirts that were placed near the body-pedestal base juncture, at least on Forms 1 and 2 (see below and Ruz 1969:fig. XL 44, 46–47, 53–56). Usually these flanges, occasionally ridges, are plain, but in some cases they are crenellated. Occasionally smaller flanges mark the neck-body juncture. These ridges and flanges differentiate Couoh Appliqué from other, better-known censers from Yucatan, which lack them. Some vessels bear traces of stucco, which was applied to the exterior of the vessel, or at least sections of it.

Forms:

1. Globular censer form with flaring bolstered rim (Figure 5.15, a–l).
2. Globular censer form with flaring direct rim (Figure 5.15, m–o).
3. Straight or slightly outcurved wall censer with direct or bolstered rim (Figure 5.16, a–f).
4. Sub-hemisperical censers with direct rim (Figure 5.16, g–h).

Figure 5.13. Couoh Appliqué: Couoh Variety ceramics.

Figure 5.14. Imí Ceramic Group ceramics: a–e. Couoh Appliqué: Couoh Variety, f–i. Couoh Composite: Couoh Variety.

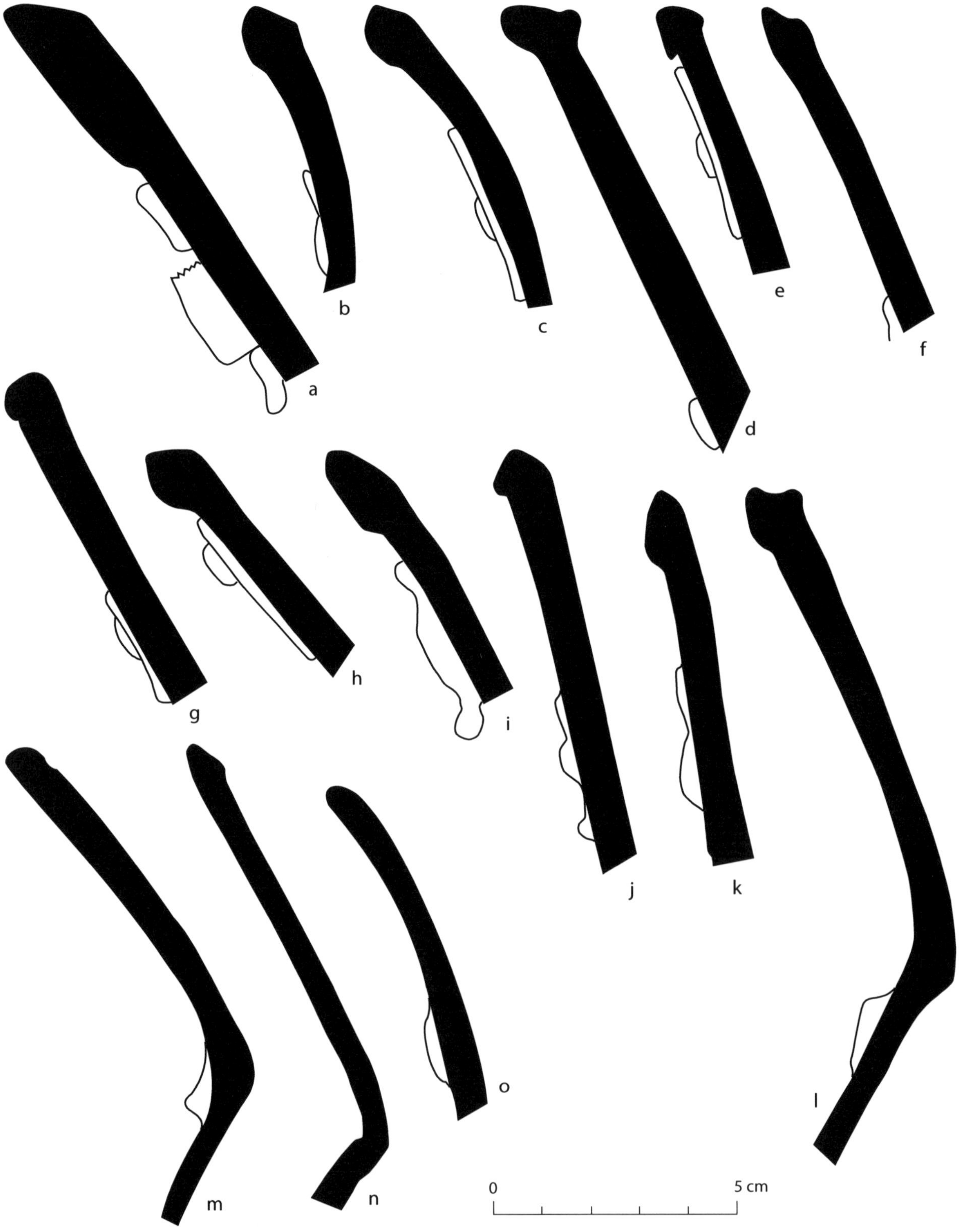

Figure 5.15. Imí Ceramic Group profile drawings—Couoh Appliqué: Couoh Variety.

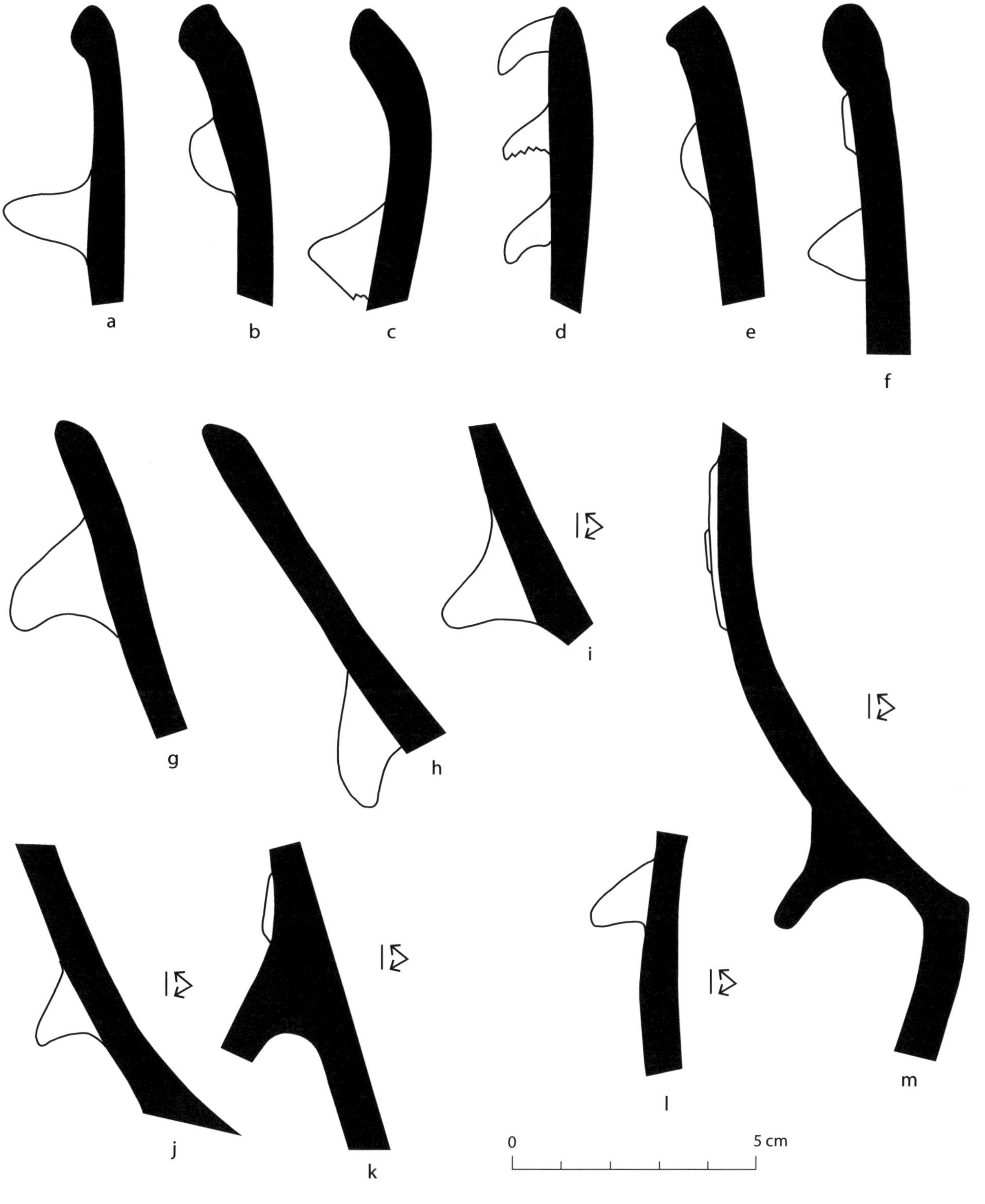

Figure 5.16. Imí Ceramic Group profile drawings—Couoh Appliqué: Couoh Variety, i–m. body sherds.

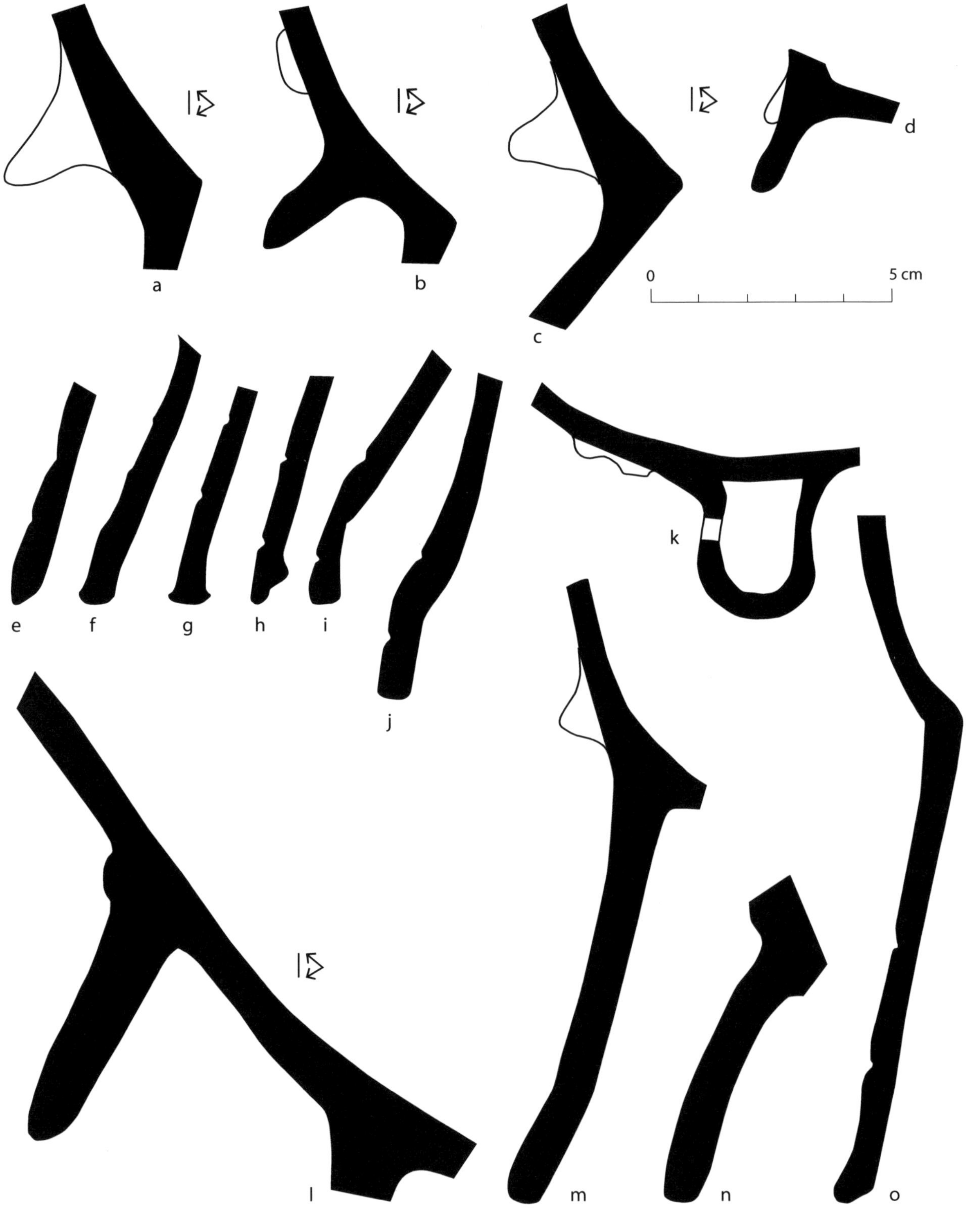

Figure 5.17. Imí Ceramic Group Profile drawings—Couoh Appliqué, a–c. body sherds, k. tripod support, d–j, l–o. pedestal bases or supports,.

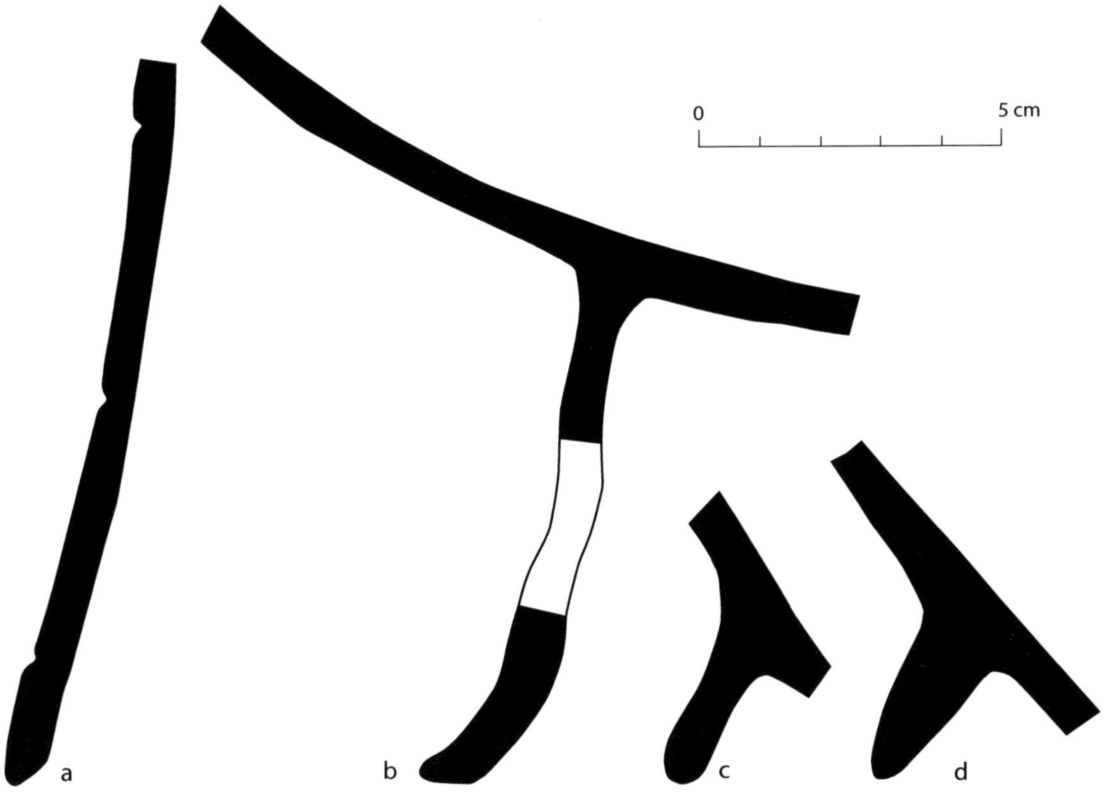

Figure 5.18. Imí Ceramic Group Profile drawings—Couoh Appliqué: pedestal bases or supports.

Bases are invariably pedestal or tripod, although the latter are rare (Figure 5.17, d-o, 5.18). The pedestal base is characteristic of this type. Such bases may be plain, but frequently bear two or three very slight chamfers just above the lip of the base (cf. Ruz 1969:Fig. XL 33-35; 50-56); compare Ruz 1969/XL 66-75 for tripod supports.

Intrasite Locations and Contexts: The same as the Imí Unslipped: Imí Variety.

Intersite Locations and Contexts: The same as Imí Unslipped: Imí Variety. See Ek (2015:502) for sites near Champotón were the type has been found.

Comment: This type is similar, but not identical, to Hunacti and/or Thul Appliqué at Mayapan (see above). The Cuouh examples have distinctive shapes and other characteristics that distinguish them from the Mayapan appliqué censers but fall into the general pattern of unslipped appliqué censers found throughout the Lowlands during the Late Postclassic period. Some analysts might wish to consider them regional variants of the Hunacti/Thul category. These censers at Champotón are quite numerous. Unlike Mayapan, the vast majority of them were apparently not painted.

Pozo del Monte Composite: Pozo del Monte Variety (for illustration see Cuouh Appliqué)

Frequency: 210 sherds (<1%; <1%)

Established: Type and variety defined in the present study. This type is certainly an analog of Cehac-Hunacti Composite at Mayapán (Smith 1971:fig. 31a–c, e, h, i, l–p). Some of Ruz's examples (1969:fig. XL 43–47, 50–56) probably also pertain to this type.

Description:

Principal Identifying Attributes: (1) unslipped, unpolished vessel surfaces; (2) cream- to light brown-colored surfaces and paste; (3) appliqué elements added to the surface; (4) basal skirts or flanges; (5) pedestal bases; (6) post-fire paint added to the surface; (7) censers.

Paste, Firing, and Temper: The same as the Imí Unslipped: Imí Variety.

Surface Finish and Decoration: The same as the Imí Unslipped: Imí Variety, except that vessel surfaces received various forms of appliqué decoration singly or in combination, identical to that of Cuouh Appliqué, and paint was added to the surface after firing. The most common paint colors were red and blue—ocassionally both. That is, the same process that was applied to Chento Painted (see above) was applied to the exteriors of these vessels. In fact, some examples counted as Chento Painted might well represent pieces of Pozo Monte vessels that lacked evidence of appliqué decoration. Painting is never found on vessel interiors.

Forms:

Same as Cuouh Appliqué

Intrasite Locations and Contexts: The same as the Imí Unslipped: Imí Variety.

Intersite Locations and Contexts: The same as Imí Unslipped: Imí Variety. See Ek (2015:502) for sites near Champotón were the type has been found.

Comment: Pozo del Monte bears the same relation to Cehac-Hunacti Composite as Cuouh does to Hunacti/Thul; however, painting on Champotón censers is quite rare, whereas in Yucatan it appears to be the norm. It is possible that painting was more common at Champotón but that the fugitive paint has weathered away. There is little compelling evidence of this, as examples of paint on these surfaces show up only in a small number of instances.

Chen Pec Modeled: Chen Pec Variety (Figures 5.19–5.22)

Frequency: 3206 sherds (11%; 8%)

Established: Type and variety defined in the present study. This type is a direct analog of Chen Mul Modeled at Mayapan (Smith 1971:24, 135) and could perhaps be considered coincident with it. Ball (1978:92–93) refers to it as such, but recognized that Chen Mul was being used in an "overly inclusive" manner. For reasons detailed below, I define the Chen Pec type for Champotón, but recognize that others may simply choose to regard it as Chen Mul—something I myself did when applying temporary monikers to potential types (cf. Ruz (1969:fig. XLV3–6 for examples of this type recovered from Champotón.) Ruz (1969:119) described elements of this type under his discussion of "Braseros" in his "Cerámica grisácea" category, beginning in the right-hand column of page 119 with "Numerosos fragmentos..."

Description:

Principal Identifying Attributes: (1) unslipped, unpolished vessel surfaces; (2) cream-to-light brown-colored surfaces and paste; (3) appliqué elements added to the surface; (4) anthropomorphic censers; (5) modeled and appliquéd elements.

Paste, Firing, and Temper: The same as the Imí Unslipped: Imí Variety. Neutron activation studies by Bishop et al. (2006:139) show that the paste of the anthropomorphic censers at Champotón are chemically the same as the rest of the unslipped pottery.

Surface Finish and Decoration: The same as the Imí Unslipped: Imí Variety. Some examples of Chen Pec bear post-fire paint on the anthropomorphic portion of the vessel, usually in red or blue, but sometimes in black, yellow, or pink, among others. The vast majority of examples, however, do not bear paint (only 54 sherds bore paint). Whether the Champotón examples were generally unpainted or whether the lack of paint is a function of weathering or some other factor is unknown.

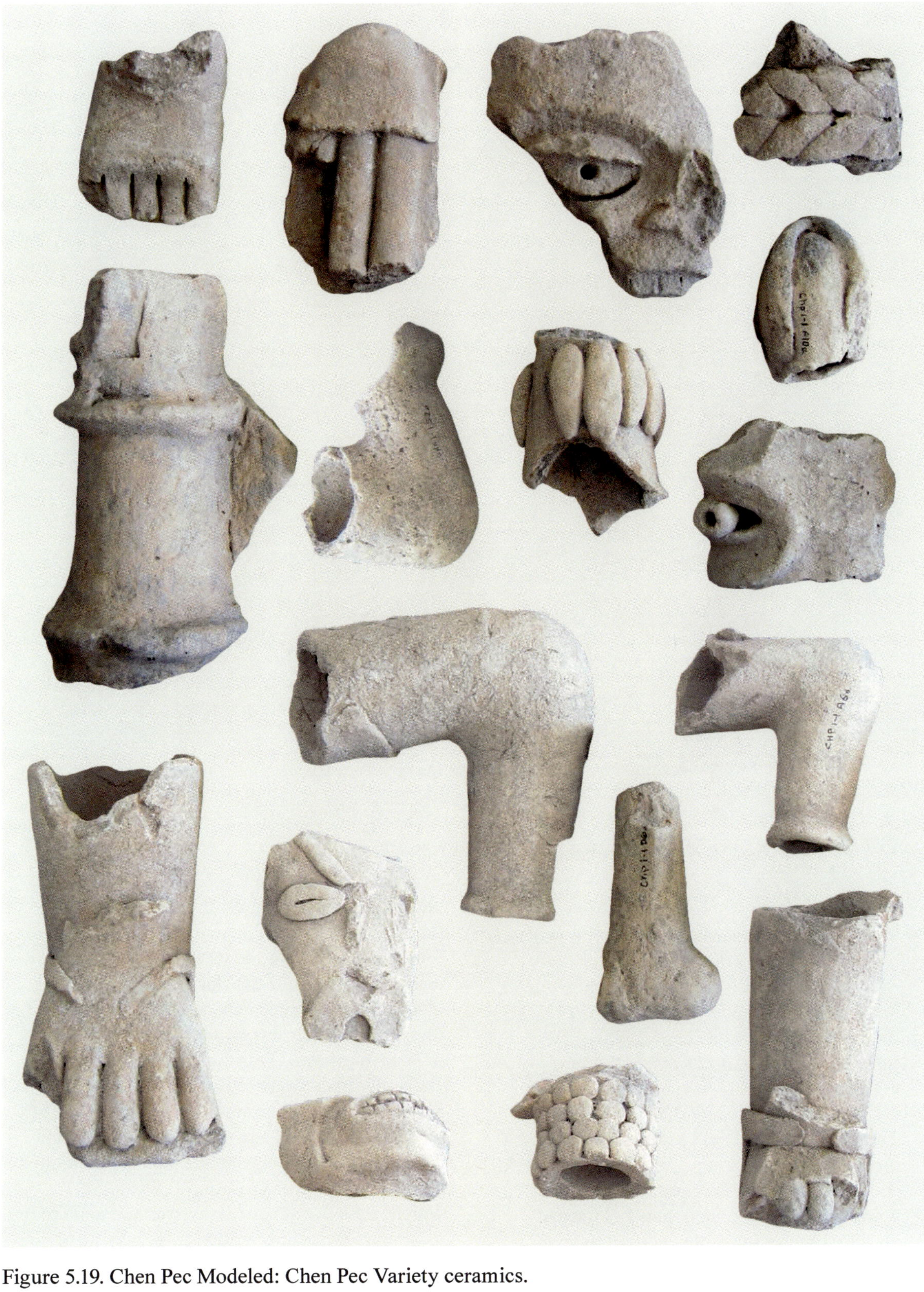

Figure 5.19. Chen Pec Modeled: Chen Pec Variety ceramics.

Figure 5.20. Chen Pec Modeled: Chen Pec Variety ceramics.

Forms:

1. Anthropompomorphic censer with pedestal-base vessel attached to back of deity figure. This is the only form known. [cf. Smith 1971:32e-pp] (Figures 5.19–5.22).

Intrasite Locations and Contexts: The distribution of this type is highly skewed in collections recovered by the UAC investigations. The 2001 and 2002 field seasons concentrated on excavations at Group 1, Structure 1 (Barrio de Guadalupe), and on parallel excavations at Moquel. Group 1, Structure 1 is located on the eastern edge of the modern town of Champotón. Excavations at this structure yielded massive amounts of Chen Pec sherds. In fact, to the west of Structure 1L (Op. L-31a) (Folan et al. 2002:fig. 5) on the Structure 1 platform was a huge deposit of large fragments of anthropomorphic censers, which seemingly represented some sort of deposition episode of only such censers. This deposit has not yet been analyzed. In addition, other excavation units on Structure 1 often contained very large quantities of Chen Pec sherds—nearly 3000 sherds—not counting the very large single deposit mentioned above. In other words, Group 1, Structure 1, which had a Late Postclassic structure abutted to it on its west side, yielded extremely large quantities of Chen Pec Modeled.

Figure 5.21. Chen Pec Modeled: Chen Pec Variety ceramics.

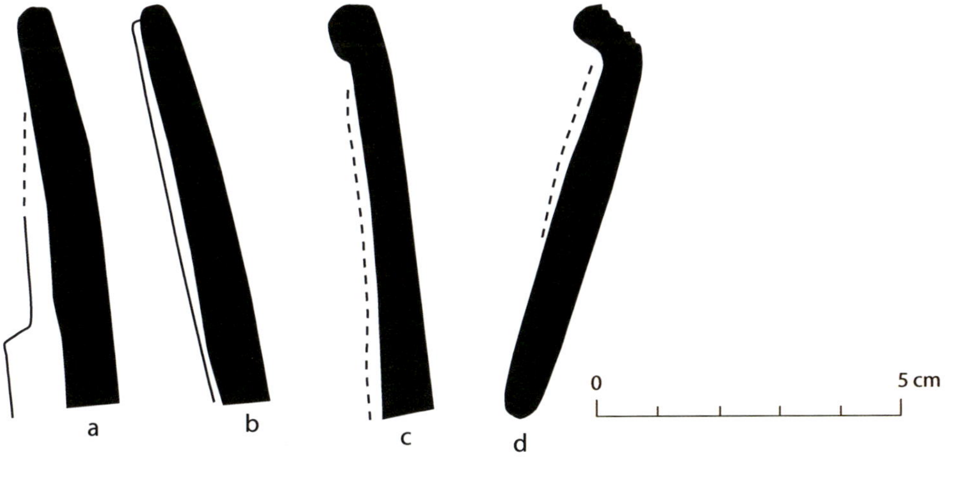

Figure 5.22. Imí Ceramic Group profile drawings—Chen Pec Modeled: Chen Pec Variety.

During the 2003 field season, the UAC team directed its efforts to the northern portion of the town of Champotón, closer to the river in the Pozo del Monte-Mercedes area (Folan et al. 2004:fig. 3). These excavations yielded only Postclassic materials, with an occasional earlier sherd incorporated in the later materials. Notably, in these deposits Chen Pec Modeled is extremely rare (287 sherds), even though the other members of the Imí Ceramic Group are present in quantity. This might suggest that Chen Pec was not a common ceramic of the everyday household inventory, but rather played a restricted role in public activities. A similar pattern has been noted in a smaller site near Champotón (Jerry Ek, personal communication, 2007).

Intersite Locations and Contexts: The same as Imí Unslipped: Imí Variety. See Ek (2015:502, 515) for sites near Champotón where the type has been found. On page 503, Ek labels this type as Chen Mul Modeled and makes it part of the Navula Ceramic Group; but on page 513, he correctly notes that Chen Pec in the Champotón region is a Chen Mul analog (see Smith 1971:24). Related Chen Mul materials or analogs are widespread throughout the Northern Lowlands, and related types, such as Kol Modeled (Chase 1982:537–538) are found in Belize, and Patojo and Idolos Modeled (Rice 1987:184–192, 195–197) were recovered in the Central Lakes region.

Comment: As indicated above, many might wish to classify what I have called Chen Pec Modeled as Chen Mul Modeled. There are certainly significant similarities, and it might be possible to see it as a variety of Chen Mul. Nevertheless, there are a couple of distinctions that have led me to separate it at the typological level. The first is that the paste is quite distinct, and, in fact, is the same distinctive paste as the Champotón Unslipped Ware. Ball (1978:92) has already highlighted that Chen Mul is in need of some classificatory subdivision and suggested paste as one criterion among others. Similarly, the anthropomorphic censers at Champotón by and large lack the extensive painting that mark Chen Mul censers, at least at Mayapan itself. At the latter site, a large proportion of the Chen Mul examples bear such paint or a thin layer of stucco or both. While both painting and stucco occur on Chen Pec images, they are not common (54 sherds out of nearly 3000), and most appear to have been plain, relying on the modeling of the complex image alone rather than painting. Moreover, their restricted distribution suggests a specialized function for them. Detailed analysis of the iconography of these censers still needs to be done. This will have to include the large sample of large pieces, as yet unanalyzed, recovered from what appears to be a ceremonial breaking or dumping between Structures 1L and 1B of Group 1, Structure 1.

Cherna Incised: Cherna Variety (Figures 5.23–5.25)

Frequency: 821 sherds (11%; 2%)

Established: Type and variety established by Ball (1978:92) but without description other than reference to Ruz (1969:118–119). The type is common at Champotón; compare with Ruz (1969:fig. XL/28–32; XLII/3). These are known in Mexico as *molcajetes* or chili grinders. Other analysts prefer to call them *raspadores* so as not to project a perhaps unwarranted function onto these vessels.

Description:

Principal Identifying Attributes: (1) unslipped, unpolished vessel surfaces; (2) cream to buff to gray-colored paste; (3) cream to buff vessel surfaces; (4) rough surface finish; (5) sub-hemispherical dish or bowl with tripod supports; (6) zoned incising in sections on interior bottom of dish or bowl.

Paste, Firing, and Temper: The same as the Imí Unslipped: Imí Variety.

Surface Finish and Decoration: The same as the Imí Unslipped: Imí Variety, except for the incising on the interior base of the bowl. Ruz (1969:118–119) provides a good description of this type under the category of "Molcajetes" in his "Cerámica grisácea." Virtually all examples have a single circumferential incised line that begins from one to three centimeters below the interior lip. It is within the circle created by this incised line that sections of hatching-like incisions were made. Each section, usually four, but not always, was incised with parallel lines, but their direction changes from one section to another. Often these incised lines are deep, and not particularly well executed, although there is, of course, considerable variability across many examples. The parallel lines are not typically evenly spaced and sometimes not particularly straight, but the overall pattern is very much like other types of molcajetes manufactured during the Late Postclassic. The area above the circumferential line, the lip, and the exterior are smoothed, but unpolished, like the surfaces of other members of the Imí Ceramic Group.

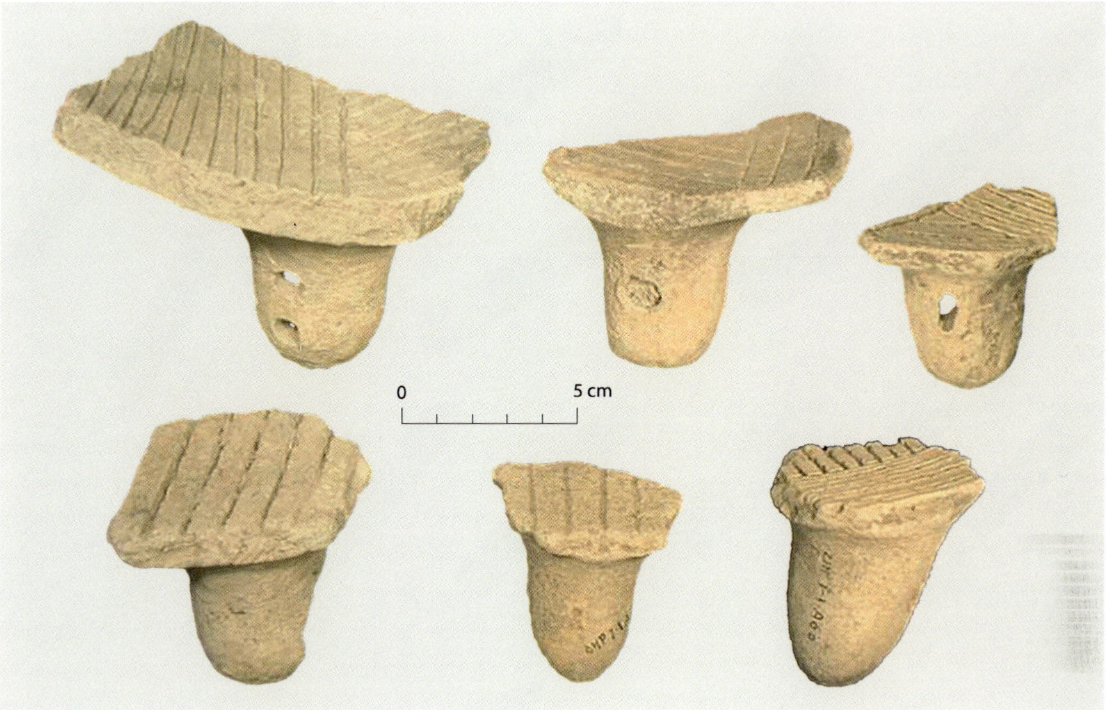

Figure 5.23. Cherna Incised: Cherna Variety ceramics.

Forms:

1. Small sub-hemispherical dish (rarely bowl) with tripod supports (Figures 5.23–5.25). This form has a rounded bottom usually with tripod supports, which may be solid or hollow. The hollow supports are quite variable; compare the foot forms to those illustrated by Ruz (1969:fig. XL/65–75). All of these hollow forms occur in this and other forms, but another form, the hollow bulbous form also occurs. Because of the rounded nature of the base, these supports are asymmetrical in shape so as to present a level vessel when resting on the supports. These vessels are generally small with rim diameters of 25 cm or less, although occasionally larger examples do occur. Rims may be direct, but usually are beveled and grooved or beveled and ridged toward the interior; compare with Ruz (1969:figs. XXXVI/32; XL/28–32). Virtually all examples have a single circumferential incised line that begins from one to three centimeters from the interior lip. It is within the circle created by this incised line that sections of hatching-like incisions were made. Each section, usually four, but not always, was incised with parallel lines, although their direction changes from one section to another. Normally these incised lines are deep and not particularly well executed, although there is, of course, considerable variability across the many examples.

Intrasite Locations and Contexts: The same as the Imí Unslipped: Imí Variety.

Intersite Locations and Contexts: The same as Imí Unslipped: Imí Variety. See Ek (2015:502, 503, 515). According to Antonio Benavides (personal communication, 2006), this variety also occurs at Seybaplaya, approximately 25–30 km up the coast from Champotón.

Comment: This type, with its distinctive lip forms, serves as a kind of diagnostic type for the Champotón region. We still do not know the

Figure 5.24. Imí Ceramic Group profile drawings—Cherna Incised: Cherna Variety.

Figure 5.25. Cherna Incised: Cherna Variety ceramics.

extent of the region in which Cherna Incised and other types and varieties of the Champotón Unslipped Ware was manufactured and/or utilized. Two sherds of Cherna Incised carry blue post-fire paint applied to the interior (Figure 5.24m). This is extremely rare, however.

Cherna Incised: Red-rim Variety (Figure 5.26)

Frequency: 76 sherds (<1%; <1%)

Established: Type established by Ball (1978:92) but without description other than a reference to Ruz (1969:118–119). The Red-rim Variety is established in the present study. The variety is less common at Champotón than the Cherna Variety but occurs consistently; compare with Ruz 1969:fig. XL/28–32.

Description:

Principal Identifying Attributes: (1) unslipped, unpolished vessel surfaces; (2) cream to buff to gray-colored paste; (3) cream to buff vessel surfaces; (4) rough surface finish; (5) sub-hemispherical dish or bowl with tripod supports; (6) red slip or paint applied to the top of the lip and sometimes a millimeter or two over either the exterior or interior rim edge or both; (7) zoned incising in sections on interior bottom of dish or bowl.

Paste, Firing, and Temper: The same as the Imí Unslipped: Imí Variety.

Surface Finish and Decoration: The same as the Cherna Incised: Cherna Variety, except for the red-painted lip top.

Forms:

1. Small sub-hemispherical dish (rarely bowl) with tripod supports (Figures 5.26). The form is identical to that described for the Cherna Variety, as this is the only form known for both varieties.

Intrasite Locations and Contexts: The same as the Imí Unslipped: Imí Variety.

Intersite Locations and Contexts: The same as Imí Unslipped: Imí Variety. Several examples of this type, but in a strongly oxidized paste, were recovered in a salvage test pit from Seybaplaya, approximately 25–30 km up the coast from Champotón. In all but firing, these are identical to Champotón examples. As noted by Ball (1978:92) they are functional analogs of the Mayapan Chenkeken Incised grater bowls (Smith 1971:fig. 33j); however, at Mayapan grater bowls tend to occur on exteriorly red-slipped vessels and only rarely on unslipped vessels. Smith (1971:195, 205) lists a total of 16 sherds from such unslipped grater bowls for the Hocabá and Tases complexes combined. Champotón, on the other hand, has large numbers of them, and Champotón correspondingly lacks red-slipped grater bowls.

Comment: This variety seems to be unique to the Champotón region. It is relatively rare, but it can be distinguished from the Cherna Variety only if a portion of the rim is present.

Other Imí Group: Incised and Painted

A total of 69 sherds that bear both incising and post-fire paint have been recovered from the Pozo del Monte-Mercedes area (63 of them came from a single excavation unit).

Almendros Ceramic Group [2203]

Almendros Mottled: Almendros Variety (Figures 5.27–5.28)

Frequency: The exact total of sherds is unknown. Almendros Mottled was not originally counted, apart from Arrocera Brushed, during the analysis of ceramics from Group 1, Structure 1 (field seasons 2001 and 2002); however, the two types were separated during the analysis of the 2003 field season. A total 436 sherds of Almendros and Arrocera sherds were recovered from the Group 1 Structure 1 excavations (field seasons 2001 and 2002), with 634 sherds of Almendros Mottled recovered from the 2003 field season. Because the exact counts for this type are uncertain, I have not provided percentages for the ceramic group and ware, as is the case for other types.

Established: Established in the present study.

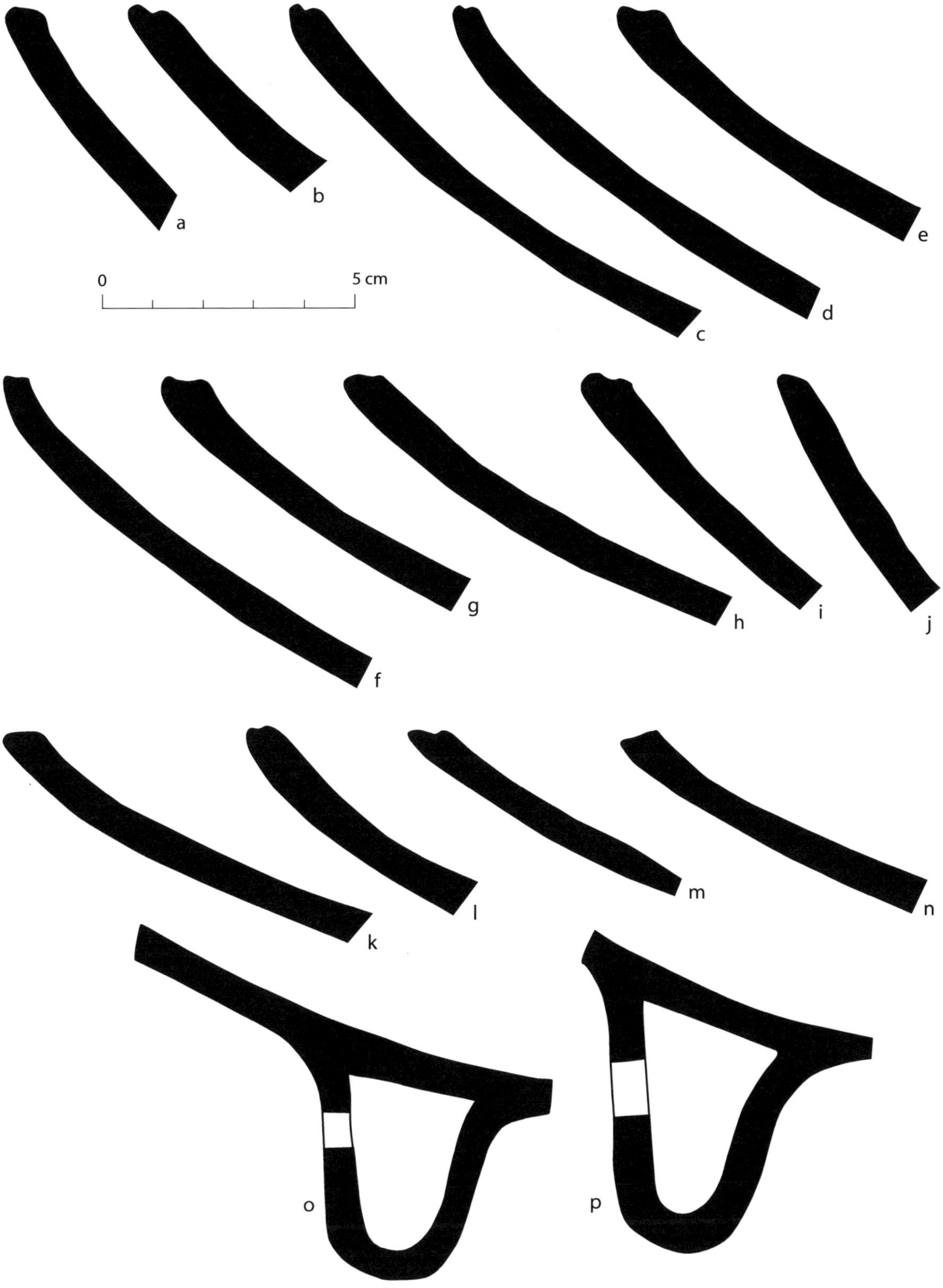

Figure 5.26. Imí Ceramic Group profile drawings—Cherna Incised: Red-rim Variety.

Figure 5.27. Almendros Mottled: Almendros Variety ceramics.

Description:

Principal Identifying Attributes: (1) unslipped, unpolished vessel surfaces; (2) red to brown to gray to cream-colored mottled vessel surfaces; (3) rough surface finish; (4) thin vessel walls; (6) small to medium jar form.

Paste, Firing, and Temper: The paste of this type is the same as that for Imí Unslipped: Imí Variety; however, the firing of the pottery often resulted in paste and surface colors quite different from that of the Imí Ceramic Group. The surfaces of this type sometimes have the cream to buff to pinkish cream color characteristic of Imí Unslipped but often tend to be mottled. There is a tendency toward gray surfaces mottled with brown to pink to reddish tones, often giving a splotchy surface appearance. In other cases the surface colors represent various shades of gray to brown. In short, surface color varies considerably within this type and suggests either variable firing conditions, or more likely, utilization in or over a fire during use. Paste texture is coarse, rarely medium. The temper is calcite, although other unidentified particles occasionally occur. Particle size ranges from 0.3 to 0.9 mm. Given the thinness of the vessel walls, the paste usually bears some large chunks of temper, although quite small pieces also are frequent.

Surface Finish and Decoration: Vessels surfaces were smoothed but not polished. They have a rough surface texture. Vessel walls are invaribly thin, perhaps averaging less than 6 mm, although this, of course, varies, depending on the part of the vessel being measured. Rims tend to be somewhat thicker than bodies.

Forms:

1. Medium-necked jar (olla) (Figure 5.28, a–l). This is the overwhelmingly dominant form for this type, and the ceramic group is characterized by this

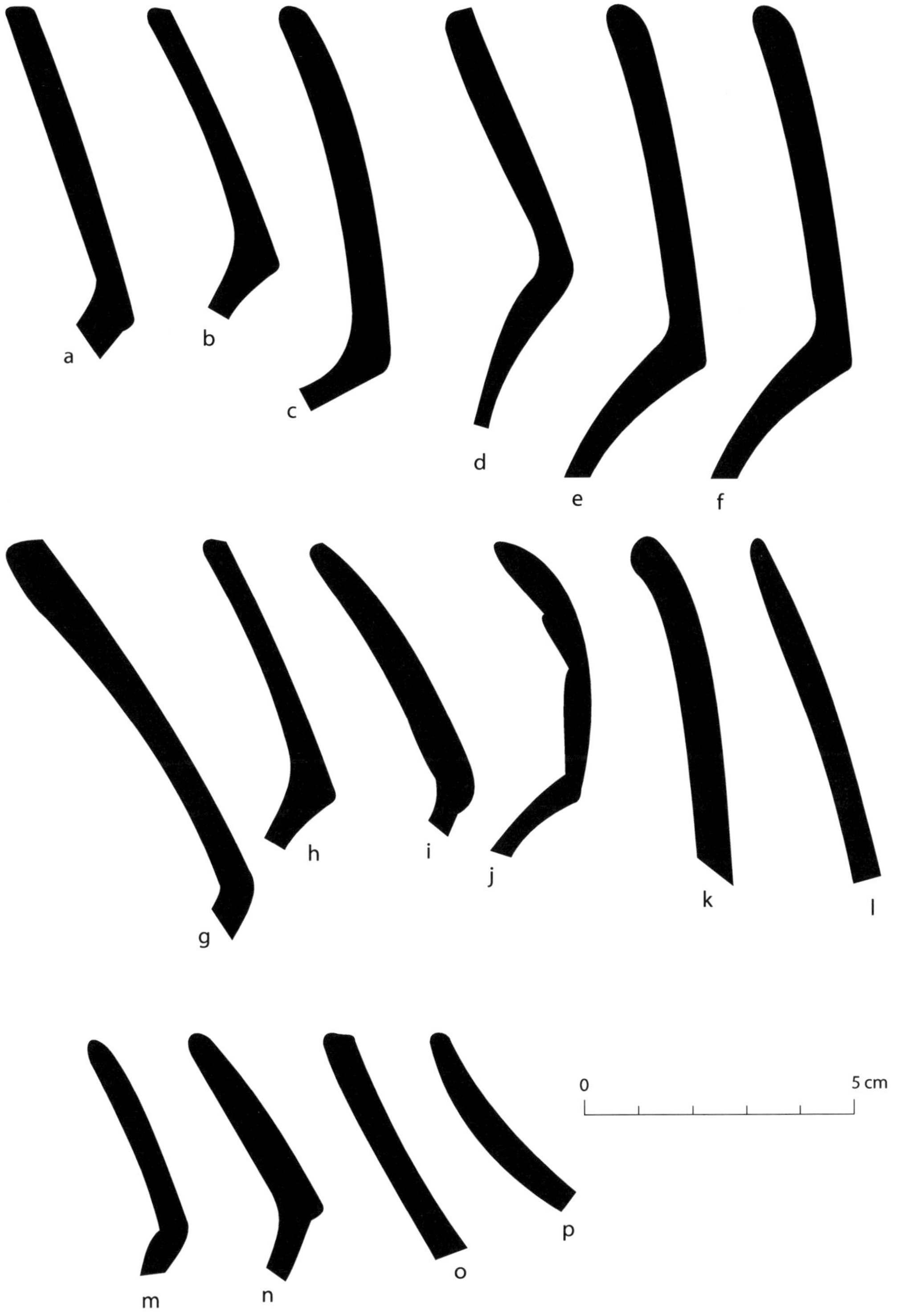

Figure 5.28. Almendros Ceramic Group profile drawings—Almendros Mottled: Almendros Variety.

form, although others do occur. Rim diameter tends to range from 12–21 cm, but there are larger examples. Lip forms are generally direct and rounded, although flattened, beveled, beveled and grooved forms also occur. Neck height averages around 4–5 cm but ranges from 3–6 cm. The jar neck flares stongly to only slightly outward from a sharp break at the neck-shoulder junction; compare with Ruz (1969:figs. XXXVI/8, 10–16).

2. Small collared jar (Figure 5.28, m–n). The jar has a squat profile. The neck or collar is generally very short, usually less than or equal to 2 cm and has a distinct break from the globular vessel. Because of the shortness of the collar, the rim diameter is only slightly smaller than the vessel diameter of the body. Bases are flat. Several examples have small, vertically placed handles with a small hole through them. These were almost certainly made for running a cord through, as not even a child's finger could fit through the tiny holes.

3. Small incurved rim bowl (no illustration). This is not a common form, but occurs consistently in this type. The rim is generally flattened or beveled. Often there is flattened, solid handle that projects outward from the upper vessel wall 1.5 to 2 cm; compare with Ruz (1969:fig. XL/25, 2 7)

4. Miscellaneous forms (Figure 5.28, o–p).

Intrasite Locations and Contexts: The same as the Imí Unslipped: Imí Variety.

Intersite Locations and Contexts: This type is known only from Champotón. It was found by Ek (2015:502, 512) at sites in or very near to Champotón. In terms of vessel wall thickness, and shape, it is, however, reminiscent of Pozo Unslipped defined by Rice (1987:170ff.) at Macanche Island in the Central Lakes region of the Peten in Guatemala, as well as found in some quantity at Flores Island (personal observation).

Comment: The Almendros Ceramic Group differs from the Imí Ceramic Group primarily in the thinness of the vessel walls and the relative limitation of vessel shape to medium- to short-necked or collared jars.

Arrocera Brushed: Arrocera Variety (Figures 5.29–5.31)

Frequency: The exact total of sherds is unknown. Almendros Mottled was not originally counted apart from Arrocera Brushed during the analysis of ceramics from Group 1, Structure 1 (field seasons 2001 and 2002); however, the two types were separated during the analysis of the 2003 field season. A total of 436 sherds of Almendros and Arrocera sherds were recovered from the Group 1, Structure 1 excavations (field seasons 2001 and 2002), with 1133 sherds of Arrocera Brushed recovered from the 2003 field season. Because exact counts for this type are uncertain, I have not provided percentages for the ceramic group and ware as is the case for other types.

Established: Established in the present study.

Description:

Principal Identifying Attributes: (1) unslipped, unpolished vessel surfaces; (2) cream to buff to gray-colored paste; (3) cream to buff vessel surfaces, but some examples have red to brown to gray-mottled vessel surfaces; (4) thin vessel walls; (5) brushing/very light striation on globular portion of vessel; (6) small to medium jar form.

Paste, Firing, and Temper: For the most part the paste of this type is the same as that for Imí Unslipped: Imí Variety. Firing is often the same as the Imí Variety also. Some examples, however, are similar to the firing of Almendros Mottled, which resulted in paste and surface colors that tend toward gray surfaces mottled with brown to pink to reddish tones, often giving the surface a splotchy appearance. In other cases the surfaces colors represent various shades of gray to brown. Still, Arrocera Brushed is more commonly a cream to buff color than is Almendros Mottled. Paste texture is similar to Almendros Mottled.

Figure 5.29. Arrocera Brushed: Arrocera Variety Vessel.

Figure 5.30. Arrocera Brushed: Arrocera Variety ceramics.

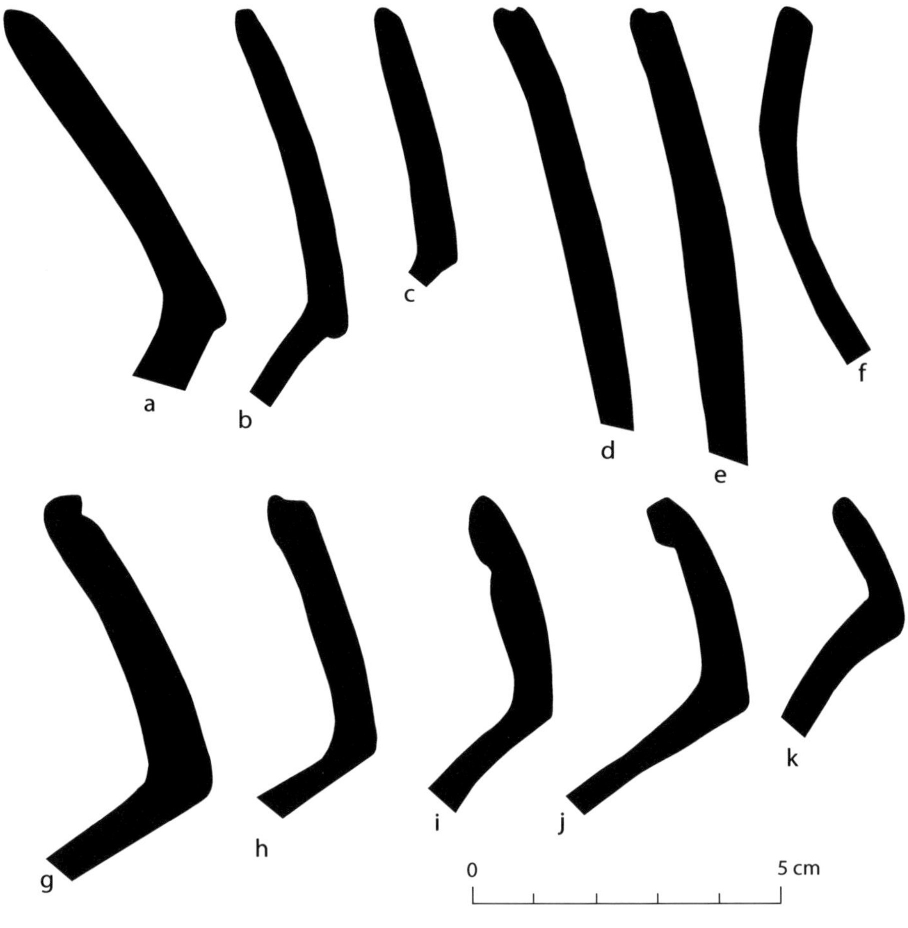

Figure 5.31. Almendros Ceramic Group profile drawings—Arrocera Brushed: Arrocera Variety.

Surface Finish and Decoration: Vessels surfaces were smoothed but not polished. They have a rough surface texture. Vessel walls are invariably thin, perhaps averaging less than 5 mm, although this varies, depending on the part of the vessel being measured. Rims tend to be somewhat thicker than bodies. The globular portion of the vessel, beginning at the neck-body juncture, was brushed yielding a lightly striated appearance. The brushing was often diagonal or horizontal, and the striations are never deep. The lightness of the striations is why I have labeled it Arrocera Brushed rather than Arrocera Striated; but the placement of the brushing, its patterning, and the principal vessel form on which it is executed is clearly a continuation of the long striated unslipped ware tradition in the Maya Lowlands.

Forms:

1. Short to medium-necked jar (olla) (Figure 5.31, a–c, g–j). This is overwhelmingly the dominant form for this type, and the ceramic group is characterized by this form, although others do occur. Rim diameter tends to range from 10–19 cm, but there are larger examples. Lip forms are generally direct and rounded, although flattened, beveled, beveled and grooved forms also occur. Neck height averages around 4–5 cm. The jar neck flares stongly to only slightly outward from a sharp break at the neck-shoulder junction; compare with Ruz (1969:figs. XXXVI/8, 10–16).

2. Small collared jar (Figure 5.31k). The jar has a squat profile. The neck or collar is generally very short, usually less than or equal to 2 cm, and has a distinct break from the globular vessel, but because of the shortness of the collar the rim diameter is only slightly smaller than the major point.
3. Small incurved rim bowl (Figure 5.31f). This is not a common form but occurs consistently in this type. The rim is generally flattened or beveled. Often there is flattened, solid handle that projects outward from the upper vessel wall 1.5 to 2 cm; compare with Ruz (1969:fig. XL/25, 27).
4. Vase Form (Figure 5.31, d–e).

Intrasite Locations and Contexts: The same as the Imí Unslipped: Imí Variety.

Intersite Locations and Contexts: This type is known only from Champotón. Ek (2015:502, 503) recovered this type, labeled as Arrocero Brushed, but does not provide distribution data on the specific type. In terms of vessel wall thickness and shape it is, however, reminiscent of Pozo Unslipped defined by Rice (1987:170ff.) at Macanche Island in the Central Lakes region of the Peten in Guatemala, and found in some quantity at Flores Island (personal observation). Nonetheless, in the Central Lakes Region brushing or striation is not found. It differs significantly from Yacman Striated at Mayapan (Smith 1971:24) and other sites in Yucatan. It is much thinner walled, occurs in forms that are smaller, and with a different rim form than most Yacman vessels; it has brushing that begins right at the neck-body junction and not a centimeter or so below the juncture, as the Yacman vessels usually do, as well as other differences. The only close parallel is that they are unslipped jars with striation. Moreover, Arrocera Brushed makes up a relatively small percentage of the unslipped pottery at Champotón, while Yacman Striated is the dominant unslipped, non-effigy type at Mayapan.

BOMAL RED WARE [3224]

Moquel Ceramic Group [3224]

Moquel Red: Moquel Variety (Figures 5.32–5.38)

Frequency: 3051 sherds (95%; 7%). See comment under Frequency for the Unslipped-exterior Variety.

Established: Established in the present study. This type constitutes the bulk of what Ruz (1969:128–129;fig. XLI/33–66,74–84; XLII/6–8) called "Cerámica roja."

Description:

Principal Identifying Attributes: (1) dull to slightly polished red slip; (2) cream to buff to gray-colored paste; (3) dishes and bowls often with basal ridge; (4) bulbous and other tripod supports.

Paste, Firing, and Temper: The paste of this type is the same as that for Imí Unslipped: Imí Variety. In fact, the red-slipped pottery at Champotón was made from the same paste as the unslipped pottery. What distinguishes it from Champotón Unslipped Ware is the addition of a red slip, presumably fired in a strongly oxidizing atmosphere that yielded its red color. Due to this strong oxidation, some sherds have a more tan-colored paste, but many retain the cream color of Champotón Unslipped Ware. Because the vessel walls are often thinner than the majority of Imí vessels, there is a tendency for the paste to be somewhat finer, and the particle size of the temper to be somewhat smaller. The paste is essentially the same, except that it is perhaps somewhat more consistent. Paste colors range from pinkish (7.5YR 6–7/2–4) to very pale brown (10YR 6–7/2–4).

Surface Finish and Decoration: Vessels surfaces were smoothed and well smoothed. A dull to moderately polished red-firing slip was applied over this (7.5R 4–5/8; 10R 4–5/6–8). This slip is thin and erodes quite easily, so that most sherds are strongly eroded. Still, in protected contexts, the slip adheres moderately well. The slip covered both the interior and

Figure 5.32. Moquel Red: Moquel Variety ceramics.

Figure 5.33. Moquel Red: Moquel Variety ceramics.

Figure 5.34. Moquel Red: Moquel Variety ceramics.

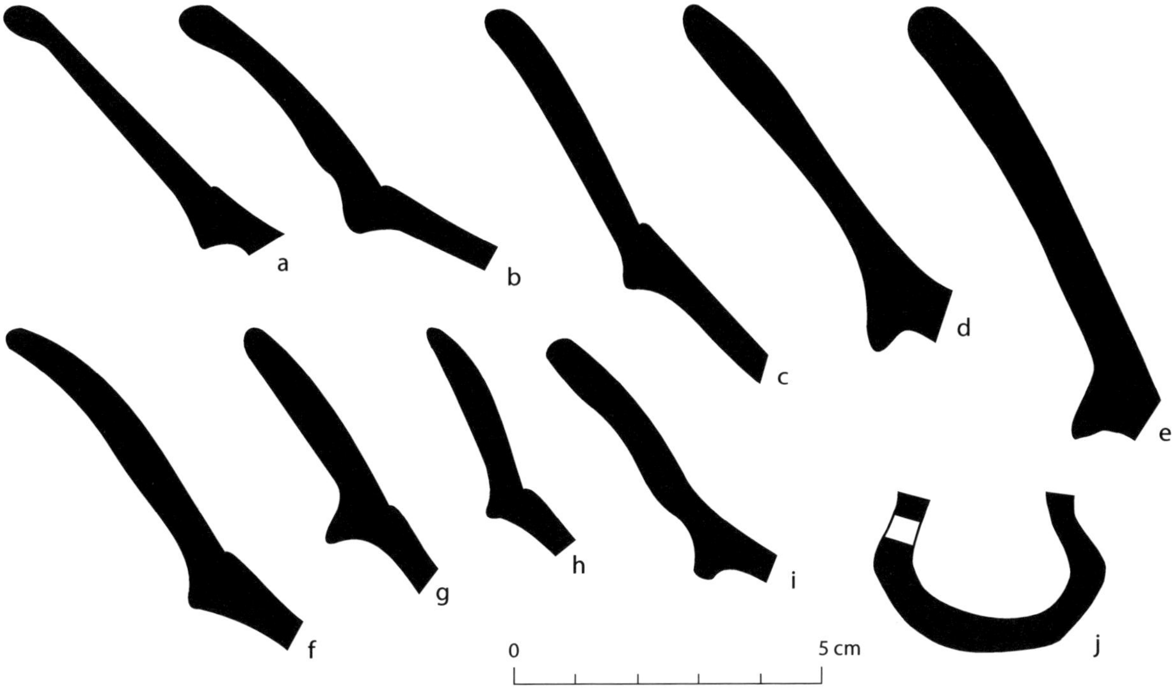

Figure 5.35. Moquel Ceramic Group profile drawings—Moquel Red: Moquel Variety.

exterior surfaces of the vessel and sometimes also the tripod supports on those vessels that had such supports. In other cases, however, the slip was only applied to the upper portion of the support. In either case, the slip on the supports tends to be washy and unpolished. Gray to black fire-clouds are not uncommon on these vessels. Whether or not it should be considered a form of decoration or not, the dominant vessel form bears a basal ridge near where the vessel wall starts to curve inward. Usually the ridges are plain but not infrequently are notched. These notches may be plain V-shaped cuts or more elaborate ones in the form of crenellation or tau-shaped notches.

Forms:

1. Basal ridge dish, occasionally bowl, with flaring or outcurving walls and tripod supports (Figures 5.35–5.36). This form is dominant for the type. Rim diameter varies between 17 and 28 cm. Lip forms are generally direct and rounded, interiorly beveled, interiorly ridged, and even occasionally beveled and grooved. Also a few examples have slightly everted lips, but these are uncommon. Bases are generally slightly rounded. There is usually, though not invariably, a break between the vessel wall and the base, often with a depression and/or interior offset. The tripod supports are usually hollow but solid supports are also known. Some have modeled serpent heads similar to those found on Matillas Orange vessels; compare with Ruz (1969:figs. XLI/56–63, 65–66) and "cajetes trípodes con moldura basal."
2. Sub-hemispherical dish (rarely bowl) with tripod supports (Figure 5.37, a–n). The rim is generally flattened or beveled but may also be rounded. Some occasionally also bear basal ridges. This form corresponds in part to Ruz's (1969:128; fig. XLI/42–44) "Cajetes de paredes convexas."
3. Dish with flaring or outcurving walls and tripod supports (Figures 5.37, q–t; 5.38, a–f). This form is similar in

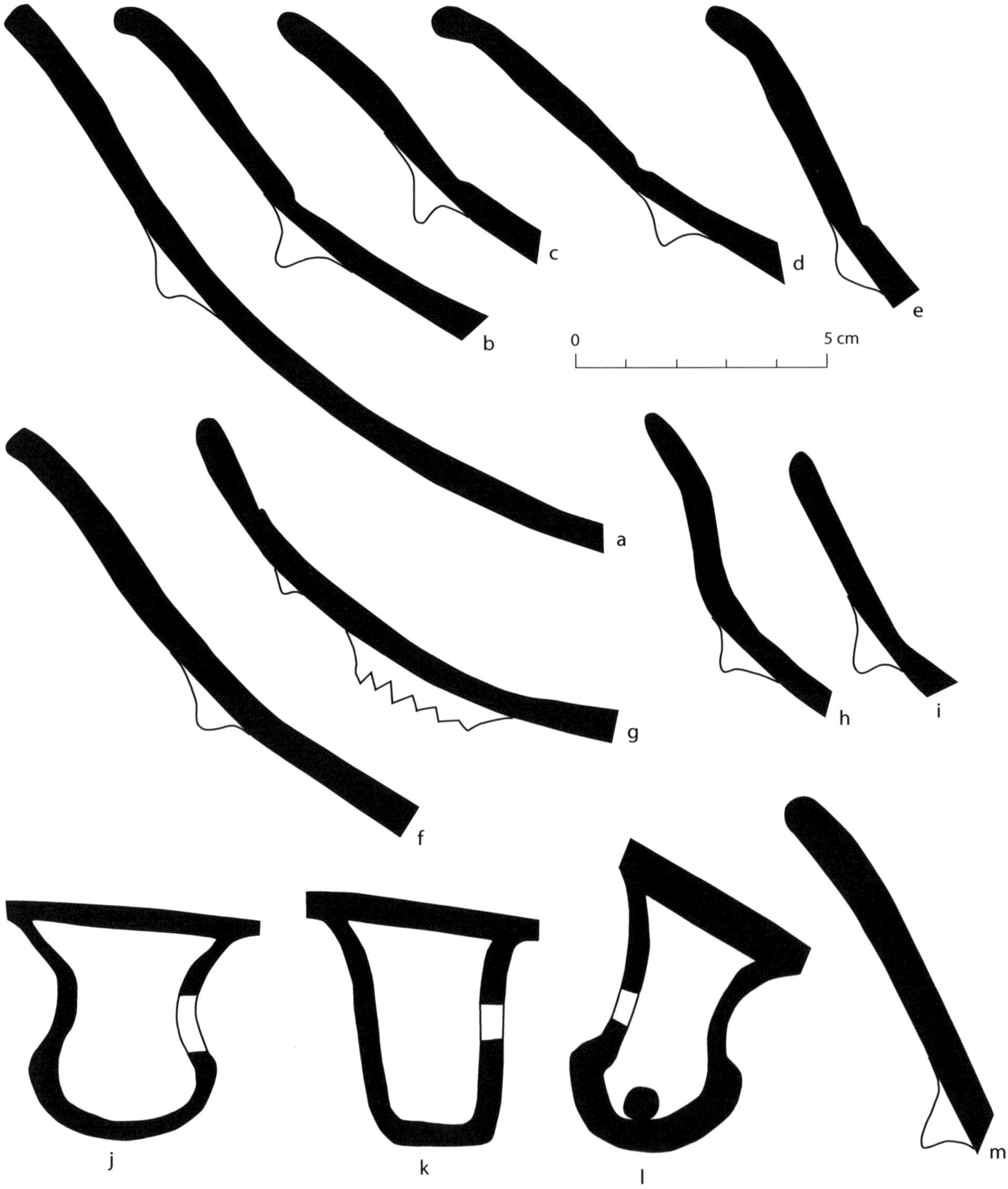

Figure 5.36. Moquel Ceramic Group profile drawings—Moquel Red: Moquel Variety.

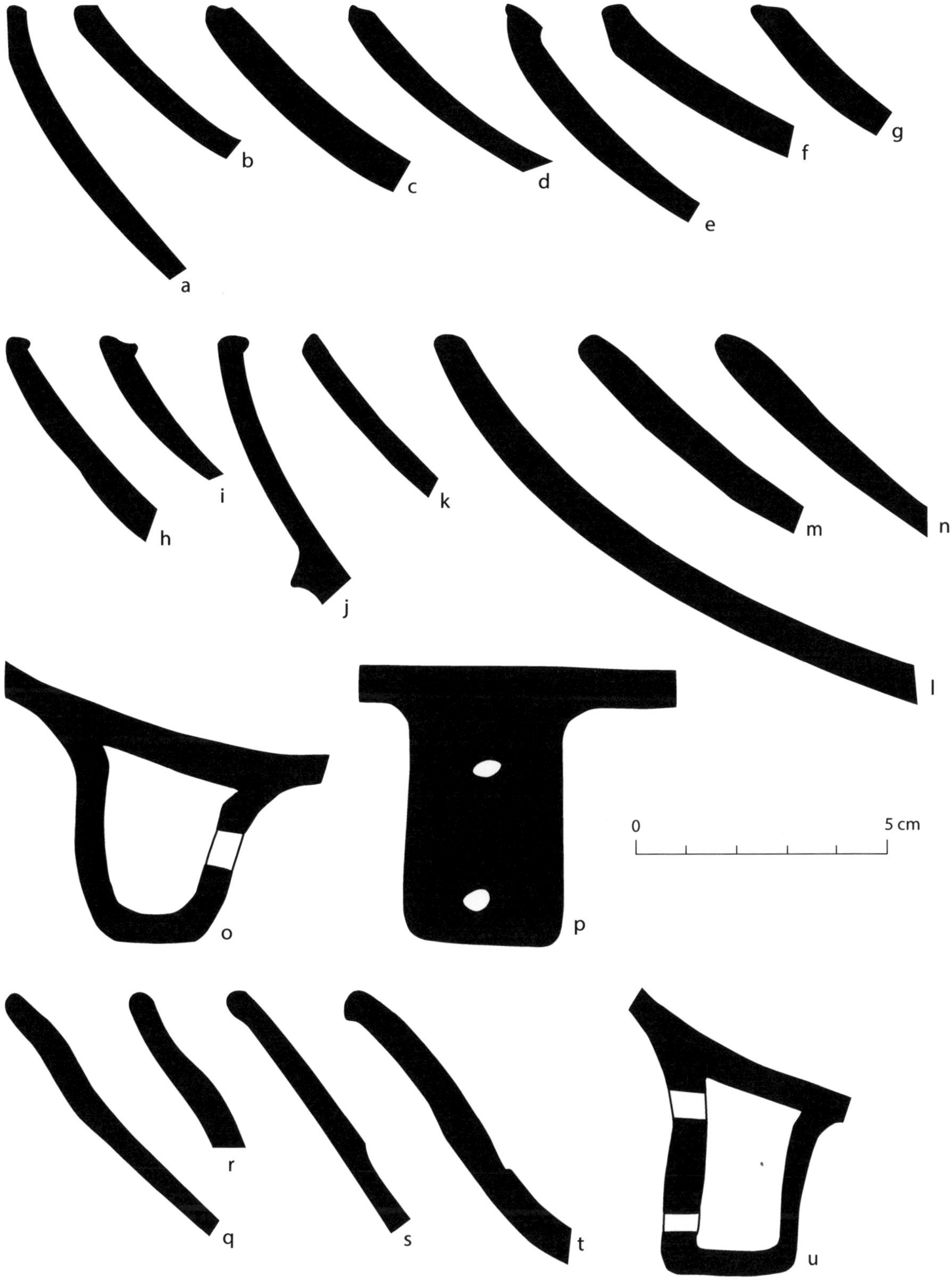

Figure 5.37. Moquel Ceramic Group profile drawings—Moquel Red: Moquel Variety (o, p, and u are foot or support forms; their vessel form is not clear).

Figure 5.38. Moquel Ceramic Group profile drawings—Moquel Red: Moquel Variety.

most respects to Form 1 but lacks the basal ridge. This form would probably also include what Ruz (1969:128; fig. XLI/47–50) called "Cajetes con silueta compuesta."

4. Short-necked jars (Figure 5.38, g–n). The body is globular and the neck flares out slightly. The vessel is slipped on the exterior. The interior body is not slipped, but there is variation with respect to the interior neck. Sometimes it is not slipped and sometimes it is. Base form is unknown. Wide strap handles, placed horizontally, sometimes occur on this form.
5. Collard bowl (Figure 5.38, o–p). This is a relatively squat, rounded vessel with a short, slightly everted rim or collar. It is not certain, but it may have had tripod supports; compare with Ruz (1969:fig. XLI/52–54)
6. Miscellaneous forms (Figure 5.38, q–t).

Intrasite Locations and Contexts: Moquel Red materials were found in almost all deposits recovered from Champotón. Pure deposits were found in a number of operations. It was recovered in unmixed deposits in the Pozo del Monte-Mercedes barrios of Champotón but occurs in some quantity in Group 1, Structure 1 (Barrio de Guadalupe) in structural fill and other contexts. For reasons not yet understood, in Guadalupe it makes up a smaller proportion of the Late Postclassic ceramics than in the Pozo del Monte-Mercedes area.

Intersite Locations and Contexts: Moquel Red is presently known only from Champotón and its environs (see Ek 2015:503, 512). It may turn out to be more widely distributed than currently indicated when greater knowledge of the Postclassic occupation of the surrounding areas is undertaken. Settlement survey by Jerry Ek in the region around Champotón indicates that this ware does not extend very far from Champotón itself. It is roughly analoguous to Mama/Panabchen Red at Mayapán (Smith 1971); however, it differs significantly from these types in vessel forms, as well as in paste. Moquel Red thus bears a horizon-level similarity to Mayapan, but constitutes its own form and paste characteristics.

Moquel Red: Unslipped-exterior Variety (Figure 5.39)

Frequency: 136 sherds (4%; <1%). The actual numbers of this variety may be larger. The Unslipped-exterior variety was not counted separately when we analyzed the ceramics from Group 1, Structure 1 (Barrio de Guadelupe) excavations. So some these sherds may have been counted as the Moquel Variety.

Established: Established in the present study. This type would fall into part of what Ruz (1969:128–129; fig. XLI/33–66, 74–84) called "Cerámica roja."

Description:

Principal Identifying Attributes: (1) dull to slightly polished red slip on interior and over onto the top of the lip and often a millimeter or so over the lip on the exterior; (2) cream to buff to gray-colored paste; (3) dishes, with or without a basal ridge; (4) bulbous and other tripod supports.

Paste, Firing, and Temper: The same as that for Moquel Red: Moquel Variety.

Surface Finish and Decoration: The same as that for Moquel Red: Moquel Variety with the exception that the red slip was applied only to the interior of the vessel. It usually covered the top of the lip and frequently came down 1–4 mm on the exterior. Below that, the surface was smoothed but not polished and is equivalent to Imí Unslipped bowls. On some vessels the slip comes down the exterior a greater distance (1–3 cm).

Forms:

1. Sub-hemispherical dish (rarely bowl) with tripod supports (Figure 5.39). The rim is generally flattened or beveled but may also be rounded. Some of these occasionally bear basal ridges. This form corresponds in part to Ruz's (1969:128; fig. XLI/42–44) "Cajetes de paredes convexas."

Figure 5.39. Moquel Ceramic Group profile drawings— Moquel Red: Unslipped-exterior Variety.

Figure 5.40. Tajonal Incised: Tajonal Variety ceramics.

Intrasite Locations and Contexts: The same as the Moquel Variety.

Intersite Locations and Contexts: Moquel Red is presently known only from Champotón and its immediate environs. See the comments under the Moquel Variety. This variety is roughly analoguous to Mama Red: Unslipped-exterior Variety at Mayapan (Smith 1971); however, it differs significantly from these types in vessel forms, as well as in paste. Moquel Red thus bears a horizon-level similarity to Mayapan but constitutes its own form and paste characteristics.

Comment: A restricted number of red incised sherds (34) were recovered from our Champotón investigations. I have chosen not to treat these as a separate type until a larger sample can be obtained. I treat them as a Special. These sherds were not counted in the final counts for the Champotón types.

Tajonal Incised: Tajonal Variety (Figures 5.40–5.41)

Frequency: 31 sherds (1%; <1%)

Established: Established in the present study. This type would fall into part of what Ruz (1969:128–129; fig. XLI/33–66, 74–84) called "Cerámica roja;" however, Ruz notes that decoration of any kind is rare on red-slipped vessels. Tajonal Incised is a relatively rare type.

Description:

Principal Identifying Attributes: (1) dull to slightly polished red slip; (2) cream to buff to gray-colored paste; (3) dishes and bowls often with basal ridge; (4) bulbous and other tripod supports; (5) incising of designs and circumferential lines on vessel exteriors but sometimes on the upper portion of the interior of flaring-walled dishes and bowls.

Paste, Firing, and Temper: The same as that for Moquel Red: Moquel Variety.

Surface Finish and Decoration: The same as that for Moquel Red: Moquel Variety; however,

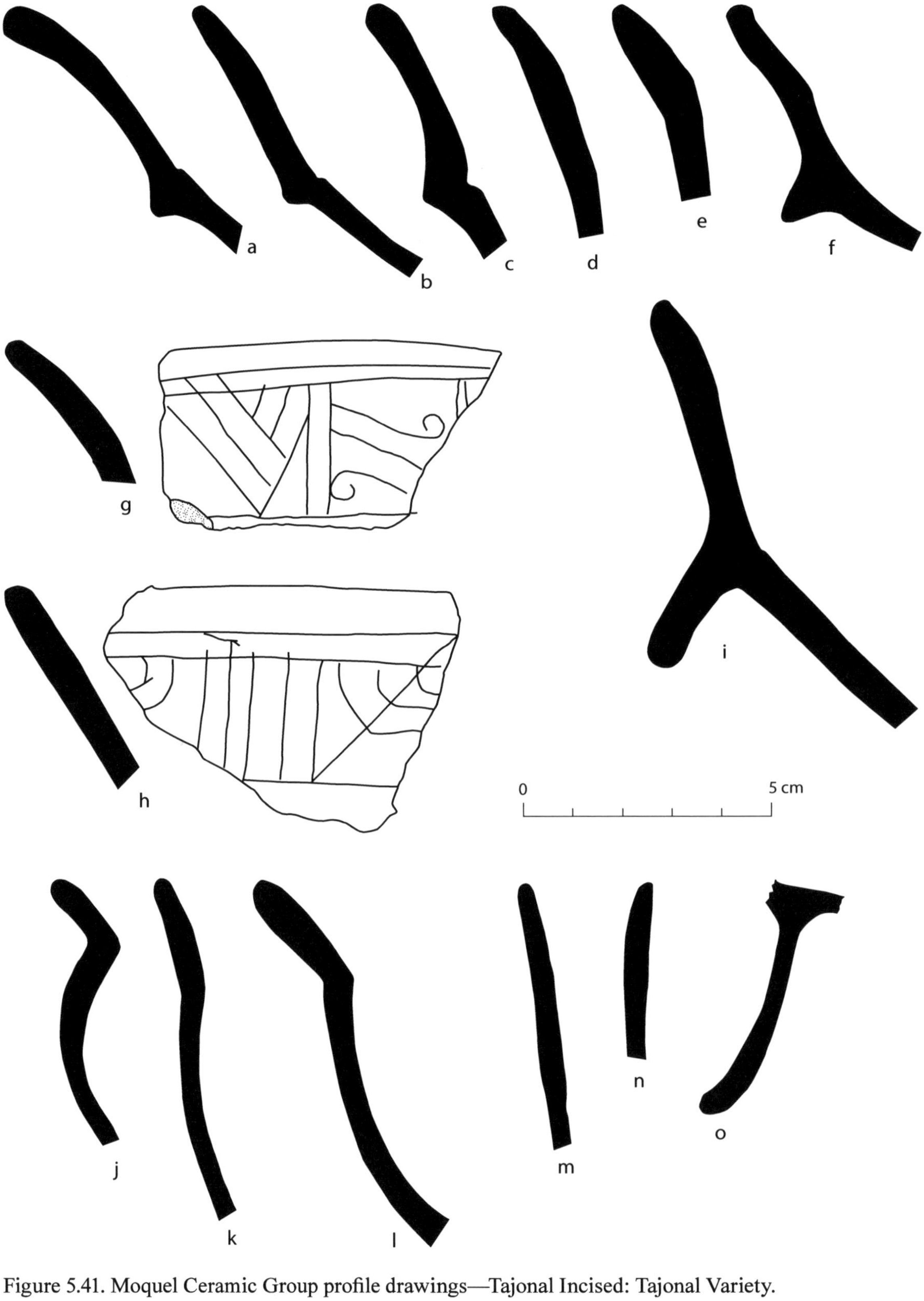

Figure 5.41. Moquel Ceramic Group profile drawings—Tajonal Incised: Tajonal Variety.

incised designs were executed on the exterior or the interior of the vessels. On vessel exteriors there is generally one to two circumferential incised lines below which more elaborate motifs were incised on the vessels. Below the incised designs, there is often a circumferential incised lines demarcating the designs from the rest of the unincised surface. Restricted vessels generally bear incisions only on the exterior of the vessel, while unrestricted forms may bear incisions on either the exterior or interior. In the latter case, they usually appear on the upper portion of the flaring-walled vessels. The incisions may be either postslip or preslip.

Forms:

1. Basal ridge dish, occasionally bowl, with flaring or outcurving sidewalls and tripod supports (Figure 5.41, a–i). This is the dominant form for this type. Rim diameter is unknown but is probably similar to the same form in Moquel Red. Bases are generally slightly rounded. There is usually, though not invariably, a break between the vessel wall and the base, often with a depression and/or interior offset. The tripod supports are usually hollow, but solid supports are also known. A small number of pedestal bases also occur in this type. Occasionally the basal ridges are crenulated; compare with Ruz (1969:fig. XLI/68–70) and "cajetes trípodes con moldura basal."
2. Collared jar (Figure 5.41, j–l). Rim diameter is unknown. The jar has a squat profile. The neck or collar is generally very short, usually less than or equal to 2 cm, and has a distinct break from the globular vessel. Bases are flat; compare with Ruz (1969:fig. XLI/52–54).
3. Miscellaneous vessel forms (Figure 5.41, m–o).

Intrasite Locations and Contexts: The same as the Moquel Variety.

Intersite Locations and Contexts: The same as the Moquel Variety.

Other Moquel Group: Black-on-red

Six sherds from Moquel Ceramic Group vessels with zoned areas bearing a black slip or paint with fine-line incised designs cut through the black paint were recovered from Champotón. A small number of Moquel Ceramic Group sherds, including two rims, bore vertical or horizontal black lines painted over the red slip.

PETO CREAM WARE [1586]

Kukula Ceramic Group [1586]

Xcanchacan Black-on-cream: Variety Unspecified (Figures 5.42–5.43)

Frequency: 1586 sherds (100%; 4%)

Established: Established by Smith (1971:26, 135–136, 200–201, figs. 51–52). This type would fall into part of what Ruz (1969:119–120, see "ollas decoradas" and "cajetes decorados;" fig. XLI/1–32) called "Cerámica grisácea-con decoración negra." See also Ochoa (1999) for a summary treatment of the ware.

Description:

Principal Identifying Attributes: (1) red to cream or buff paste; (1) slipped or well-smoothed vessel surfaces; (3) cream to buff vessel surfaces; (4) black trickle paint on exterior and/or interior of vessels; (5) jar forms.

Paste, Firing, and Temper: The paste is generally coarse although thin-walled vessels have a medium texture with smaller temper particles. There is considerable difference in this respect between vessels, although the larger vessels, usually jars, tend to have the coarsest paste. Temper appears to be white to gray crushed calcite. Some examples may well have been made from the same paste as the Imí Ceramic Group, but most seem to have either been made from a different paste or at least fired differently to give many of them a strong red to reddish brown paste color. This produces a pinkish color on many, but not all, of the vessel surfaces as the reddish brown paste shows through the thin cream slip. Paste colors tend to

Figure 5.42. Xcanchacan Black-on-cream: Variety Unspecified ceramics.

fall into two distinct modes: one is red/brown hues (10R 4/6, 6/6; 2.5YR 5–6/6–8), while the other is buff/very pale brown (10YR 6–7/3–4). Some examples were not oxidized all the way through the vessel wall, leaving dark cores. In a few cases the whole cross-section of the paste is dark (10R 2.5/1; 10R 4/1).

Surface Finish and Decoration: Surfaces were generally, though not invariably, moderately smoothed. A thin slip, made from the same clay as the paste, was apparently applied to the surface. At times, it is difficult to determine that there is, in fact, a slip, while in other cases it is more obvious. At Champotón some of these vessels may have been manufactured from the same clay as the unslipped and red-slipped pottery. In some cases there, in fact, may have been no slip, and the decoration simply added to the smoothed surface of the vessel. Surface color is similar to that for Imí Unslipped, except that well-slipped and preserved examples may have a slightly more pinkish hue to them (5 YR 8/2–37.5YR 8/2–3). Others have a tan to light brown or even gray color, but these colors are not common (10YR 8/1–2). The slip weathers readily, and sometimes makes it difficult to determine if there was a slip at all. This same pattern obtained on examples of Peto Cream Ware from Mayapan (personal observation, 2006, ceramoteca, Centro INAH-Yucatan). Decoration was executed by applying black paint to vessel surfaces, usually the exterior, but occasionally also to the interior. The black paint is very dark (2.5YR 2.5/0), but it also weathers readily, and therefore is often badly faded. The overwhelming majority of the decoration is trickle painting, a well-known form of painted decoration in the Northern Lowlands. This may begin at the neck of the vessel, but on most jars, the overwhelmingly most common form, it often starts below the neck-shoulder juncture. On some examples there is one or two solid black lines circling the vessel neck near the neck-shoulder juncture. Other designs or applications involve reverse angles, scrolls, dots, parallel lines, curvilinear or straight, rim ticking (what Smith [1971:76] calls "finger dabbing," dots, and others). The designs are, however, relatively simple and not particularly well executed. Usually the black paint is a strong black, although it tends to weather fairly readily. In other cases the paint tends to be watered down and weak. Typically, the paint seems to cover a significant portion of the vessel surface so that a sherd of any size will exhibit a good deal of paint. In other cases, however, the paint on a moderate to large sherd will consist of a single thin line or two thin parallel lines. By and large, the black paint fits well within the established tradition of this type.

Forms:

1. Short to medium-necked jars with or without exterior rim bolster (Figure 5.43, a–e). The neck usually flares outward, but some are nearly vertical. Bases are presumably flat. Horizontal strap handles, often quite large, occur on these vessels. The handles also have trickle, or other, decoration on them. The form corresponds most closely to what Smith (1971:200, fig. 52) calls water jars, and Ruz (1969:119–120) calls "ollas decoradas."

2. Dishes or bowls with interior interiorly beveled, folded, or direct rims (Figure 5.43, h–m). These may have been tripod vessels, but this is not definitive. The interiors usually bear the trickle and/or other decoration, although trickle decoration may continue down the exterior some one or two centimeters. In a few cases the exterior may carry the black decoration. The form corresponds most closely to what Smith (1971:200, fig. 52) calls tripod dishes, and Ruz (1969:119–120) calls "cajetes decorados."

3. Incurved rim bowl or basin (Figure 5.43, n–o). The orifice is slightly restricted and some examples have horizontal strap handles located approximately 3–4 cm below the rim.

4. Tall necked jar (Figure 5.43, f–g). This form is similar to Form 1 except for the great height of the neck, 10–12 cm.

Intrasite Locations and Contexts: This type is found in both the Group 1, Structure 1 (Barrio

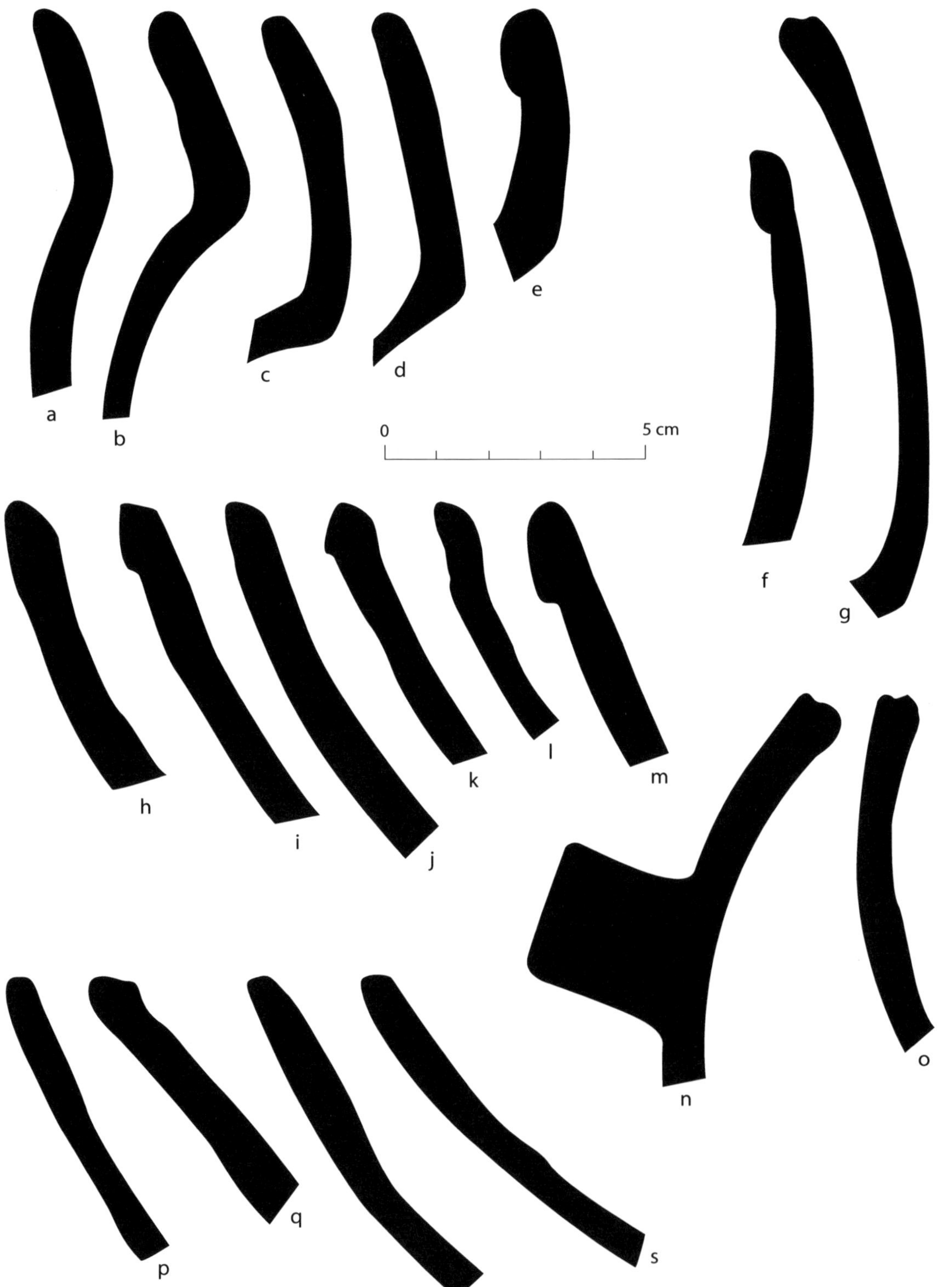

Figure 5.43. Kukula Ceramic Group profile drawings— Xcanchacan Black-on-cream: Variety Unspecified.

de Guadalupe) area and in the Pozo del Monte-Mercedes portion of Champotón. In the former it seems to be particularly concentrated in Group 1, Structure 1, A and C excavation areas, but it is relatively rare in this area in that we recovered only 228 sherds of the type. In the Pozo del Monte-Mercedes area of Champotón it was found in particularly high quantities in Group 5 (1215 sherds). As should be obvious the distribution of this type is quite uneven. While most other types of the Pabox Complex occur frequently and together in almost all excavation lots, Xcanchakan Black-on-cream occurs only in certain lots and sometimes in considerable quantities in those lots. What this means in terms of production, use, chronology or otherwise is not clear. I have not been able to conclusively demonstrate any obvious chronological differences as yet, given the lack of clear stratigraphy; Ek (2015:513), however, who has better stratigraphic evidence, has argued that it occurs in an early facet of his Complex 7 period. This would correspond with what Smith (1971) asserted for Mayapan. So a chronological difference may account for the uneven distribution of the type in our collections.

Intersite Locations and Contexts: This type is well known on the basis of material from Dzibilchaltun, Chichen Itza, and Mayapan. It apparently also occurs in numerous sites in Yucatan (see Ball 1978:117 and Ochoa 1999), as well as along the coast of Quintana Roo. Champotón, I believe, is the southernmost occurrence of it in any quantity on the Bay of Campeche. Ochoa (1999:53) suggests that it is present at Los Guarixes (Isla de Carmen) and equates Ruz's "Coarse Slate" (1969:97) with this ware. While this may indeed be the case—I have tried to locate Ruz's collection from 1949, but have been unable to do so—according to Ruz, this pottery was very rare. Its presence at Champotón makes the probability of it also being present at Los Guarixes more likely. See Ek (2015:513) for a discussion of the chronology of this pottery.

Comment: A single example of what Smith (1971:201, fig. 52s) called the sharp-incised variety was recovered from Champotón. It is essentially a Cherna Incised grater bowl that bears black trickle from the top of the lip down to the beginning of the incising. This sherd was not included in the final counts for the Champotón types.

Other Kukula Ceramic Group: Incised

Several examples of Xcanchacan Black-on-cream grater bowls occurred in the Champotón collection (Figures 5.43, p–s). These appear to be similar to what Smith (1970:135, 201; fig. 52s) called the "sharp-incised variety" of Xcanchacan. These sherds were not counted in the final counts for the Champotón types.

FINE ORANGE WARE [5846]

Matillas Ceramic Group [5846]

Matillas Orange: Matillas Variety (Figures 5.44–5.49, a–f)

Frequency: 3558 sherds (62%; 9%). The actual numbers of this variety may be fewer. The red-slipped variety was not counted separately when we analyzed the ceramics from Group 1, Structure 1 (Barrio de Guadelupe) excavations. So some of the sherds counted as the Matillas Variety almost certainly should be categorized as the red-slipped variety.

Established: Established by Smith (1971:20–21, 136, 201–202, 234–238, figs. 55–56). This type would fall into part of what Ruz (1969:128–129; figs. XXXVI/41–93; XXXVII–XXXVIII; XLII/1–2, 4–5; XLIII/1–2; XLIV/1–5, 8–18; XLV/2,7,8; XLVI/2) called "Cerámica anaranjada," including both his "mediana" and "delgada" sub-categories.

Description:

Principal Identifying Attributes: (1) fine paste; (2) orange to brown paste color; (3) orange slip, often weathered; (4) serpent head supports.

Paste, Firing, and Temper: The paste is fine. There is no temper. Firing took place in an oxidizing atmosphere that resulted in orange paste (2.5 YR 6–7/6–8; 5YR 6–7/6–8, 5YR 6/4;

Figure 5.44. Matillas Orange: Matillas Variety ceramics.

Figure 5.45. Matillas Orange: Matillas Variety vessel.

7.5YR 6–7/4; see also Smith 1971:20 for other Munsell readings). Still, a not insignificant number of vessels were either reduced in firing, or subsequent to firing, resulting in brown to dark brown paste colors (5YR 4/2; 7.5YR 4/3). This dark brown coloration is fairly unique to Matillas Ceramic Group sherds. That is, it occurs infrequently on Altar, Balancán or Silhó Ceramic Group vessels. Occasional sherds also have grayish surfaces (2.5YR 5/2). The paste is chalky, and, like most Fine Orange Ware sherds, tends to leave an orange chalk-like residue when scraped on a hard surface. Although many of these vessels were oxidized all the way through the vessel wall, and thus have an orange to pink-colored paste, many were clearly only partially oxidized, sometimes only a millimeter or two on the surface. Thus, this type often has dark cores, sometimes gray (Gley N3/), but quite frequently a deep, stark black (Gley N2.5/). This is a fairly common characteristic of the Matillas Fine Orange that is infrequent in earlier Fine Orange Ware vessels.

Surface Finish and Decoration: As indicated by Smith (1971:20) the vessel surfaces were well smoothed and generally covered with a slip made from the same clay as the paste. Surfaces were lightly polished but not to any great extent. The surfaces are matte rather than brilliant. Smith (1971:20) argued that all of these vessels were slipped an orange, red, black, or cream color; however, the examples from Champotón suggest that the brown and cream examples are not a slip in the sense that the orange and red are. The former tend to be applied only to zones or sections of the exterior of the vessels, leaving significant portions of the interior and/or exterior uncovered. Thus, they tend to be part of decorated types. The Matillas Variety at Champotón is therefore defined as having an orange-colored surface, covered with a slip made from the same clay as the vessel, and distinguishable from it only when in an excellent state of preservation. When such is the case, the slipped surfaces tend to have a slightly darker tone than the underlying paste. In many cases though, the vessels were not slipped at all, but the surfaces were polished, which brought finer clay particles to the surface. This yielded a slightly darker orange surface. The bases of most vessels, including tripod dishes, were left unslipped or unpolished. In addition, this ware tends to weather easily and most of the vessel surfaces are badly eroded. This is common in Matillas group pottery. Those examples that bear a red-firing slip, distinct from the orange-surfaced vessels, are treated as a different variety (see below). Nonetheless, given the high level of erosion, it can often be difficult to differentiate the two, in which case the sherds were classified as the Matillas Variety.

Forms:

1. Tripod dish or bowl with basal ridge (Figure 5.46). The rim is slightly thickened either interiorly or exteriorly or, commonly, both. Tripod supports are almost invariably hollow and usually serpent effigies. Sometimes human or other effigy supports occur, as, occasionally, do plain supports. The basal ridge is usually plain, but sometimes notched or crenellated. Some vessels, perhaps most, seem to have been unslipped below the basal ridge. Bases may be flat or rounded. This form corresponds in part to Ruz's (1969:122; fig. XXXVI/58–73) "Cajetes trípodes con moldura basal o lateral."

2. Tripod dish or bowl without basal ridge (Figures 5.47). These are similar to Form 1, but also include vessels with flaring walls. They also usually have similar tripod supports; compare with Ruz (1969:fig. XXVI/44, 46, 48–50).

3. Jars with extremely high outflaring necks (Figure 5.48, a–c). The height of the neck is usually as high as, or sometimes occasionally higher, than the globular part of the jar. These are characteristic and diagnostic Matillas Ceramic Group forms.

4. Round-sided bowls (Figure 5.48d). Rims are generally rounded. Although some examples are unrestricted, others have rims that curve inwards slightly, making the rim slightly restricted.

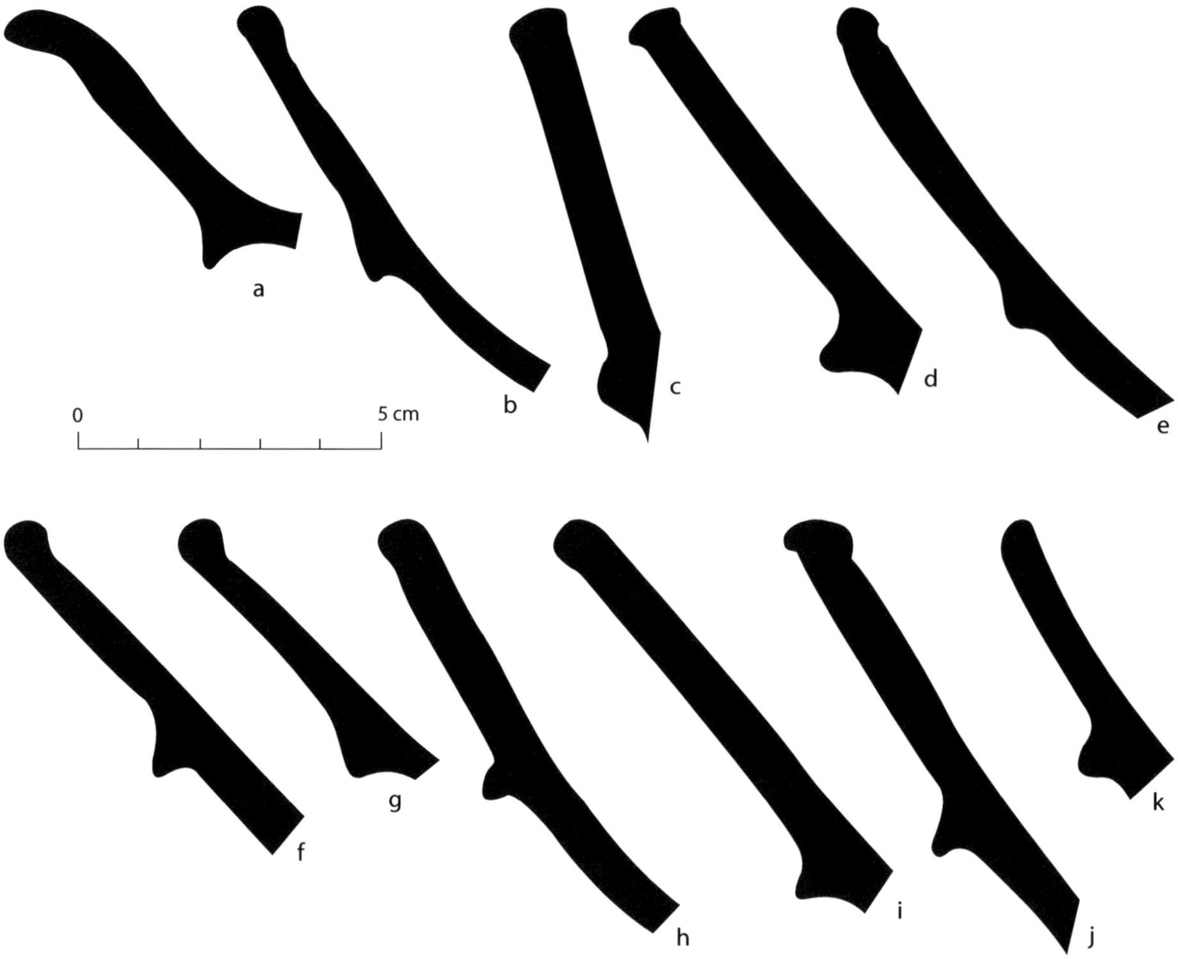

Figure 5.46. Matillas Ceramic Group profile drawings—Matillas Orange: Matillas Variety.

5. Bowls or jar with rounded sides and pedestal base (no illustration). The exact form is unknown, but examples of the pedestal bases and portions of the vessel bottom occur.

6. Miscellaneous forms (Figure 5.48, e–g).

Intrasite Locations and Contexts: Matillas Orange materials were found in many deposits recovered from Champotón, with pure deposits in a number of operations. It was recovered in unmixed deposits in the Pozo del Monte-Mercedes barrios of Champotón, along with other materials of the Pabox complex, but it also occurs in some quantity in Group 1, Structure 1 (Barrio de Guadalupe) in structural fill, and other contexts. This is a very common type at Champotón, and the Matillas Ceramic Group constitutes the primary serving ware at the site, exceeding in quantity the red-slipped pottery.

Intersite Locations and Contexts: Matillas Orange (and the Matillas Ceramic Group) is a well-known class of pottery that is frequently used as a marker for the Late Postclassic. It was probably manufactured somewhere in the lower Usumacinta drainage and probably in more than one location, but its exact provenience is not known (Bishop et al. 2006:139). It was first defined formally at Mayapan (Smith 1971) but is a rare import at that site (Smith 1971:237,

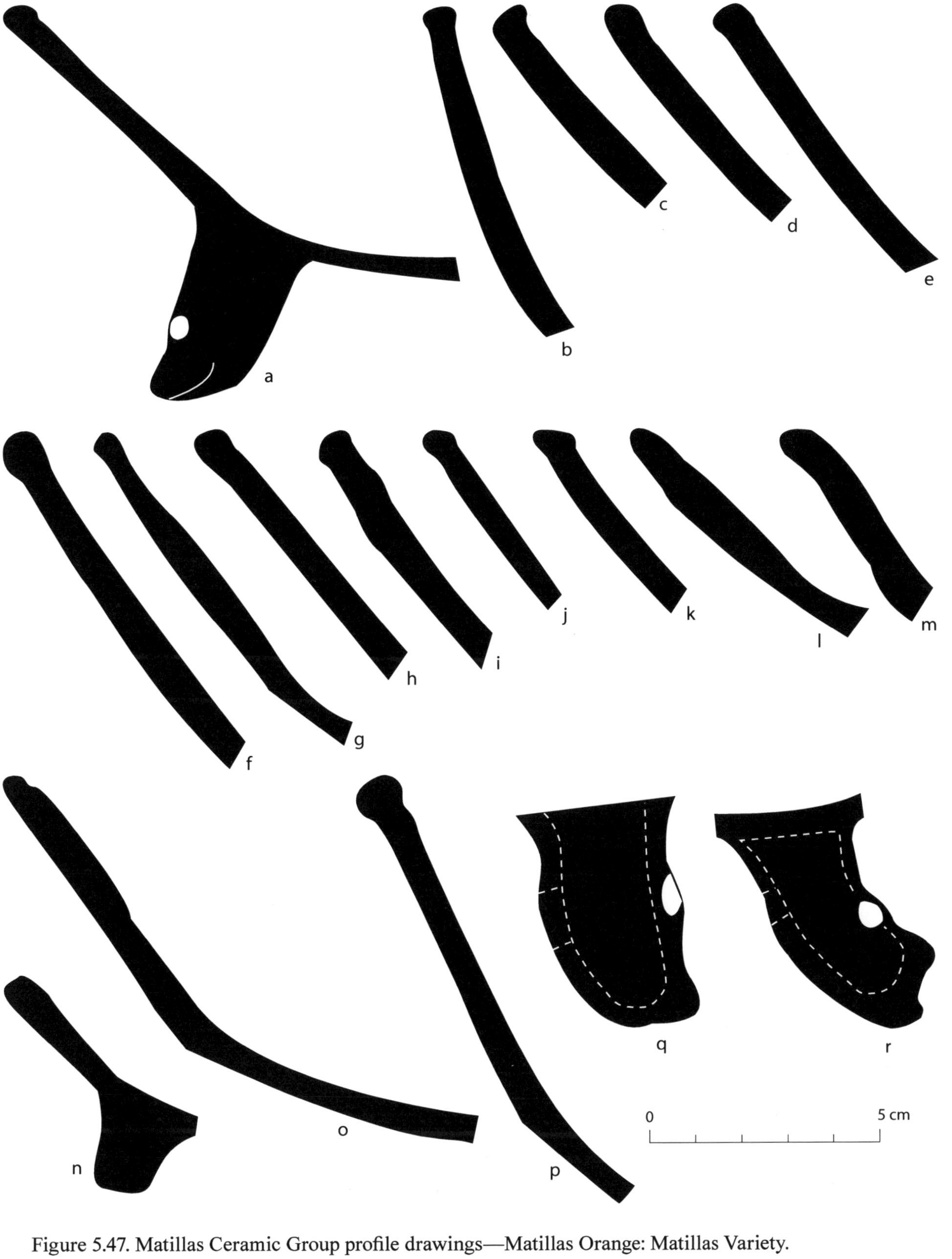

Figure 5.47. Matillas Ceramic Group profile drawings—Matillas Orange: Matillas Variety.

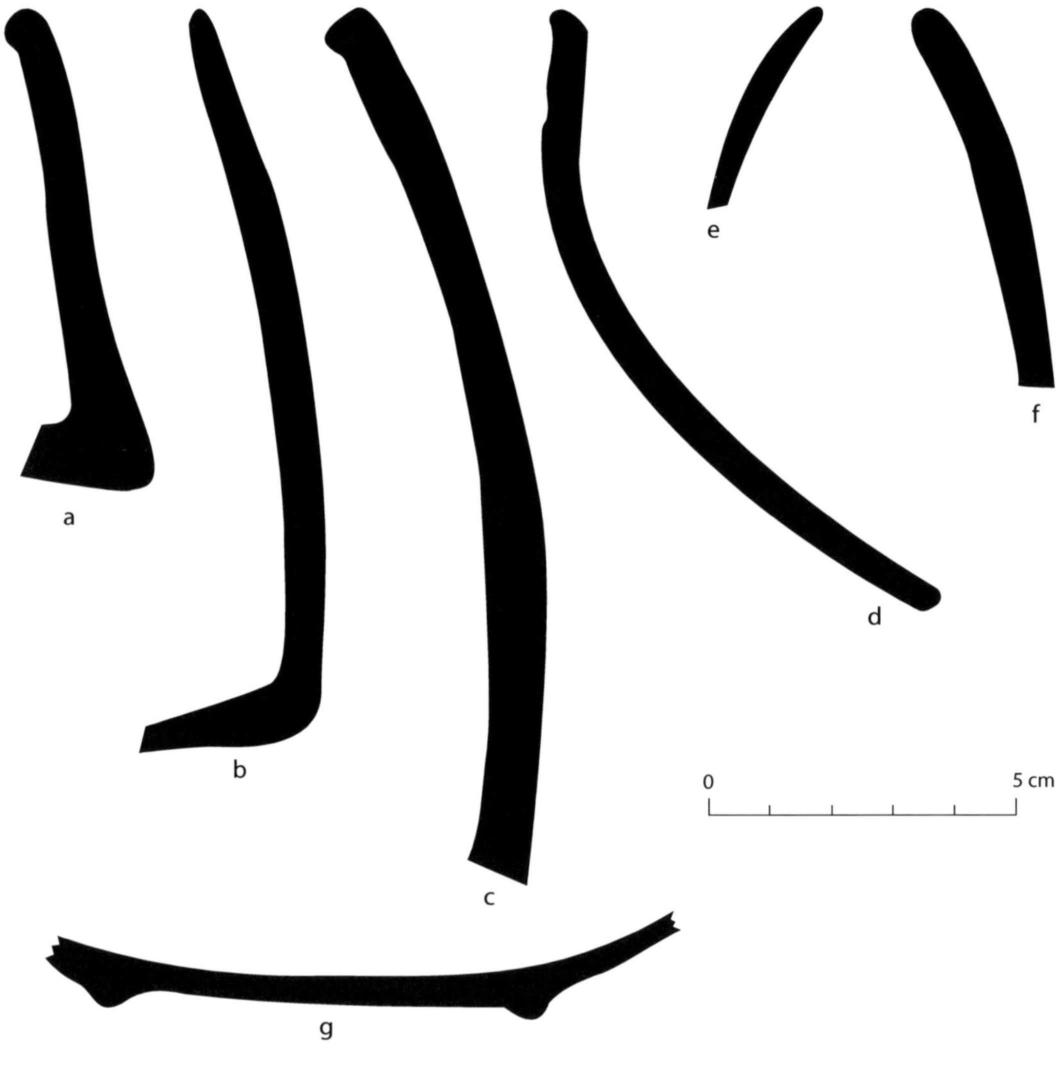

Figure 5.48. Matillas Ceramic Group profile drawings—Matillas Orange: Matillas Variety.

243–244), making up about 0.3 percent of the ceramic total at Mayapan. Similarly, extremely small amounts of Matillas Orange and other members of the ceramic group are found widely throughout the Maya Lowlands, indicating that it was a widespread, but limited trade ware. It occurs as such in numerous sites in Yucatan and Quintana Roo. It also occurs in small quantities in the Central Lakes region of the Peten (personal observation). It has been reported in large quantities, however, only from Champotón (Ruz 1969:128–129), Tixchel (Ruz 1969:109–111; fig. XXXIV/50–77), Aguacatal (Matheny 1970:93–98), and apparently at El Tigre (Delgado 2002; Piña Chán 2003:332). See Ball (1978:91) for other sites. Many other sites have also reported small amounts of this pottery, such as Xcambo (Jiménez 2002:300). Ek (2015:503, 509–510) discusses Matillas pottery from sites in the Champotón region.

Comment: Despite its function as a horizon marker, the Matillas group is poorly known and understood in its area of manufacture. Almost no full ceramic complexes in which Matillas group pottery formed a major element have been described or defined. Champotón is the first such occurrence. Aguacatal (Matheny 1970) yielded a considerable amount of the material, but the Plantación Complex at that site is probably not a full complex in the sense defined by Adams (1973:133–135). See Bishop et al. (2006:141) for a discussion of the source area for the Matillas Ceramic Group materials.

Matillas Orange: Red-slipped Variety (Figure 5.49–5.52)

Frequency: 1094 sherds (19%; 3%). The actual numbers of this variety may be greater, as the red-slipped variety was not counted separately when we analyzed the ceramics from Group 1, Structure 1 (Barrio de Guadelupe) excavations. So some of the sherds counted as the Matillas Variety almost certainly should be categorized as the red-slipped variety.

Established: Type established by Smith (1971:20–21, 136, 201–202, 234–238, figs. 55–56). Smith did not distinguish what I am calling the red-slipped variety because he argued that all Matillas Orange vessels were always slipped with either an orange, red, black, or cream slip (Smith 1971:20). In the Champotón collection, however, the Red-slipped Variety was rather common and obviously different from the Matillas Variety (see above). Black or cream slips, or paints, were extremely rare, and usually occurred only when other forms of decoration were present. This was particularly so in the excavations from the Pozo del Monte-Mercedes excavations carried out during the 2003 field season. Much of the Matillas pottery from Group 1, Structure 1 (Barrio de Guadalupe), as well as other Postclassic types, was badly weathered, and the difference was not stark or obvious. Like the Matillas variety, this variety would fall into part of what Ruz (1969:128–129; figs. XXXVI/41–93; XXXVII–XXXVIII; XLII/1–2, 4–5; XLIII/1–2; XLIV/1–5, 8–18; XLV/2, 7, 8; XLVI/2) called "Cerámica anaranjada," including both his "mediana" and "delgada" sub-categories.

Description:

Principal Identifying Attributes: (1) fine paste; (2) orange to brown paste color; (3) red slip; (4) serpent head supports.

Paste, Firing, and Temper: Same as Matillas Orange: Matillas Variety.

Surface Finish and Decoration: Same as the Matillas Variety with the exception that a red-firing, rather than an orange, slip was applied to the surface of the vessels. This slip contrasts with the orange paste underneath. The slip tends to be matte but does reach a slight polish sometimes. Slip color varies from light red to red (7.5R 4–4.5/6–8, 5–5.5/6–8; 10R 4/6–8). The slip tended to be applied on surfaces on unrestricted vessels, and on the exterior, and sometimes the interior neck, of restricted vessels; but on dish and bowl forms the lower portion of the exterior was often unslipped, particularly near, at, or below the exterior basal ridge.

Forms:

1. Tripod dish or bowl with basal ridge (Figure 5.51, c–e). The rim is slightly thickened either interiorly or exteriorly or, commonly, both. Tripod supports are almost invariably hollow and typically serpent effigies. Sometimes human or other effigy supports occur, as, occasionally, do plain supports. The basal ridge is usually plain but sometimes notched or crenellated. Some vessels, perhaps most, seem to have been unslipped below the basal ridge. Bases may be flat or rounded. This form corresponds in part to Ruz's (1969:122; fig. XXXVI/58–73) "Cajetes trípodes con moldura basal o lateral."
2. Tripod dish or bowl without basal ridge (Figures 5.51, a–b, f–g). These are similar to Form 1 but also include vessels with flaring walls. They also usually have similar tripod supports; compare with Ruz (1969:fig. XXVI/44, 46, 48–50).
3. Small to medium round-sided bowls (Figure 5.51, h–l). Rims are generally rounded. Although some examples are unrestricted, others have rims that curve inwards slightly, making the rim slightly restricted.

Figure 5.49. Matillas Orange ceramics: a–f. Matillas Variety; g–h. Red-slipped Variety.

Figure 5.50. Matillas Orange: Red-slipped Variety ceramics.

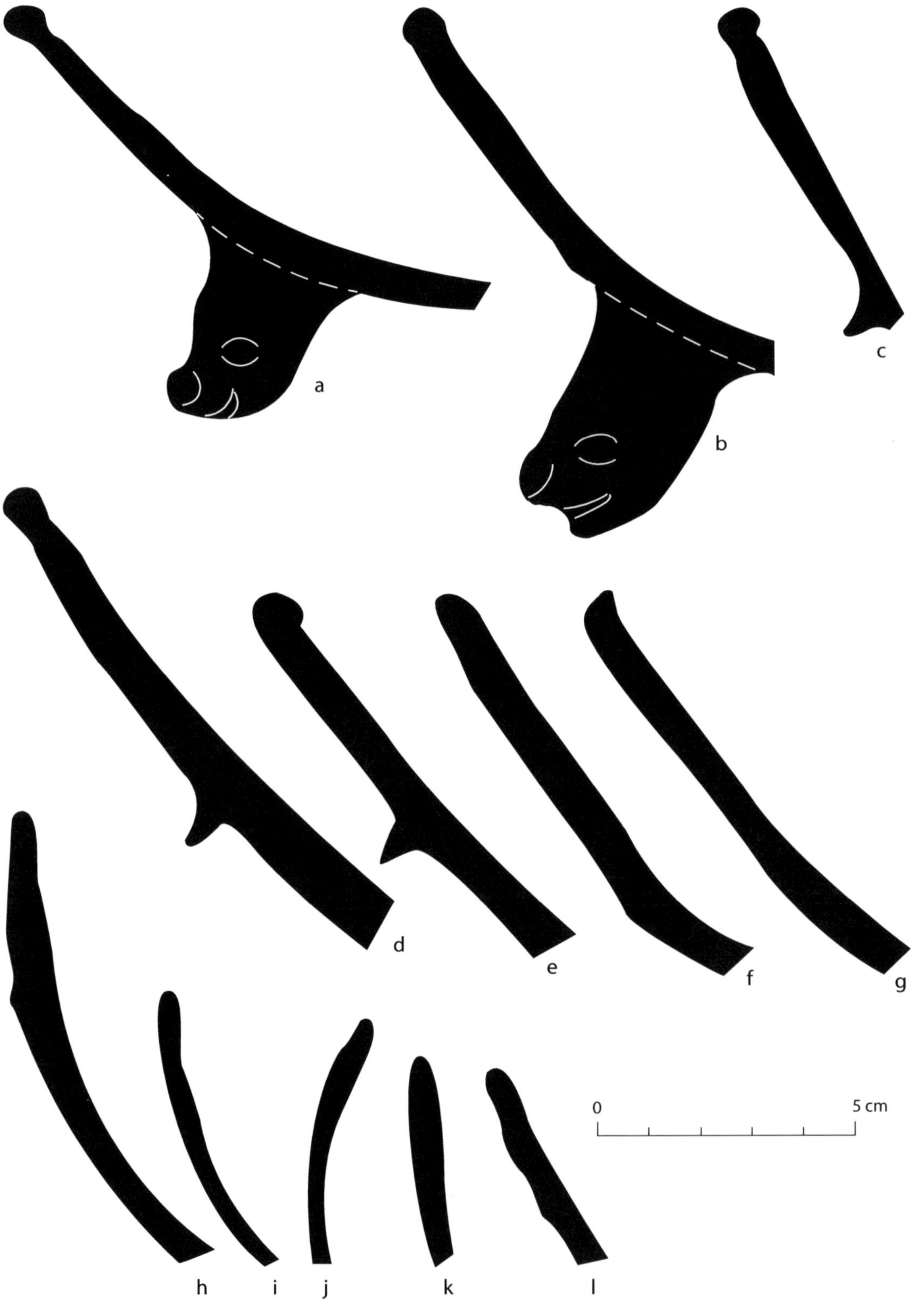

Figure 5.51. Matillas Ceramic Group profile drawings—Matillas Orange: Red-slipped Variety.

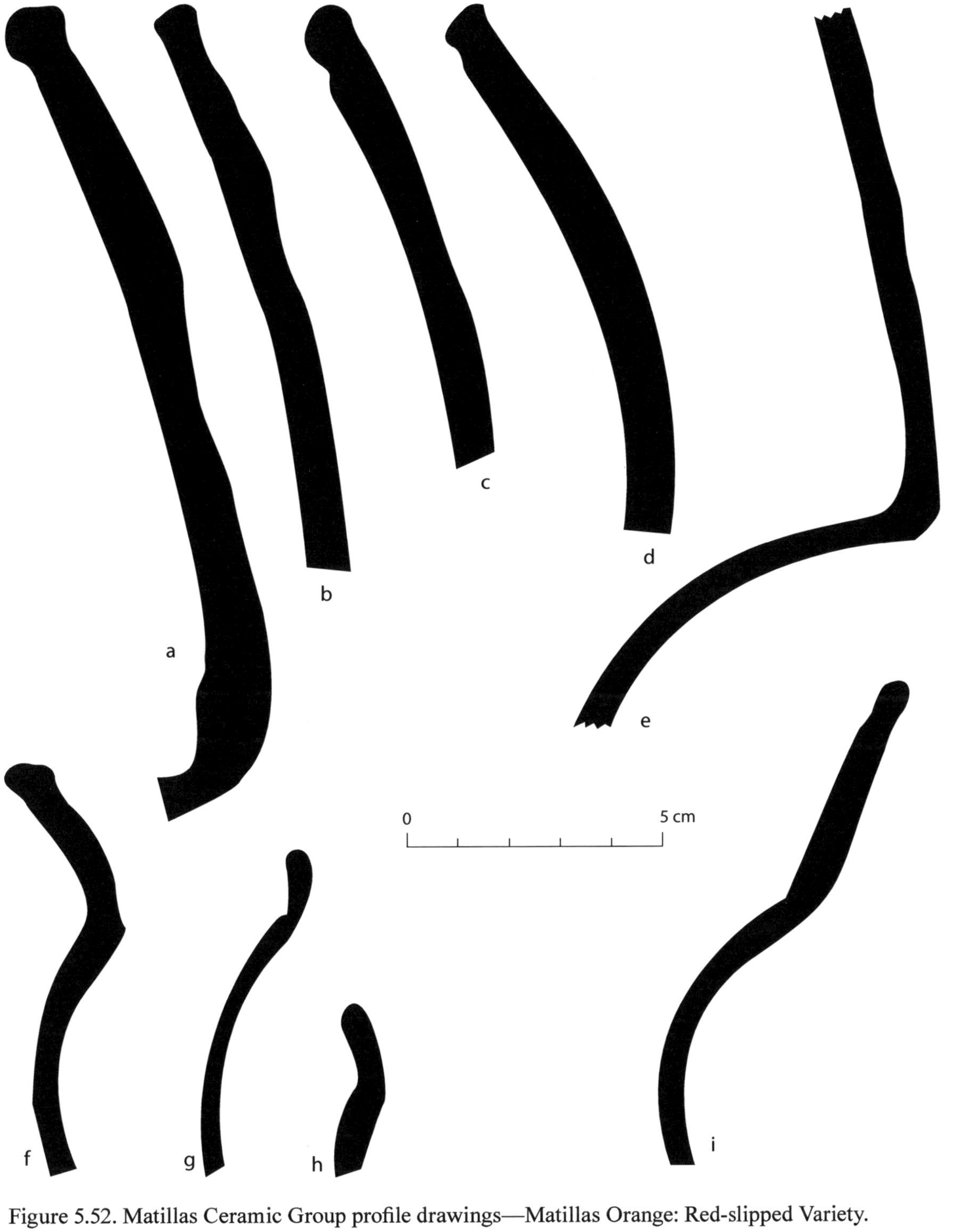

Figure 5.52. Matillas Ceramic Group profile drawings—Matillas Orange: Red-slipped Variety.

4. Jars with extremely high outflaring necks (Figure 5.52, a–e). The height of the neck is usually as high as, or sometimes occasionally higher than, the globular part of the jar. These are characteristic and diagnostic Matillas Ceramic Group forms.
5. Short-necked jars (Figure 5.52, f–h). These are generally medium to small-sized.
6. Inslanted-neck jars (Figure 5.52i). This form is rare.

Intrasite Locations and Contexts: Same as Matillas Variety.

Intersite Locations and Contexts: See Matillas Variety discussion. I have separated out the Red-slipped Variety from the more general Matillas Variety. Presumably, the Red-slipped Variety is also found at sites where Matillas Orange has been identified.

Villahermosa Incised: Villahermosa Variety (Figures 5.53–5.55)

Frequency: 418 sherds (7%; 1%)

Established: Type established by Smith (1971:20–21, 136, 201–202, 235–238, fig. 55b2, 4, 7–11). This type falls into part of what Ruz (1969:128–129) called "Cerámica anaranjada," including both his "mediana" and "delgada" sub-categories. For examples of Villahermosa Incised, see Ruz (1969:XXXVII 1–6; also see fig. XXXVI, 77–93) for examples of incising on the basal ridge. Not all of these examples are necessarily Villahermosa Incised, however.

Description:

Principal Identifying Attributes: (1) fine paste; (2) orange to brown paste color; (3) orange or red slip, often weathered; (4) fine to medium-line incision (5) serpent head supports.

Paste, Firing, and Temper: Same as Matillas Orange: Matillas Variety.

Surface Finish and Decoration: The surface finish is the same as Matillas Orange with the exception that this type bears incisions on the exterior and/or interior of vessels. Both orange and red-slipped vessels are included in this type (see Comment section below). The incision was usually fine to medium-line and executed postslip, but pre-fired. Smith (1971:82) says that the incisions at Mayapan were preslip, although the Champotón examples are postslip. The vast majority of examples consist of rather simple, formalistic designs—chevrons formed by parallel lines, often with a central incised circle, straight parallel lines, hooked lines and rectangles, also sometimes with incised circles in the middle. More complex hatched and diamond-shaped designs also occur but are rare and found mostly on jars or other restricted forms. On tripod dishes and bowls the placement of the incision is highly predictable; it is located on the upper portion of the exterior vessel above the basal ridge or on the upper half of the interior of the vessel or both. When found on both the interior and exterior, there is usually some difference between the designs on the two sides. Sometimes, however, the only incision on the vessel is found on the outer surface of the basal ridge itself and nowhere else on the vessel. Oftimes there are from one to three parallel circumferential lines beginning near the rim of the vessel below which is the main design; but this is not invariable. Most incisions are only lightly cut into the paste, but in a few cases they are deeper and wider. The interior base of unrestricted vessels only rarely received incision. There are some curvilinear designs, like interlocking scrolls, circles with interior dots, etc. There are a few examples, however, that have only one to three circumferential lines, generally on the exterior. A few pieces exhibit groove-incising, but this is rare. Restricted bowl forms bear incised designs on the uppermost portion of the exterior, while the very tall-necked jars tend to have one or two circumferential lines on the globular body 2–3 cm down from the neck-body juncture.

Forms:

1. Tripod dish or bowl with basal ridge (Figure 5.54, a–i). The rim is slightly thickened either interiorly or exteriorly or, commonly, both. Tripod supports are almost invariably hollow and

Figure 5.53. Villahermosa Incised: Villahermosa Variety ceramics.

usually serpent effigies. Sometimes human or other effigy supports occur, as, occasionally, do plain supports. The basal ridge is usually plain but sometimes notched or crenellated; however, in this type, the upper portion of the ridge is often, though not invariably, incised. Some examples bear incising only in this area. Some vessels, perhaps most, seem to have been unslipped below the basal ridge. Bases may be flat or rounded. This form corresponds in part to Ruz's (1969:122; fig. XXXVI/58–73) "Cajetes trípodes con moldura basal o lateral." This is an extremely common form for almost all of the Matillas Group types. It is by far the most dominant one in Villahermosa Incised.

2. Tripod dish or bowl without basal ridge (Figures 5.54, j–l). These are similar to Form 1 but also include vessels with flaring walls. They also usually have similar tripod supports; compare with Ruz (1969:fig. XXVI/44, 46, 48–50).
3. Jars with extremely high outflaring necks (Figure 5.55, a–b). The height of the neck is usually as high as, or sometimes occasionally higher than, the globular part of the jar. These are characteristic and diagnostic Matillas Ceramic Group forms. This form is rare in Villahermosa Incised.
4. Small round-sided bowls with slightly restricted necks (Figures 5.55, c–e). Rims are generally rounded. Although some examples are unrestricted, others have rims that curve inwards slightly, making the rim slightly restricted.
5. Short-necked jars (Figure 5.55, f–g). These are generally medium- to small-sized.

Intrasite Locations and Contexts: Same as Matillas Orange.

Intersite Locations and Contexts: Same as Matillas Orange.

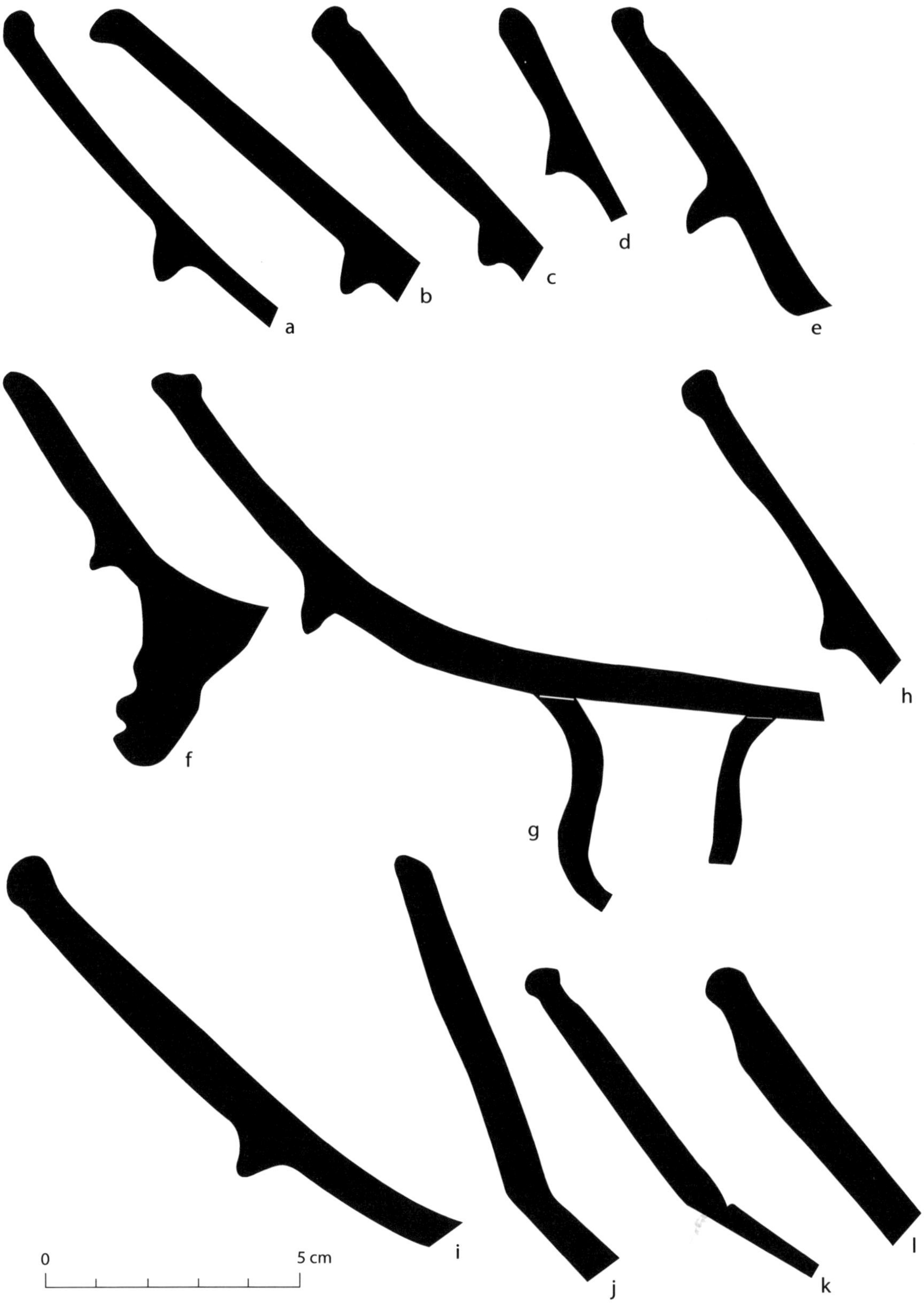

Figure 5.54. Matillas Ceramic Group profile drawings—Villahermosa Incised: Villahermosa Variety.

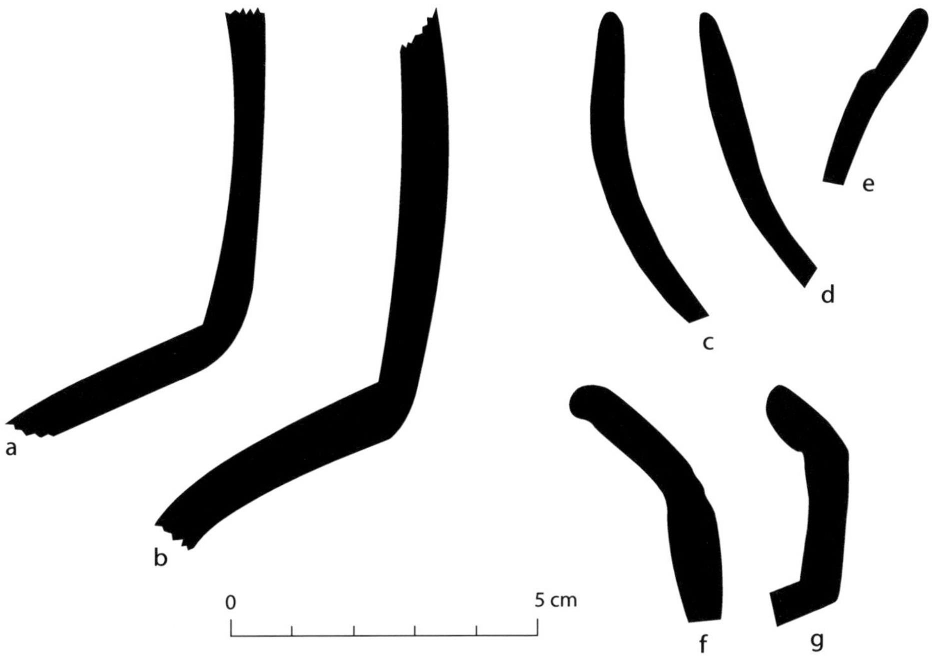

Figure 5.55. Matillas Ceramic Group profile drawings—Villahermosa Incised: Villahermosa Variety.

Comment: This type could reasonably be divided into two varieties on the basis of slip color in that some examples seem to have an orange slip (or perhaps just a degree of polishing that produces a slip-like finish), while others were slipped red. I have not chosen to make this distinction here, but it would certainly be consistent with the separation made in Matillas Orange.

Nacajuca Black-on-orange: Nacajuca Variety (Figure 5.56, a–g)

Frequency: 190 sherds (3%; <1%)

Established: Type established by Smith (1971:20–21, 136, 201–202, 235–238, fig. 55d1–3, 5–6). This type falls into part of what Ruz (1969:128–129) called "Cerámica anaranjada," including both his "mediana" and "delgada" sub-categories. For examples of Nacajuca Black-on-orange, see Ruz (1969:XXXVIII 1, 4-5, 10-11; XXXIX 1).

Description:

Principal Identifying Attributes: (1) fine paste; (2) orange to brown paste color; (3) orange or red slip, often weathered; (4) black-painted lines and designs on orange background.

Paste, Firing, and Temper: Same as Matillas Orange: Matillas Variety.

Surface Finish and Decoration: The surface finish is the same as Matillas Orange except for the addition of paint to the surface of the vessel in black to brown paint (2.5YR 2.5/0–2; 2.5YR 4–5/2). The most common form of decoration is from one to a spaced series of circumferential lines running horizontally around the vessel (see Smith 1971:fig. 55d3 and Ruz 1969:fig. XXVIII 1–3 for examples). Sometimes vertical and/or diagonal lines were added as well (see Smith 1971:fig. 55d1–2, 6, and Ruz 1969:fig. XXVIII 4, 10–11 for examples). The width of these lines vary from 1–8 mm, depending on the vessel. More complex designs also sometimes occur (see Ruz 1969:XXXIX 1–2).

Forms:

1. Tripod dish or bowl with basal ridge (Figure 5.56, a–b). The rim is slightly thickened either interiorly or exteriorly or, commonly, both. Tripod supports are

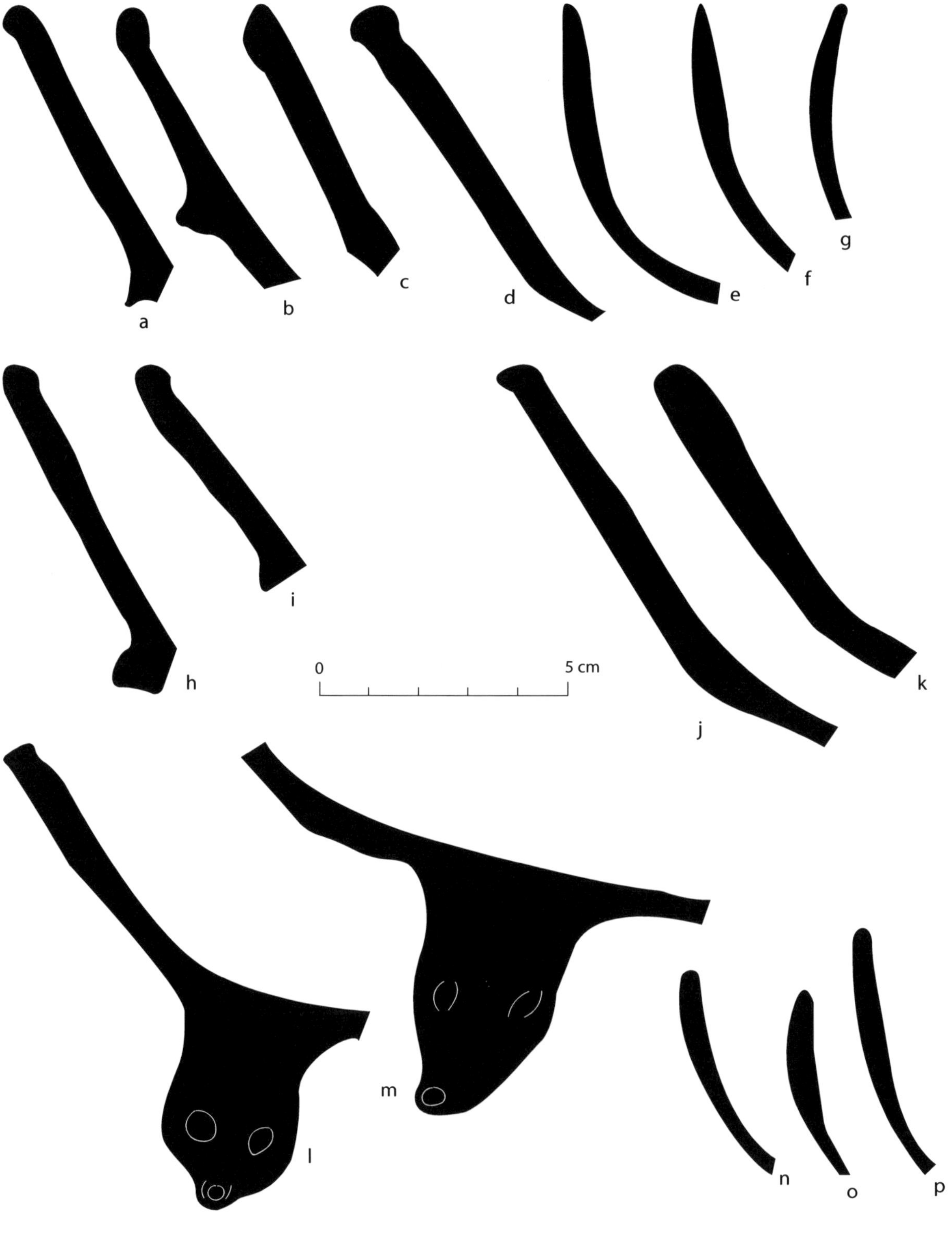

Figure 5.56. Matillas Ceramic Group profile drawing—a–g. Nacajuca Black-on-orange: Nacajuca Variety; h–p. Sayula Polychrome: Sayula Variety.

almost invariably hollow and usually serpent effigies.

2. Tripod dish or bowl without basal ridge (Figure 5.56, c–d). These are similar to Form 1 but also include vessels with flaring walls. They also usually have similar tripod supports.
3. Small round-sided bowls (Figure 5.56, e–g). Rims are generally rounded. Although some examples are unrestricted, others have rims that curve inwards slightly, making the rim slightly restricted.

Intrasite Locations and Contexts: Same as Matillas Orange.

Intersite Locations and Contexts: Same as Matillas Orange.

Sayula Polychrome: Sayula Variety (Figure 5.56, h–p)

Frequency: 162 sherds (3%; <1%)

Established: Type established by Smith (1971:20–21, 136, 201–202, 235–238, fig. 55d4). This type falls into part of what Ruz (1969:128–129) called "Cerámica anaranjada," including both his "mediana" and "delgada" sub-categories. For examples of Sayula Polychrome, see Ruz (1969:XXXVIII 14, 17–18), although some of the others illustrated may also fall into this category.

Description:

Principal Identifying Attributes: (1) fine paste; (2) orange to brown paste color; (3) orange or red slip, often weathered; (4) zoned polychromy on vessel surface(s).

Paste, Firing, and Temper: Same as Matillas Orange: Matillas Variety.

Surface Finish and Decoration: The surface finish is the same as Matillas Orange except for the addition of paint to the surface of the vessel in two or more colors. The polychrome effect on Sayula is quite different from that associated with Classic period types. It is actually zoned trichromy. That is, the different colors are not placed to form an integrated design but are placed in bands and blocks to contrast with other colors. The major pattern is vertical, with a series of horizontal bands that contrast in color running around the vessel. A good example of this can be seen in Smith (1971:fig. 55d4). The major colors are red, white, black, and orange, the latter being the underlying color of the vessel. Another pattern is horizontal—a series of alternating panels or blocks of different colors that encircle the vessel (e.g., red alternating with black and/or orange (see Smith 1971:fig. 55b1 for an illustration of this effect). On some examples, however, simple designs in red and black or black and white alternate in this way (see Ruz 1969:fig. XXXVIII 17–18). In others, the designs are vertically banded (see Ruz 1969:fig. XXXVIII 14–16, 19), but nevertheless, create a design in one color on a background of a different color. The vessels with simple designs are far less common than those with zoned areas of color, which contrast with the adjacent zones, whether running vertically or horizontally. The red color tends to be a strong, thick layer that sometimes attains a light sheen, although this is not common. It is the same color as the Red-slipped Variety slip (7.5R 4–4.5/6–8, 5–5.5/6–8; 10R 4/6–8). The black and white colors, on the other hand, are often matte. The white paint is usually a weak white but sometimes can be a strong, adherent white (Gley N 9/). The black color varies considerably (2.5YR 2.5/0–2) and is often actually a dark brown color (2.5YR 4–5/2). All tend to weather readily.

Forms:

1. Tripod dish or bowl with basal ridge (Figure 5.56, h–i). The rim is slightly thickened either interiorly or exteriorly or, commonly, both. Tripod supports are almost invariably hollow and usually serpent effigies. Sometimes human or other effigy supports occur, as, occasionally, do plain supports. The basal ridge is usually plain but sometimes notched or crenellated. Some vessels, perhaps most, seem to have been unslipped below the basal ridge. Bases may be flat or rounded. This form corresponds in part to Ruz's (1969:122;

fig. XXXVI/58–73) "Cajetes trípodes con moldura basal o lateral."

2. Tripod dish or bowl without basal ridge (Figure 5.56, j–m). These are similar to Form 1 but also include vessels with flaring walls. They also usually have similar tripod supports; compare with Ruz (1969:fig. XXVI/44, 46, 48–50).
3. Small round-sided bowls (Figure 5.56, n–p). Rims are generally rounded. Although some examples are unrestricted, others have rims that curve inwards slightly, making the rim slightly restricted.

Intrasite Locations and Contexts: Same as Matillas Orange.

Intersite Locations and Contexts: Same as Matillas Orange.

Chilapa Gouged-incised: Chilapa Variety (Figure 5.57)

Frequency: 146 sherds (2%; <1%)

Established: Type established by Smith (1971:20–21, 136, 201–202, 235–238, figs. 55c2–4, 7–8, 11–12, 14, 18–19). This type falls into part of what Ruz (1969:128–129) called "Cerámica anaranjada," including both his "mediana" and "delgada" sub-categories. For examples of Chilapa Gouged-incised, see Ruz (1969:XXXVII 11, 13, 17–20, 22; XLII 5), although some of the others illustrated may also fall into this category.

Description:

Principal Identifying Attributes: (1) fine paste; (2) orange to brown paste color; (3) orange or red slip, often weathered; (4) fine to medium-line incision combined with gouge-incision.

Paste, Firing, and Temper: Same as Matillas Orange: Matillas Variety.

Surface Finish and Decoration: The surface finish is the same as Matillas Orange with the exception of the incised decoration on part of the surface. Chilapa differs from Villahermosa Incised in three significant ways. One is that the fine to medium-line incisions are combined into a single overall design with areas that are gouge-incised away from the background to give a more three dimensional appearance to the design. Most incisions are still, in fact, of the fine to medium variety (i.e., like Villahermosa Incised), although small areas of the vessel surface were cut away to emphasize the outline of the design. The gouge-incised areas are small and cover a very small portion of the vessel surface. They usually have the effect of outlining an incised element, such as a circle or emphasizes the corners of a rectangle. One can see this cut-away effect in Smith (1971:fig. 55c12, 14). In some respects, it is a less well-executed development out of the use of cutting away the background as seen in Provincia Plano-relief in earlier times. The second way in which it differs from Villahermosa Incised is that the designs are generally more complex and better integrated. Villahermosa designs seem simple and not particularly well executed in many cases, although this is not true for all. Chilapa designs, on the other hand, tend to take up more of the vessel surface and have more sophisticated design schemes. The exception to this generalization is noted below. The third way in which Chilapa differs from Villahermosa is with respect to vessel form. In Villahermosa Incised, the most common vessel form is the tripod dish or bowl with basal ridge, which bears relatively simple designs. This form is rare in the Chilapa Gouged-incised type. Instead, variants of round-sided, thin-walled bowls, unrestricted or slightly restricted, are much more common in the latter. This is not an absolute distinction, as the same forms can be found in both types, but there is a noticeable statistical difference. Perhaps for this reason, Chilapa seems to have more complex designs. These more complex and integrated designs tend to occur on thin-walled bowls to a much greater extent than on the basal-ridge tripod bowls. For this reason, examples of Villahermosa thin-walled bowls also tend to have more complex design patterns. In other words, they resemble Chilapa in this respect more than do Villahermosa basal-ridge tripod bowls.

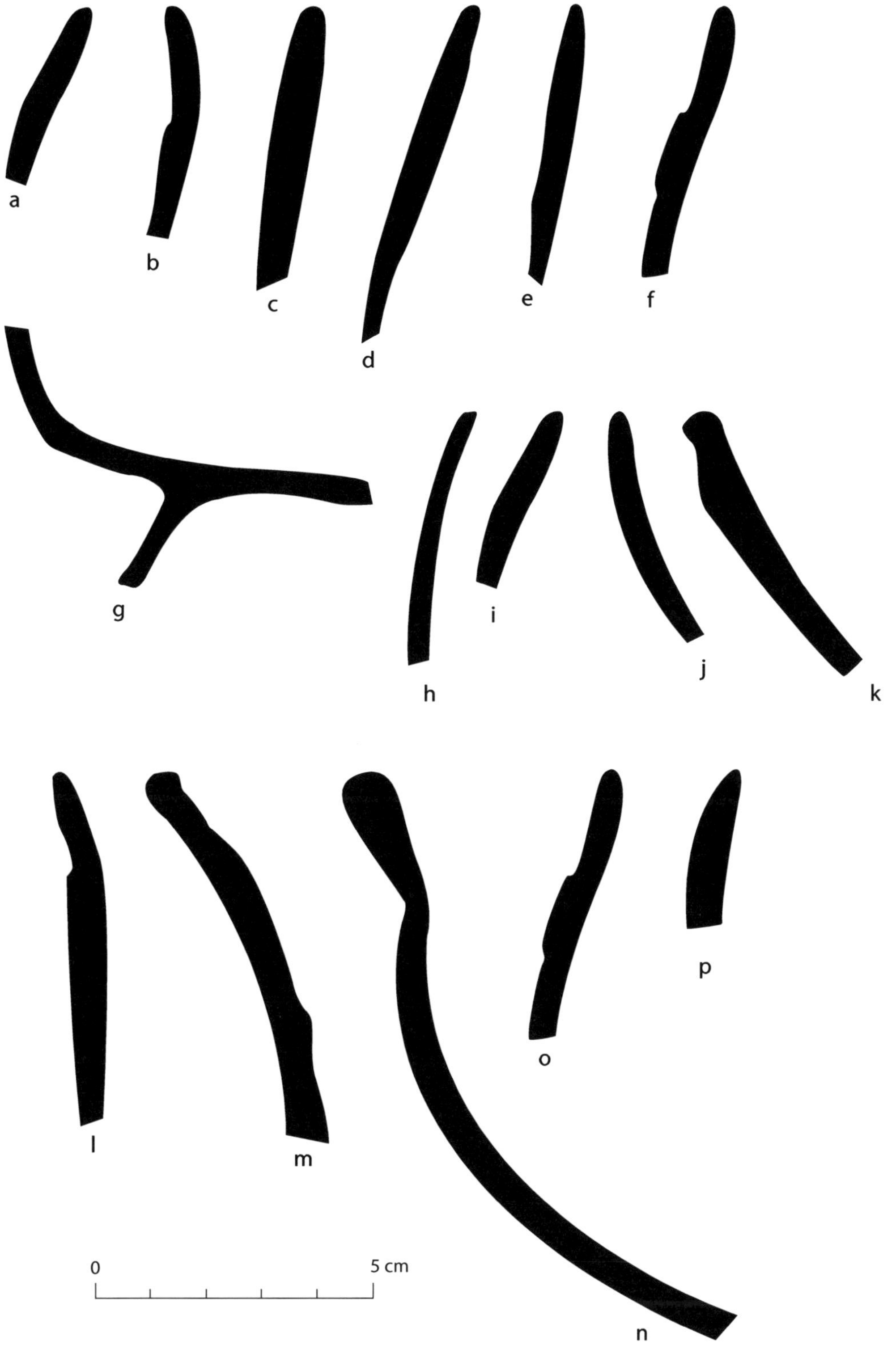

Figure 5.57. Matillas Ceramic Group profile drawings—Chilapa Gouged-incised: Chilapa Variety.

Designs are overwhelmingly geometric and consist of circles or ellipses, often with other circles or ellipses inside of them, braided elements, rectangles, T-shaped elements, and others.

Forms:

1. Small round-sided bowls with unrestricted or slightly restricted necks (Figure 5.57, h–k). Rims are generally rounded. Although some examples are unrestricted, others have rims that curve inwards slightly, making the rim slightly restricted; compare with Smith (1971:fig. 55c14, 16, 19) and Ruz (1969:fig. XXXVIII 14–19). The examples in Ruz are not Chilapa Gouged-incised but are of the same form as this.

2. Deep, thin-walled bowl with restricted orifice (Figure 5.57, a–g). These are similar to Form 1 but are deeper and often bear a pedestal base. They also usually have similar tripod supports; compare with Smith (1971:fig. 55c5, 7, 9, 11 for the shape).

3. Miscellaneous forms (Figure 5.57, l–p).

Intrasite Locations and Contexts: Same as Matillas Orange.

Intersite Locations and Contexts: Same as Matillas Orange.

Salto Composite: Salto Variety (Figures 5.58–5.59)

Frequency: 158 sherds (3%; <1%)

Established: Type established by Smith (1971:20–21, 136, 201–202, 235–238, fig. 55clm, 5m, 6m, 9–10, 13, 15–17). This type falls into part of what Ruz (1969:128–129) calls "Cerámica anaranjada," including both his "mediana" and "delgada" sub-categories. For examples of Salto Composite, see Ruz (1969:XXXVII 17–20), although some of the others illustrated may also fall into this category.

Description:

Principal Identifying Attributes: (1) fine paste; (2) orange to brown paste color; (3) orange or red slip, often weathered; (4) zoned polychromy on vessel surface(s); (5) incised and gouge-incised designs.

Paste, Firing, and Temper: Same as Matillas Orange: Matillas Variety.

Surface Finish and Decoration: The surface finish is the same as Matillas Orange except for the addition of paint to the surface of the vessel in two or more colors combined with regular Villahermosa-like incision and gouge-incision. In this respect Salto Composite is a combination of the decorative techniques found on Sayula Polychrome and Chilapa Gouged-incised. So, the description of the surface finish of those two types apply to this type, since they are combined together in this type. As with the Chilapa and Villahermosa types, the incised designs are often found on the upper portion of the interior, particularly on tripod bowls. They can also sometimes be found on the interior bottom of such vessels, as well as on exterior vessel walls.

Forms:

1. Tripod dish or bowl with basal ridge (Figures 5.58, a-g). The rim is slightly thickened either interiorly or exteriorly or, commonly, both. Tripod supports are almost invariably hollow and usually serpent effigies.

2. Tripod dish or bowl without basal ridge (Figure 5.59, a–j. These are similar to Form 1 but also include vessels with flaring walls. They also usually have similar tripod supports.

3. Small round-sided bowls (Figure 5.58, h–l). Rims are generally rounded. Although some examples are unrestricted, most have rims that curve inwards slightly, making the rim slightly restricted.

4. Miscellaneous forms (Figure 5.59, k–l).

Intrasite Locations and Contexts: Same as Matillas Orange.

Intersite Locations and Contexts: Same as Matillas Orange.

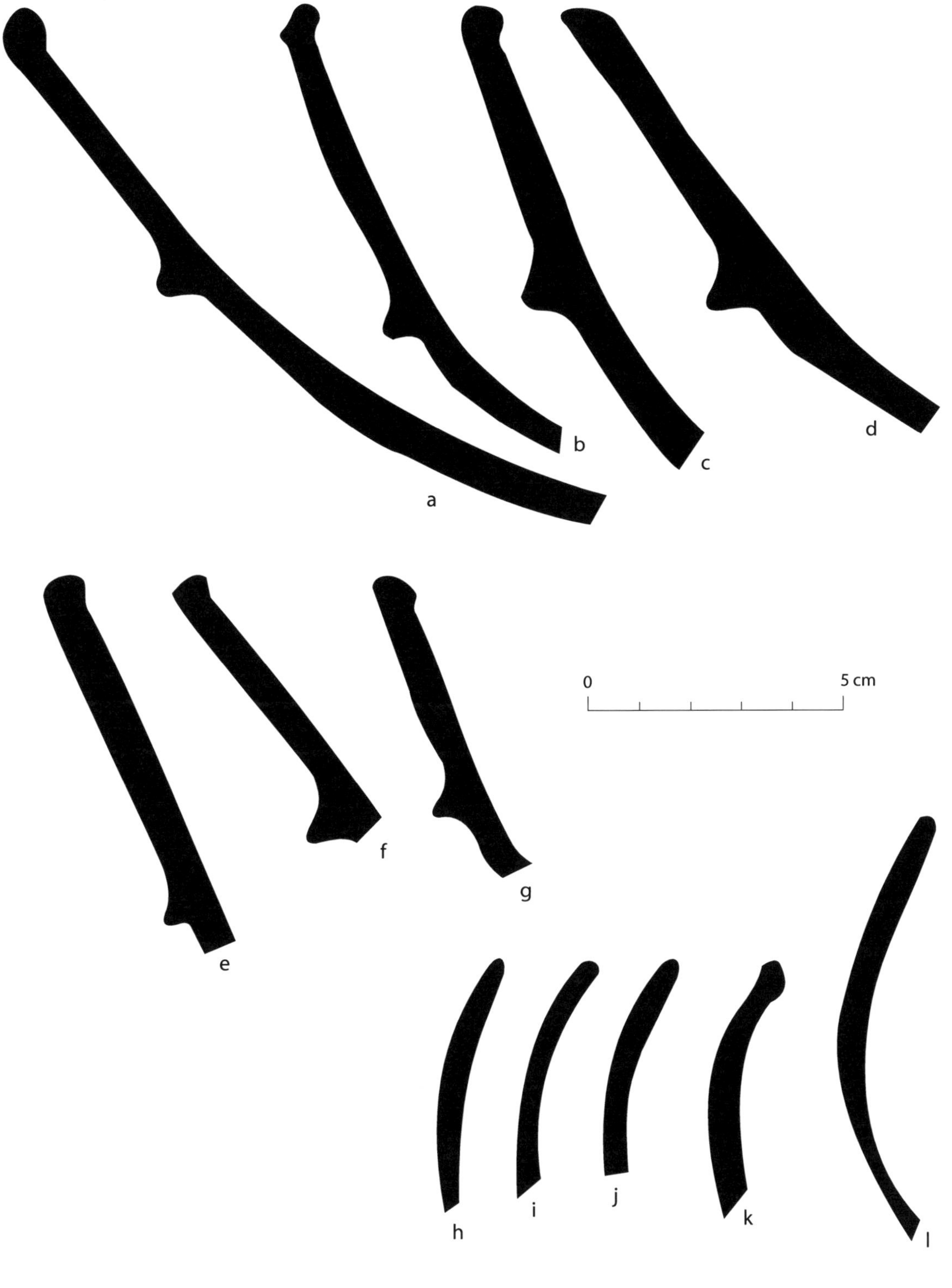

Figure 5.58. Matillas Ceramic Group profile drawings—Salto Composite: Salto Variety.

Figure 5.59. Matillas Ceramic Group profile drawings—Salto Composite: Salto Variety.

Figure 5.60. Grijalva Incised-polychrome: Grijalva Variety ceramics.

Comment: I have treated only those sherds, which have both gouge-incision and regular incision combined with dichromy or polychromy as members of Salto Composite. Judging from Smith's (1971:236; fig. 55b3, 5-6) treatment of this type, he apparently included in it examples of plain incision when it occurred on a black or white surface. This is not altogether clear, however. Unfortunately, Smith did not provide type descriptions of his named categories in anything like the normal manner. Instead, one has to infer the characteristics that define the types from his descriptions of illustrated examples. For what it is worth, I am treating examples bearing only regular fine to medium incision (e.g., like Villahermosa Incised) combined with polychromy as Grijalva Incised-polychrome.

Grijalva Incised-polychrome: Grijalva Variety (Figures 5.60–5.61)

Frequency: 32 sherds (1%; <1%)

Established: Type established by Smith (1971:20–21, 136, 201–202, 235–238, fig. 55b1). This type falls into part of what Ruz (1969:128–129) called "Cerámica anaranjada," including both his "mediana" and "delgada" sub-categories.

Description:

Principal Identifying Attributes: (1) fine paste; (2) orange to brown paste color; (3) orange or red slip, often weathered; (4) zoned polychromy on vessel surface(s); (5) incised designs.

Paste, Firing, and Temper: Same as Matillas Orange: Matillas Variety.

Surface Finish and Decoration: The surface finish is the same as Matillas Orange except for the addition of paint to the surface of the vessel in two or more colors combined with

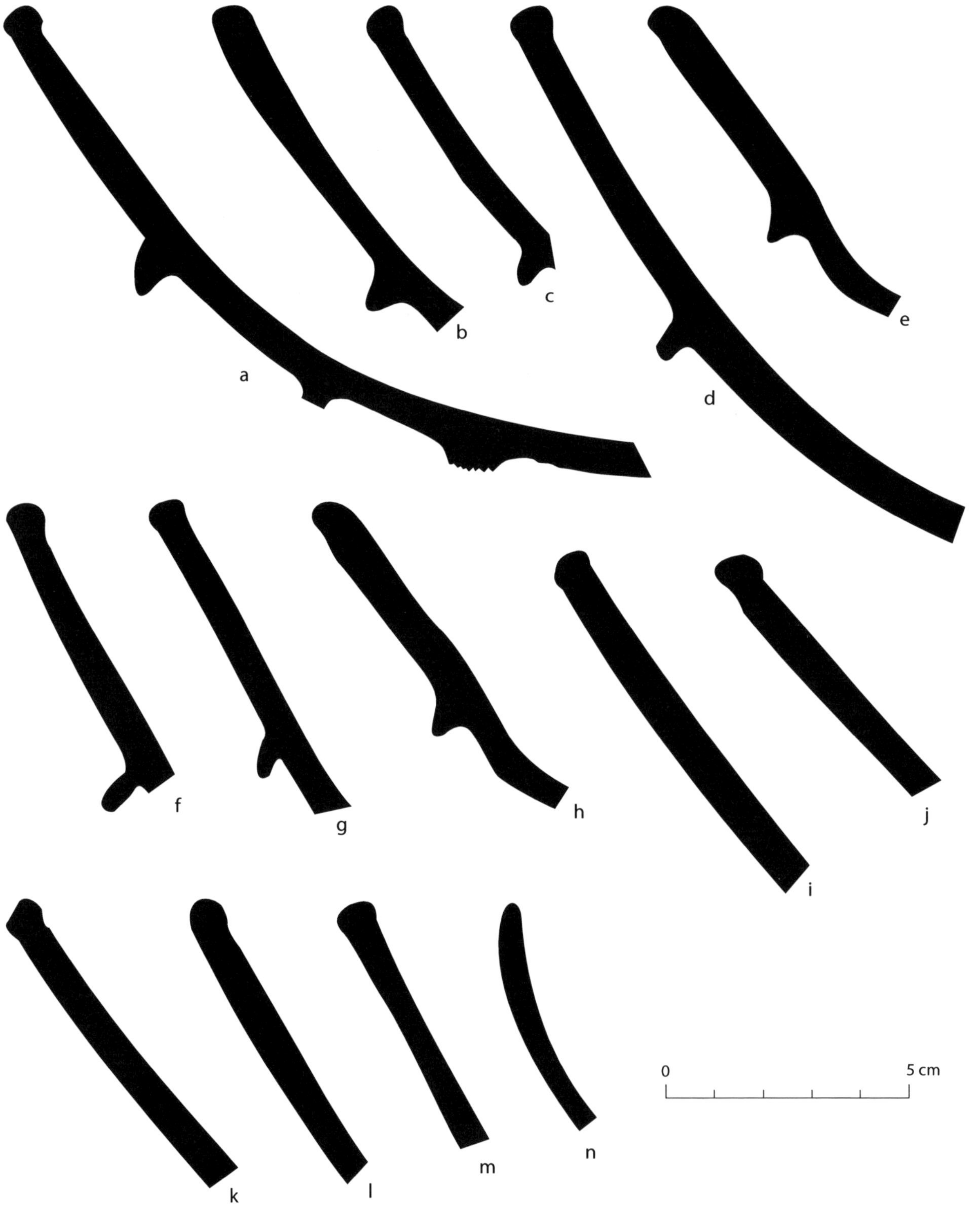

Figure 5.61. Matillas Ceramic Group profile drawings— Grijalva Incised-polychrome: Grijalva Variety.

regular Villahermosa-like incision. In this respect, Grijalva Composite is a combination of the decorative techniques found on Sayula Polychrome and Villahermosa Incised. So, the description of the surface finish of those two types apply to this type, since they are combined together in this type. As with the Villahermosa Incised and other types, the incised designs are often found on the upper portion of the interior, particularly on tripod bowls, although designs are not necessarily confined to that area.

Forms:

1. Tripod dish or bowl with basal ridge (Figure 5.61, a–h). The rim is slightly thickened either interiorly or exteriorly or, commonly, both. Tripod supports are almost invariably hollow and usually serpent effigies.
2. Tripod dish or bowl without basal ridge (Figure 5.61, i–m). These are similar to Form 1 but lack the basal ridge. They also usually have similar tripod supports.
3. Small round-sided bowls (Figure 5.61n). Rims are generally rounded. Although some examples are unrestricted, others have rims that curve inwards slightly, making the rim slightly restricted.

Intrasite Locations and Contexts: Same as Matillas Orange.

Intersite Locations and Contexts: Same as Matillas Orange.

Comment: I have treated all those examples that have multilple color schemes on orange that also bear fine to medium-line incisions as part of Grijalva Incised-polychrome. Some of these Smith (1971:236; fig. 55b3, 5–6) seems to have treated as Salto Composite. In the Comment section under Salto Composite, I explained that I did not follow the reasoning of Smith on this, even if I have interpreted what he had to say correctly. Examples of one color-on-orange (i.e., black, white, or red) with Villahermosa-like incisions I have classified as Villahermosa Incised, not Salto Composite.

Examples of sherds with polychromy, but exhibiting no other type class, such as gouge- or fine to medium-incision I have classified as Sayula Polychrome. Because the broken nature of sherds often does not necessarily exhibit the whole design of a vessel, some sherds with two colors were sometimes classified as Sayula. Chilapa Gouged-incised lacked color additions to the surface of the vessel and exhibited both gouge and fine to medium-incision. Salto Composite I treated as a combination of the type classes found on Chilapa Gouged-incised together with the type class found on Sayula Polychrome. That is, gouge and fine to medium-incision combined with three or more color polychromy. I classified those sherds with only fine to medium-incision combined with three or more color polychromy as Grijalva Incised Polychrome. Whether or not this fits with Smith's (1971) original intent I cannot be certain because he provided no type descriptions. In any case, the categories are less than clear because, as is the case with most members of a ceramic group, a given sherd may be classed as one of these types given what the analyst can see on the sherd but actually be part of a vessel that, if found intact, would be classified as a different type within that ceramic group.

Other Matillas Group: Groove-incised

A small number of Matillas Ceramic Group sherds bear incised-line decoration in a manner like Villahermosa Incised; however, the incised lines are sufficiently wide to be considered groove-incision. All six of these sherds are illustrated in Figure 5.62. Perhaps these might be considered a variety of Villahermosa Incised. They did not occur in large numbers, and I have not formally named them. They are not included in the table.

Other Indeterminate Matillas Group

There were 88 Matillas Ceramic Group sherds that could not be placed in a type. I could only tell that they were Matilas, and not one of the other Fine Orange groups.

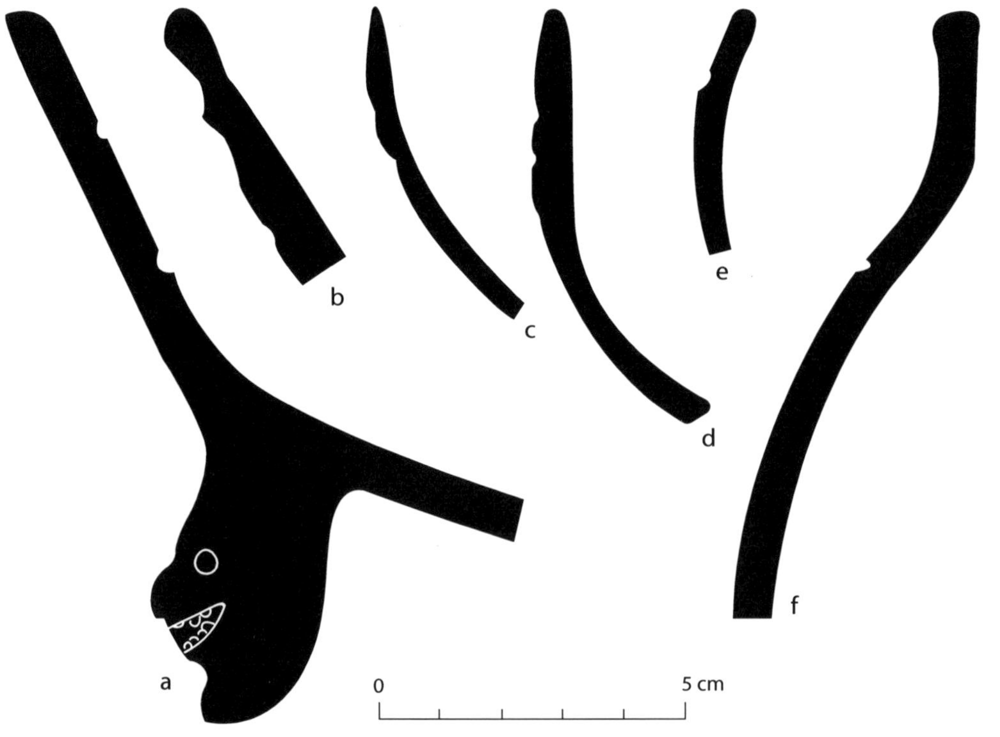

Figure 5.62. Matillas Ceramic Group profile drawings—Other Matillas Group: Groove-incised.

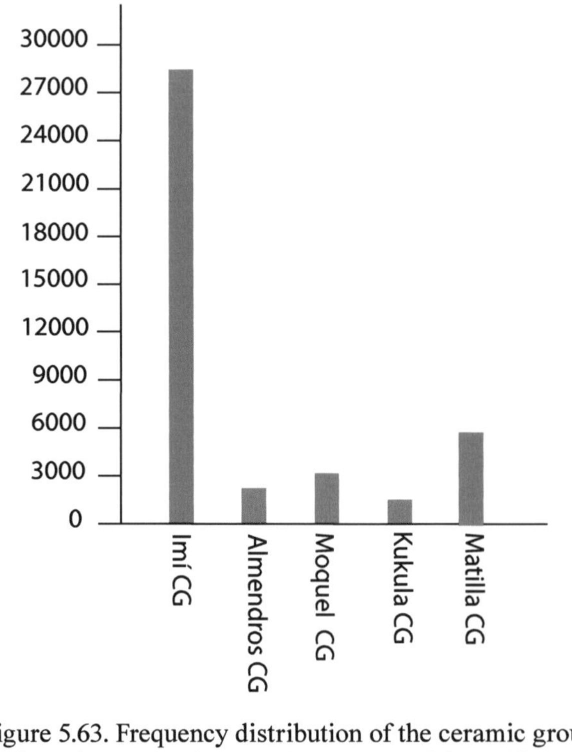

Figure 5.63. Frequency distribution of the ceramic groups of the Pabox Ceramic Complex recovered from Champotón, Campeche, México

Table 5.1. Late Postclassic ceramic type count.

CHAMPOTÓN UNSLIPPED WARE	30878
Imi Ceramic Group	**28675**
Imi Unslipped: Imi Variety	19860
Imi Unslipped: Kaymuch Variety	72
Chento Painted: Chento Variety	277
San Patricio Incised: San Patricio Variety	247
Couoh Appliqué: Couoh Variety	3837
Pozo del Monte Composite: Pozo del Monte Variety	210
Chen Pec Modeled: Chen Pec Variety	3206
Cherna Incised: Cherna Variety	821
Cherna Incised: Red-rim Variety	76
Other Imi Group (painted & incised)	69
Almendros Ceramic Group	**2203**
Almendros Mottled: Almendros Variety	790*
Arrocera Brushed: Arrocera Variety	1413*
BOMAL RED WARE	3224
Moquel Ceramic Group	**3224**
Moquel Red: Moquel Variety	3051
Moquel Red: Unslipped-exterior Variety	136
Tajonal Incised: Tajonal Variety	31
Other Moquel Group: Black-on-red	6
PETO CREAM WARE	1586
Kukula Ceramic Group	**1586**
Xcanchacan Black-on-cream: Variety Unspecified	1586
FINE ORANGE WARE	5846
Matillas Ceramic Group	**5846**
Matillas Orange: Matillas Variety	3558
Matillas Orange: Red-slipped Variety	1094
Villahermosa Incised: Villahermosa Variety	418
Nacajuca Black-on-orange: Nacajuca Variety	190
Sayula Polychrome: Sayula Variety	162
Chilapa Gouged-incised: Chilapa Variety	146
Salto Composite: Salto Variety	158
Grijalva Incised-polychrome: Grijalva Variety	32
Other Indeterminate Matillas Group	88
Total	41534

*some of these sherds were not counted separately (see pp, 160, 164).

CHAPTER 6

INTERPRETATION

All of the ceramic materials described here were recovered from within the city limits of modern Champotón, Campeche, Mexico. These ceramics came from only a small area of the present, and almost certainly, the Precolumbian and Contact period site. The following summary of the complexes is based on that collection. Much of the material came from Group 1 Structure 1, which had a complex architectural development. For these reasons very fine-grained stratigraphical analysis was not possible. Although not from Champotón proper, Jerry Ek (2015, 2016) did carry out excavations in numerous sites in the Champotón region. Some of these excavations had considerably finer chronological control. Ek's work was able to do finer gradations of complexes than I could do with the materials from Champotón itself, particularly with the earliest ceramics in the region and also with the ceramics from the Late/Terminal Classic period. For the most part, however, Ek's materials correlate well with the Champotón ceramics, indicating that Champotón-style ceramics were used over a considerable region around the site as his work illustrates.

Although our typologies correspond very well, there are a few discrepancies between the type names used in this work and those given by Ek. In part this is because Ek recovered materials that were not found at Champotón, and in other cases because of differing classification approaches. Although for the most part we have agreed on the nomenclature of types, Ek's publication (2015) has some types that do not appear in our Champotón Project collections, and vice versa. This is particularly true of Ek's Champotón 1A period for which we, in our collection, found no evidence. Ek's ceramic data lack detailed type descriptions and deal with the quantitative data at the ceramic group level, rather than at the type level as given here. However, it must be understood that Ek's work was not primarily a ceramic study but was part of a much larger study for which the ceramics were only one element in a much more comprehensive report. This fact to some degree accounts for the different approaches. In fact, anyone interested in the archaeology of the Champotón region and it's cultural development will find his work invaluable. But if the reader sometimes may be frustrated because of some perceived incompatibility of the two sets of data, this could not be avoided. Anyone interested in the ceramics from this region should pay close attention to Ek's contribution and not regard the current volume as sufficient.

While there are some unique, or at least not previously described in type-variety terms, ceramics at Champotón, they do fall within the framework of other sites and regions in the Northern Lowlands and present a developmental sequence long established in the Maya area. The collection, however, does not equally represent all periods of the sequence. By far the strongest complex in our sample is the Pabox complex, followed by the Late/Terminal Classic and Petentun complex. The Middle Preclassic—Ek's (2016:529–530) Champotón IB—and Early Classic periods are only weakly represented, while Ek's Champotón IA period is absent.

The following account of the ceramic complexes is a summary of their content and archaeological significance relative to the Prehispanic occupation of the site. It should be taken as a preliminary statement, rather than a definitive conclusion concerning the site.

THE MANTILLA CERAMIC COMPLEX (LATE MIDDLE PRECLASSIC)

This is a tentative complex. The small number of sherds recovered from our investigations would normally not be sufficient to define a whole ceramic complex. Ek, however, recovered evidence of a more robust occupation in sites outside of Champotón. He labeled this complex IB in his dissertation and in a subsequent publication (Ek 2015:412, 426 ff; 2016:529–530). At Champotón, La Mantilla ceramics were recovered only from mixed deposits, although there were indications that they may have been present in a pure deposit buried very deeply under at least one of the large platforms at Moquel, just across the Champotón River from the city. This pottery seems to most closely resemble the Malecon Complex encountered previously at Edzná (Forsyth 1983:16–32). It consists exclusively of waxy-slipped vessels in red, black, and cream. No unslipped ceramics from this period were recognized, although they may have been present. Unslipped ceramics from this period are difficult to distinguish from those that immediately follow. While the data are tenuous due to the small sample, the presence of this material may indicate that Champotón was participating, at least ceramically, in the same cultural processes that were becoming so widespread in the Maya Lowlands at this time.

PETENTUN CERAMIC COMPLEX (LATE PRECLASSIC)

Late Preclassic pottery is relatively abundant in the collections of the Champotón Project. Although also found in quantity at Moquel, the majority of this pottery was recovered from Structure 1 of Group 1 in the Barrio of Guadalupe. Investigations carried out in 2001 and 2002 in the Barrio de Guadalupe in Champotón by the Universidad Autónoma de Campeche (UAC) revealed that Structure 1 in Group 1 was constructed during Petentun times. The structure was a monumental platform measuring 54 by 54 m constructed of enormous cut-stone blocks. According to Folan et al. (2003:67):

> The Great Platform, that represents a jewel of Maya archaeology, [was] constructed with five distinct sets of megalithic stairs, all different in their details, with the largest on the north face [of the building and] measuring seven meters wide at its base. The other four megalithic stairways [are] inset in each corner [of the structure]...

Not only were the stairways constructed of megalithic stone, but the walls of the structure were formed by such stones as well. This platform was built during the Late Preclassic. On its top were constructed at least one, and probably three, structures (1-A-sub), formed using large stones and perhaps roofed using perishable materials (Folan et al. 2003:67). In association with the platform and structure(s) were considerable quantities of Chicanel ceramics (Forsyth and Jordan 2003:58). This pottery is very similar to that manufactured contemporaneously at Edzná and other sites of central Campeche. The monumental size of the structure, as well as its form, suggests that the population of Champotón would have had to have been quite large. It is highly likely that there were other public buildings that dated to the Preclassic. In fact, Ek (2015:317–318, 436) has also encountered pyramids with a strong occupation during this period in Rancho San Carlos—an area immediately to the east of the modern urban zone of Champotón. Unfortuantely, subsequent occupation, especially the growth of the modern city, has probably destroyed or obscured other examples of large-scale Preclassic culture. Nonetheless, it is probable that Champotón was one of the largest sites on the Campeche coast in the first few centuries before the current era.

Moquel, a site near Champotón (Figure 1.4), also produced evidence of occupation during the Late Preclassic (Forsyth and Jordan 2003). In addition to the investigations by the UAC at Champotón, Jerry Ek (2015, 2016) has undertaken a program of survey and study of the settlement patterns in the region around Champotón. According to Ek (2015:434):

> The spatial distribution of Champotón 2 [Late Formative] ceramics reflects a major expansion of populations across the Río Champotón drainage... All sites investigated in the region have substantial Late Formative occupations. The sites of Ulumal and San Dimas grew in size and importance during this period, with the latter likely representing large settlements

> and political centers. Populations along the coast swelled to their maximum density during Champotón 2, which (sic) extensive yet dispersed settlement at the coastal sites of Niop and Rancho Potrero Grande. Settlement survey along the coastal margin revealed a near continuous distribution of residential groups, with nearly all tested structures having Late Formative occupation.

Other investigations along the coast immediately to the southwest of Champotón have also yielded significant evidence of Late Preclassic occupation at Playa Esmeralda and Villamar (Suárez et al. 2010; Ojeda and Suárez 2012:217–233; Ancona 2012:145–160; Ancona et al. 2010:261–263).

Moreover, in 1993 archaeologists working for the INAH Center in Campeche "carried out surveys and excavations in various archaeological mounds that were to be impacted as a result of the construction of a highway that linked...Campeche and Champotón" (Zapata 1997:406). These investigations in the town of Villa Madero (Figure 1.4), the largest site of the zone, produced evidence of a significant Late Preclassic occupation. The primary evidence for this occupation was the recovery of ceramics that date to that period. In fact, the ceramic types represented at Villa Madero make up a complete ceramic complex—that is, a suite of vessels that would satisfy "the total number of functional needs for pottery in a specific time and place" (Adams 1973:134), indicating something much more than a short-term settlement. The excavators also found buried inside a large mound (Platform 6) at Villa Madero three Sierra Red plates but apparently in a secondary context. Because of the nature of the investigations at Villa Madero, it is not possible to determine with exactness the size or intensity of the early occupation of the site. Still, Zapata (1997:408) classifies it, along with Jaina, Campeche, and Champotón, as a "monumental site," without specifying that that description is necessarily applicable to the Late Preclassic occupation. Eaton (1978:27–28), in his survey of the coast, also encountered evidence of Chicanel ceramics near the site, which he labeled Kilometer 165 (Acapulquito). Likewise, the sites of Sihoplaya and Haltunchén yielded evidence of occupation during the same period (Eaton 1978:27; Ball 1978:79; Rivera et al. 1982:18, 20, 48–49). Therefore, it would appear that the central part of the Campeche coast first attained a significant population during the Late Preclassic.

Likewise, investigations by Alberto Ruz (1969) in the 1940s reported a significant occupation at Tixchel to the south of Champotón.

All of this suggests strongly that by the time of the Late Preclassic period, Champotón and its surrounding area was characterized by a significant population and that Champotón and the area around it were participating in the same cultural processes that have been established in other regions of the Maya Lowlands.

In terms of ceramics, the Petentun complex pertains to the widespread Chicanel Ceramic Sphere, constituting definite, full membership as defined by Ball (1976:323). The ceramic inventory is constituted by the now familiar wares and types of Paso Caballo Waxy Ware, characterized by waxy red, black, and cream slips, and Achiotes Unslipped Ware, consisting mostly of unslipped jars, both of which are distributed over a very large area of the Maya Lowlands, and which define the sphere.
The monochrome pottery is marked by the dominance of the Sierra Ceramic Group, which comprises the overwhelming majority of the monochrome sherds during this time. This group is in turn dominated by the type, Sierra Red. The Sierra group bears a red-firing slip with a waxy feel—a characteristic of almost all of the Late Preclassic slipped ceramics in the Southern Lowlands. Sierra Red at Champotón is distinguished at the varietal level from the more southernly complexes because the Champotón Sierra Red material is more like that found at Edzná (Forsyth 1983:33–37). The Chon Variety differs from the Sierra Variety with regard to differing percentages of some forms and modes (Forsyth 1983:37). Such differences characterize a slightly different selection of form and other modes, rather than their presence or absence in one or the other of the varieties.

Black-slipped ceramics of the Polvero Ceramic Group constitute the second most common slipped monochrome class, followed by the less frequent Flor Ceramic Group. Although there are sometimes statistical frequency differences in forms with each of the groups, they were essentially manufactured in the same forms and using most of the same surface modification modes.

The Petentun unslipped pottery, on the other hand, presents an anomaly. Although typologically, and in terms of forms and modes, they are similar to the same types found at Edzná, the Champotón collection is atypical. In most complexes this pottery makes up a large percentage of the ceramic complex, often around 30 percent. At Champotón, on the other hand, unslipped pottery was nowhere near as frequent, constituting less than 10 percent of the complex. This may be due to the architectural context from which the pottery from this period was recovered, but it is difficult to understand why there would be such a differential occurrence of slipped and unslipped pottery even in this context.

Towards the end of the Chicanel period, a number of new modes, forms, decorative schemes, and slip colors were added to the standard Chicanel repertoire. They appear at numerous sites in the Maya Lowlands. They have often been characterized as marking a distinct period, referred to as the Protoclassic. The concept of the Protoclassic has long been a problematical issue in Maya archaeology (Willey 1977:391; Brady et al. 1998:18). Brady et al. (1998) have tried to bring some order and synthesis to the concept. They divided the period into two successive but perhaps overlapping facets—Facet 1, characterized by the introduction of the above characteristics, and Facet 2, which was more directly ancestral to the slipped ceramics of the Early Classic. The ceramics recovered from the Champotón Project pertain to what they designate as Facet 1, which I prefer to label the Terminal Preclassic.

Only a small number of such sherds from the Terminal Preclassic have been recovered from Champotón. Based on better data from other regions, it seems probable these materials do not replace the Chicanel technology and types, but constitute an addition to it, with the new characteristics added to and sometimes modifying the old standard Chicanel ceramics. I have considered these materials to be part of the Petentun complex, rather than a separate complex. Ek (2015:435; n.d: Champotón 2) likewise considered them as part of his Champotón 2 period. Where this material is found in greater quantity and in better contexts, this may not be the case, and a late complex, or at least facet, may be in order. This distinction cannot be made on the basis of the materials from the Champotón Project.

The new ceramic types of the Terminal Preclassic consists mostly of less than 50 sherds from Iberia Orange and a handful of other sherds of Caramba Red-on-red-orange and Sacluc Black-on-orange.

THE EARLY CLASSIC

The Champotón ceramics have yielded very little evidence of an occupation during the period between the Late Preclassic and the Late Classic. This fact might indicate that the site was mostly abandoned during this time or, alternatively, reflect the limited nature of the coverage of the site in the Champotón Project. Notably, Ek's (2015) more extensive coverage of sites in the region around Champotón encountered the same pattern. So it is possible that there was considerable depopulation at Champotón and the surrounding area at this time. In addition to the possibility of abandonment, Ek (2015:439) has also proposed a different possibility, suggesting that the Champotón region might have continued to manufacture and use Chicanel ceramics into Early Classic times when new kinds of pottery had replaced the old Chicanel pottery in most other areas of the Maya region. Unfortunately, neither of these hypotheses can be resolved on the basis of the ceramic data at hand. It is possible, of course, that the apparent absence of a distinctive Early Classic ceramic complex is a function of skewed sampling and that such evidence might be found in the future. If all the evidence relative to this issue came only from the Champotón Project, I would be inclined to think so, but given Ek's more comprehensive data, the issue remains a conundrum.

The examples of Early Classic ceramics from Champotón itself consist almost exclusively of small numbers of Peten Gloss Ware. These are mostly fine ware serving vessels and evidence for more utilitarian vessels is extremely rare.

THE LATE CLASSIC/TERMINAL CERAMICS

Because of the nature of the ceramic collection from this period, it has not been possible to define an internally consistent ceramic complex or set of complexes. It is likely that this material can be divided into two or more complexes. Ek (2015:458–511, 2016:532–542) has certainly attempted to do so based on stratigraphic evidence, and his analysis has much to recommend it. At Champotón proper though, it was not possible to separate this material due to the fact that it seemed to be mixed as architectural fill. For this reason I have considered this material as a kind of place holder category, rather than a full-fledged complex with consistent and well-defined ceramic content that characterizes a more specific time horizon at the site.

It is clear, nevertheless, that after the potential decline in population at Champotón at the end of the Terminal Preclassic, there emerge strong indications of substantial occupation at the site during the Late Classic period, at least as indicated by ceramic deposits. In contrast to the Petentun complex, in which the ceramics pertained to a well-known and widespread ceramic sphere throughout the Maya Lowlands, the Late Classic ceramics do not seem to form a clear-cut pattern but reflect a mixture of types and varieties from different regions together with locally produced materials. Some of these ceramics are like those found at Edzná in the Agua Potable complex, while perhaps the majority are part of the Canbalam sphere, a regional ceramic area apparently limited to the coastal area from south-central Campeche northward including the northwest coast of Yucatán (Ball 1978:135; Jiménez 2002:301; Jiménez, Ceballos et al. 2006). In fact, Jiménez includes in her Canbalam sphere some of the types that characterized the Agua Potable complex. This may in fact be the case. Ek (2016:532–533), however, separates the more Agua Potable-like materials in his Champotón 4 period from Canbalam proper—his Champotón 5 period. The materials recovered from the Champotón Project cannot help to resolve such issues, as the collections are too mixed to allow fine chronological or other distinctions. Some of these types would also be part of Ek's Champotón 6 period. Thus our Late Classic/ Terminal Classic ceramics correspond more or less to Ek's (2015) Champotón 4 through 6.

The dominant types of this period clearly fall within the parameters of the above-mentioned Canbalam sphere. The most frequent pottery in the collections belongs to the Baca Ceramic Group, forming 33 percent of all the sherds recovered from this admittedly long period. On the other hand, Nimun Ceramic Group sherds are rare, forming only 1 percent of the total. This contrasts with other sites such as Dzibilchaltún and Xcambó where Nimun pottery made up roughly 20–25 per cent of Celestún Red Ware. Such may not be the fact at other sites (see, for example, the varying percentages from sites in Ek's regional survey [Ek 2015:496 table 7.14]). Whatever the situation, red-paste Baca group is the most frequent of the ceramic groups recovered in the Structure 1, Group 1 excavations.

It is followed in frequency by Fine Gray Ware, with the Chablekal Ceramic Group dominating overwhelmingly, while the Tsicul Ceramic Group is much rarer.

These two wares form the main elements of the Canbalam Sphere. Our collection also has another element common to the sphere in Isla Fina Fine Buff Ware in moderate quantities. Still, as Ek (2015:472) has pointed out, Canbalam is less a distinct ceramic sphere in the traditional sense,

> However, it is important to note that the Canbalam sphere is not a monolithic entity, but instead a set of tradewares that linked coastal centers between the Chontalpa region of Tabasco, coastal Campeche, and parts of the northern Yucatecan coast. Thus, the term 'sphere' is perhaps not entirely accurate since many of the shared ceramic wares and groups among a coastal network of sites are more likely a subassemblage of

trade wares that were combined with local ceramics. Thus, the 'Canbalam Pheonomon' (sic) is perhaps best understood as a horizon or tradeware subassemblage.

However that may be, Champotón was clearly participating in this phenomenon.

On the other hand, there are other ceramics that do not fit this pattern. Mixed in with this material is a considerable quantity of Campeche Gloss Ware ceramics, particularly Charote Group vessels, with their highly burnished red surfaces, and Simochac polychrome vessels. Simochac vessels are the Campeche analogue of the Saxche/Palmar orange-polychromes in the Southern Lowlands. I have described under the type the issues relating to this material; however, until the niceties of classification are finally worked out with respect to Campeche Gloss Ware polychromes, it was not possible to separate this pottery from the Canbalam materials in any clear way. They may represent influences or actual trade from inland sites, as they are found in some quantities at Edzná and Ulumal. A limited number of other Campeche polychromes were recovered but in small quantities. Also note that Jiménez, Ceballos et al. (2006:350–351, 362–367) include both Charote Group materials, as well as the Campeche polychromes (Saxche, Cui, Chimbote, Sayan) as part of the Canbalam Sphere.

Also found mixed together with the above ceramics are moderate amounts of Fine Orange pottery. While Silhó Ceramic Group sherds are the most numerous, Altar and Balancán group totals are not far behind. They, like Isla Fina Buff Ware, were traded into Champotón from further along the south coast of Campeche or eastern Tabasco.

The Unslipped pottery in the collection pertains to several different wares. By far the most common is the Acapulquito Ceramic Group dominated by Yakatzib Striated. This central Campeche group is analogous to the Cambio/Encanto pottery in the Southern Lowlands and probably to Chum/Yokat pottery of the Northern Lowlands. Large striated jars are a major form found throughout the Maya Lowlands during this time period. Chencan Brown-on-orange and Keste Incised, as well as Neza Unslipped were recovered in modest amounts. Neza Unslipped is known only from the Champotón area at present, as are Tajonal Unslipped and an undesignated Buff/brownware—the latter two relatively infrequent in the collections.

One of the notable characteristics at Champotón is the general lack of typical Terminal Classic wares so common in interior sites and in the Northern Lowlands. Puuc Slate Ware occurs in small quantities, and Puuc Red and Thin Slate Wares are nearly absent.

PABOX CERAMIC COMPLEX

The Postclassic ceramics recovered from Champotón make up the overwhelming majority of all the pottery recovered from the site by the Champotón Project. It is possible that this reflects the fact that the Postclassic period represented the largest occupation of the site during its long history. On the other hand, this dominance may be somewhat misleading given the restricted coverage of the Champotón Project investigations. The Guadalupe excavation yielded ceramics from all of the periods, Late Preclassic through the Postclassic, although in differing quantities, whereas the northern area of the city produced almost exclusively Postclassic pottery. A more comprehensive coverage of the site might produce a somewhat different interpretation of the occupational history of the site. Nevertheless, on the basis of the current data it would seem that Champotón was indeed a major Postclassic site on the Campeche coast.

The Pabox Ceramic Complex consisted of a very uniform and regular group of types and varieties and formed what Adams (1973:133–134) called "usage complementarity." That is, the complex represents "the total number of functional needs for pottery in a specific time and place." Moreover, it is possible to compare the materials from the Champotón Project with those reported by Alberto Ruz (1969) from Champotón, which he recovered in excavations in the 1940s. Unfortunately, the comparison to Ruz must be made only on the basis of his publication (Ruz 1969:117–141), given that Ruz's actual collection has apparently disappeared.

Although Ruz used a different classification scheme, and some of the details of his descriptions do not necessarily correspond closely with ours, it is possible to see that his 13,000 sherd sample is similar to those recovered by us, particularly when his illustrations are compared to ours. Thus, the Pabox complex is perhaps the best defined and circumscribed of all of the complexes found at the site.

The vast majority of the Pabox ceramics recovered from the site consists of unslipped pottery belonging to Champotón Unslipped Ware. This pottery made up 74 percent of the Postclassic total sample. The unslipped pottery collected by Ruz (1969:117–118) constituted 82 percent of his collection (Ruz's "cerámica café" and "cerámica grisácea"). In fact, Champotón Unslipped Ware encompasses both of these categories defined by Ruz. The Imi and Almendros groups' surface color varies considerably from light beige to brown to occasionally gray. The predominant color, however, is a creamy white to very light beige color and is distinctive to Champotón and its environs. Similar pottery at some other sites in the region seem to have been manufactured with a different paste or at least fired in a more strongly oxidizing atmosphere.

One of the distinguishing characteristics of the Champotón Postclassic unslipped pottery is the relative lack of striated vessels. Unlike Mayapán in Yucatán, where Yacman Striated outnumbered Navula Unslipped by more than 2.5 times, Imi Unslipped outnumbered Arrocera Brushed, a lightly striated unslipped type at Champotón, by a factor of 14. Heavy striation was lacking entirely, but even the lightly striated (brushed) pottery was not very common at Champotón.

Another characteristic is that, although the general assemblage with respect to forms, and presumably functions, parallels those found at other Postclassic sites in both the Northern and Southern Lowlands, Champotón retains a distinctiveness from other, better known sites. Among the shared characteristics are the heavy dominance of unslipped ceramics relative to slipped types, the importance of red-slipped monochrome vessels, the use of rounded-bottomed tripod bowls, the strong emphasis on the manufacture and utilization of censers in the ceramic inventory, and in the use of a number of widespread decorative modes applied to vessel surfaces. Within those similarities, however, Champotón differs by often creating its own distinctive forms and usages. For example, the Champotón censers, while they have a general similarity to those manufactured in other areas of the Maya Lowlands, are not just copies of those found in other regions but take their own unique form. Although clearly analogous to the better known Cehac-Hunacti Appliqué censers at Mayapán, the Cuouh Appliqué vessels retain their own regional distinctiveness. Likewise, the Chen Pec Modeled censers are similar to the better known Chen Mul Modeled but have characteristics which differentiate them from the Chen Mul examples. Milbrath and Peraza (2007:13) have described some of the differences. Among the most important are the limited range of deities represented in comparison to Mayapán, the limited contexts in which they are found at Champotón, the relative lack of painting on Champotón effigy censers, and the lesser detail expended on the digits and eyes.

At Champotón Chen Pec Modeled effigy censers are rare in the majority of Postclassic contexts at the site. Although nearly as numerous as Cuouh Appliqué in absolute quantity of sherds analyzed by us—these do not represent all of the effigy censers recovered at Structure 1, Group 1—this is entirely due to the fact that the Postclassic Maya deposited thousands of these Chen Pec censer fragments in special deposits and debris associated with a single structure, Structure 1 Group 1 in the Barrio de Guadalupe (see Appendix 1). Nearly 92 percent of all Chen Pec sherds counted by us came from this location.

Another distinctive characteristic of Champotón is the occurrence of unslipped grater bowls. The surfaces of these vessels are always the light beige to grayish color of Campeche Unslipped Ware and, unlike the situation of these kinds of vessels at Mayapán where they are normally slipped red (see Smith 1971:fig. 46a), the Champotón examples are always unslipped. Ball (1978:92) recognized the difference in treatment of these kinds of vessels from others on the peninsula and gave them the name of Cherna Incised. Ball indicated that Cherna was an analog to Chenkeken Incised at Mayapán, an unslipped grater bowl. Given the sparsity of Chenkeken at Mayapán, however, only 47 sherds out of nearly 250,000, Chenkeken should perhaps be considered an analogue of Cherna Incised, which is much more frequent in the Champotón Project collection.

An additional category of unslipped pottery consisted of small jars with thin vessel walls. The thinness of the walls together with the small size of the jars, and the relatively sparse frequency of these vessels, suggest that they may have had some specialized function.

With respect to slipped pottery, Postclassic complexes overwhelmingly are dominated by red wares, primarily monochrome reds, thus continuing the long-lived uninterrupted red ware tradition in the Maya Lowlands. In almost all of the Postclassic ceramic complexes in the Lowlands, red-slipped vessels are overwhelmingly the most frequent of the slipped ceramics. Ceramic groups such as Mama, Payil, Paxcaman, Topoxte, and Rita tended to dominate the slipped pottery at the sites where they were found, generally constituting between 20 and 35 percent of the ceramic complexes they belonged to. In contrast, at Champotón red-slipped pottery made up only 6 percent of Ruz's collection, and a little less than 8 percent of the Champotón Project complex.

Despite this difference, Champotón nevertheless participated in the trade component of the ceramic complex, and they still did not constitute the dominant serving vessel function.

Instead, the occupants of Champotón utilized Fine Orange Ware pottery to a far greater extent than any other known site, at least outside of the lower Usumacinta drainage. In fact, it appears to be the most numerous of the "finer" wares utilized at the site. This pottery belongs to the Matillas Ceramic Group and occurs in large quantities across a large number of types. Matillas Group pottery constitutes 14 percent of the Pabox complex total, and 54 percent of the slipped/fine wares at the site. This contrasts sharply with other sites such as Mayapán where Matillas Group pottery is 1 percent of the slipped/fine wares and 0.3 percent of the total ceramic inventory. At most sites in the Northern Lowlands, Matillas Group pottery is almost always a small percentage of the complex—a specialty item traded over long distances. In fact, this pottery is almost always quite rare at most Late Postclassic Maya sites, except for those in or near the area of production.

Neutron activation studies carried out by Bishop et al. (2006:141) indicate that the Matillas Group pottery is likewise an import into Champotón. Like other Fine Orange Ware pottery, Matillas ceramics were manufactured in or near the Usumacinta River drainage. According to them:

> ...based on the chemistry of the paste, the production area is located outside the region of Champotón, and the principle zone of the production of fine orange is the lower and middle Usumacinta River Basin. Comparisons with Matillas ceramics with other fine pastes in the database indicate similarities with other Matillas Fine Orange ceramics from the site of Tierra Colorada, located near Lake Matillas [Laguna Matillas], approximately 25 km. southeast of the modern city of Villahermosa, Tabasco.

While the specific location, or locations, of manufacture of Champotón Matillas pottery cannot at present be specified, it is clear that they were produced in the area around Villahermosa from soils produced in a lacustrine/riverine environment.

Although Matillas Group ceramics have long served, and continue to serve, as an easily recognized marker for the Late Postclassic in the Maya Lowlands, at the overwhelming majority of sites this pottery never constituted more than a small percentage of the ceramic complexes of which it was part. In short, Matillas ceramics formed a class of imported vessels with an exceptionally wide distribution but of very limited usage—as was the pattern with its precursors, Balancán and Silhó. Only in the Usumacinta drainage and nearby sites did it form a significant part of the pottery inventory. Indeed, it may well be that much of this pottery was manufactured precisely for export. Nevertheless, the pattern at Champotón is quite different from most other Maya sites on the peninsula. Here, Matillas pottery played a much more important role than in sites where it has been encountered outside of its zone of production. It would appear that Matillas ceramics fulfilled functions that at other sites were filled by red-slipped pottery. At Champotón Matillas pottery is the dominant serving ware, followed by red ware pottery, which was certainly manufactured at or near Champotón. So it seems clear that the function of Matillas pottery at the site was a utilitarian one, rather than merely for more restricted uses, although these are not mutually exclusive. It seems clear it functioned as ordinary pottery used daily by the inhabitants of the site. If this is correct, then it is likely that the ceramic industry at Champotón formed an integral part of the system of production and distribution in the coastal wetland regions in southwestern Campeche and far eastern Tabasco during the Late Postclassic, given that the Champotóneros imported a significant portion of their ceramic needs from this zone.

This is, however, a difficult argument to sustain with a high degree of certainty because eastern Tabasco and southwestern Campeche constitute one of the most poorly investigated portions of the Maya Lowlands. Little is known about the sites, and their ceramic inventories, in this zone. In fact, it is primarily due to the uniqueness of Fine Orange pottery and its chemical signature that allow us to know where it was manufactured. Although recognized as a distinctive pottery, by Ruz (1969) and others, few excavations in the area of its production—eastern Tabasco and/or far southwestern Campeche—have been undertaken. Berlin (1956:136) briefly described some of this pottery from excavations carried out by him at Atasta on the Xicalango Peninsula (also known as the Atasta Peninsula) in far southwestern Campeche. The typological characterization of it was published by Smith (1970:20–21, 136, 234–237, fig. 55) based on pottery from Mayapán. Although Smith did apply type-variety names to the Matillas pottery from Mayapán, he did not describe the criteria used for distinguishing the various types and varieties, nor did he give clear descriptions of them. The reader must try to discern what these criteria were from listings of examples and from consulting the illustrations.

Except for investigations carried out by Berlin (1956), and at Aguacatal (Matheny 1970; Ruz 1969:51–59, 81–87) and on the Xicalango Peninsula (Vargas 1994; Ochoa and Terreros 1997) the area is principally known through surface reconnaissance or limited excavations. Because of this, although it is possible to say that there is sufficient ceramic information to establish that there was indeed a Postclassic occupation in the area, we have very little in the way of concrete data concerning the nature and internal development of these occupations (see Ball 1978:141–142; Vargas 1985; 1994:35; Ochoa and Terreros 1997:93–96). Apart from the work of those investigators mentioned above, most of our information about this area consists of ceramic data, and those data present considerable difficulty in understanding what the Postclassic ceramic complexes in the area were actually like.

Based on excavations carried out at Aguacatal, first by Ruz (1969) in the 1940s, and then by Brigham Young University in 1958 and 1961, Matheny (1970:93–99) named the Late Postclassic occupation at the site the Plantación Ceramic Complex. This complex, however, was a very unusual one in that it consisted entirely of Fine Orange pottery of the Matillas and Cunduacan groups. It is virtually unknown for a ceramic complex to consist of only one ware, and one at that which lacks an unslipped or utilitarian component. Matheny noted this anomaly, suggesting that it was due to the fact that the Plantación materials came almost exclusively from surface contexts. That is, it was not possible to associate the Fine Orange surface pottery with other wares. The Matillas and Cunduacan ceramics could be dated to the Late Postclassic only because this pottery is an easily recognizable horizon marker due to its unique characteristics. Thus, the Plantación complex is not really a complete complex in the sense that Adams (Adams 1973:133–135) defines it.

The Aguacatal situation is paralleled by other sites along the southwest Campeche littoral in which the Late Postclassic is recognized by the presence of Matillas group ceramics—for example, Tixchel (Ruz 1969:fig. 34; Ball 1978:141). More recent investigations carried out by the Centro de Estudios Mayas, directed by Lorenzo Ochoa, encountered a similar situation (Vargas 1985:101–17, 1994:35; Jiménez Valdez 1987:119; Ochoa and Vargas 1987:100; Ochoa and Terreros 1997:93–96). At sites where the Matillas group ceramics show up, they appear to be quite numerous, and it can be hypothesized that they probably constituted the primary, or at least an important, serving vessel class at those sites. Nevertheless, it is not yet possible to define a functionally complete ceramic complex for this zone during this horizon. For this reason it is not possible to determine how similar or different the Champotón Pabox Ceramic Complex was compared to these other sites further along the southwest littoral of Campeche and far eastern Tabasco.

Fortunately, portions of this area have been undergoing considerable development in recent years, resulting in more recent investigations, and we may have a clearer picture as to whether the occupants of sites further south and west of Champotón had a similar pattern of usage with respect to Matillas group pottery.

Perhaps another class of Postclassic Champotón ceramics that should be addressed is Peto Cream Ware. Recognized as a distinct class of pottery for a long time, it has nevertheless played an outsized role in the interpretation of the transition from the Classic to Postclassic. Known by various, names, it was R. E. Smith (1971:26, 200–202, 232–234, fig. 52) who provided the Peto Cream Ware name for it, as well as for its overwhelmingly dominant type, Xcanchakan Black-on-cream. There has been a decades-long debate about the chronological placement and developmental significance of Peto Cream pottery. I will not rehearse all of these arguments. The reader can review these debates and analyses if interested. For a general summary of the issues and the distribution of this ware, see Virginia Ochoa (1999). For a more recent summary of the various arguments, see Pérez de Heredia (2010:272–294). Suffice it to say that the current view of Peto Cream Ware is that it was produced over a long period of time and persisted into the early to middle Postclassic.

The latter interpretation is derived originally from the work of Robert E. Smith on the ceramics recovered in the 1950s by the Carnegie Institution of Washington at Mayapán in Yucatán, Mexico. The overwhelming majority of ceramics recovered there pertained to the Postclassic period. Smith's interpretation divided the ceramics into two sequent phases, named Hocaba and Tases. According to Smith (1971:112; 135–136, 200–202, 232–234), Peto Cream Ware was a marker for the earlier Hocaba complex. Although when Smith counted the total number of Peto Cream Ware sherds Peto Cream Ware was about half as common in the Tases phase as in the Hocaba phase; when he examined a much smaller number of sherds from locations within stratigraphic cuts, he found that Peto Cream Ware dominated the earlier (bottom-most) layer, and diminished into the middle and late (upper) lots (see Smith 1971:234, and vol. 2: 130 [Table 24]). This led Smith to regard Peto Cream Ware as a marker for his Hocaba phase. Despite much discussion on the chronological position of Peto Cream Ware, most ceramic analysts still continue to regard Peto Cream Ware types as markers for an earlier facet or phase of the Northern Lowlands Postclassic period.

This was also the position that Ek (2015:526) took in the interpretation of the ceramics from the region surrounding Champotón.

> … the distribution of Peto Cream was highly variable, constrasting with the very homogeneous frequencies of other Postclassic types found within the region. Contexts with high frequencies of Xcanchakan Black-on-Cream were thus provisionally attributed to the early facet of the Postclassic: Champotón 7a. (Ek 2015:526)

In the Champotón Project collections, a similar pattern was noted. The Xcanchakan type is really the only member of the Kukula Ceramic Group to be found in any quantity. Likewise, it is rare in most of the excavation contexts carried out by the UAC at Champotón, and it did not occur in a particular stratigraphic context. As in Ek's sample above, the presence of Xcanchakan sherds was variable and contrasted "with the homogenous frequencies of other Postclassic types" (see Ek above). There is one exception, however. The excavations carried out in Structure 1 of Group 5 yielded a very large number of sherds of the Xcanchakan Black-on-cream type. In fact, over 75 percent of all the Peto Cream Ware sherds were recovered from this area. In at least one excavation, they were found sealed under each of three sequent floors. Unfortunately, this stratigraphy did not aid in unequivocally establishing the date of these ceramics relative to other excavation contexts because the Peto Cream pottery was found throughout the stratigraphic column, although it did seem to be more frequent below the floors. But wherever it was found, it was always accompanied by the standard repertoire of the more common Late Postclassic ceramic groups—Imí, Moquel, and Matillas.

Another interesting fact about the Structure 1, Group 5 excavations is that these same strata were accompanied by examples of Moquel Red: Unslipped-exterior Variety. In fact, nearly 90 percent of all unslipped-exterior variety sherds came from the G5 excavation units. It is interesting in light of Smith's (1971:112) findings in stratigraphic cuts at Maypan in which the analogue of Moquel Red: Unslipped-exterior Variety, Mama Red: unslipped exterior variety is regarded as a Late Postclassic marker. There is, of course, no reason why Champotón pottery production should necessarily mirror that of Mayapán. So the unslipped exterior pottery may not serve as a horizon marker, but the parallel in surface treatment on the major red ware is intriguing. Moreover, it is interesting that both the unslippped exterior variety of Moquel Red and Xcanchakan Black-on-cream attained their highest frequencies by far in the same group.

SUMMARY

The investigations carried out by the UAC in 2001–2003 have demonstrated that Champotón had a much longer occupation than had previously been recognized, beginning during the Middle Preclassic period. The following Late Preclassic period, corresponding to the Petentun complex, was one of significant occupation at the site, although its extent and intensity cannot be determined with any real accuracy. Petentun ceramics have been recovered in quantity from both Structure 1, Group 1 and from Moquel, suggesting that the occupation was probably not restricted to a small area of the site.

Following the Late Preclassic period, on the other hand, there is little ceramic evidence of an Early Classic occupation. There was evidence to indicate that ceramics were being used in the Terminal Preclassic and the Early Classic proper; but there was very little of it, suggesting either that the site was not occupied to any great extent during this time or, if otherwise, that the bulk of the ceramic assemblage was very different from the standard modes and types characteristic of this period. Ek (2015:439) has raised the possibility of this, although based on current evidence it remains an hypothesis. It is also possible that there was a significant occupation at Champotón itself, but that it concentrated in areas of the site not investigated by the Champotón Project. Given the fact that Ek (2015:412–413, 439, 447–448; n.d.:Champotón 3) likewise failed to find evidence of a strong occupation in his settlement survey of the region around Champotón tends to weaken that possibility.

It has not been possible given the ceramic contexts to differentiate the Late Classic from the Terminal Classic materials from Champotón, and I have treated them together. Ek (2015; 2016) has attempted to work out a ceramic chronology for the region based on his work in the settlement patterns around Champotón, and it is the best hypothesis available at this time. The Champotón Project collections contain most of the same types that Ek defines but are all from mixed contexts, and therefore do not provide a clear chronological pattern. What can be said is that Champotón and Moquel certainly participated strongly in the Canbalam sphere or phenomenon during this time, but there is also evidence of other local or regional ceramics that are or may be part of other complexes. The jumbled nature of the Champotón collections does not permit further elaboration. Still, the ceramics recovered do indicate that there was a substantial occupation at the site, although it is not possible to determine its extent.

There is no evidence of a transition from the Late/Terminal Classic at the site into the Postclassic. In fact, we have not been able to subdivide the Postclassic period into subdivisions. Ek (2015:526) has suggested that Peto Cream Ware may be a marker for the earlier portion of the Postclassic, but the Champotón Project materials cannot confirm that (see discussion above). What can be said is that the Postclassic ceramics at the site make up a very clear set of types, modes, and pastes that are found in all of the excavations areas investigated, although it is not as common at Moquel as in Champotón proper. These ceramics have been found in association with large-scale architecture of considerable sophistication. The fact that the inhabitants of the site were importing a significant proportion of their ceramics from outside the production zone suggests that they were participating in a large-scale coastal exchange system involving ceramics and obsidian (Folan et al. 2015:101–102), and perhaps much else. The ceramics recovered from Champotón certainly reinforce the conclusions of Ruz (1969) and Ball (1978), as well as the Spanish historical documents that Champotón was indeed a major Postclassic site on the Campeche coast.

APPENDIX

THE EFFIGY CENSERS OF CHAMPOTÓN

INTRODUCTION

During the investigation at Structure 1, Group 1 in the Guadalupe barrio, carried out by the Autonomous University of Campeche (UAC), at Champotón, Campeche between 2001 and 2003 (Figure 1.2), Dr. Folan and colleagues (2002; 2003) recovered a large quantity of Late Postclassic ceramics (Forsyth and Jordan 2003; Forsyth 2004). This was hardly surprising since previous investigations at Champotón, first by Ruz (1969:117ff.) in 1949, and later by Eaton (1978:26) in 1968 (see also Ball 1978:90-93) confirmed the historic sources from the time of the Spanish Conquest that the city was an important Postclassic site. Although the UAC investigations recovered evidence that Champotón had a much longer occupation, beginning in the Preclassic period and extending to the present (Forsyth and Jordan 2003; Forsyth 2004), they also reconfirmed that the site "played an important role during the Postclassic, especially during the Late and Terminal Postclassic" (Forsyth 2004:33).

DEPOSITS OF ANTHROPOMORPHIC CENSERS

At Structure 1 the investigations, directed by Dr. William Folan, recovered a large quantity of Late Postclassic pottery. During excavations, they encountered deposits that consisted almost exclusively of numerous large fragments of effigy censers similar to those found at Mayapan. According to Folan and Florey de Folan (personal communication), these special deposits of censers were found in two main locations on Structure 1. One was located on the west side of Structure 1-L in an area between Structures 1-L and 1-B (Figure 1.3). It appears that the inhabitants of the site placed an enormous quantity of broken anthropomorphic censers. The other primary location that produced evidence of numerous large fragments was the principal stairway of the great platform of Structure 1. This stairway was modified during the Postclassic, and the accumulation of anthropomorphic censer fragments might suggest some sort of activity similar to that which resulted in the deposit to the side of Structure 1-L. These kinds of ritual dumps of censers have been found at other sites (see Russell 2017:70).

The nature of these deposits suggests that the effigies were deposited in a single episode for some unknown reason. Although it is not possible to determine with certainty, it would appear that the censers were broken somewhere else and intentionally deposited afterwards, where they were found by the archaeologists, rather than being broken in place—a practice also known from Mayapan and Aventura in Belize (Milbrath et al. 2008:106). This pattern of depositing a large quantity of ceramic fragments in a special place, perhaps not in the same locale as where they were broken, appears to have been a not infrequent practice among the Maya since at least the Early Classic (Matheny 1986:344; Forsyth 1993:44) if not earlier. Perhaps these deposits were part of some now lost ritual related to the construction, dedication, use, or termination of Postclassic buildings that form part of Structure 1.

THE POSTCLASSIC CONSTRUCTIONS

According to Folan et al. (2002:13-14), the inhabitants Postclassic Champotón undertook constructions or left deposits in four main zones on Structure 1. One of these was Structure 1-G, a platform measuring 25 by ± 5.50 m attached to the west side of the Great Platform forming Structure 1 (Figure 1.3), although they found no evidence of any kind of superstructure on this building. On the opposite, east side of the Structure 1 great platform, more or less opposite

Structure 1-G, the Champotóneros dumped a great quantity of sascab and soil containing large amounts of ceramics rising to a height of 3 m and measuring 25 m long. It appears that if this material was intended to form the hearting of some new structure, it was never completed. In fact, it is not possible to determine why they dumped this material there.

Another contemporaneous building was Structure 1-L (Figure 1.3), constructed immediately north of Structure 1-A (Folan et al. 2002:14). Still other modifications were carried out on the principal stairway of the great platform. Moreover, the Postclassic inhabitants of Champotón also deposited 17 burials (Figure 1.3) along the northeast base of the great platform, seven of them directly in front of or on the stairway near the northeast corner of the platform (Folan et. al. 2002:14). Given the nature of these burial deposits, the investigators concluded that all the burials consisted of sacrificed individuals (Gomez et al. 2002:21).

These data attest to the fact that the Postclassic inhabitants of Champotón continued to use and modify the Structure 1 platform that was originally constructed in Preclassic times. It was precisely in some of these locations that heavy deposits of Chen Pec anthropomorphic censers were encountered.

Given the scale of Postclassic construction at the great platform, it is not surprising that the project recovered a great deal of ceramics and other artifacts from this period. Large quantities of Late Postclassic ceramics were encountered in the locations described previously. However, the amount of fragments of anthropomorphic censers found in these deposits was surprising. This was especially so when compared to the remains recovered from Groups 5-9 in the northern portion of the city (Figure 1.3), which also produced large quantities of almost exclusively Late Postclassic ceramics. In these latter contexts remains of effigy censers were quite rare, constituting less than 1 percent of all the Postclassic ceramics. In the Guadalupe Barrio, on the other hand, they made up 15 percent of the recovered Late Postclassic ceramics. This discrepancy in the quantity of these censers does not even take into consideration the dozens of kilos of large censer fragments from the special deposits that were not included in the counts of Postclassic censers from the general refuse deposits. This all suggests that Structure 1 was the object of special rites or activities resulting in the deposition of numerous effigy censers, while their use in other locations of the city was not very common. This contrasts significantly with the Tases Phase occupation at Mayapan, where the effigy censer fragments made up more than 50 percent of the ceramic complex (Smith 1971) and were recovered from a much wider set of contexts.

Anthropomorphic censers were recovered in great quantities from two main types of contexts at Structure 1. One of these consisted of the two special deposits (between Structures 1-L and 1-B, and on the principal stairway), comprising mostly effigy censer fragments. The other contained general refuse with the whole range of Late Postclassic ceramic types but with a large number of effigy censers fragments as part of the refuse. These latter contexts were probably secondary deposits. For this reason the censer fragments from these contexts were generally much more fragmented than was the case of those recovered from the special deposit contexts. The largest quantity of anthropomorphic censers from fill material were recovered from the area around the special deposit near Structure 1-L. Both Structure 1-A and 1-B produced large accumulations of effigies. The north side of the platform near the special deposit on the stairway and the sacrificial burials yielded many examples. Finally, the area of sascab and soil on the east side of the platform produced a very large quantity of fragments also. Structure 1-G was an exception given that it yielded few examples.

The prodigious quantity of anthropomorphic censers found at Structure 1, both in special deposits, as well as in other contexts in comparison to other contemporaneous buildings investigated by the project, would suggest that Structure 1 was the object of some sort of special worship or activity. It is possible that there are other contexts or areas of the site that might produce a similar pattern to that of Structure 1 but which were not investigated by the project. On the basis of current available data, the concentration of these censers at Structure 1 seems to suggest that it was the object of special reverence by the inhabitants of Champotón, perhaps due to it great antiquity. It might also imply that the anthropomorphic censers fulfilled a much more restricted function in the life of the Champotóneros than they did at sites like Mayapan, where they appear to have a much more extensive distribution.

THE ANALYSIS OF CHEN PEC MODELED ANTHROPOMORPHIC CENSERS

One of the principal goals of the analysis was to determine how the Chen Pec Modeled censers were constructed (Noble & Forsyth 2009:193-202). All of the examples recovered were broken. No intact examples were found; however, given that a significant number of large fragments were recovered from the special deposits, it was possible to reconstruct the process by which the manufacturers made the effigies. We did not make a technical analysis of the paste of the ceramics other than to note the color, but Bishop and colleagues (2006) have published a study of the chemical composition of the paste of the ceramic group to which Chen Pec Modeled belongs. The chemical composition indicates that the censers were made of the same materials as other ceramic vessels of Champotón Unslipped Ware.

In addition to analyzing the construction methods of the censers, the form of surface decoration, especially the details of the features of the personages, and of their clothing, including biological elements, and the application of paint to the effigies was undertaken.

RESULTS

The Chen Pec Modeled fragments have a relatively uniform surface color that varies from light brown to a cream color, at times achieving an almost white shade. Given the uniformity of the firing, one might infer that the makers probably used a kiln or protected firing chamber of some sort, although this cannot be demonstrated.

The censers are smooth on all surfaces and appear to have been constructed manually rather than with the use of molds. They were manufactured first in sections, according to the details of physiognomy and dress of the personage being represented and then joined together to form the final figure. The manufacturers used plastic clay to join the pieces and hide the joints. That is, various parts of the body of the effigy were preformed and then joined together. Among the sections or preforms that have been identified are the hands, the feet, the forearms, the upper arms, and the legs. It is likely that the faces were also preformed, and possibly the torsos as well. With respect to the torsos though, the lack of intact examples—only one was found in the Champotón collections—does not permit a definitive conclusion. We suppose that they also were preformed in sections distinct from the rest of the figure.

The heads of the figures were made up of two main segments—the face and the headdress. The head was connected to the neck and torso at the level of the jaw, and the majority of mandible fragments had a visible joint scar where the two pieces were united. Occasionally, however, no evidence of such a union between the face and the neck was apparent. The faces took both anthropomorphic and zoomorphic forms, although the anthropomorphic form was much more common.

Among the common elements of the figures' faces are the incisor teeth, usually formed by incision and generally exaggerated in size in that they are proportionally longer than those of a normal person. Sometimes the canine teeth are represented as well and usually take the form of a hook or volute. They are longer than the other teeth and appear to represent fish fins, possibly a symbol of divinity.

Another way of indicating the mouth is without any teeth at all, showing only the gum inside the mouth. This sometimes has the effect of making the personage appear to be elderly, although not in all cases. A third form of representing the teeth consists of the use of little balls or ceramic beads. A series or rows of little clay balls were inserted into the mouth to give the appearance of teeth, or at least where the teeth would normally be. The little balls were not uniform in size though and required less precision than the incising method.

Sometimes, similar balls were used to form the iris of the eye. When the bead method was used in this way, the pupil was not indicated by a punched hole as was the case in more common forms of representing the eye. When the ball form was used for the eye, the eye consisted of only the eye socket and the bead inside of it. Possibly this form of eye was used to represent a zoomorphic face, but this is only speculation.

The cheeks can vary between two typical forms, gaunt and full. The gaunt cheek forms give the impression of death and age, possibly representing a death deity. The full form gives the figurine a youthful look but is also very uncommon. The full cheek form also requires more time and attention to detail by the manufacturer.

The headdresses of the figurines vary in their detail, but there are several common themes. On all of the headdresses there is complex decoration of some sort. Some are decorated with appliqué beads; others are decorated with cross-hatching bands. The headdresses can also have appliqué layers that create a fold-like appearance in the headdress. There are many elements that can make up the headdresses and most are highly elaborated. On several, there is a pattern that resembles the Mexican year sign.

Another important aspect of the finish and decoration of the effigies is the frequency of painting. At Mayapan the majority of the analogues to Chen Pec vessels—Chen Mul Modeled—bore postfiring painting applied to the exteriors. In contrast, the overwhelming majority of Chen Pec censers, both in the special deposits, as well as in fill contexts, lack evidence of painting. This led us to conclude that, in general, the effigies at Champotón were not painted. Still, some of the fragments in all of the deposits yielded evidence of paint in red, blue, and black. The proportion of examples that provide this evidence, however, is small. Of course, given the fugitive nature of the paints used at Champotón—and postfire painting often suffers from the problem of adherence when subjected to weathering—it is possible that much of the paint has weathered away. The most feasible interpretation of the evidence, however, suggests that the great majority of the censers were not painted.

According to Milbrath and Peraza (2007), the Champotón censers lack certain elements or details that are common on the better known Mayapan censers, such as the representation of nails on the hands and feet of the personage. At Mayapan these were made by incision and presented in a realistic manner. In contrast, the digits of the Champotón censers are much simpler lacking much indication of detail. Nevertheless, such indications do exist on a small number of Champotón effigies. Moreover, a few Chen Pec examples bore evidence of nails represented not by incising but by the application of a small separate piece representing the nail. These are very rare, however, and it is not known how common this practice was. In summary, it would appear that the effigies at Champotón were manufactured with less attention to detail than was the case with the more famous Mayapan censers.

Milbrath et al. (2008) also points out that the range of deities represented at Champotón is more restricted than was the case at Mayapan.

With respect to the manufacture of the Chen Pec censers it seems evident that the preformed pieces were put together after they were dry. It would appear that the effigies were manufactured by means of a systematic process whereby the sections were preformed, and after drying, joined together using plastic clay to hold the pieces together and hide the evidence of the joints. Finally, the appliqué elements and forms of decoration were added.

As to the function of the effigies, the seemingly restricted context in which they were deposited suggests they were used for some special and limited function. The similarity of Chen Pec vessels to those of Mayapan and other areas of the Maya area does suggest some connections in belief and ritual. On the other hand, the differences between them and their contexts may also indicate considerable variation in their meaning and usage during Late Postclassic times.

REFERENCES CITED

ADAMS, RICHARD E. W.

1971 *The Ceramics of Altar de Sacrificios.* Papers of the Peabody Museum of Archaeology and Ethnology 63(1). Harvard University, Cambridge.

1973 Maya Collapse: Transformation and Termination in the Ceramic Sequence at Altar de Sacrificios. In *The Classic Maya Collapse,* edited by T. Patrick Culbert, pp. 133–163. University of New Mexico Press, Albuquerque.

ÁLVAREZ AGUILAR, LÚIS FERNANDO

1985 *El sitio arqueológico Los Guarixés.* Gobierno Municipal Ciudad del Carmen, Ciudad de Carmen, Campeche.

ANCONA ARAGÓN, ILIANA

2012 La cerámica del Preclásico en la costa de campeche. In *Arqueología de la costa de Campeche: La época prehispánica*, coordinated by Rafael Cobos, pp. 145-160. Ediciones de la Universida Autónoma de Yucatán, Mérida.

ANCONA ARAGÓN, ILIANA, AND SOCORRO DEL PILAR JIMÉNEZ ÁLVAREZ

2005 Las cerámicas gris y negra fina como marcadores de interacción en el litoral campechano. In *Encuentro Internacional "Los Investigadores de la Cultura Maya"* 13:209–227. Universidad Autónoma de Campeche, Campeche.

ANCONA ARAGÓN, ILIANA, VICENTE SUÁREZ AGUILAR, AND SOCORRO JIMÉNEZ ÁLVAREZ

2009a La cerámica preclásica de Constitución, un sitio al sur de Campeche. In *Encuentro Internacional "Los Investigadores de la Cultura Maya"* 18(1):233–252. Universidad Autónoma de Campeche, Campeche.

2009b La cerámica del periodo Preclásico en Cerros de los Muertos, Campeche. In *XXIII Simposio de Investigaciones Arqueológicas en Guatemala*, editado por Bárbara Arroyo, Adriana Linares Palma, and Lorena Paiz Aragón, pp. 1111–1124. Museo Nacional de Arqueología y Etnología, Ministerio de Cultura y Deportes, Instituto de Antropología e Historia, Asociación Tikal, Guatemala.

ANCONA ARAGÓN, ILIANA, VICENTE SUÁREZ AGUILAR, AND HEBER OJEDA MÁS

2010 La secuencia cerámica del sitio Playa Esmeralda, Campeche. In *Los investigadores de la cultura maya* 19:257–275. Universidad Autónoma de Campeche, Campeche.

BALL, JOSEPH W.

1975 Cui Orange Polychrome: A Late Classic Funerary Type from Central Campeche, Mexico. *Contributions of the University of California Archaeological Research Facility* 27:32–39. Berkeley.

1976 Ceramic Sphere Affiliations of the Barton Ramie Ceramic Complexes. In *Prehistoric Pottery Analysis and the Ceramics of Barton Ramie in the Belize Valley*, edited by James C. Gifford. Memoirs of the Peabody Museum of Archaeology and Ethnology 18:323–330. Harvard University, Cambridge.

1977 *The Archaeological Ceramics of Becán, Campeche, Mexico.* Middle American Research Institute, Pub. 43. Tulane University, New Orleans.

1978 Archaeological Pottery of the Yucatan-Campeche Coast. In *Studies in the Archaeology of Coastal Yucatan and Campeche, Mexico.* Middle American Research Institute, Pub. 46. Tulane University, New Orleans.

BARBA MEINECKE, HELENA

2003 Una visita al Proyecto Arqueológico Jaina en Campeche. In *Investigadores de Mesoamérica* 3:52–72. Universidad Autónoma de Campeche, Campeche.

Benavides Castillo, Antonio
2002 Principales hallazgos de la Temporada 2000 en Jaina. In *Encuentro Internacional "Los Investigadores de la Cultura Maya"* 10:88–101. Universidad Autónoma de Campeche, Campeche.

Berlin, Heinrich
1956 *Late Pottery Horizons of Tabasco, Mexico.* Contributions to American Anthropology and History 12 (59). Pub. 606, Carnegie Institution, Washington, DC.

Bishop, Ronald L.
2003 Five Decades of Maya Fine Orange Ceramic Investigation by INAA. In *Patterns and Process: A Festschrift in Honor of Dr. Edward V. Sayre*, edited by Lambertus van Zelst, pp. 81–91. Smithsonian Center for Materials Research and Education, Suitland.

Bishop, Ronald L. and Robert L. Rands
1982 Maya Fine Paste Ceramics: A Compositional Perspective. In *Analyses of Fine Paste Ceramics: Excavations at Seibal*, edited by Jeremy A. Sabloff, pp. 283–314. Memoirs of the Peabody Museum of Archaeology and Ethnology 15(2). Harvard University. Cambridge.

Bishop, Ronald L., Erin L. Sears, and James Blackman
2005 Jonuta: Una ventana a la producción y distribución de pasta fina a finales del Clásico maya. In *Encuentro Internacional "Los Investigadores de la Cultura Maya"* 13:174–187. Universidad Autónoma de Campeche, Campeche.

Bishop, Ronald L., James Blackman, Erin L. Sears, William Folan, and Donald W. Forsyth
2006 Observaciones iniciales sobre el consumo de la cerámica de Champotón. In *Encuentro Internacional "Los Investigadores de la Cultura Maya"* 14(1):137–145. Universidad Autónoma de Campeche, Campeche.

Boucher, Sylviane, and Sara Dzul G.
2006 La secuencia tipológica preliminar de la cerámica del Proyecto Arqueológico Calakmul, Campeche (temporadas 1993–2000). In *Los mayas de ayer y hoy: Memorias del Primer Congreso Internacional de Cultura Maya*, edited by Alfredo Barrera Rubio and Ruth Gubler, pp. 584–616. Universidad Autónoma de Yucatán, Mérida.

Boucher, Sylviane, and Yoly Palomo
1989 Estilo regional en cerámica polícroma de Campeche. In *Memorias del Segundo Coloquio Internacional de Mayistas: 17–21 de agosto de 1987, Campeche*, pp. 485–516. Centro de Estudios Mayas, UNAM, Mexico.

Brady, James E., Joseph W. Ball, Ronald L. Bishop, Duncan C. Pring, Norman Hammond, and Rupert Housley
1998 The Lowland Maya "Protoclassic": A Reconsideration of Its Nature and Significance. *Ancient Mesoamerica* 9:17–38.

Brainerd, George W.
1941 Fine Orange Pottery in Yucatan. *Revista de Estudios Antropológicos* 5:163–183.

1958 *The Archaeological Ceramics of Yucatan.* Anthropological Records, Vol. 19. University of California Press, Berkeley and Los Angeles.

Chase, Arlen F.
1984 The Ceramic Complexes of the Tayasal-Paxcaman Zone, Lake Peten, Guatemala. *Cerámica de Cultura Maya* 13:27–41. Philadelphia.

Chase, Arlen F., and Diane Z. Chase
n.d. The Ceramics of the Tayasal-Paxcaman Zone, Lake Peten Itza, Guatemala. Photocopy, Department of Anthropology, University of Pennsylvania, 1983.

Chase, Diane E. Zaino
1982 *Spatial and Temporal Variability in Postclassic Northern Belize.*

Ph.D. dissertation, Department of Anthropology, University of Pennsylvania, Philadelphia.

CHRISTENSEN, ROSS T.
n.d. Archaeological Investigations of Brigham Young University in Southern Mexico in 1958. Manuscript on file, Brigham Young University. Provo, 1960.

CHUNG, HEAJOO, ALFREDO VICTORIA MORALES, AND JESÚS ARENAS ALATORRE
1998 La cerámica pizarra: Variedades identificadas mediante análisis petrográfico y por microscópia eletrónica de barrido. In *Encuentro Internacional "Los Investigadores de la Cultura Maya"* 6(2):241–257. Universidad Autónoma de Campeche, Campeche.

CULBERT, T. PATRICK
n.d. Descriptions of the Preclassic Ceramics, Tikal, Guatemala. Manuscript, Department of Anthropology, University of Arizona.

DELGADO SALGADO, ANGÉLICA
2002 *Itzamkanac en el tiempo: Secuencia cerámica de El Tigre, Campeche.* Licenciatura thesis in Archaeology, Escuela Nacional de Antropología e Historia, Mexico.

EATON, JACK D.
1978 Archaeological Survey of the Yucatan-Campeche Coast. In *Studies in the Archaeology of Coastal Yucatan and Campeche, Mexico.* Middle American Research Institute Pub. 46:1–67. Tulane University, New Orleans.

EK, JERALD
2015 *Resilience in the Midst of Collapse: A Regional Case Study of Socio-Ecological Dynamics in the Río Champotón Drainage, Campeche, Mexico.* Unpublished Ph.D. dissertation, Department of Anthropology, State University of New York, Albany.

2016 Pottery and Politics: Contextualizing the Classic to Postclassic Transitions in Champotón, Campeche. *Latin American Antiquity* 27(4):527–548.

n.d. The Champotón Regional Settlement Survey Regional Ceramic Sequence. Accessed January 22, 2019. http://www.campechearchaeology.com/regional-ceramic-sequence.html

FOIAS, ANTONIA
1996 *Changing Ceramic Production and Exchange Systems and the Classic Maya Collapse in the Petexbatun Region.* Unpublished Ph.D. dissertation, Department of Anthropology, Vanderbilt University, Nashville.

FOLAN, WILLIAM J., ABEL MORALES, MA. DEL ROSARIO DOMÍNGUEZ, ROBERTO RUIZ, RAYMUNDO GONZÁLEZ, JOEL D. GUNN, LYNDA FLOREY, M. BARREDO, J. HERNANDEZ, AND DAVID BOLLES
2002 La ciudad y puerto de Champotón, Campeche: Una encrucijada del Golfo de México y su corredor eco-arqueológico. In *Encuentro Internacional "Los Investigadores de la Cultura Maya"* 10(1):8–27. Universidad Autónoma de Campeche, Campeche.

FOLAN, WILLIAM J., LYNDA FLOREY, ABEL MORALES, RAYMUNDO GONZÁLEZ, JOSÉ HERNÁNDEZ, MA. DEL ROSARIO DOMÍNGUEZ, VERA TIESLER, DAVID BOLLES, ROBERTO RUIZ, AND JOEL D. GUNN
2003 Champotón, Campeche: Su presencia en el desarrollo cultural del Golfo de México y su corredor eco-arqueológico. In *Encuentro Internacional "Los Investigadores de la Cultura Maya"* 11(1):64–71. Universidad Autónoma de Campeche, Campeche.

FOLAN, WILLIAM J., ABEL MORALES, JOSÉ ANTONIO HERNÁNDEZ TRUJEQUE, RAYMUNDO GONZÁLEZ HEREDIA, LYNDA FLOREY FOLAN, DAVID BOLLES, JOEL D. GUNN, AND MA. DEL ROSARIO DOMÍNGUEZ CARRASCO
2004 Recientes excavaciones en el antiguo Barrio de Pozo del Monte-Las Mercedes en la ciudad y puerto de

Champotón (Chakan Putún) Campeche: Un lugar central del Preclásico Medio a Posclásico en la costa oeste de la península de Yucatán y su corredor eco-arqueológico e histórico. In *Encuentro Internacional "Los Investigadores de la Cultura Maya"* 12(1):38–53. Universidad Autónoma de Campeche, Campeche.

Folan, William J. Abel Morales L., Raymundo González H., Donald Forsyth, Vera Tiesler B., David Bolles, Joel D. Gunn, G. Villanueva, Ma. del Rosario Domínguez C.

2015 Champotón, Campeche: El desarrollo de un sistema costero resiliente durante dos milenios de cambios climáticos. In *Pasos largos al futuro: La resiliencia socio-ecológica de los mayas de Campeche en relación a los cambios climáticos*, coordinated by Betty B. Faust and William J. Folan, pp. 95–108. Universidad Autónoma de Campeche, Campeche.

Forsyth, Donald W.

1983 *Investigations at Edzná, Campeche, Mexico: Ceramics.* Papers of the New World Archaeological Foundation, No. 46 (2). Brigham Young University, Provo.

1989 *The Ceramics of El Mirador, Peten, Guatemala.* Papers of the New World Archaeological Foundation, No. 63. Brigham Young University, Provo.

1993 The Ceramic Sequence at Nakbé, Guatemala. *Ancient Mesoamerica* 4:31–53.

1996 La secuencia cerámica en La Isla Flores, Petén. *Mayab* 10:5–14.

2004 Reflexiones sobre la ocupación postclásica en Champotón a través de la cerámica. In *Encuentro Internacional "Los Investigadores de la Cultura Maya"* 12:32–37. Universidad Autónoma de Campeche, Campeche.

2006 El desarrollo cultural de la Cuenca Mirador a través de la cerámica. In *XIX Simposio de Investigaciones Arqueológicas en Guatemala, 2005,* edited by Juan Pedro Laporte, Barbara Arroyo, and Hector E. Mejía, pp. 447-455. Ministerio de Guatemala City Deportes.

n.d. a The Archaeological Ceramics of Flores, Peten, Guatemala. Manuscript in preparation, 2009.

n.d. b The Ceramics of Nakbé. Manuscript in preparation.

Forsyth, Donald, and Zachary Hruby

1997 Análisis de la cerámica arqueológica de Piedras Negras: Temporada de 1997. In Proyecto Arqueológico Piedras Negras: Informe Preliminar No.1, Primera Temporada 1997 edited by Hector L. Escobedo and Stephen D. Houston), pp. 207–212. Report submitted to the Instituto de Antropología e Historia, Guatemala.

Forsyth, Donald W., and Aaron Jordan

2003 La secuencia cerámica de Champotón, Campeche: Un ensayo preliminar. In *Encuentro Internacional "Los Investigadores de la Cultura Maya"* 11:56–63. Universidad Autónoma de Campeche, Campeche.

Gifford, James C.

1976 *Prehistoric Pottery Analysis and the Ceramics of Barton Ramie in the Belize Valley.* Memoirs of the Peabody Museum of Archaeology and Ethnology, No. 18. Harvard University, Cambridge.

Gómez, María José, Araceli Hurtado, Cecilia Medina, Lucy Medrano, Marlene Pérez, and Vera Tiesler Blos

2002 Recientes hallazgos óseos en el Edificio I del Grupo I de Champotón, Campeche. In *Encuentro Internacional "Los Investigadores de la Cultura Maya"* 10:18–27. Universidad Autónoma de Campeche, Campeche.

Hermes, Bernard

2000 Industria cerámica. In *El sitio maya de Topoxté: Investigaciones en una isla del* lago Yaxhá, Petén, Guatemala*, edited by Wolfgang W. Wurster, pp. 164–202. Verlag Phillipp Von Zabern, Mainz.

INURRETA DÍAZ, ARMANDO

2004 *Uaymil un puerto de transbordo en la costa norte de Campeche.* CONACULTA/INAH, Campeche.

2006 Isla Piedras: A Northern Campeche Coast Seaport as Part of a Regional Polity. Report submitted to FAMSI. Accessed January 22, 2019. http://www.famsi.org/reports/03053/index.html

JAKEMAN, M. WELLS

1952 An Archaeological Reconnaissance of the Xicalango Area of Western Campeche, Mexico. *Bulletin of the University Archaeological Society* 3. Brigham Young University, Provo.

n.d. Preliminary Report of Archaeological Investigations of Brigham Young University in the Xicalango Region of Southwestern Campeche, Mexico, in 1961. Manuscript on file, Brigham Young University, Provo, 1961.

JIMÉNEZ ÁLVAREZ, SOCORRO DEL PILAR

2002 *La secuencia cerámica de Xcambó, costa norte de Yucatán: Complejo cerámico Xcambó y complejo cerámico Cayalac.* Tésis Profesional, Facultad de Ciencias Antropológicas, Universidad Autónoma de Yucatán, Mérida.

JIMÉNEZ ÁLVAREZ, SOCORRO, ROBERTO BELMAR, THELMA SIERRA, AND HEAJOO CHUNG

2006 Estudio tecnológico de la cerámica de pasta fina "Chabekal Temprano e Isla Fina" del sitio costero de Xcambó, Yucatán. In *Encuentro Internacional "Los Investigadores de la Cultura Maya"* 14(2):502–515. Universidad Autónoma de Campeche, Campeche.

JIMÉNEZ ÁLVAREZ, SOCORRO, TERESA CEBALLOS, AND THELMA SIERRA

2006 Las insólitas cerámicas del litoral noroeste de la península de Yucatán en el Clasico Tardio: La esfera cerámica Canbalam. In *La producción alfarera en el México antiguo, Volumén III: La alfarería del Clásico Tardío (700–1200 d.C.)*, coordinated by Beatriz Leonor Merino Carrión and Ángel García Cook, pp. 345–371. Instituto Nacional de Antropología e Historia, Mexico.

JIMÉNEZ VALDEZ, GLORIA MARTHA

1987 Algunas consideraciones arqueológicas sobre la península de Xicalango, Campeche. *Anales de Antropología* 24:115–126.

JOHNSTONE, DAVE

2001 *The Ceramics of Yaxuna, Yucatan.* Unpublished Ph.D. dissertation, Department of Anthropology, Southern Methodist University, Dallas.

KOSAKOWSKY, LAURA J.

1987 *Preclassic Maya Pottery at Cuello, Belize.* Anthropological Papers. University of Arizona, Tucson.

2001 Preliminary Report on the Ceramics from Holmul, Guatemala: Year 2000 Season. In Archaeological Investigations at Holmul, Guatemala: Report of the First Field Season, May-June 2000 by Francisco Estrada-Belli, with contributions by Jason Gonzales, Marc Wolf, Laura Kosakowsky and Justin Ebersole. FAMSI. Accessed January 22, 2019. http://www.famsi.org/reports/98010/index.html

LÓPEZ VARELA, SANDRA L.

1989 *Análisis y clasificación de la cerámica de un sitio maya del Clásico: Yaxchilan, México.* BAR International Series 535, Oxford.

MATHENY, RAY T.

1970 *The Ceramics of Aguacatal, Campeche, Mexico.* Papers of the New World Archaeological Foundation, No. 27. Brigham Young University, Provo.

1986 Investigations at El Mirador, Petén, Guatemala. *National Geographic Research* 2(3):332–353.

MILBRATH, SUSAN AND CARLOS PERAZA LOPE
2007 Los incensarios efigie de Mayapán: Iconografía, contexto y conexiones externas. Paper presented at the VII Congreso Internacional de Mayistas, July of 2007. A somewhat revised version of this paper with additional authors can be found at FAMSI. Accessed January 22, 2019. http://www.famsi.org/reports/05025/Chen_Mul_final.pdf

MILBRATH, SUSAN, JAMES AIMERS, CARLOS PERAZA LOPE, AND LYNDA FLOREY FOLAN
2008 Effigy Censers of the Chen Mul Modeled Ceramic System and their Implications for the Late Postclassic Maya Interregional Interaction. *Mexicon* 20 (October):104–112.

MUÑOZ, ARTURO RENÉ
2004 The Ceramic Sequence of Piedras Negras, Guatemala: Type and Varieties. Report submitted to FAMSI. Accessed January 22, 2019. http://www.famsi.org/reports/02055/section05.htm

NOBLE, TRENT, AND DONALD W. FORSYTH
2009 Los incensarios efigies de Champotón, Campeche, Mexico. In *Encuentro Internacional "Los Investigadores de la Cultura Maya"* 17:193–202. Universidad Autónoma de Campeche, Campeche.

OCHOA, LORENZO, AND ELADIO TERREROS
1997 *Renunciar al paraíso: Paisaje y arqueología en la tierras bajas pantanosas de la cuenca del San Pedro y San Pablo y Xicalango, Campeche.* Gobierno del Estado de Campeche, Instituto Campechano, and Instituto de Cultura de Campeche, Campeche.

OCHOA, LORENZO, AND ERNESTO VARGAS
1987 Xicalango. Puerto chontal de intercambio: mito y realidad. *Anales de Antropología* 24:95–114.

OCHOA RODRÍGUEZ, VIRGINIA JOSEFINA
1999 *Spatial Distribution of Peto Cream Ware on the Yucatan Peninsula.* M.A. thesis, Department of Geography and Anthropology, Louisiana State University, Baton Rouge.

OJEDA MAS, HEBER AND SUÁREZ AGUILAR, VICENTE
2012 Playa Esmeralda: Un asentimiento prehispánico temprano de la costa central de Campeche. In *Arqueología de la costa de Campeche: La época prehispánica*, coordinated by Rafael Cobos, pp. 217–233. Ediciones de la Universidad Autónoma de Yucatán, Mérida.

PÉREZ DE HEREDIA PUENTE, EDUARDO J.
2010 *Ceramic Contexts and Chronology at Chichen Itza, Yucatan, Mexico.* Unpublished Ph.D. dissertation, School of Historical and European Studies Archaeology Program, La Trobe University, Bundoora, Victoria, Australia. Digital version available, accessed January 22, 2019. http://www.wayeb.org/download/theses/perez_2010.pdf

PIERREBOURG, FABIENNE DE
2003 La cerámica de Balamkú desde el Preclásico hasta el Clásico Temprano. In *Encuentro Internacional "Los Investigadores de la Cultura Maya"* 11(II):334–353. Universidad Autónoma de Campeche, Campeche.

PIÑA CHÁN, ROMÁN
1968 *Jaina: La casa en el agua.* Instituto Nacional de Antropología e Historia, Mexico.

2003 Los orígenes. In *Enciclopedia Histórica de Campeche, Tomo I.* Gobierno del Estado de Campeche, Mexico.

PRING, DUNCAN
1977 *The Preclassic Ceramics of Northern Belize.* Unpublished Ph.D. dissertation, Institute of Archaeology, London University, London.

RICE, PRUDENCE
1979 Ceramic and Nonceramic Artifacts of Lakes Yaxhá-Sacnab, El Petén,

Guatemala. Part 1. The Ceramics. Section B, Postclassic Pottery from Topoxté. *Cerámica de Cultura Maya* 11:1–85. Philadelphia.

1987 *Macanché Island, El Petén, Guatemala: Excavations, Pottery, and Artifacts*. University of Florida Press, Gainesville.

Rivera, Miguel, José Luis De Rojas, and Emma Sánchez
1982 Exploraciones arqueológicas en Haltunchén, Campeche. *Revista española de antropología americana* 12:9–110. Madrid.

Russell, Bradley W.
2017 *Postclassic Pottery Censers in the Maya Lowlands: A Study of Form, Function and Symbolism.* Institute of Mesoamerican Studies Occasional Publication 17. University at Albany, Suny, New York. See https://www.albany.edu/ims/Publications/Occasional%20Publications/17_IMS_OcPub17.pdf

Ruz Lluillier, Alberto
1969 *La costa de Campeche en los tiempos prehispánicos*. Instituto Nacional de Antropología e Historia, Mexico.

Sabloff, Jeremy A.
1975 *Excavations at Seibal: Ceramics.* Memoirs of the Peabody Museum of Archaeology and Ethnology 13(2). Harvard University, Cambridge.

Sauri, Brenda, Socorro Jiménez, and Antonio Benavides
2005 La Naranja Fina "X" de Jaina, Campeche, como parte de un sistema cerámico. In *Encuentro Internacional "Los Investigadores de la Cultura Maya"* 13(1):229–243. Universidad Autónoma de Campeche, Campeche.

Shepard, Anna O.
1968 *Ceramics for the Archaeologist.* Pub. 609, Carnegie Institution. Washington, DC.

Simmons, Michael
n.d. The Archaeological Ceramics of Dzibilchaltún, Yucatan, Mexico. The Ceramic Typology. Unpublished manuscript, 1980.

Smith Robert E.
1955 *Ceramic Sequence at Uaxactun, Guatemala.* 2 vols. Middle American Research Institute, Pub. 20. Tulane University, New Orleans.

1957 The Marquez Collection of X Fine Orange and Fine Orange Polychrome Vessels. In *Notes on Mesoamerican Archaeology and Ethnology, Carnegie Institution of Washington, Department of Archaeology* 5(131):135–181. AMS Press, New York.

1958 The Place of Fine Orange Pottery in Mesoamerican Archaeology. *American Antiquity* 24(2):151–160.

1971 *The Pottery of Mayapan: including Studies of Ceramic Material from Uxmal, Kabah, and Chichen Itza.* Papers of the Peabody Museum of Archaeology and Ethnology, No. 66. Harvard University, Cambridge.

Smith, Robert E. and James C. Gifford
1966 *Maya Ceramic Varieties, Types, and Wares at Uaxactun: Supplement to 'Ceramic Squence at Uaxactun.'* Middle American Research Institute, Pub. 28, pp. 125–174. Tulane University, New Orleans.

Suárez Aguilar, Vicente, Heber Ojeda Más, and Iliana Ancona Aragón
2010 Economía y subsistencia en Playa Esmeralda, Champotón, durante el Preclásico. In *XXIII Simposio de Investigaciones Arqueológicas en Guatemala, 2009*, edited by B. Arroyo, A. Linares, and Lorena Paiz, pp. 750–766. Museo Nacional de Arqueología e Ethnología, Guatemala.

Valdez, Fred, Jr.
1987 *The Prehistoric Ceramics of Colhá, Northern Belize.* Unpublished

Ph.D. dissertation, Department of Anthropology, Harvard University, Cambridge.

1988 The Ceramics of Colha, Belize. *Ceramica de Cultura Maya et al.* 15:41–50. Temple University, Philadelphia.

VARGAS PACHECO, ERNESTO

1985 Arqueología e historia de los mayas-chontales de Tabasco. In *Olmecas y mayas en Tabasco: Cinco acercamientos,* coordinated by Lorenzo Ochoa, pp. 485-516. Gobierno del Estado de Tabasco, Villahermosa.

1994 Síntesis de la historia prehispánica de los mayas chontales de Tabasco-Campeche. *América Indígena* 54 (1–2):15–61.

2001 *Itzamkanac y Acalan: Tiempos de crisis anticipando el futuro.* Universidad Nacional Autónoma de México, Mexico.

WILLEY, GORDON R.

1977 The Rise of Maya Civilization. In *Origins of Maya Civilization,* edited by R. E. W. Adams, pp. 383–423. University of New Mexico Press, Albuquerque.

WILLIAMS-BECK, LORRAINE A.

1999 *Tiempo en trozos: Cerámica de la región de los Chenes, Campeche, México.* Universidad Autónoma de Campeche, Campeche.

ZAPATA P., RENÉE LORELEI

1997 Arqueología de algunos sitios de la costa central de Campeche. In *Encuentro Internacional "Los Investigadores de la Cultura Maya"* 5:406–411. Universidad Autónoma de Campeche, Campeche.

ZARAGOZA BALDERAS, ELIZABETH, AND ALMA MARTÍNEZ DÁVILA

2002 Jaina, más allá de la inhumación y exhumación. In *Encuentro Internacional "Los Investigadores de la Cultura Maya"* 10:102–108. Universidad Autónoma de Campeche, Campeche.